Directions in Applied Linguistics

Directions in Applied Linguistics
Essays in Honor of Robert B. Kaplan

Edited by
Paul Bruthiaux, Dwight Atkinson,
William G. Eggington, William Grabe
and Vaidehi Ramanathan

Orient BlackSwan

DIRECTIONS IN APPLIED LINGUISTICS

ORIENT BLACKSWAN PRIVATE LIMITED

Registered Office
3-6-752 Himayatnagar, Hyderabad 500 029 (A.P.), INDIA
e-mail: centraloffice@orientblackswan.com
Other Offices
Bangalore, Bhopal, Bhubaneshwar, Chennai, Ernakulam, Guwahati, Hyderabad, Jaipur, Kolkata, Lucknow, Mumbai, New Delhi, Patna

©2005 Paul Bruthiaux, Dwight Atkinson, William G Eggington, William Grabe and Vaidehi Ramanathan and the authors of the individual chapters

This edition of **Directions of Applied Linguistics** is published by in arrangement with **Multilingual Matters, imprint of Chanel View Publications Ltd** and is for sale only in the following territories: **India, Pakistan, Bangladesh, Bhutan, Nepal, Sri Lanka, and the Maldives only, not for export.**

First Published in India by
Orient Blackswan Private Limited, 2009

ISBN 13: 978 81 250 3655 5

Printed in India at
S.D.R. Printers
Delhi

Published by
Orient Blackswan Private Limited
1/24 Asaf Ali Road
New Delhi 110 002
e-mail: delhi@orientblackswan.com

Contents

Contributors vii

Part 1: Perspectives on Applied Linguistics

Introduction
Paul Bruthiaux. 3

1 Applied Linguistics, Interdisciplinarity, and Disparate Realities
 Henry G. Widdowson. 12

2 Is Language Policy Applied Linguistics?
 Bernard Spolsky 26

Part 2: Language Education

Introduction
Vaidehi Ramanathan 39

3 Sharing Community Languages: Utopian Dream or Realistic Vision?
 Michael Clyne 42

4 Documenting Curricular Reform: Innovative Foreign Language Education in Elementary School
 Rocío Domínguez, G. Richard Tucker and Richard Donato 56

5 Research Perspectives on Non-native English-speaking Educators
 Lía D. Kamhi-Stein 72

Part 3: English for Academic Purposes

Introduction
Dwight Atkinson 87

6 Reflections of a 'Blue Collar Linguist:' Analysis of Written Discourse, Classroom Research, and EAP Pedagogy
 Dana R. Ferris 91

7 English for Academic Purposes: Issues in Undergraduate Writing and Reading
 Ann M. Johns 101

8 'Ear' Learners and Error in US College Writing
  Joy Reid 117

9 Teachers' Perceptions of Lexical Anomalies: A Pilot Study
  Cheryl Boyd Zimmerman 131

Part 4: Contrastive Discourse Analysis

Introduction
William Grabe................................. 149

10 *Tertium Comparationis:* A Vital Component in Contrastive Rhetoric Research
  Ulla M. Connor and Ana I. Moreno 153

11 Structure and Style in the Narrative Writings of Mexican-American and African-American Adolescents
  Ann Daubney-Davis and Genevieve Patthey-Chavez 165

12 Functions of Personal Examples and Narratives in L1 and L2 Academic Prose
  Eli Hinkel 186

13 Cross-cultural Variation in Classroom Turn-taking Practices
  Deborah Poole 201

Part 5: Language Policy and Planning

Introduction
William G. Eggington........................... 223

14 Micro Language Planning
  Richard B. Baldauf Jr 227

15 The Englishization of Spanish in Mexico
  Robert J. Baumgardner 240

16 Including Discourse in Language Planning Theory
  Joseph Lo Bianco............................... 255

17 World-Language: Foreign Language Policy in Hungary
  Péter Medgyes.................................. 264

References 279
Robert Kaplan: Biography and Publications 310
Index 324

Contributors

Dwight Atkinson is an applied linguist and ESL teacher currently working at Temple University Japan. His research interests include culture theory, second language writing, postmodernism, qualitative research methodology, and sociocognitive approaches to language and culture. He received his PhD in applied linguistics under Robert B. Kaplan at the University of Southern California in 1993.

Richard B. Baldauf, Jr is Associate Professor of TESOL in the School of Education at the University of Queensland and is a member of the Executive of the International Association of Applied Linguistics (AILA). He has published numerous articles in refereed journals and books. He is co-editor of *Language Planning and Education in Australasia and the South Pacific* (Multilingual Matters, 1990) and a series of areal volumes on *Language Planning and Policy in...* (Multilingual Matters, 2004). He is co-author (with Robert B. Kaplan) of *Language Planning from Practice to Theory* (Multilingual Matters, 1997) and *Language and Language-in-Education Planning in the Pacific Basin* (Kluwer, 2003).

Robert J. Baumgardner is Professor of Applied Linguistics at Texas A&M University-Commerce, where he teaches courses in Sociolinguistics, History of the English Language, and Teaching ESL. He earned his PhD in Linguistics from the University of Southern California in 1982. He is editor of *ESP in the Classroom: Practice and Evaluation* (Macmillan, 1988), *The English Language in Pakistan* (OUP, 1993), and *South Asian English: Structure, Use, and Users* (University of Illinois Press, 1996) and is author of numerous articles on Pakistani English, US Americans in Mexico, and the English language in Mexico.

Paul Bruthiaux has written on language education in *Journal of Multilingual and Multicultural Development, International Journal of the Sociology of Language, TESOL Quarterly, International Journal of Applied Linguistics, Language Problems and Language Planning, Current Issues in Language Planning,* and *Journal of Asian-Pacific Communication*. His work in discourse analysis has appeared as *The Discourse of Classified Advertising: Exploring the Nature of Linguistic Simplicity* (OUP, 1996) and in *Language and Communica-*

tion, *Applied Linguistics*, and *English Today*. Currently at the Hong Kong Institute of Education, he has taught at Texas A&M University, National University of Singapore, University of Southern California, and City University of Hong Kong.

Michael Clyne is Professorial Fellow in Linguistics at the University of Melbourne. His research interests are language contact/multilingualism/language policy, sociolinguistics, inter-cultural communication, and second/third language acquisition. His publications include *Dynamics of Language Contact* (CUP, 2003), *Undoing and Redoing Corpus Planning* (editor, Mouton de Gruyter, 1997), *The German Language in a Changing Europe* (CUP, 1995), and *Inter-Cultural Communication at Work* (CUP, 1994).

Ulla M. Connor is Karl R. and Barbara E. Zimmer Chair in Intercultural Communication and Director of the Indiana Center for Intercultural Communication in the School of Liberal Arts at Indiana University Purdue University Indianapolis. Her research interests include contrastive rhetoric, English for specific purposes, discourse analysis, and corpus linguistics. Her articles have appeared in journals such as *Text*, *TESOL Quarterly*, *English for Specific Purposes*, and *Journal of Second Language Writing*. Her books include the singly authored *Contrastive Rhetoric* and the co-edited books *Writing Across Languages* (with Robert B. Kaplan), *Coherence* (with Ann M. Johns), and *Multiliterate Lives* (with Diane Belcher).

The late **Ann Daubney-Davis** received her PhD in applied linguistics under Robert B. Kaplan at the University of Southern California. Ann was an enthusiastic and dedicated ESL teacher, researcher, volunteer worker, parent, spouse, and advocate of language-minority students. A few weeks before her death from cancer at the age of 38, Ann casually remarked to a co-editor of this volume that she had taken on a new Spanish-speaking tutee, a young woman who had fallen through the cracks of the US education system, and that it was 'time to get to work.' The chapter in this volume is based on Ann's dissertation data, lovingly reconstituted and written up by Genevieve Patthey-Chavez.

Rocío Domínguez, who earned her PhD at Carnegie Mellon University, is a consultant for the GTZ (Deutsche Gesellschaft für Technische Zusammenarbeit) regarding bilingual education programs in Peru. She worked with the Spanish Program in Chartiers Valley, Pennsylvania for two years in a variety of initiatives including the design of the 5th, 6th, and 7th grade Spanish curricula, the teachers' professional development, and students' foreign language assessment. For the past 8 years, she has taught various language courses at college level. In 2002, she earned the Carnegie Mellon's Graduate Student Teaching Award for her contributions in teaching and mentoring undergraduate students.

Richard Donato gained his PhD at the University of Delaware and is currently Associate Professor of Foreign Language Education at the University of Pittsburgh, where he directs graduate programs in foreign language education and ESL. He is the recipient of the Pennsylvania State Modern Language Association Teacher of the Year Award (1996) and, with Tucker and Antonek, also the recipient of the MLJ/ACTFL Paul Pimsleur award for foreign language learning research (1997). He has received (with Adair Hauck) the Freeman Award (2003) and the French Institute of Washington Award for the best article on foreign language teaching to appear in the *French Review* in 2002.

William G. Eggington is Professor of Linguistics and English Language at Brigham Young University, Provo, Utah. He is a member of the Board of Directors of TESOL (2003–2006), serving as convention chair for TESOL 2005. Originally from Australia, he received his doctorate in linguistics from the University of Southern California in 1985, with Robert B. Kaplan serving as his dissertation chair. He has researched and published in language planning in Australia, the USA, South Pacific, and general contexts, his most recent co-edited volume (with Joan Kelly Hall) being *The Sociopolitics of English Language Teaching* (Multilingual Matters, 2000).

Dana R. Ferris is Professor of English at California State University, Sacramento, where she teaches linguistics, TESOL, and ESL composition courses, and coordinates the ESL program. She is the author of four books and 25 articles and book chapters on second language writing. Her research interests are feedback on student writing, error correction, and the characteristics of Generation 1.5 writers and their texts. Her most recent book is the second edition of *Teaching ESL Composition* (with John Hedgcock) published by Lawrence Erlbaum (2005).

William Grabe is Professor of English at Northern Arizona University and teaches in the Applied Linguistics PhD and MA-TESL program. His interests include reading, writing, written discourse analysis, and literacy. He recently co-authored a book with Fredricka Stoller, *Teaching and Researching Reading* (Longman, 2002). He was President of the American Association for Applied Linguistics (AAAL) from 2001 to 2002 and he was editor of the *Annual Review of Applied Linguistics* from 1991 to 2000 (CUP).

Eli Hinkel has taught ESL and applied linguistics and has also trained teachers for almost 25 years. She has published books and numerous articles on learning a second culture, second language grammar, writing, and pragmatics. Her recent books deal with the effects of culture on second language learning, approaches to teaching L2 grammar, syntactic and lexical features of L2 written text, and practical techniques for teaching L2 academic writing. She is the editor of the Lawrence Erlbaum Associates ESL and Applied Linguistics Professional Series of books and textbooks for teachers and graduate students.

Ann M. Johns is Professor Emerita of Linguistics and Writing Studies at San Diego State University. She has published more than 50 articles and chapters on issues of academic literacy and has also published five books, including *Text, Role, and Context: Developing Academic Literacies* (CUP, 1997), *Genre in the Classroom: Multiple Perspectives* (Lawrence Erlbaum, 2002), and *Diversity in College Classrooms: Practices for Today's Campus* (University of Michigan, 2004). She has consulted on English for Specific Purposes and presented plenaries in 15 countries, and is currently completing a writing textbook for university students.

Lía D. Kamhi-Stein is Associate Professor in the Charter College of Education at California State University, Los Angeles, where she teaches in the TESOL MA Program. She is editor of *Learning and Teaching from Experience: Perspectives on Nonnative English-speaking Professionals* (University of Michigan Press, 2004), and she has published articles in *TESOL Quarterly, TESOL Journal, Journal of Adult and Adolescent Literacy, Lectura y Vida*, and other professional journals. She is currently on the Board of Directors of TESOL, serving as Director-At-Large (2004–2007). She received the 2003–2004 Outstanding Professor Award at California State University, Los Angeles.

Joseph Lo Bianco is Professor of Language and Literacy Education at the University of Melbourne. His recent books include *A Site for Debate, Negotiation and Contest of National Identity: Language Policy in Australia* (2004), *Teaching Invisible Culture: Classroom Practice and Theory* (2003, edited with C. Crozet), *Voices from Phnom Penh: Language and Development* (editor, 2002), *Australian Policy Activism in Language and Literacy* (2001, edited with R. Wickert), and *Australian Literacies: Informing National Policy on Literacy Education* (2001, with P. Freebody).

Péter Medgyes works as Deputy State Secretary in the Hungarian Ministry of Education. In this post, he is responsible for international relations and the promotion of foreign language education. During his long teaching and academic career, he has written numerous professional books and articles, including *The Non-native Teacher* (MacMillan, 1994; winner of the Duke of Edinburgh English Language Book Competition), *Changing Perspectives in Teacher Education* (Heinemann, 1996; co-edited with Angi Malderez), *The Language Teacher* (Corvina, 2004), *Criss Cross* (Hueber Verlag, 1998/99), and *Laughing Matters* (CUP, 2002).

Ana I. Moreno is Lecturer in English and Contemporary Models of Description of English in the Department of Modern Languages at the University of León, Spain. Her main research interests are contrastive rhetoric, discourse analysis, and needs analysis for language teaching. She has published in *ESP Journal*, *Text*, and *English for Specific Purposes*. She is participating in a research project financed by the Spanish Ministry of Science and Technology entitled 'Contrastive analysis and specialized English-Spanish translation: Applications and tools (ACTRES).' She collaborates with Ulla Connor in teaching the doctoral course 'Research Methods in Spanish-English Contrastive Analysis' at the University of León.

Genevieve Patthey-Chavez became interested in language policy and planning and written communication under Robert B. Kaplan's guidance. She has explored the relationships between activity, task, text, and talk in educational enterprises ranging from fourth grade language arts to computer problem solving and college composition in higher education to eighth grade mathematics in seven countries. She also founded an intersegmental research consortium to follow the progress of developmental students in both composition and mathematics across institutional boundaries, and she has been leading a faculty action research team aiming to improve writing instruction at Los Angeles City College.

Deborah Poole is Associate Professor in the Department of Linguistics and Oriental Languages at San Diego State University, where she teaches a variety of courses in applied linguistics, coordinates the ESL composition program, and administers an after-school 'Fifth Dimension' program based on Vygotskyan principles. Her current research focuses on the linguistic characteristics of speech-writing interplay in school-based literacy events, and she has a long-held interest in the pedagogical and cultural dimensions of classroom discourse.

Vaidehi Ramanathan is Professor in the Department of Linguistics at the University of California at Davis. Her research interests span all aspects of first and second language literacy and language teacher education. Her recent publications include *The Politics of TESOL Education: Writing Knowl-*

edge, Critical Pedagogy (Routledge Falmer, 2002) and *The English-Vernacular Divide: Postcolonial Language Politics and Practice* (Multilingual Matters, 2005). Her work has also appeared in mainstream journals such as *TESOL Quarterly, Applied Linguistics, Journal of Second Language Writing,* and *Language and Society.*

Joy Reid recently retired from her position as Professor of ESL and Composition in the English Department at the University of Wyoming, where she prepared teachers, directed the ESL support program, and taught composition, ESL, and linguistics. She currently teaches at Maui Community College (Hawaii). She has published textbooks and teacher-resource books about ESL writing as well as edited anthologies about students' learning styles. She recently co-edited an ESL series for Houghton Mifflin (in press) focused on the needs of immigrant students. Her research interests include discourse analysis, the process of change in learning, and the study of student errors.

Bernard Spolsky was born and educated in New Zealand. He received his PhD from the University of Montreal and taught at McGill University, Indiana University, and the University of New Mexico. He became Professor of English at Bar-Ilan University in 1980, retiring in 2000. He was co-founding editor of Applied Linguistics in 1980, and more recently of the journal *Language Policy.* He is editor-in-chief for ASIA TEFL. He has been president of TESOL and ILTA and secretary-treasurer of AAAL. He has published over 230 books and articles. His most recent books include *Concise Encyclopedia of Educational Linguistics* (Elsevier, 1999), *Sociolinguistics* (OUP, 1998), and *Language Policy* (CUP, 2004).

G. Richard Tucker, who gained his PhD at McGill University, is Paul Mellon Professor of Applied Linguistics and Head of the Modern Languages Department at Carnegie Mellon University. Prior to joining Carnegie Mellon, he served as President of the Center for Applied Linguistics (1978–1991) and as Professor of Psychology and Linguistics at McGill University (1969–1978). He has published more than 200 books, articles, and reviews concerning diverse aspects of second language learning and teaching. In addition to his work in North America, he spent five years as a Language Education advisor for the Ford Foundation in Southeast Asia, the Middle East, and North Africa.

Henry G. Widdowson is Professor Emeritus at the University of London and Honorary Professor at the University of Vienna. He was a founding editor of the journal *Applied Linguistics,* and author of a number of books including *Teaching Language as Communication* (1978), two volumes of *Explorations in Applied Linguistics* (1979, 1984), *Aspects of Language Teaching* (1990), *Practical Stylistics* (1992), and *Linguistics* (1996), the last being a title in the series *Oxford Introductions to Language Study*, of which he is the editor. His most recent books are *Defining Issues in English Language Teaching* (2003) and *Text, Context, Pretext* (2004).

Cheryl Boyd Zimmerman is Assistant Professor in the MS TESOL Program at California State University, Fullerton. Her publications relate to second language vocabulary acquisition, and have appeared in *Text, TESOL Quarterly, Studies in Second Language Acquisition,* the *Conference Proceedings of the Georgetown University Roundtable,* and in edited collections. She has contributed to vocabulary textbooks and teachers' resources, and is a frequent invited lecturer for teachers on lexical issues. Her research interests include incremental word learning, derivational knowledge, lexical issues related to high school writing success, and other issues of particular relevance to English for Academic Purposes.

Part 1
Perspectives on Applied Linguistics

Part 1
Introduction

PAUL BRUTHIAUX

Because the field of applied linguistics is concerned with bridging theory and practice, it affects our understanding of the relationship between language form and language use. As a result, applied linguistics is of direct relevance to the practices of a range of professionals, including language educators and language policy makers. Making informed decisions affecting language education, for example, requires (among other things) an understanding of the formal structure of language, its psycholinguistic correlates in individuals, and its sociolinguistic manifestations in groups. This often means that applied linguists need to be versed not only in syntax, phonology, and semantics but also in interdisciplinary areas such as second language acquisition, learning theory, crosscultural communication and pragmatics. At the micro-level, applied linguists engaged, for example, in the effective and humanistic delivery of writing instruction must not only consider variation in discourse strategies across individuals and groups, but must also theorize the very nature and scope of literacy.

This vision of the role of applied linguistics in bridging theory and practice and the dividend accruing from holding a broad view of the field has been evident in the work of Robert B. Kaplan throughout his career, as both a linguist and an educator. Over the period during which applied linguistics came of age as a field, Kaplan's name has been most widely linked with the notion of 'contrastive rhetoric,' that is, the study of variation in written discourse across cultures. Contrastive rhetoric has its source in an article Kaplan published in 1966 in the journal *Language Learning* – a piece that generated intellectual and pedagogical explorations among a generation of applied linguists. Like all powerful conceptualizations, it also attracted a lively critique. Taken together, the writings of both supporters and detractors over the best part of four decades add up to a solid testimony to the power of Kaplan's original insight. Yet, the impact of that insight should not detract from the rich contribution made by Kaplan in other areas of applied linguistics, including language education, academic writing, and especially language policy and planning, all of which are represented in this volume.

As he built up a record as a scholar of international repute, Kaplan also won and retained the affection of countless colleagues and graduate students. Thus, it is fitting that a lifetime of scholarship, insightful research, persuasive writing, pedagogical commitment, and personal loyalty should be celebrated by those who benefited from his professional and personal engagement. In this sense, this book is a tribute to a scholar, mentor, and friend. A second motivation behind this volume is to present to a wider public a broad perspective on applied linguistics that might act as a guide to past developments, current debates, and future trends in the field. Given the personal nature of the tributes included here, this volume unavoidably presents a plurality of views, interests, and styles. Yet, it is also limited in scope in that it naturally focuses on those areas most closely associated with Kaplan's lifelong work, namely *Language Education, English for Academic Purposes, Contrastive Discourse Analysis,* and *Language Policy and Planning.*

The collection opens with a pair of pieces that reflect on the nature of applied linguistics and provide a conceptual framework for the more narrowly-focused discussions that follow. In Chapter 1, Henry Widdowson searches for the conditions that would have to be met for applied linguistics to be a unitary field rather than a cluster of language-related activities. Somewhat counter to the dominant academic *zeitgeist* (and, incidentally, to Kaplan's own views on the matter), Widdowson argues against interdisciplinarity and in favor of a search for methodological consensus that might counteract diffuseness and promote conceptual unity. A distinctive feature of this consensus, Widdowson argues, should be an emphasis on applying linguistics, that is, on examining how the abstractions favored by applied linguists can be tested rigorously and systematically against the actuality of everyday existence. This, Widdowson argues, would set applied linguistics apart from academic disciplines that aim instead to draw data from everyday existence in an effort to construct increasingly abstract theories.

In Chapter 2, Bernard Spolsky reviews the development of the subfield of language policy and planning, an area in which he and Kaplan share an abiding interest, and which Spolsky regards as a paradigmatic example of applied linguistics in that it aims to unite all the fields relevant to language education under his preferred label of 'educational linguistics.' In this, he shares with Widdowson the belief that applied linguistics does not consist solely of applying theory downward in an attempt to solve societal problems. Spolsky does, however, seem less troubled by the partial overlap between applied linguistics and sociolinguistics in that problem solving requires applied linguists to go beyond language use while sociolinguists often stop at description and theory without application. He also welcomes the interdisciplinarity he sees at the heart of language policy and planning since any attempt to influence language behavior inevitably draws on a range of academic fields.

Perspectives on Applied Linguistics: Introduction

These introductory chapters set the scene for a robust debate regarding the nature and scope of applied linguistics. Vaidehi Ramanathan introduces the theme of *Language Education* by noting the common concern for educational change that runs through this section. Appropriately, she does this by couching her comments in a metaphor-rich style that challenges the hallowed conventions of Anglo-American academic writing. Noting that the inevitably institutionalized experience of language education can lead to a sense of powerlessness in players of small parts within a large machinery, Ramanathan introduces three papers that set out to show that focused activism and a willingness to challenge institutional forces can lead to beneficial educational change.

The first illustration of this proposition is from Michael Clyne, who argues in Chapter 3 that the sharing of community languages in deeply multicultural societies is no utopia, but a realistic policy aim with tangible benefits in extending cultural horizons, promoting understanding, and easing communication. In chronicling the key role played by the promotion of community languages in the initial elaboration and later defense of a language policy in Australia, Clyne provides an example of applied linguistics firmly grounded in practice as he shows how little theory can achieve unless minds are won and practicalities attended to among all interested parties, from policy makers to language users and learners at grassroot level.

In Chapter 4, Rocío Domínguez, Richard Donato, and Richard Tucker describe how one school district is experimenting with curricular reform for its K–5 Spanish as a Foreign Language program, and they analyze some of the key factors involved in introducing curricular innovation. They show that applied linguists specializing in foreign language curriculum design need to take into account the range of sociocultural variables that form the context in which all language-in-education planning takes place. For foreign language curricular innovation to succeed, Domínguez, Donato, and Tucker argue, vision and context – or, if you prefer, theory and practice – need to continuously inform each other.

Finally, in Chapter 5, Lía Kamhi-Stein addresses the thorny question of the native/non-native speaker construct and its effect on perceptions of ESL/EFL (English as a second language / English as a foreign language) teachers by the teachers themselves, their students, and program administrators. She reviews research which shows that the cogs in Ramanathan's educational machinery have indeed been turning and that earlier views of the native/non-native speaker construct as a sharp dichotomy are being superseded by a view of these variables as continuous rather than dichotomous. Kamhi-Stein also argues that language educators need to be assessed on a range of factors that include not only language proficiency but also (and often more importantly) professionalism, empathy, and interactional skills.

In his introduction to the section devoted to *English for Academic Purposes* (EAP), Dwight Atkinson takes a resolutely personal view of Robert B. Kaplan's life work. He argues that Kaplan not only made a significant personal contribution to applied linguistics through his writings but that he also encouraged the development of a body of scholars and educators whose own contribution to the field can be traced directly back to the attentive mentoring they received as graduate students. While Kaplan was never shy of engaging in debates over the nature and value of theories of applied linguistics, he never lost sight of the fact that no amount of theorizing would have any effect – that is, would work as applied linguistics – unless it was accompanied by personal devotion to inducting developing scholars into the profession. Clearly, all four chapters in this section reflect the gratitude expressed by Atkinson toward Kaplan as a mentor.

In Chapter 6, Dana Ferris narrates her personal journey from theory-driven to practice-driven applied linguistics and back again. In a piece rich in personal narrative, she relates how a typical applied linguist *experiences* the nature of applied linguistics in the course of a career rather than merely *reflecting* on that nature, with reflection informing experience and vice versa. Ferris's response to the bewilderingly broad scope of applied linguistics she encounters as her career unfolds is to call, not for methodological unity (as Widdowson does) or even close cooperation (interdisciplinarity by another name), but simply for applied linguists to grant each other a modicum of mutual respect and appreciation.

Ann Johns in Chapter 7 also considers the bond between theory and practice – between research and application – as it relates to the apprenticeship of academic writing by college students. She anchors her discussion firmly in the world of classrooms as she discusses the impact a succession of dominant paradigms have had on the practices of EAP professionals over the years. She argues that, while all major paradigms have made a lasting contribution to the profession, the most beneficial contribution has come from social constructivists, who see texts as socially situated and the writing of texts as influenced by a range of situational factors, including content but also audience, writer purpose, and genre. However, in addition to relating and interpreting current theory as it may apply to real-world problems, Johns discusses the specifics of EAP pedagogies both in terms of the specific social situations from which they emerged and in terms of their potential for informing theory.

In contrast, in Chapter 8 Joy Reid tackles the specific language learning needs of what she calls 'US resident' learners, a population that typically combines a high level of communicative fluency and persistent accuracy problems, both derived from having acquired the language as 'ear' learners. Reid contrasts this population with its counterpart, those 'eye' learners whose early experience of English language learning took place mostly in classrooms, where accuracy was often promoted at the expense of fluency. She discusses the types of errors that EAP teachers typically encounter in the writing of 'ear' learners, and then invokes second language acquisition theory and research in an attempt to explain some of the causes of these errors. Finally, she proposes practical pedagogic approaches to the remediation of these errors, thus concluding a classic applied linguistics process of problem identification, appeal to theory and research, and blueprint for remediation and amelioration.

A similar approach is evident Chapter 9, in which Cheryl Zimmerman discusses the issue of identification of lexical errors by second language writers and assessment of teachers' awareness of lexical errors in their students' writing. Like Reid, Zimmerman starts from the theoretical end of the applied linguistics continuum and goes on to review possible applications of this information to remediating a specific learning problem. First she discusses a range of semantic and collocational features of vocabulary. She then argues that effective remediation of student difficulties with lexical knowledge requires teachers to familiarize themselves with lexical concepts and metalanguage so that they can better provide students with generalizations and learning strategies. This, Zimmerman argues, implies that teacher preparation programs should not focus exclusively on broad educational issues at the expense of applied linguistics. Instead, teacher preparation programs should incorporate what applied linguistics can offer teachers in terms of essential language awareness so that they can better apply theory to practice.

Introducing the section on *Contrastive Discourse Analysis*, William Grabe notes that Kaplan's original insight grew out of an essentially practical observation: the academic writing of students working in English as a second language reflects discourse patterns often unfamiliar to readers steeped in Anglo-American academic discourse and is most likely influenced by different discourse patterns absorbed as part of an earlier L1 (first language) education. Whether, as Grabe discusses, it is more appropriate to view Kaplan's insight and its ramifications as a 'hypothesis,' a 'notion,' or a 'proposal,' theorizing was clearly at the core of the contrastive analysis of academic discourse from the start, with theory emerging from practice. In this sense, contrastive discourse analysis is a case of application informing linguistics, with insights flowing from theory back to application.

In Chapter 10, for example, Ulla Connor and Ana Moreno focus on methodological issues and propose an approach to contrastive discourse analysis that is not only rigorous in the criteria it sets out for the selection and analysis of comparable texts but also takes the analysis beyond formal criteria by factoring in functional meaning, whether explicitly encoded or not. This model, we are left to infer, will most likely have specific applications in second language writing research and translation studies (among others), but this is not stated explicitly. Nor should it necessarily be. Perhaps the most valuable contribution of Kaplan's original insight is that it continues to inform 'pure' research of the Connor and Moreno type as well as the work of researcher-educators more concerned with, for example, the remediation of educational disadvantage.

Among those spanning the range from social theory to educational remediation is Patthey-Chavez, whose Chapter 11, which is based on the work of the late Ann Daubney-Davis, contrasts the narrative writing of Mexican-American and African-American adolescents. In her discussion of data drawn from Daubney-Davis' field work, Patthey-Chavez confirms key generalizations made by previous research in crosscultural discourse, especially as regards the tendency of African-American writers to integrate dramatic effect into their narratives in contrast to the Mexican-American preference for report-like formats. However, Patthey-Chavez notes considerable within-group variation regardless of home background in the use of writing techniques best described on aggregate as 'style,' and she warns that contrastive generalizations – however broadly valid – might encourage stereotyping and make it more difficult for educators to spot and foster writing talent. The result is a paper that exemplifies the mutually beneficial interchange that can occur between theoretically grounded, research aware, and data based contrastive analysis at one end of the spectrum and educational remediation at the other.

In Chapter 12, Eli Hinkel also takes as a starting point the classic contrastive rhetoric proposition that the output of L2 (second language) writers of academic English will to some extent reflect discourse conventions absorbed as part of their L1 education, and she tests the proposition further in a study of exemplification in the academic writing of Asian L2 writers of English. Having shown that these writers resort to exemplification in ways that reflect Asian discourse patterns and thus differ significantly from the practices of her native-speaker control group, Hinkel proposes modifications to L2 academic writing instruction to take into account students' discourse backgrounds. The result is a take on the field that is both applied in that it offers remediation of a specific language education issue *and* linguistic in that her study makes a data-based contribution to the continuing theoretical debate over Kaplan's original proposition.

In Chapter 13, Deborah Poole departs from the conventional approach to contrastive rhetoric and its traditional concern with academic writing as she reviews studies of variation in the way teachers cue interactional turns in second and foreign language classrooms across a range of sociocultural contexts. She innovates also in drawing from a methodology normally associated with conversation analysis and adapting it to the comparative study of classroom interactions across a range of languages. In this sense, Poole's work exemplifies Widdowson's view that interdisciplinarity in applied linguistics is less a merging of equals than a judicious borrowing from one field for the benefit another. More conventionally within applied linguistics, Poole concludes her review by offering recommendations for practical problem-solving in the area of cross-cultural teacher–student interactions.

While Bob Kaplan's contribution to discourse analysis has been both far-reaching and – perhaps unavoidably – controversial, his work in the area of *Language Policy and Planning* has been no less significant, though less hotly contested. In his introduction to the final section in this volume, William Eggington notes that Kaplan's work in this area has always had a strong theoretical underpinning, specifically in the form of eight major constructs, and he proceeds to show how each of the four chapters he introduces takes one or more of these constructs as its departure point. Fittingly in the context of this volume, these papers span theory and practice, but also add specificity to the view that applied linguistics should be concerned with bringing theory to bear on language-related problems while allowing practitioners to test their theories against systematically collected data.

In Chapter 14, Richard Baldauf – a long-time collaborator of Kaplan's in the field – restates their joint (and well-known) view that language policy and planning is the prime example of applied linguistics. To clarify the kind of applied linguistics he has in mind, Baldauf reviews an extensive literature and finds that it overwhelmingly describes top-down efforts to change language behavior, moving linearly from plan to problem. Even when the language problem under remediation is narrowly defined (or micro), language planning typically refers to the use of a situational methodology that tests whether macro theory fits micro problems. In arguing instead for a needs-driven approach to language policy and planning that allows macro theory to evolve out of the solution of specific micro problems, Baldauf offers an integrated view of applied linguistics in which practice informs theory as least as much as the converse.

Picking up on Baldauf's argument, in Chapter 15 Robert Baumgardner illustrates the perils of conducting language policy with neither theoretical nor methodological expertise and above all, as repeatedly pointed out by Baldauf (and of course Kaplan), without the consent of the population that the policy is meant to benefit. In his overview of the 'Englishization' of Mexican Spanish, Baumgardner shows that the operation of a government commission charged with safeguarding language purity was short-lived and ineffective, for several reasons: it was based on unsubstantiated fears of lexical imports whose numbers were greatly exaggerated; it was backed up by neither sociolinguistic data nor a recognizable theory of languages in contact, language policy and planning, or anything else that would have been relevant; and it was imposed on a population that did not appear to share the purists' concerns in the least. As an illustration of how *not* to conduct language policy and planning – and by extension, applied linguistics – Baumgardner's paper offers a salutary lesson.

For his part, in Chapter 16 Joseph Lo Bianco shifts the debate over the proper domain of language policy and planning by arguing that the conventional practices of the discipline contribute to confining its domain in ways that exclude potentially critical areas, including the discourse of language policy and planning itself. Specifically, Lo Bianco argues that language policy and planning professionals must move beyond analyzing language behavior in purely correlational, sociolinguistic terms before proposing more advantageous alternatives. Instead, they should include in their analyses the very discourse of language policy and planning that overtly identified these language behaviors as a proper domain for action. Lo Bianco's proposal also connects directly with Baldauf's recommendation that the discipline should not restrict itself to the imposition of policy downward from a macro social level but should promote policy upward from the micro level of daily interactions. It also echoes Kaplan's own work in contrastive rhetoric, which, Lo Bianco argues, should be extended to include the study of the formation and consolidation of contrastive professional discourses through the operation of ideologies and power relations. In brief, Lo Bianco's piece suggests that Widdowson's call for a common methodology – or at least, a common approach – for applied linguistics may be an achievable goal.

Finally, in Chapter 17 Péter Medgyes returns to the roots, as it were, of language policy and planning by presenting a detailed account of the process of planning, implementing, and evaluating an integrated set of measures designed to boost the teaching of foreign languages in Hungary. The critical importance of this sequence (from plan to implementation to evaluation, with negotiation taking place at each step and each step feeding information back into the other two components) has of course been stressed repeatedly by Kaplan himself. Here, Medgyes provides an illustration by describing the national and historical background, the rapid shift in preferences for foreign language education that took place in Hungary once free of Soviet constraints, and the need to redirect national priorities toward Western Europe. Medgyes also details the specifics of a program put into place to enact these changes in foreign language education at school level, as well as the myriad reactions that the project generated. Of all the contributions in this volume, this paper presents the clearest view of the practicalities of decision-making in matters of language use.

So what, in the end, is applied linguistics, and does this volume provide more than a fragmented picture of the discipline based on a medley of views and experiences connected only by the fact that they all relate to Robert B. Kaplan's work and in some way deal with language in use? To return to Widdowson's opening remarks and his call for a common methodology that would give unity to the field, two broad trends emerge. One is a growing interest among applied linguists in discourse as a major dimension within which to frame a range of activities, including language education and language policy and planning. A key implication for applied linguistics is that priority will be given to more descriptive and social approaches to linguistics than to theorizing. While linguistic theories undoubtedly play a key role in applied linguistic research, there is a range of domains where such theorizing will have only limited value, in contrast to applications of discourse analytic approaches. However, while the promotion of discourse as a major theme in applied linguistics is certainly an important approach, it would be overstating the case to argue that it provides a consistent methodology.

A second trend, which is represented even more strongly in this volume, points to a bidirectional approach to applied linguistics in that constructs derived from linguistics (broadly understood) are tested against everyday realities while those realities and the inherent language-related problems they contain are examined and ameliorated in the light of theory. In this sense, working in applied linguistics no longer consists of moving linearly from theory to practice but of a cyclical process that shuttles insights continuously between the two. To the extent that this volume, as its title implies, offers a representative snapshot of current directions in applied linguistics, the picture presented here is one of refreshingly lively exploration and ongoing renewal, crucially informed by theory but never far from the social concerns that draw most applied linguists to the profession.

Our hope, then, is that this volume will make a valuable contribution to the continuing debate over the nature and scope of applied linguistics while at the same time honoring the work of Robert B. Kaplan, a key participant in this debate. It remains for me to thank all those who contributed their expertise and support to bringing this volume to publication: co-editors (and fellow USC alumni) Dwight Atkinson, Bill Eggington, Bill Grabe, and Vaidehi Ramanathan; our 20 authors and co-authors for convincingly articulating their views on key issues in applied linguistics; Marjukka and Mike Grover of *Multilingual Matters* and Series Editor John Edwards for their support throughout the project; Jim Lantolf, for giving us a chance to present some of the highlights of this book in a special colloquium at the 2004 meeting of the American Association for Applied Linguistics (AAAL); and Kelsey Savage and Ian Richard for their thorough proofreading; and Fung Shuk Ling for her creative work on the book cover. Finally, all those who know her will no doubt wish to take this opportunity to salute Audrey Kaplan for the part she has played in keeping the good ship RBK on course over many productive years and for extending her warm friendship to so many of Bob's colleagues and students.

Chapter 1
Applied Linguistics, Interdisciplinarity, and Disparate Realities

HENRY G. WIDDOWSON

Robert Kaplan and I, both recently retired from the academic fray, have been busy professing and promoting something called applied linguistics all our professional lives. Every now and again I feel the need to take up a critical position and reflect on just what it is that defines this field of enquiry we have been working in. Retirement is a good time for reflection. And what better place could there be for doing it in public than in a book honoring a scholar who has himself reflected on applied linguistics to such good effect over a long and distinguished career, culminating in the editorship of what must be the most comprehensive coverage of the field within one volume (Kaplan, 2002).

In his preface to that voluminous work, Kaplan notes that the diversity of topics included within the field has the consequence that 'applied linguistics is a difficult notion to define' (Kaplan, 2002: vii), and he makes it clear that it is not his purpose to provide a definition. Elusive of definition though it may be, however, there are two things that are generally said to characterize work that is undertaken in the name of applied linguistics. One is that it deals with problems in the 'real world:' 'problems in the world in which language is implicated,' as Cook puts it (2003: 5). The second is that it is, of its nature, interdisciplinary; it does not, in spite of its name, draw only on linguistics, but on a much wider range of scholarly enquiry. The two features are taken to be related in that the second follows by implication from the first: to solve real world problems you need to be interdisciplinary. This is made quite explicit in a recent editorial in one of the principal journals in the field:

> It is perhaps uncontroversial to claim that applied linguistics, in becoming more interdisciplinary, is better prepared for the principled handling of a range of distinct types of real world issues, and more critically aware of its methodologies. (Bygate & Kramsch, 2000: 2)

The claim here is that the more interdisciplinary applied linguistics is, the more capable it becomes of dealing with problems in the real world.

This might be taken as uncontroversial, but that does not make it valid. And it seems to me that, on closer inspection, it turns out to be a very questionable claim indeed, and that, far from interdisciplinarity leading to a critical awareness of methodological issues, it actually distracts attention from them.

The belief in interdisciplinarity as the essential enabling feature of applied linguistics rests, I think, on rather shaky foundations. But a belief does not have to be valid to be effective as a basis for action, and I want to stress that, in raising questions about this belief, I do not deny the value of the work that has been inspired by it. I recognize that much has been achieved in the field of applied linguistics through the publications and associations that bear its name.

One such association is the British Association of Applied Linguistics (BAAL), which provides an indispensable service in all kinds of ways, and has many an achievement to its credit. I would not want to question this. What I am concerned with, however, is how it defines what it stands for. As we might expect, interdisciplinarity figures prominently. As stated in its newsletter, BAAL's aims 'are to promote the study of language in use,' and 'to foster interdisciplinary collaboration' to that end. It has indeed incorporated the first of these aims in the slogan 'promoting understanding of language in use.' This statement of aims prompts a number of questions. One might ask, for example, where the study of language learning and teaching comes in. This has perhaps been too exclusive a preoccupation of applied linguistics in the past, but that does not seem a good reason for now excluding it completely. One might argue, of course, that learning is a 'kind' of language use, but this surely smacks of casuistry. But leaving that aside, and returning to the main issue, one might ask what is distinctive about applied linguistics as described here. If its scope is to be confined to the study of language in use, then how does it differ from the discipline that defines its aims in the same terms, namely sociolinguistics? It is not a matter, it would seem, of collaborating with this discipline but of incorporating it, in which case one wonders why there is a need for applied linguistics at all.

At this point we might invoke the first feature that is routinely said to characterize applied linguistics: its concern with real-world problems. But there is no mention of this in the BAAL statement of aims. Furthermore many sociolinguists would take the view that real-world problems fall within their purview as well and that their responsibility is not only to promote an understanding of language in use, but to intervene in linguistic affairs by correcting attitudes, for example, or protecting language diversity (see Trudgill, 2002; Nettle & Romaine, 2000). Labov (1988) goes so far as to say that the essential purpose of linguistic enquiry is to produce theories that can be used to 'resolve questions about the real world,' and he indicates what kinds of question he has in mind:

A sober look at the world around us shows that matters of importance are matters of fact. There are some very large matters of fact: the origin of the universe, the direction of continental drift, the evolution of the human species. There are also specific matters of fact: the innocence or guilt of a particular individual. These are the questions to answer if we would achieve our fullest potential as thinking beings. (Labov, 1988: 182)

Some of what Labov refers to as matters of fact, the origin of the universe, for example, can be seen as so remote from language as to be outside the scope of applied linguistics, no matter how comprehensive its conception. Others, like guilt and innocence, are not matters of fact of the same kind at all, and this brings up a crucial issue that I shall return to later. But the point to be made at present is that sociolinguistics would appear to be already engaged in what BAAL defines as the field of applied linguistics, and is indeed even taking on the problem-solving role that BAAL's statement of aims actually makes no mention of at all.

For Labov the prime motivation for his enquiry is how problematic matters in the real world might be resolved. There is no such motivation evident in the BAAL statement. Hence there is no indication of how dealing with 'real world problems' might require the fostering of interdisciplinary collaboration. Here, one might suggest, there is too much concern with interdisciplinarity, and not enough with the real world. Elsewhere, there are conceptions of applied linguistics that take adequate account of neither. An example would be recent pronouncements about the necessary relevance of corpus descriptions to the design of language curricula. Thus Sinclair (1997) proposes a number of precepts for language teachers that derive directly and unilaterally from linguistic findings:

> The precepts centre on data, and arise from observations about the nature of language. They are not concerned with psychological or pedagogical approaches to language teaching. (Sinclair, 1997: 30)

The precepts are directed at resolving questions in the real world of language classrooms, but no account is taken of this reality, nor of the other disciplines that might conceivably bear on these questions. Paradoxically, these precepts invoke the concept of reality: the first enjoins teachers to 'present real examples only' (Sinclair, 1997: 30). The reality invoked here, however, is that of native speaker users, not that of learners of the language in the contexts of classrooms. But it is this latter reality that pedagogy has to be concerned with: the problem to be addressed is not how one goes about describing the ways in which people actually use their own language, but how learners can be induced to learn a language that is not their own.

The confusion of two realities that is exemplified here brings us back to the two defining features of applied linguistics that I mentioned at the beginning, and to their relationship. The 'real world' problems that applied linguistics purports to deal with arise from a direct experience of language in everyday life. Their reality is what I shall call that of the practical domain. It is the reality as lived and apprehended by what Niedzielski and Preston (2003) refer to as the 'folk.'[1] The other reality is that which is abstracted by the expertise of people initiated into the particular principles and procedures of enquiry that define a discipline. The realities of domain and discipline do not, of course, correspond (there would be no point in the discipline if they did), and, where there is a conflict, it is generally the disciplinary expertise that is taken to represent the truth of the matter and the ideas of the folk, based on direct experience, that are taken to be mistaken.

And often, of course, they are. Developments in the disciplines of the 'hard' physical sciences have demonstrated just how wrong the folk can be. The sun does not go round the world every day, as folk might fondly imagine. What can be transmitted in sight and sound is not restricted by the natural physiological limitations of the organs of eye and ear. Things can be temporally present, and spatially absent at the same time. And so on. Although the folk may sense that there is a world beyond what they directly experience – 'strange sights, things invisible to see,' as John Donne has it – it is a mysterious one beyond human control. Puck, in Shakespeare's *A Midsummer Night's Dream*, may miraculously 'put a girdle round the earth in forty minutes,' but he had magical powers quite beyond human reach. Nowadays, the earth is girdled round a million times in seconds by means of electronic technology, and there is nothing miraculous about that. So expertise in the physical sciences, borne out by technological application, reveals the limitations of folk belief based on experience, and it is easy to dismiss it as the quaint vestige of unfounded superstition, remote from the real world of hard fact, and to be dispelled wherever possible.

And this is precisely how such belief does tend to be dismissed when it comes to matters of language. As Niedzielski and Preston put it:

> Folk linguistics has not fared well in the history of the science, and linguists have generally taken an 'us' versus 'them' position. From a scientific perspective, folk beliefs about language are, at best, innocent misunderstandings of language (perhaps only minor impediments to introductory linguistic instruction) or, at worst, the bases of prejudice, leading to the continuation, reformulation, rationalization, justification, and even development of a variety of social injustices. (Niedzielski & Preston, 2003: 1)

The common assumption is that accounts of language provided by disciplinary enquiry will necessarily, as with the 'hard' physical sciences, go beyond appearances and reveal some underlying essential reality that the folk have hitherto failed to appreciate. Where folk ideas are out of step, they are misconceived. One difficulty with this assumption of privileged access to the truth is that linguistic accounts of language are not infrequently out of step with each other. Structuralist accounts of a taxonomic kind are, according to generativists, misconceived, and generativist accounts in their turn are, according to functionalists, also misconceived. Corpus linguists tell us that any grammar not based on the observation of actually occurring language behaviour is a misrepresentation. The authors of the recent *Cambridge Grammar of English* (Huddlestone & Pullum, 2002) claim that they have come up with a correct description of some aspects of English that all preceding grammarians got wrong. Other linguists tell us that there are no rules of grammar at all, so that presumably any attempt to describe them at all is futile.

By what criteria, then, are we supposed to decide which of these alternative versions of linguistic reality is to be taken as authoritative, as revealing where the folk are in error? For disciplinary enquiry seems on the face of it to be just as prone to misunderstanding and prejudice as the unenlightened beliefs it is supposed to dispel. Perhaps the difference lies in the fact that the discipline is indeed disciplined in that its theories and findings are under strict conceptual control, intellectually rigorous, and rationally well-founded, quite unlike the rather random intuitive notions of the folk. But this does not always seem to be the case either.

Linguists, for example, will routinely assert that, contrary to popular belief, all languages are equal. This may be a morally laudable position to take, but it is not one for which any substantiation, rigorous or otherwise, is provided, and it difficult to see how it could be. It is a matter of faith, not a matter of fact. Indeed, as a matter of fact, the folk position would seem to be more tenable: all languages are certainly not equal in terms of their perceived relative complexity or of their status in particular communities. Again, sociolinguistics will routinely argue that language variation and change are natural social processes and that it is futile to impede them, as the folk not infrequently do by complaining about linguistic abuse and deploring the decline in standards. But this argument is only applied in support of linguistic diversity. When precisely the same process of adaptation to changing social circumstances leads to a diminishing of diversity and an increasing 'homogenization,' as with the case of the global spread of English, the argument apparently no longer applies (see again Nettle & Romaine, 2000; Trudgill, 2002).

Homogenization is, one might note, an odd concept to invoke, for it suggests that variation and change are not necessary and natural linguistic processes after all, but cease when homogenization sets in. The argument now is that when the survival of declining languages is at stake, it is no longer futile or foolish to intervene to prevent change. The goal posts seem to have been shifted.

To say this is not at all to deny the *cause* of linguistic diversity but to question the basis on which the *case* for it is presented. For this rests ultimately on moral belief and not on the consistent application of a principle of disciplinary enquiry. In short, the basis is one of prejudice – positive, benevolent, laudable – but prejudice all the same.

So, though their proponents might wish to suggest otherwise, disciplines that deal with language are changeable, unstable, not always internally consistent. They are indeed very much like language itself, and it is not surprising to find that the factors and forces that Thomas Kuhn (1962) identifies as responsible for shifts in disciplinary paradigms should parallel those adduced by sociolinguistics to account for language variation and change. In spite of the imprimatur of academic authority that the disciplines bear, whatever truth they reveal is always provisional and partial, and the imprimatur often has the effect of preventing us from noticing this.

Linguistics, like all disciplines, devises ideal models of one kind or another – abstract constructs that give selective prominence to certain features of the experienced world and leave others out of the reckoning. It deals essentially in simplified constructs, versions of reality perceived from different perspectives and positions, that cannot of their nature capture what language actually is for the folk who experience it. This is very obviously the case with formalist models, of course, and they have been much criticised over recent years on that account. But it is also the case, less obviously, with linguistic descriptions that claim a closer involvement with how language actually functions in use. Thus, as we have noted, corpus linguistics claims to describe the actual facts of real language. But what is presented is an analysis of the language usage that folk produce in the pragmatic process of social interaction, and this is not at all the same as the process itself. The concordance is an analytic construct and as such is no closer than constituent analysis to what the folk actually experience as language (for further discussion, see Widdowson, 2000a, 2003). Of course the concordance gets closer to what goes on in the real world in the sense that it deals with the data of actually occurring behaviour. As Labov says:

> It seems natural enough that the basic data for any form of general linguistics would be the language as it is used by native speakers communicating with each other in everyday life. (Labov, 1972a: 184)

But taking language use as data does not, of course, mean that the description based on it represents the experience of the native speakers using it.

Different areas and eras of the discipline of linguistics, then, present us with different kinds of abstraction, all of them at a remove from the actual domains of use from which they are abstracted. Perceptions shift as to what is of central importance about the nature of language, acted upon by a range of influences: sociopolitical attitudes, commercial interests, technological developments, and so on. And as perceptions shift, so the perspectives of other disciplines will be seen as relevant as potential collaborative partners, and various kinds of interdisciplinary 'hyphenated linguistics' will emerge in consequence (Spolsky, 1998). Psychology has in the past been the preferred partner, and in the generative era, linguistics was taken to be a branch of cognitive psychology, language being seen essentially as something in the mind (e.g. Chomsky, 1972). Latterly sociology has been seen as the more relevant discipline for linguistics to collaborate with, language being seen as essentially a mode of social action (e.g. Fairclough, 1992). But there are three points about interdisciplinary collaboration that we need to note.

The first is that the collaboration tends to be unilateral and to result in a hybrid that is not always recognised as a legitimate issue by both parties. The appropriation of ideas from another discipline will involve some readjustment whereby they are recontextualized to fit a conceptual scheme that is bound to be different in some respects from the one they originally belonged to. Interdisciplinarity sounds like something that is intellectually liberating, but it also has its reductive side. For it is not simply a matter of coupling two disciplines together, with each retaining its own identity and integrity, but of one discipline assuming a dominant role and drawing from the other whatever can be conveniently accommodated within its scheme of things. As a consequence, of course, the adaptation will always be open to the charge of distortion. Thus, for example, Bernstein suggests that Labov's sociolinguistics is sociologically flawed (Bernstein, 1990), and Bernstein's own excursion into linguistics has in its turn been subject to criticism on similar grounds of disciplinary naivety (Stubbs, 1980, 1983). Such criticism might sound captious, based on too purist and protectionist an attitude. But it is, after all, the purpose of disciplines to establish particular modes of abstraction and to define what is proper to their enquiry and what is not. They have no *raison d'être* otherwise. In this respect it seems entirely reasonable for scholars to defend them from abuse. At the same time it will not do for scholars to be too protective of their patch, for this would be to deny the possibility of any change at all. An interesting illustration of this occurred some ten years ago, when the name of the French philosopher Jacques Derrida was put forward for an honorary doctorate at Oxford. In a letter in *The Independent* newspaper (May 9, 1992) a number of senior academics express their objections. The tone to begin with is relatively measured:

> M. Derrida describes himself as philosopher, and his writings do indeed bear some of the marks of writings in that discipline. Their influence, however, has been to a striking degree almost entirely in

fields outside philosophy – in departments of film studies, for example, or of French and English literature.

In the eyes of philosophers, and certainly among those working in leading departments of philosophy throughout the world, Derrida's work does not meet accepted standards of clarity and rigour.

In the eyes of the philosophers, then (or the philosophers at Oxford, at any rate), Derrida's work is philosophical only in pretence, for it has compromised the proper principles of that discipline by seeking to link it with others, including some of very doubtful character (film studies, for example). The Oxonians feel that the 'standards of clarity and rigour' in their custody are under threat, and the tone of the letter becomes increasingly agitated and acerbic. Reference is made to Derrida's 'antics,' his 'academic tricks' and 'Dadaist gimmicks,' and to his 'semi-intelligible attacks upon the values of reason, truth, and scholarship.' The attitude of the philosophers is far from philosophical in an idiomatic sense: they bristle in defence of their discipline.

The first point about interdisciplinary collaboration, then, is that it tends to be one-sided, with the consequence that the resulting hybrid is often seen as compromising the integrity of the donor discipline. A second point closely follows it: quite simply, if ideas are successfully absorbed, then their interdisciplinary nature disappears. If sociological or psychological concepts get integrated into linguistics, then you get a different perspective on language, and a different kind of linguistics. Interdisciplinarity is a notion that commands universal commendation, 'a consummation devoutly to be wished,' in that it seems to provide for the possibility of seeing things more comprehensively from a diversity of perspectives. This is an appealing idea, but it is also largely an illusion. For it is simply not possible to see things from two different perspectives at the same time. You can, of course, shift from one perspective to another at different times, and this can often prove enlightening, if only to show how incomplete and partial different representations of reality can be. But the requirement for disciplinary consistency and coherence must set limits on how much diversity you can accommodate, and how comprehensive your vision can be. The fact of the matter is that if you want to see things steadily, you cannot see them whole.

And you cannot see them as they really are. Here, we come to the third point about interdisciplinary collaboration: it necessarily takes place at a level of abstraction far removed from what the folk experience in the practical domains of the real world. When we are concerned with linguistics, hyphenated or not, what is abstracted from this reality has to be referred back to it to provide empirical substantiation. This reality is transformed into language data that is drawn upon selectively to serve as evidence for theoretical or descriptive statements. Thus the enquiry remains at the level of ideal abstraction: it does not seek to represent language as experienced by the folk. Indeed, as suggested earlier, if it did, it would have no point and would serve no purpose.

Now if we consider the claim that applied linguistics is an interdisciplinary area of enquiry, we come across two obvious difficulties. The first is that, unlike linguistics, there is no host discipline, so to speak, to be modified by ideas from other disciplines, no given perspective to be adjusted. If one takes linguistics as the host, then applied linguistics ceases to be distinctive because it simply becomes a hyphenated version. The only reason for indulging in interdisciplinarity would appear to be that it provides a way of meeting the second criterial feature of applied linguistics, namely that of engaging with real world problems. But then we come up against the second difficulty: interdisciplinary enquiry does not of its nature deal with such problems.

We have the contradiction, then, that the interdisciplinarity that is invoked to deal with language problems in the 'real world' actually prevents any engagement with this reality. For this involves not the linking of ideas across the same plane of abstraction, but the mediating of a relationship between two quite different planes of reality: that of the abstract discipline and that of the actual domain where the folk experience of language is to be found. The essential issue for applied linguistics is whether, how, and how far the ideas and findings that have been refined out of actual data by idealisation and analysis can be referred back reflexively to the domains of folk experience whence they came and be made relevant in practice. You can indulge in interdisciplinary collaboration to your heart's content without ever getting involved in this issue.

Mediating between disciplinary expertise and folk experience is, of course, a tricky thing to do, and given the authority accorded to experts and the low esteem in which folk ideas are held, it is not something everybody would think worth doing anyway. It is much easier to assume that solutions to problems can be unilaterally provided. A case in point would be the precepts proposed for language teaching discussed earlier: what teachers themselves might think, or what the particular circumstances of different pedagogic domains might be, are not taken into account. No mediation here. Nor is there much sign of it in a great deal of the research that has been undertaken into second language acquisition (SLA). Just as corpus linguists have tended to suppose that their procedures of analysis can yield an intrinsically real language that has pedagogic validity whatever the local circumstances might be, so SLA researchers have tended to suppose that there is an intrinsically real language learning process that can be identified, as soon as they get their theories sorted out, and that can at last provide a universally reliable basis for course design and methodology. In both cases, the assumption is that hitherto the folk, in this case teachers, with only their own wit and experience to depend upon, have got things wrong. What Sinclair says about language expresses the SLA assumption about language learning as well:

> We are teaching English in ignorance of a vast amount of basic fact. This is not our fault, but it should not inhibit the absorption of new material. (Sinclair, 1985: 252)

This talk about fact takes us back to the remarks of Labov (1988) cited earlier. He too talks about matters of fact but in reference not to those of linguistic analysis but to 'the world around us,' and he distinguishes between 'very large' ones and those that are 'specific.' It is of interest to note that all the large ones that Labov mentions are all matters dealt with by the 'hard' scientific disciplines: the origin of the universe by astrophysics, the direction of continental drift by geology, the evolution of the human species by genetics. These disciplines operate at a level of abstraction that is a long way removed from immediate experience and can claim to reveal an empirically well-founded factuality inaccessible to folk awareness and quite remote from their 'real world.' What the folk might think is quite irrelevant to how these disciplines conduct their enquiries, and conversely, their findings might be quite irrelevant to the folk's way of thinking. What Labov refers to as 'specific matters of fact' are altogether different. The example he gives is 'the innocence or guilt of a particular individual.' But this is not something like continental drift that can be objectively established. What we have here is a matter not of fact but of belief: what counts as guilt or innocence is a figment of a particular set of sociocultural conventions. You can treat such matters as factual only by subscribing to such conventions and accepting the values they embody. Clearly facts of this kind (if they can indeed be so called) cannot be established without reference to what the folk think, and different communities of folk will think about these things in very different ways. They belong not to scientific disciplines but to social domains.

It is these 'facts' that applied linguistics has to somehow deal with if it is to engage with problems in the 'real world:' relative values, varying – and often opposing – beliefs and attitudes that constitute different ways of thinking and living. This, of course, is a difficult thing to do, and it is very tempting to simplify matters. One way of doing this is to just ignore the diversity of local domains, as with the kind of unilateral imposition of disciplinary ideas and findings we considered earlier. Another way is to assign preferential status to one set of domain values and assume that all others can, and should, be brought into line. The complex variety of the 'real world' is in this case simplified and made more manageable not by idealisation but by ideology. Such a strategy has its attractions. There are ways of thinking and living that on the face of it seem self-evidently more enlightened and more moral than others, and it is surely only right and proper that these should be promoted. And so we get applied linguistics committed to a good cause. One obvious difficulty about this is that it is not at all self-evident whether a cause is good or not. Often it turns out to be weighted with self-interest and to be rather better for its promoters than for its putative beneficiaries.

And even if one discounts ulterior motives, the goodness of a cause may not be realisable in socio-cultural contexts other than that in which it originated. The point made earlier about the difficulties of transferring ideas across disciplines applies also to the transference of values across domains. Pennycook, among others, has advocated a critical applied linguistics, one that has a mission and is committed to a particular socio-political ideology: applied linguistics, as he calls it, 'with an attitude' (Pennycook, 2001). But having a preconceived attitude is not likely to make you open to an understanding of other values, and commitment is likely to preclude a critical appraisal of your own position. Some of the work that goes under the name of critical discourse analysis is a good illustration of this: texts are assigned interpretations from a particular ideological point of view and no consideration is given to how other readers, with other pretextual assumptions, might understand them (for further discussion, see Widdowson, 1998, 2004).

Applied linguistics is said to deal with those problems to do with language that crop up in 'real world' domains. But these are infinitely many and diverse. The diversity is reduced by the abstractions of disciplinary enquiry, thereby putting itself at a remove from folk experience, and no amount of interdisciplinarity can close that gap. The diversity can also be reduced by paying selective attention to certain domains and the socio-cultural values associated with them, and then extrapolating to others. But, of course, this, too, involves the disregard of reality as experienced by the local folk. So on this account it would seem that the claim that applied linguistics engages in the investigation of real world problems by means of interdisciplinary collaboration is questionable, to say the least.

What goes on under the name of applied linguistics is acknowledged to be highly diverse, and this is seen to be positive. But it can also be seen, somewhat less positively, as a rather motley assortment of activities. The term seems to be used as a convenient designation for any discussion about observed language data from any source, and from any disciplinary perspective. There is no agreed set of principles and procedures that one would normally expect of an area of enquiry, and that would provide some measure of consistency and coherence to such activities. Indeed it has been suggested that any such agreement would be undesirable in that it would make applied linguistics too academic and too restrictive in scope (see Rampton, 1997).[2] Any attempt to give explicit consideration to how the field might be defined tends to be dismissed as unnecessary agonising: let us not worry about what we are doing, is the common cry; let us just get on with it, whatever it might be. The diversity of the field, especially if it can be associated with interdisciplinarity, is, in this view, its most commendable feature. If it is diffuse in consequence, then that, apparently, is a price worth paying.

But it does not follow that, if the scope of enquiry in applied linguistics is to range over a diversity of language phenomena, it should be correspondingly diffuse as a *mode* of enquiry. On the contrary, it would generally be the case that the reason why a field of enquiry can deal with diversity is precisely because there is some consensus about how this is to be done. The diversity is reduced by the very consistency of the methodology used to deal with it. One can readily accept that the problems concerning language in the 'real world' that applied linguistics should seek to address are many and diverse. But that is all the more reason why there should be some degree of uniformity of approach, some set of agreed principles about how to proceed. Otherwise, 'applied linguistics' is simply a term without substance, a label that we find it expedient to attach, like a flag of convenience, to almost any activity that concerns itself with language.

It seems to me that the only way of establishing what is distinctive about applied linguistics is to recognize that, as a mode of enquiry, it has conditions of accountability to meet that are very different from those of disciplinary study. All disciplines are necessarily concerned with reality as actually experienced since this provides the data that has to be empirically adduced as substantiating evidence for the underlying abstractions that are drawn from them. And so it is that in linguistics, however hyphenated, there has to be what Firth (1952/1978: 19) referred to as a 'renewal of connection' with language as it actually occurs in the real world. But the connection is selectively renewed only with those aspects of language that can serve as relevant evidence. Applied linguistics cannot be selective in this way. If it claims to engage with language problems in the real world, it cannot just reduce these to data to substantiate some theory or other. Its procedures must somehow work in reverse: instead of looking at how actual language experience can be used to substantiate abstraction, it must look at how abstraction can be used to take a different fix on actuality. We renew connection with folk realities, not so as to use them as data, but to see them in alternative terms, to reformulate what is problematic about them in the light of a detached disciplinary perspective.

But to do this, we need to be quite clear about what kind of 'truth' or 'factuality' disciplinary expertise can, and cannot, provide us with. And here we encounter the paradox that folk experience in the domains of the 'real world' can only be described in terms that in some degree misrepresent the experience. The paradox is nicely expressed in a passage from Bruce Chatwin's *The Songlines* (1987):

Kidder, expanding on his theme, said that sacred knowledge was the cultural property of the Aboriginal people. All such knowledge which had got into the hands of the white man had been acquired either by fraud or by force. It was now going to be de-programed.

> 'Knowledge is knowledge,' I said. 'It's not that easy to dispose of.'
>
> He did not agree.
>
> To 'de-program' sacred knowledge, he said, meant examining archives for unpublished material on Aboriginals; you then returned the relevant pages to the rightful 'owners.' It meant transferring copyright from the author of a book to the people it described; returning photographs to the photographed (or their descendents); recording tapes to the recorded, and so forth.
>
> I heard him out, gasping in disbelief.
>
> 'And who,' I asked, 'will decide who these 'owners' are?'
>
> 'We have ways of researching that kind of information.'
>
> 'Your ways or their ways?'
>
> He did not reply. (Chatwin, 1987: 43)

The de-programing of knowledge that is expertly abstracted cannot possibly recover knowledge in its pristine, unrecorded state as originally, or aboriginally, conceived as sacred by the folk. The photographs and tapes necessarily misrepresent it: in returning the record, you obviously do not thereby restore the experience recorded. And the folk are not consulted about how the records are to be returned, any more than they were consulted when the records were made in the first place. The knowledge that Kidder wants to return to its owners cannot be returned, because they do not own it. It is a construct of ethnographic enquiry. This does not render it invalid, of course. On the contrary, it is because such an enquiry is at a remove from the immediacy of folk experience that it can reveal aspects of it from an outsider's perspective.

There is confusion here, then, between two kinds of knowledge, two kinds of reality: that of disciplinary expertise and that of domain experience. Each has its own legitimacy, and each can draw support from the other: expertise uses experience as data to substantiate its abstractions and experience can be reformulated in reference to the expertise. But the crucial point is that if these reformulations are to be effective, they cannot simply be unilaterally imposed. They must also take local 'real world' conditions of relevance into account. Hence the need to mediate across these two realities without giving undue primacy to either.

The two realities correspond, of course, to the two features that, as I said at the beginning, are generally taken to be distinctive of applied linguistics: interdisciplinarity and a concern with problems in the real world. Although we are told (in the editorial cited earlier: Bygate & Kramsch, 2000) that it is uncontroversially the case that interdisciplinarity serves as a preparation for the handling of real-world issues, there is no indication as to how it is supposed to do this. I have argued that interdisciplinarity, itself a very tenuous concept, cannot actually provide such a service since it operates on a level of abstraction remote from actualities as experienced by the folk. If we are to engage with real-world issues, we need to develop a methodological approach that mediates between these two orders of reality of discipline and domain.

One might argue, of course, that in practice this is what a vast amount of work in applied linguistics does anyway, inspired and not inhibited by the wider transcendental vision suggested by manifesto statements. In this case, there is no need to press for more explicitness in the specification of methodological principles. Good work will continue to be done, and whether you call it applied linguistics or something else does not matter much. What, after all, is in a name?

There is, no doubt, something to be said for this pragmatic view. But if, every now and then, and on reflection, one feels the need to be rather more specific about what applied linguistics is all about, then one might be led to the conclusion that, if our field is to have any distinctive character, it must surely rest on the claim that it is a particular mode of enquiry that is not only not essentially interdisciplinary but not essentially disciplinary at all, because it does not deal with abstractions per se and with what data can be adduced as evidence for them. Rather, it takes an approach that is the reverse of this in that it explores how the problems that folk experience with language in real-world domains might be clarified, reformulated, made more amenable to solution by reference to the abstract representations of language that linguistics (hyphenated and otherwise) has to offer.

Notes

1. I intend this term in the sense in which Niedzielski and Preston (2003) use it to refer to people without specialist knowledge of the phenomena they experience. As they put it:
   We use *folk* to refer to those who are not trained professionals in the area under investigation (although we would not for one moment deny the fact that professional linguists themselves are a folk group, with their own rich set of beliefs). We definitely do not use *folk* to refer to rustic, ignorant, uneducated, backward, primitive, minority, isolated, marginalized, or lower status groups or individuals. (Niedzielski & Preston, 2003: xviii)
   The term is then a relative one, and people who are expert in one particular discipline will be the folk in regard to another.
2. Rampton's paper prompted a lively exchange of views about the nature of applied linguistics, and is reprinted in Seidlhofer (2003).

Chapter 2
Is Language Policy Applied Linguistics?

BERNARD SPOLSKY

A Somewhat Personal Introduction

Robert Kaplan and I have been acquainted professionally and personally for something like 40 years, although in that time we have written only one piece together (Spolsky & Kaplan, 1976), and that a somewhat polemic one. Nonetheless, the parallels in our careers and interests give a certain poignancy to the invitation to write a piece for his Festschrift. For both of us, our early research dealt with teaching English as a foreign language and, while I chose to concentrate on language testing (Jones & Spolsky, 1975; Spolsky, 1968, 1971), Kaplan developed the field of contrastive rhetoric (Kaplan, 1963, 1966, 1972). Soon, however, we both seem to have realized that our concern with teaching English required us, if we were to work in a wider theoretical framework, to attempt to place language teaching and pedagogy in the context of applied linguistics.

It was a short step then to start asking, what is applied linguistics? Both of us come back to this question regularly (Kaplan, 1980a, 2002; Spolsky, 1973, 1980, 1990). I argued for an intermediate field called educational linguistics (Spolsky, 1978), a term now being picked up by others (see the new book series edited for Kluwer by Leo van Lier and university programs with that name at the University of Pennsylvania, the University of Lancaster, the Monterey Institute of International Studies, the University of Groningen, the University of Sydney, and the University of New Mexico, to list the first half-dozen that appear on a Google search).

Not satisfied with this, both Kaplan and I were increasingly attracted by the field that I call language policy (Spolsky, 2004) and Kaplan calls language policy and language planning (Kaplan, 1994; Kaplan & Baldauf, 2003). The move was no doubt logically necessary, for we both came to recognize that teaching English as a foreign language implied teaching English to speakers of other languages, just as the naming of TESOL – the international organization in which we were both active and each served a term as president – proclaimed. It was a short step to recognize that teaching English to speakers of other languages was the kind of language policy that Robert Cooper (1989) later sagely defined as language acquisition policy, and that Kaplan regularly refers to as language-in-education policy. Understanding that language education policy does not exist in a vacuum, it seems logical that both of us have become increasingly interested in the wider field.

In this brief chapter, I do not intend to reiterate all the steps involved in these arguments, nor to trace and resolve the probably quite minor technical or theoretical differences in our approaches and terminology. Rather, I will first quickly sketch the multiple connections between applied linguistics and language policy, suggesting that a good understanding of the latter draws on the widest resources of the former. This done, I will try to analyze the various approaches of linguists (and by definition applied linguists) to language policy over the past half-century or so, placing Kaplan (and incidentally but inevitably, myself) somewhere inside the range of possible varieties.

What is Applied Linguistics?

What differentiates applied linguistics from linguistics? The simplest answer seems to be that linguists are mainly interested in the nature and structure of language, some going so far as to treat it as completely autonomous and connected to the outside world only because it is located inside the brain of human beings. An oversimplified and dangerously erroneous extension of this approach was what I have characterized as the 'little boy with the hammer' belief that this knowledge of language can be directly applied to a task such as the teaching of languages. Too many language learners have suffered through lessons in formal, structural, or transformational grammar without this in any way improving their competence in language use. This is certainly not to argue that language teaching cannot benefit from our understanding of the implications of this knowledge (Spolsky, 1970), but that it needs to be interpreted and modified by all the other kinds of knowledge relevant to a theory of language pedagogy.

Applied linguistics then would seem to be another case of the problem that linguists have with terms, as Ferguson once remarked in an unpublished talk at the 1978 meeting of the American Association for Applied Linguistics (AAAL). He reminded us that we insist on our own idiosyncratic meaning for the name of our profession, so that we are constantly forced to explain to lay people that a linguist studies languages but does not necessarily speak very many. In much the same way, Chomsky's (1965) choice of 'competence' as the term for grammatical knowledge has produced all sorts of confusion for those talking about language proficiency.

The trouble with *applied* linguistics is its suggestion that linguistics comes first and application later. Defined in this broad way, it seems that just as any use of mathematical knowledge in practical matters can be considered applied mathematics, so any field involving language might benefit from applying theories and knowledge derived from the scientific study of language, namely linguistics.

Take an illustrative case. When people realized that a major gap in international communication could be met by machine translation, it was natural to draw on current theories of language to attempt to build translation devices. By the early 1960s, it was evident that a major impediment was the failure of contemporary theory to provide a basis for automatic parsing, the first step in such a process, and so research was virtually halted for the next decade (Hutchins, 2001). More recently, developments in machine translation have included using human assistance, building tools to help human translators, training people to write translatable texts (Bernth & Gdaniec, 2001), and building programs that allow correction of and learning from erroneous output (Frederking et al., 2000).

The case of machine translation models the relationship between linguistics and its applied fields. Knowledge developed by the scientific study of language turns out to be useful and relevant to the applied field, but direct application is rare, and limited to specific areas. The successful solution of language-related problems depends on the blending of linguistic knowledge with knowledge derived from other fields, and so in time leads to the formation of hyphenated fields, as Voegelin (n.d.) named them. For machine translation, the hyphenated field is computational linguistics, and it lives happily in its own domain, closer to engineering and information theory than to core linguistics.

The field of language teaching presents much the same picture. While there are certain approaches to language teaching that place the main emphasis on grammar and so reveal the direct influence of changes in grammatical theory, the relationship is generally more indirect. Attempts in the 1940s to re-establish the teaching of the spoken language that had been at the core of the Direct Method fashionable at the end of the 19th century drew heavily on (then) current methods of analyzing and describing spoken languages, and combined with behaviorist notions of learning, led to the ill-fated but faddishly popular Audiolingual method. Misunderstanding the implications of the Chomskyan revolution, at least one trendy foreign language textbook writer replaced his structural drills ('I see the book. He: He sees the book. They: They see the book.') with so-called transformationalist drills ('I see the book. Not. I did not see the book. Question. Did I see the book?').

A more sophisticated but ultimately equally misguided, approach involved accepting Chomsky's attack on Skinner as weakening all claims for grammar learning, and adopted Chomsky's use of the term 'acquisition' and his search for innate universal grammars in order to condemn all efforts to teach languages, glorifying automatic acquisition through exposure to the next needed form (Krashen, 1981). This had major effects on the profession, justifying the building of a new sub-field to study 'second language acquisition,' most recently encapsulated in Doughty and Long (2003) and privileging the teaching of functions rather than forms (Finocchiaro, 1983; Wilkins, 1976), with correctives in a new 'focus on form' (Long, 2000). It is important to note that this too was not 'application' in the narrow sense, but rather implication. For those to whom second language acquisition was somewhat limited in parenthood, another new field developed, namely educational linguistics (Spolsky, 2003), which aims to unite all the fields relevant to language education.

Language Policy: Beginnings

Essentially, language policy as a field of study grew in a similar way. Early on, linguistics had been shown to be relevant to language management activities such as orthography development and language standardization: Panini with Sanskrit grammar and the medieval Arabic grammarians applied their linguistic knowledge to the preservation of classical sacred texts. Phonetics and later phonology were often naively assumed to be all that was required to develop a workable orthography, but sociolinguists such as Ferguson (1968a) showed that other factors (social, religious, political, nationalist) needed to be involved in the successful creation and modification of writing systems. Working with languages with a well-developed literature, the process that the Prague schools linguists called *cultivation* (Prague School, 1973; Garvin, 1973) seemed to need only linguistics to find out what was the norm. But the standardization of spoken languages required going beyond the core elements of non-hyphenated linguistics into a concern with social and political factors – witness the struggle over the selection of writing systems in the Soviet Union and its successor states (Grenoble, 2003). Although linguists working for the Summer Institute of Linguistics (now SIL International) were among those that initially thought that the phonemic principle was all that was required to develop an orthography (Gudschinsky, 1976), they modified this by adding a preference for script and spelling conventions derived from the regional official language, and have increasingly added 'socio' to their linguistics (Robbins, 1992). A similar logic led to what was to be a study of literacy teaching based on a sociolinguistic survey (Spolsky, 1974, 1980).

Accordingly, there has developed a number of hyphenated and ancillary fields, the core of which is a search for a relevant balancing of the claims of linguistics and other disciplines to deal with the problems of language in use. Among these subfields, Fishman (1991) discusses the field of sociolinguistics, arguing that it has failed to deal adequately with ideas from sociology.

It is the willingness to consider other disciplines as relevant that marks the hyphenated fields, including applied linguistics. A working distinction might be to say that linguistics is concerned with language itself, while applied linguistics is interested in the uses (and so users) of language. Such a distinction makes clearer why linguistics is taken to include all the parts of the field that study the nature and structure of language itself, such as phonetics, phonology, morphology, syntax, and semantics, while applied linguistics in its widest sense includes not just fields such as language teaching, translation, and language management but also Voegelin's hyphenated linguistics, including sociolinguistics.

Language policy fits into applied linguistics, not just because of the practical implications of language management, but also because the study of its two other components, language practice and language beliefs or ideology, requires looking at language in use and studying its users. True, the first of those areas is also covered by sociolinguistics and the ethnography of speaking (Hymes, 1974), and the second is dealt with by social psychology. However, to exclude them from language policy means leaving out two of the major domains in which language policy is embodied and by which language management is constrained. In societies lacking explicit written language policy, the place to seek it is in language practice (the consensually accepted rules of appropriate language choice) or in language ideology (the social beliefs about desirable language practices). Language management itself, the effort by individuals, groups, or institutions with (or claiming to have) authority to modify the language practices or beliefs of other speakers, is at the very core of applied linguistics. Although many language planners considered what they called corpus planning to be the prototypical language management activity, once Cooper (1989) added language acquisition policy to the original dichotomy proposed by Kloss (1969) between status planning and corpus planning, it became obvious that language education policy was probably the most extensive branch of language management.

It is true, as Kaplan and Baldauf (1997) point out, that language education policies are commonly inconsistent with national language policies and that they regularly exist in the absence of an explicit national policy. Perhaps one of the principal tasks of language policy scholars is to clarify the lack of fit between language education and language policy. In the United States for example, this shows up in the regular failure of language education policy to produce citizens with the kinds of language proficiency demanded by the country's international responsibilities and activities (Brecht et al., 1995; Brecht & Ingold, 1998). During the Second World War, an attempt to fill the gap left by the educational establishment's abdication of responsibility for teaching foreign languages was first made by a few linguists led by J. Milton Cowan at the American Council for Learned

Is Language Policy Applied Linguistics? 31

Societies and then briefly undertaken by the US Army (Keefer, 1988; Spolsky, 1995). Since then, the various branches of the Federal Government have run their own language schools (the Foreign Service Institute of the State Department, the Defense Language Institute, the language schools of the Central Intelligence Agency, the National Security Agency, and the Federal Bureau of Investigation). In recent years, the Defense and Intelligence communities have attempted to overcome the shortages of speakers of strategically important languages (it is estimated that they have 30% of the needed capacity) produced by the continued ideological commitment of state departments of education to monolingualism (Brecht & Walton, 1994, 2000). Problems like these are produced in part by the absence of carefully developed national language policies, including language education policies, consistent with the language situation, as Kaplan and Baldauf (1997, 1999, 2000, 2003) regularly demonstrate, and in part by a reluctance to commit the resources needed to implement policies when they are developed.

Language Policy People

Arguing, therefore, that language policy is a paradigmatic example of applied linguistics in that it must draw on a range of academic fields to develop practical plans to modify language practices and beliefs, in the rest of this chapter I want to explore this notion by sketching out the involvement of linguists in language policy over the last century or so. As is so often the case in this kind of analysis, it is possible to recognize a number of stages in the historical progression, all the time realizing that there has been and continues to be a considerable chronological overlap.

Language guardians and reformers

The first category of linguists working in the general sphere of language policy was probably linguists and grammarians turned language reformers. These scholars, generally studying the literary and standard form of their own mother tongue, went beyond efforts to describe the language and its grammar and moved on to provide ways of purifying or cultivating the language. Discovering as they did the patterning and regularities of the language and developing strong respect for the literary value of the best writers, it was not unnatural that they should become advocates of 'correct' language. Perhaps it was their concern for the maintenance of tradition that added purism to normativism, but more probably it was the influence of the nationalistic Zeitgeist. The most elaborated analysis of this approach was in the work of the Prague school, for whom cultivation of the language was seen as a central task of the language planner.

Purism becomes especially important during a time of language cultivation and modernization in that it provides a criterion for the choice of new lexicon. Annamalai (1979, 1989) defines purism as concerned with sources: purism favors native sources and tries to close off non-native sources. As Haugen (1987: 87) notes, 'purism is closely connected with national feeling and has blossomed in periods of patriotic fervor.' It occurs in a situation of language contact and is generally associated with elite bilingualism and efforts to maintain boundaries. For Neustupný (1989: 211), it is 'one of many corrective processes directed towards culture.' It has parallels, Neustupný notes, in similar concerns for keeping foreign influence out of music, literature, and architecture.

Cultivation is a term that was coined in English by Garvin (1973) to translate the term *Sprachkultur*. Cultivation deals with establishing and modifying the norms of a literary or standard language. The main problems concerning the norms of the literary language are 'flexible stability' and 'functional differentiation.' Neustupný (1989: 212) describes the cultivation approach as 'characterized by interest in questions of correctness, efficiency, linguistic levels fulfilling specific functions, style, constraints on communicative capacity, etc.'. This approach was crystallized in the work of Prague School linguists, who focused on the linguistic modifications that followed the selection of a literary language. It dealt with the form of the language itself and looked at the changes that became necessary when a spoken language was given formal functions, including being written. It was thus more appropriate to the case of those European languages whose selection as national languages dates back to earlier centuries than to the solution of urgent 20th century post-independence language questions.

> By the cultivation of good language we mean the conscious fostering of the standard language; this can be done by (1) theoretical linguistic work, (2) language education in the schools, and (3) literary practice... At the root to the successful cultivation of the standard language must be the theoretical understanding of the real norm of the contemporary standard language. (Prague School, 1973: 102–103)

Notice how the Prague School avoided appealing to some arbitrary criteria of correctness such as native or foreign but rather took pragmatic note of language practice. But not just anyone's practice. The 'real norm' must be based on 'the average literary language practice over the past fifty years' (Prague School, 1973: 103). It assumed, in other words, the existence of an established practicing literary elite that used the language in a consensually standard way, something that was seldom to be found in the languages competing for official status in the newly independent states of Africa and Asia in the 1960s when the language planning model was developed. Clearly, it was a Eurocentric approach, and one that, when applied elsewhere, might well distort local realities.

Language planning experts

Cultivation might do for European languages with literary traditions, but the problems faced by the newly independent countries of Asia and Africa in the mid- to late-1960s were quite different. A second category of linguists, who might be labeled the language planning experts, consisted of an international cluster of young scholars who developed the American School of language planning. Often working with Ford Foundation support (Ford Foundation, 1975), they studied and advised newly independent countries and their governments. Among them were Charles Ferguson, Joshua Fishman, Jyotirindra Das Gupta, Joan Rubin, and Bjorn Jernudd. Generally trained in linguistics (Fishman being the exception), they saw their task as understanding the nature of language policy, a concern that led them to be among the founders of the field of sociolinguistics.

There were of course many others (Paulston & Tucker, 1997), but the group named above shared in an exceptional research project (Rubin et al., 1977), the aim of which was to study the nature and effectiveness of language planning. The International Research Project on Language Planning Processes, which lasted from 1968 to 1972, was the first major effort to describe and evaluate the work of language planning agencies. During the first year, four of its research leaders spent the year together working on preliminary studies and developing a research design (Rubin & Jernudd, 1971). The study itself was subsequently carried out in India by Das Gupta, in Israel by Fishman, in Indonesia by Rubin, and in Sweden (after the planned fieldwork in East Pakistan was abandoned) by Jernudd. Each of these studies looked both at language planning agencies and at specific issues of terminological development. Today, this pioneering study retains its importance as one of the few objective efforts to investigate and evaluate the implementation of language management in the area of terminological development. In addition, this is an area where evaluation would seem easiest. The definition of the relevant data is straightforward: the management decisions (usually lists issued by an academy or terminology committee) are explicit; the effects (usage in newspapers or other publications, or knowledge of words shown through questionnaires and interviews) comparatively easy to specify. The fact that there have been very few attempts to replicate the study probably says something important about the area called corpus planning: people argue for it, and, with or without government support, do it; but few people have time or interest to see if it works. These difficulties lead Kaplan and Baldauf (1997) to conclude that the assessment of language planning is complex and difficult and that status planning and corpus planning cannot in fact be usefully divided.

Language rights activists

There are, as I have implied, many linguists who continue to work in the tradition of the language planning experts. More recently, there has developed a new group that might be labeled language policy experts or, more precisely, language rights activists. Among these are scholars who started by describing some of the complex and damaging effects on minority and indigenous groups of what they labeled imperialist (Phillipson, 1992) or colonialist (Pennycook, 1998) language policies, and went on to develop arguments based on theories of linguistic and human rights (Skutnabb-Kangas, 2000; Skutnabb-Kangas & Cummins, 1988; Skutnabb-Kangas & Phillipson, 1995) and the need to preserve linguistic diversity. To their theoretical models and descriptions, they added strong advocacy of specific language policies, and attempted to influence the governments and supranational bodies into recognizing these rights and adopt different policies. A few of those who work on linguistic rights are lawyers rather than linguists – such as Del Valle (2003), but most in this category combine advocacy and scholarship.

Protectors of endangered languages

A related but generally separate category is made up of those scholars who, commonly as a result of studying and describing smaller indigenous languages, have become involved in efforts to resist language shift and maintain these languages. Primarily linguists, their first concern is usually the preservation of linguistic diversity. Two pioneers in the field were the late Kenneth Hale (Hale, 1991; Hinton & Hale, 2001) and Michael Krauss (Krauss, 1991, 1998). While many of these people may be satisfied with developing a grammar and a dictionary of the threatened language to preserve knowledge of it for linguistic science, others often become involved in other management activities, such as the development of a writing system, the teaching of the language to children and other members of the ethnic group, and the collection of cultural materials written in the language. Originally, this interest arises out of the field of anthropological linguistics, with its assumption that the major task of linguists is to describe all existing languages. With growing sensitivity to issues of intellectual ownership and the rights of indigenous people, it becomes clear that it is not enough to take a description of the language back to university and record it in the form of a dissertation or grammar in the library, but that it is appropriate and ethical to be concerned about repaying the speakers of the language (once called informants but now called collaborators or co-workers) for providing material. Although the quality and effect of the work of this group have varied, at its best it has produced native speakers of the languages in question able to take responsibility for both the description and preservation of their language. These include Paul Platero, a leading Navajo linguist, and Patrick Hohepa, who studied linguistics with Ken Hale at MIT and returned to New Zealand to become professor of Maori and later Maori Language Commissioner.

Missionary linguists

A fifth group, also not directly motivated by interest in language policy but exerting considerable influence on it, is made up of Christian missionaries who combine the study of previously unstudied languages with preparations for conversion of the speakers. As Ferguson (1982) noted, missionaries had a major influence on the diffusion of writing systems and the standardization of countless languages. In the largest number of cases, these activities included the development of alphabets, the translation of the Bible and other religious texts, and the teaching of literacy, with the Summer Institute of Linguistics (now SIL International) being a major force in this area. In recent years, these activities have involved not just linguistic training but also a growing sensitivity to sociolinguistic and language policy matters, as shown in studies like Brye (2003) and Diller et al. (2002), which report on sociolinguistic surveys conducted to assess the status of and prospects for two indigenous languages in Cameroon in order to determine the value of starting Bible translations.

Government language managers

Another category, harder to locate because the work is often conducted anonymously within bureaucracies, is that of the linguists working in various official national or supranational language agencies and responsible for a range of language management activities: preparing and implementing laws and regulations, developing and publishing terminological innovations, studying and improving language maintenance programs, or publicizing and supporting language revival activities. Some of the better known are involved in government-supported activities that aim to reverse language shift in Quebec, the Spanish autonomous regions, Friesland, and New Zealand. If one were to include in this group all those administrators, inspectors, and teachers actually busy with the largest language management enterprise of all, the teaching of first, second, and foreign languages, it is clear that this group would in fact overwhelm all the others in terms of numbers.

Language policy scholars

The final category consists of those whose fundamental interest is in the nature and process of language policy, spending their time collecting and publishing empirical evidence that characterizes the field and developing theoretical models to account for what appears to happen in it. Often criticized by activists as socially irresponsible, they are starting to build on the work of scholars in the other categories to create an emerging model of the complexity of language policy. Kaplan's own work is now a paradigmatic example. Since his publication with Baldauf of a detailed account of the field (Kaplan & Baldauf, 1997), he has started a journal *(Current Issues in Language Planning)* and a related book series whose aim is to build up a sufficiently broad and detailed collection of empirically-based studies of language policy and planning to justify the development of a robust theory of the field. Others who follow this approach are Schiffman (1996), Paulston (1988; Paulston & Peckham, 1998), and Barbour (Barbour & Carmichael, 2000), to name a few.

A More Abstract Conclusion

In the long run, the definition of a field can reasonably be explored by looking at the professionals involved in its study. In the area of language policy, most are trained in various aspects of language (especially applied linguistics) and very few are trained in specific policy fields (politics, administration, perhaps even law). That, too, helps account for the overlap.

But this again raises the possibility of better defining applied linguistics. Fifty years ago, the practitioners were generally trained as linguists and then assumed to be qualified to apply that training to solving language-related problems. Linguistics was the theoretical discipline expected to produce linguists able to work in all the hyphenated fields, beginning with foreign language teaching. But as the hyphenated fields have clarified their own boundaries and accepted the need for education in disciplines other than core linguistics, so professionals too have been trained in each appropriate field – second language acquisition, sociolinguistics, computational linguistics, psycholinguistics, language policy, language testing, etc. Thus applied linguistics has developed from being an in-group name for foreign language teaching to being a cover term for a sizeable group of semi-autonomous disciplines, each dividing its parentage and allegiances between the formal study of language and other relevant fields, and each working to develop its own methodologies and principles.

Those, like Kaplan, who have been pioneers in the field of applied linguistics have thus been engaged in an ongoing expansion and redefinition of the field, one that is united with other subfields by its central concern for understanding the nature of language use, and the relevance to society of that understanding.

Part 2
Language Education

Part 2
Introduction

VAIDEHI RAMANATHAN

The idea that educational systems worldwide are elaborate machineries that seem to have lives of their own is a resonant one at some level. All of us – students, teachers, researchers, mentors – engaged in various aspects of the enterprise have realized, at different points and with varying degrees of frustration, that the educational endeavor seems at times overwhelming, and that our roles as (potential) educators may sometimes seem to be only minimal. And yet most of us applied linguists hold on to the hope that it is in part in noting language-related problems in our collective machineries and in finding ways to alleviate them that our professional commitment lies. I use this metaphor of our educational machineries, not to highlight education's sometimes mechanistic nature, but because it allows us, if only for a few fleeting moments, to step back from our participation and to view the alignment and synchronicity of the various cogs and subcogs churning together. It also permits occasional glimpses into how all of us, with divergent backgrounds and interests, participate in creating 'knowledge' in our 'disciplinary thought collectives' (Ramanathan, 2002), and how aspects of our collective's constructed 'knowledge' sometimes can become a naturalized part of the larger machinery.

This view of larger socio-educational machineries being 'outside' us is not intended to convey a sense of machineries being fixed; neither is it intended to suggest that we are not embedded in them. Indeed, because the socio-educational enterprise churns and mutates, change is written into its nature and, as researchers, we are embedded in and partially responsible for any change. All three chapters in this section address various aspects of change, some more directly than others, some concentrating more on 'problems,' others more on solutions. I offer below a summary of each of the chapters.

In Chapter 3, entitled 'Sharing community languages: Utopian dream or realistic vision?' Clyne offers a partial historical exploration of language policies on the teaching of English as a second language and languages other than English (LOTEs) in Australia. Clyne notes how particular language policies have traditionally kept one group of people from sustaining their bilingualism while spending huge amounts of money toward making others bilingual by teaching them a language other than English. Documenting implicit negative policies towards languages other than English, Clyne discusses ways in which LOTEs were relegated to an 'elitist' realm that designated these languages as 'foreign.' Clyne also discusses the refragmentation of community-language issues into 'single-policy' issues (such as Asian language policy or literacy policy). The chapter concludes with a call for change in several realms, including working toward cultivating a society that is free of xenophobia and linguistically more aware, and that validates and rewards multilingualism.

The theme of transformation also characterizes Chapter 4, on curricular reform, by Domínguez, Donato, and Tucker. Following the sometimes uneven journey of curricular reform in foreign language education in US elementary schools (FLES), the authors report on a two-year-long research project involving the introduction of reading and writing skills in the K–5 (kindergarten to grade 5) curriculum. The study documents how teachers participating in an early literacy program (PACE) come to realize that their current focus on teaching only speaking is limited and how they attempt to integrate literacy skills by drawing on stories, folktales, and legends. Throughout, the study highlights the complex confluence of social factors competitively influencing the educational context: political climate, historical and economic conditions, administrative and institutional support, and language planning factors and policies. The research captures the unfinished, ongoing nature of all reform – including its travails and problems – while remaining steadfastly committed to the need for reform itself.

The need to question existing (sub)cogs in our collective's socio-educational machinery and to think about ways to bring about educational change marks Kamhi-Stein's piece as well. In Chapter 5, taking on the recently politicized 'native-non-native' dichotomy, Kamhi-Stein reviews the variety of different pockets in which this divide is played out, especially as it applies to the role of 'non-native' language teachers in language education. Far-ranging and comprehensive, her discussion explores sensitive areas: how program administrators and language learners perceive 'non-native' teachers, how the linguistic competence and literacy skills of these teachers permit them to work as double agents, and how past debates regarding these issues have tended to override latent complexities. By chronicling the diverse ways in which the dichotomy has grown and changed over the years, Kamhi-Stein simultaneously advocates more questioning and more transformation.

To return to the metaphor of socio-educational machineries in our thought-collectives, each of these chapters isolates one facet in a much larger set of interconnected cogs for closer examination and possible change. For all of us who know Robert B. Kaplan and his work, the themes of these chapters echo strains that distinctly mark his own work. Each chapter not only reverberates views and issues that Bob Kaplan has consistently upheld in his own writing, but also underscores his commitment to multilingualism and language reform as well as his questioning of dichotomies. The chapters in this section, as indeed in the entire book, constitute a tribute to Kaplan's unswerving pledge to question some key sites in our thought collectives.

Chapter 3
Sharing Community Languages: Utopian Dream or Realistic Vision?

MICHAEL CLYNE

Bob Kaplan, whom we honor in this volume, has not only provided exemplary models and analyses of languages-in-education policy. He has also acted as a catalyst for actual policy development. His several visits to Australia and New Zealand have resulted in new initiatives inspired by interactions with a person of such vision and foresight. I can recall, for instance, how a workshop organized by Terry Quinn around Bob in 1980 caused a number of us who had been trying to get an immersion program off the ground to proceed with Melbourne's first such program and a research and evaluation project to accompany it.

More than two decades later, the impetus provided by that visit continues to be felt in the mainstreaming of community languages to the benefit of those who have ethnic links to these languages and of others who enjoy them instrumentally, integratively, and above all, intrinsically (Gardner & Lambert, 1972; Ellis, 1995). In a recent paper (Clyne, 2003), I suggest that in some cases an identity and a community may be created around a language (rather than the other way around). In this chapter, I will also discuss impediments to the utilization of the linguistic capital of bilingual students and to the spread and sharing of community languages. The term 'community languages,' coined in 1975, refers to languages other than English (LOTEs) as well as to indigenous languages used in the Australian community. Its use legitimizes such languages. The term corresponds to 'heritage language' employed in Canada and to a lesser extent in the US. In fact, 'heritage language' includes languages no longer active in a community, whereas there is a more dynamic semantic component in 'community language.' However, there is often a continuing interest among people of a particular ethnic background in learning their ancestors' language, and perhaps there would be some value in employing the two terms with a differentiated semantic range.

It is traditional in predominantly English-speaking countries to discourage one group of people from maintaining their bilingualism while at the same time spending large sums of money in an attempt to make others bilingual by teaching them the same or different LOTEs. This was the case for most of the period of postwar mass immigration into Australia and has been the case again in the US since the repeal of the Bilingual Education Act (c.f., García, 2002). In Australia we have the paradox of 27% of the residents of Melbourne and 29% of those of Sydney speaking a LOTE in their homes (the percentage is higher if we count those who speak a LOTE regularly but not in their own homes). Meanwhile, very few students continue the study of a LOTE into the final year of schooling and, contrary to government policy, many schools do not make such a study compulsory beyond Year 8. A statement made by the Australian Linguistic Society in 1978 in an unpublished letter to the then Prime Minister expresses some lingering attitudes:

> It appears to be widely believed in Australia that foreign languages (*sic*) are essentially unlearnable to normal people, and that Australians have a special innate anti-talent for learning them. English, on the other hand, is learnable, and even those other languages which a normal person and especially an Australian could never learn can be learnt easily and effortlessly by people whose first language is not English.

Assimilation: LOTEs as Deficit

For most of the 20th century, Australia had an implicit negative policy toward LOTEs as part of an assimilation policy and a policy emphasizing the British (meaning English) heritage. This meant that LOTEs were designated exclusively as 'foreign languages' and were treated as elitist subjects at school. French was the 'foreign language' normally taught at school, sometimes along with Latin and occasionally German. Where German – or in rare cases Russian or Italian – was taught, care was taken not to offer it in schools where there were students who had a home background in the language. Discriminatory assessment systems were devised to ensure that those with a home background involving that language did not obtain better scores than those without such an advantage (Clyne *et al.*, 1997). Up to the 1980s, several states of Australia maintained legislation dating from World War I prohibiting bilingual education. Television was an almost monolingual medium and most public libraries were monolingual. Until 1973, there were severe restrictions on radio transmissions in community languages and, until 1956, newspapers published in community languages had to include sections in English. For much of the era of postwar mass immigration, speaking a LOTE was considered not only un-Australian but also an indicator of social deprivation, of a deficit in English, the all-powerful language of education and socioeconomic mobility.

Emancipation in the Interest of Social Justice and National Identity

The reformist Labor government led by Gough Whitlam (1972–75) proclaimed cultural diversity as an important feature of the national identity of an independent Australia as well as a demographic reality. Also, as part of its commitment to social justice, there was a celebration of bilingual Australians being at least as good and loyal citizens as monolinguals (Clyne, 1991). This was part of the process that Lo Bianco (2002: 9) terms the 'reconstructive optimism' that 'drives forward national interests.' As the government also created a Schools Commission that aimed at improving education for everyone and at opening up the radio airwaves to far more stations – including government multi-ethnic and public access stations, some of which were multilingual – LOTEs and related maintenance efforts were emancipated from the private sphere. A telephone interpreter service was established. Federal grants enabled universities, recently transferred from state to federal responsibility, to introduce programs in community languages and their cultures. Grants were available for community language schools run by ethnic communities. Many of these measures were a response to demands from ethnic groups, educators, trades unions, and others.

Mainstreaming

At the same time, some states substantially increased the number of languages accredited as (external) examination subjects at high school graduation to include many community languages, and also extended the number of languages taught in mainstream schools, gradually including some primary schools. Even bilingual programs were introduced, some for students of all ethnic backgrounds. This started the process of 'mainstreaming community languages,' something that continued with the establishment by the conservative government under Malcolm Fraser (1977-83) – which was equally supportive of multiculturalism – of a second government television channel, with films largely in LOTEs with English subtitles.

Perhaps the most significant exercise in mainstreaming community languages was the development of the National Policy on Languages (NPL) (Lo Bianco, 1987). This resulted from a concerted grassroot campaign involving teachers, academic linguists, and ethnic, indigenous, and deaf groups. A parliamentary committee with equal representation from the two major parties conducted hearings in all states and territories, and received submissions. Its final report (Senate, 1984) determined the scope of national languages policy: English as a first, second, and foreign language, indigenous, community (immigrant) and sign languages, and languages in education, the media, and translating and interpreting. This established the complementarity of English and all other languages used in Australia. The report also proposed the guiding principles of Australian language policy, which found their way into much future policy development:

(1) English competence for all;
(2) the maintenance and development of indigenous and community languages;
(3) provision of services in community and indigenous languages;
(4) opportunities to learn second languages.

The NPL presented an irresistible case for multilingualism in terms of social equity, cultural enrichment, and economic strategies, based on Australian and international research and the Australian experience. It also proposed implementation strategies, including budgetary recommendations, which were accepted.

Economic Strategies

By this time, the tide had begun to turn away from social agendas and, before long, neo-liberalism ('economic rationalism' in Australian English) had taken a firm grip on government. This meant cost-cutting, user pays, and a strong emphasis on making money, with the social agenda being relegated to the background. While the NPL drew on the work and deliberations of activists committed to languages, the Australian Language and Literacy Policy [ALLP] (Dawkins, 1991) was the work of a minister aspiring to the Treasury portfolio, who had formed the amalgamated Department of Employment, Education, and Training. It is not surprising that the objectives were short-term export and labor market goals. Languages of economic importance to Australia and literacy, conceptualized as English-only literacy, were seen as linguistic capital. In 1992, the then Prime Minister, Paul Keating, launched the policy of Productive Diversity, encouraging business and industry to utilize and value the diverse linguistic and cultural resources of the workforce. In the 1990s, those with language skills working in the Public Service were able to obtain a supplementary allowance by passing an examination in that language. A total of 14 languages were 'prioritized,' and each state had to select eight of these as their priority languages. Schools and education systems were paid A$300 per head for each student passing the Year 12 examination in a language prioritized by their state.

Heller (1999) and Pomerantz (2002) address from Canadian and American perspectives the commodification of language and how it can transform a symbol of ethnic identity into an asset in the economic market place. In Australia, the emphasis was placed on languages of economic significance. The Rudd Report entitled *Asian Languages and Australia's Economic Future* (Rudd, 1994), which became the focus of a joint policy of the Commonwealth and the states, closely matched the Keating government's thrust toward the economic integration of Australia into Asia. The policy created the 'super-prioritization' of four Asian languages: Chinese (Mandarin), Indonesian, Japanese, and Korean. This policy did not include Thai or Vietnamese, both among those 14 languages available for prioritization by the states in the ALLP and, despite the fact that Vietnamese had been prioritized by four out of six states on the basis of enrolment numbers. Among the completely unprioritized Asian languages were Hindi, an important language of wider communication in India and beyond as well as a community language of increasing significance in Australia, and Filipino, the national language of the Philippines and the ninth most widely used community language in Australia. The policy provided for the four 'super-prioritized' languages to be taught to 60% of Australian school children by 2006 and for the other 40% to take one another language. This has not yet been nearly achieved. In 2000, barely 6% were taking one of the prioritized Asian languages in Year 12 and 7% one of the other languages (DETYA, 2003). As a result of funding for the National Asian Languages and Studies in Australian Schools (NALSAS) strategy ensuing from the Rudd Report, many schools were attracted to one or more of the Asian languages, with the aim of replacing a European language. This was particularly harmful to community languages of relatively little significance internationally, such as Macedonian, Turkish, and Maltese, and to a lesser extent Greek. Arabic, neither a European language nor an Asian one but both an international language and a community language of importance, continues to receive little support and is taught very little in mainstream government schools. Little attention was paid to the importance of resources in the four prioritized languages provided by recent immigration. The interest was focused on those learning an Asian language from scratch.

Since the early 1990s, language policy has been characterized by declining federal government commitment, refragmentation into single-issue policies (such as Asian languages policy, literacy policy and, interpreting and translating policy), and the disabling of change, all of which were underpinned by economic liberalism and anti-social and anti-intellectual agendas. Lo Bianco (2001) refers to the current context as 'anti-policy' as government now shows an aversion to explicit policy development, especially anything resembling a bottom-up policy of the 1980s variety.

As school education is a state responsibility within Australia's federal system of government, languages-in-education policy has continued to evolve at the state level with each of the six states and two territories developing their own policy. Victoria's policy is the most supportive of LOTEs, which are seen as a key learning area and are expected to be studied for the seven years of primary school and the four compulsory years of secondary education, although these expectations are not fulfilled throughout all (state or non-state) schools (Victoria, 2002).

Changes in Immigration and Language Demography

Following the dismantling in the early 1970s of the White Australia Policy that had restricted the immigration of people of non-European background, a non-discriminatory immigration intake policy based on a points system was introduced. Changes in the Australian economy entailed a need for skilled and professionally qualified immigrants, rather than unskilled factory workers as had been the case in the 1940s to 1960s. This, together with the declining significance of some of Australia's traditionally European sources of immigrants, led to the arrival of large numbers of people using the very languages that were being declared of special importance to Australia.

In the period between the 1996 and 2001 censuses, the number of home users of Mandarin nationwide increased by 51.3%, Indonesian by 42.4%, Korean by 32.1%, Japanese by 10.2%, and (incidentally) Hindi by 40.7%, although – interestingly – this was not one of the prioritized languages. These (apart from Serbian[1] and Australian Sign Language[2]) were the languages with the greatest increases. While the four languages specially prioritized in the Rudd report are often designated in educational discourse as Asian languages or trade languages and not as community languages, there is no doubt that they also exercise that function. This has reopened the debate on how to treat students with a home background in a language they are taking as an examination subject. Due to limitations of space, I will focus here on how this debate plays out in the state of Victoria (of which Melbourne is the capital).

Differentiating and Discriminating

Discrimination against students with a home background in German, Italian, and Russian ended in Victoria in 1966, when a new Schools Board considered it none of their business to ascertain why students did as well as they did and gave the examiners in each language the opportunity to grant more 'A' results in accordance with their estimate of how many students were advantaged by their background (Clyne et al., 1997).

However, the issue of differentiation between learners on the basis of background reemerged in the 1990s. At the end of secondary school, examinations in four languages (Chinese/Mandarin, Indonesian, Japanese, and Korean) are taken by many students who have been educated in the language at overseas schools as well as many who have no ethnic, family, or national background in the language, and different examinations are now set for first and second language learners.[3] A thorough investigation of the students' background, overseas experience, and schooling in the language is conducted through a form completed by the student and signed by both a parent and the school principal. In these languages, eligibility for the second language (L2) subject is determined through a points system, and by no means do all those required to take the more difficult First Language (L1) examination attend secondary schooling conducted in the language nor do they sit for the English as a Second Language examination.

The legalistic character of this exercise causes bitterness and cannot motivate children to maintain their family language (see also Clyne et al., 1997). For instance, students of Hong Kong descent sometimes have to argue for permission to take the Chinese (Second Language) rather than the Chinese (First Language) examination by providing declarations from their kindergarten in Hong Kong to prove that their early schooling was not conducted in Mandarin. On the other hand, there is an assumption among many students who do not have a home background in a language spoken by the wider community that they will not be able to continue with the language until the final year of secondary school because that is only possible if they speak the language at home. The Victorian Curriculum and Assessment Authority, which is responsible for public examinations, has decided on a further differentiation of second language learners into those with and without a home background in the language they are studying. However, this could be achieved only through intrusive surveys, and through students with limited home language backgrounds being discouraged from maintaining the community language. Far from rewarding determined maintenance, the language subject might reduce the students' Tertiary Entry score and decrease their chances of entering the university or faculty of their choice. In an action research project involving secondary school programs in Mandarin, Greek, Arabic, and Spanish, the proportion of students without a home background in the language they are studying once a LOTE is no longer compulsory is receding (Clyne et al., 2004).

Because school programs and materials seldom cater for the needs of all students, the L1/L2 distinction is useful in identifying those who have recently arrived from overseas and have received a substantial proportion of their secondary education through the medium of the target language. However, the L1/L2 dichotomy is often misleading when it comes to describing the rest of the population because of the wide range and degree of backgrounds since, wherever we draw the line, we discriminate and demotivate (Clyne et al., 1997; Elder, 2000). Studies of learners of community languages (Clyne et al., 1997; Clyne et al., 2004) have identified the following main groupings of students according to language background (or absence thereof):

(1) students with an active home background in the language and (some) overseas experience of formal education through the language as a medium of instruction;
(2) students with an active home background in the language and some formal instruction (in primary and/or ethnic school) in Australia;
(3) students with an active home background in the language and no formal instruction prior to secondary school;
(4) students with an active home background in a non-standard variety of the language in which classes are conducted formally or informally in Australia or elsewhere (examples are Cantonese, or the various national varieties of spoken Arabic);
(5) students with a passive home background in the language;
(6) students with no home background in the language but formal instruction in it in primary school;
(7) third language (L3) learners;
(8) students with a passive family background (usually one parent or grandparent/s) and no formal instruction in the language prior to secondary school;
(9) students with a passive family background in a variety of the language and no formal instruction in the standard language prior to secondary school;
(10) students with no home background and no prior knowledge of the language.

This whole issue needs to be seen in terms of attitudes to language learning. For as long as bilingualism was treated as a deficit, bilinguals were encouraged to become monolingual English speakers, and monolingual English speakers retained their position of power. Now that bilingualism is sometimes considered to have a market value (Bourdieu & Passeron, 1979), the 'unfairness' of ethnic groups possessing such an asset needs to be moderated by discriminatory assessment procedures. At the same time, no interrogation takes place regarding a child's early access to computers, sport, music, or the theater. The 'fairness' issue has discouraged other states from carrying out what Victoria has done, namely giving all students passing the Year 12 test in a LOTE a 10% bonus toward university entry.

Practical Aspects of Sharing Languages

The alternative to discrimination against any group of learners, whether second language learners or bilinguals with a limited home background, is a sharing of community languages in which those who already speak a language are recognized as possessing a commodity of national significance and can be helped to advance their skills, while those who do not can benefit from the first group's use of the language within the community.

This in turn provides motivation for those with a background, as we found in a Spanish program outlined below. Parents at a focus group meeting indicated that their children's interest in the language had been enhanced by the fact that their friends from non-Spanish-speaking families were bothering to learn it. While educational institutions (primary and secondary schools, part-time ethnic schools, universities, adult education courses) offer the best opportunities for such sharing to take place, they can be supported by the existing media in community languages (radio, TV, newspapers). Moreover, input/output opportunities and cultural knowledge could be enhanced by local cultural tourism around areas of cities where particular languages are concentrated and where business transactions are conducted in the language. Whether such possibilities exist or not, ethnic community centers – social and cultural societies, religious entities, and part-time ethnic schools, even country guest houses serving the respective language community – could become community language resource centers. They could function as havens for the use of the language, providing an authentic environment, even for young people. An important component of the population in this context is the elderly, for many of whom the first language and culture have regained much of their importance and many of whom are seeking opportunities for socializing and interacting with younger people. One Melbourne primary school with a German/English bilingual program has time-tabled classes in the nearby German old people's home, which benefits the students both linguistically and culturally. A number of Greek classes similarly visit Greek old people's homes. There are many other ways in which young learners can interact with a community of speakers. For instance, Greek classes in another primary school have produced children's segments for the Greek program of a multilingual radio station. Conversely, one university has for many years held a week of German immersion for its students and brought in people from a multiplicity of professional backgrounds within the community to give talks and lead discussions in German on topics in which they have expertise (Clyne, 2002). At the individual level, an existing scheme that could act as a model in some cases is the Home Tutor Scheme, which enables people with native or near-native proficiency in English to provide input/output opportunities and cultural knowledge for immigrants who wish to improve their English. This is a community outreach activity complementing the government's free 510 hours of ESL (teaching of English as a second language) for those who have recently arrived.

In addition, the new technologies such as the Internet – making available email, radio programs, and daily newspapers – as well as satellite TV programs and videos provide further input and authentic interaction opportunities with countries where the language is the majority language. These technologies make it possible for young people – regardless of whether they have a home background in the language – to interact with a peer group in the target language even though English is the language for peer group communication among the young in Australia, both within and across ethnic groups.

A Schools Project

The Research Unit for Multilingualism and Cross Cultural Communication at the University of Melbourne, in conjunction with the Victorian Department of Education and Training and the Catholic Education Commission of Victoria, has been conducting an action research project[4] involving four Melbourne secondary schools, three co-educational state schools, and one Catholic girls' school. The project studies the role of secondary schools in the maintenance, development, and spread of community languages – in this case Arabic, Chinese (Mandarin), Greek, and Spanish, in one school each. The project primarily aims to develop models and practices to help schools cater for the diversity of students taking community language subjects. Each school is multicultural in its composition, and three of the four are situated in areas in which speakers of the respective community language are concentrated. The fourth school, which teaches Spanish, is easily accessible to areas in which Spanish is used, not far from the city center. This enables us also to explore the feasibility of utilizing community resources in the language, both within and beyond the school, in the interest of all students' language competence and cultural knowledge, especially those of students without a family background in the language.

Apart from various research issues such as biliteracy and third language learning, one of the foci of the project has been the development of activities that will encourage collaboration between students of different types and degrees of language background as well as the utilization of community resources. At School S,[5] the students have visited a day care center for the Spanish-speaking elderly and engaged in conversations with them. Our Spanish-speaking research assistant has helped the students produce an electronic newsletter each term on which groups of students collaborated on specific tasks such as writing, editing, and design. The articles covered issues such as Spanish music, singers, festivals, clubs, films and videos, food, shopping, and controversial topics. At Schools C and G, the research assistants worked with the teachers to develop age-appropriate units of work covering routines needed to conduct business transactions in a local shopping center, including asking for directions. Students were organized into small groups, and the tasks differentiated according to proficiency levels.

Finally, we have been working on comparative analyses to facilitate the development of strategies for students with Cantonese or a rural Lebanese dialect of Arabic to enable them to switch when need be to Mandarin and Modern Standard Arabic, respectively. In School A, we explored how this can be facilitated by the presence in Year 11 of two recently arrived Lebanese students who received all their prior education in Modern Standard Arabic and did not share the dialect of most of the other students (who are second-generation Australians).

Impediments to Sharing

The sharing of community languages may be a Utopian ideal, but it also has practical value in extending cultural horizons, promoting understanding, and easing communication in the era of globalization. However, there are a number of impediments in the way of this ideal becoming a reality under normal circumstances. Turning first to an attitudinal dimension, there is a widespread misunderstanding of the nature of the home and family background and a related fear of those with an 'unfair advantage.' Such misunderstanding is rife among teachers, fellow students, and, in some cases, the students themselves. This often becomes a self-fulfilling prophecy, sometimes enhanced by different names for two groups, such as 'beginners' and 'advanced,' with 'beginners' continuing to be so designated even after studying the language for ten years. In School C, however, there are several success stories of students without any Chinese background who excelled in the language through their motivation and aptitude and, while benefiting from the presence of Mandarin language and Chinese culture in the community within and beyond the school, performed better than most of those with a home background. Such students are not deterred by myths or misconceptions about fellow students enjoying an 'unfair advantage.' At the same time, there were those who built on their home background in Mandarin or a passive background in Cantonese together with their Chinese cultural background to acquire excellent competence in Mandarin (while dominant in English). In School S, L3 learners are outperforming L2 learners regardless of whether or not their community language is related to Spanish. These students are also continuing with Spanish for longer than L2 learners. This underlines the importance of attitudinal factors in promoting both multilingualism and the metalinguistic awareness of bilinguals. We hope that our project will provide information and models that can counteract entrenched attitudes and practices across the entire education system.

The second type of impediment relates to the low status of LOTEs in the school curriculum despite their recognition as a key learning area. This is epitomized in two figures of speech: the 'language/literacy' dichotomy and the 'overcrowded curriculum.' The 'language/literacy' dichotomy was introduced by Minister John Dawkins in his *Australia's Language: The*

Australian Language and Literacy Policy (Dawkins, 1991) which, as we have seen, introduced economic goals as the main purpose of language policy. It also had the ultimate effect of refragmenting language policy. A tension was created between 'language,' which included both English and at least some other languages, and 'literacy,' which assumed monolingual English. As Kaplan and Baldauf (1997: 146) sensibly assert: 'To the extent that literacy remains ill-defined [or defined] in terms of a single language, [language-in-education planning] is not likely to succeed.' A minority of submissions received for the review of LOTEs in Victorian government schools (Victoria, 2002) argued that the level of English literacy of some students was too low for them to afford the time to acquire another language. There is even in some educational circles in Australia the belief that literacy standards (i.e. English literacy or English spelling) are falling and that this is due to children spending too much time – typically 1 to 1.5 hours a week – learning Japanese or Italian. In fact, there are schools in which English literacy (for those needing special assistance) is timetabled *against* LOTEs. Yet, the international literature shows that:

(1) there is an underlying literacy skill that can be acquired in any language and transferred to any another and involves strategies needed to make meaning from a text and recognizing its the internal structure;
(2) literacy can be acquired in more than one language;
(3) literacy can be enhanced by the acquisition of additional languages (see, for example, Cummins, 1978, 1979; Cummins & Swain, 1989; Baker, 2001; Koda, 2002).

Meanwhile, the metaphor 'crowded curriculum' heard frequently in Australian educational circles presents LOTEs as intruders, having been comparatively recent additions to the primary curriculum and having functioned for a long time as gatekeepers for a student elite at secondary level. In many primary schools, this means that, in terms of time on task and frequency of classes, languages are not provided for in such a way as to encourage positive and successful outcomes. It must be acknowledged that there is also a profound staffing problem in this area. Many state secondary schools offer languages only as an elective from Year 9 alongside such attractive options as self-defense, cake decoration, air brushing, photography, and ceramics. As one submission to the Victorian LOTE review put it:

> The crowded curriculum is due to the fact that too many schools are trying to integrate what should be considered extra-curricular activities into the core curriculum.

In response, it is sometimes rationalized that, because English is a world language, it is unnecessary for English speakers to learn other languages – which is hard work. This situation creates a rift, especially in state schools, between monolingual and bilingual sections of the population, and accentuates the paradox between Australian multilingualism and the limited number of second language learners at the upper secondary school able to share in community languages.

The third impediment is a demographic one, which has become influential because of its link with changing patterns of urban distribution. The teaching of community languages in schools has been rationalized on the basis of geographical concentrations in particular areas of Australian cities. So, for instance, Greek has been taught to students from Greek and non-Greek backgrounds in schools with a large Greek population. But now that the Greek community has changed from being highly concentrated to widely dispersed throughout metropolitan areas, the local-base argument for offering it as a school subject has been lost, and many schools have dropped it. Greek is now studied mainly on Saturdays at state schools that act as centers for the Saturday Languages initiative in Victoria, New South Wales, and South Australia. As in after-hours ethnic schools, the main takers are those with a home background, and others with a special interest in the language. The declining opportunities to study community languages at university, which affects the flow-on of teachers at primary and secondary schools, is due to funding costs and the reluctance of most universities to keep programs that do not 'earn their keep.'

Concluding Remarks

In spite of these impediments, the sharing of languages goes on in Australia and many other parts of the world on a daily basis, as shown, for example, in work on 'crossing' such as Rampton (1995). However, there is a need to extend this work. The first step is to develop a collaborative agenda that, like the initial push for a national languages policy, is bottom-up (from ethnic groups, teacher and linguistics groups, trades unions, and some business interests) and supported by government. This agenda needs to be based on:

(1) a more linguistically aware society;
(2) a school environment that is free of xenophobia and mistrust;
(3) a prominent role for L3 learners, who can act as mediators;
(4) ethnic community institutions being seen as active community language resource centers for younger people of the same and different ethnicities;
(5) financial incentives and actual employment benefits for multilingualism.

Ironically, all aspects of this agenda will be greatly enhanced by the outcomes of each individual aspect. The first point is quite crucial. There have been better times in Australia's history. However, I am encouraged by the number of submissions to the Victorian LOTE review requesting a public awareness campaign, and it is hoped that such a campaign will be carried out by the Victorian Government. More than two decades after Bob Kaplan's 1980 visit to Australia, his beneficial influence lives on.

Notes

1. Due in part to the speakers' changing designation of the language. In earlier censuses, many speakers designated their language as Yugoslav (or Serbo-Croatian).
2. This was probably due to confusion over the census question 'Does this person *speak* a language other than English in the home?' which may have led to a gross underclaiming of Auslan (Australian Sign Language) as a home language.
3. This measure was introduced for Chinese in 1995, and subsequently in the other three languages.
4. This project is funded by the Australian Research Council and described in Clyne et al. (2004).
5. School S is the one in which we have been researching the Spanish program, and Schools A, C and G the ones in which we were studying the Arabic, Chinese, and Greek programs, respectively.

Chapter 4

Documenting Curricular Reform: Innovative Foreign Language Education in Elementary School

ROCÍO DOMÍNGUEZ, G. RICHARD TUCKER AND RICHARD DONATO

Introduction

As foreign language programs in elementary school (FLES) expand nationwide (Rhodes & Branaman, 1999), the need for careful attention to matters of curricular content and articulation becomes critical to the health and longevity of these programs. It is fair to say, that despite their recently renewed status in the elementary school curriculum, FLES programs have not received the same amount of curricular attention in the form of commercially-published textbooks as their middle and secondary school counterparts. Although the K–12 (kindergarten to grade 12) National Foreign Language Resource Center and the Center for Applied Linguistics have made significant contributions in producing materials for FLES programs, their work tends to reach only limited numbers of dedicated professionals. Access to summer institutes is not always possible for teachers, who may not be made aware of the resources available to them. The unfortunate result is that FLES instructors are often left on their own to develop curricula, to establish coherent and well articulated objectives across the elementary school years, and to assess whether standards are being met.

One area of particular concern, which serves as the focus of this study, is foreign language literacy in elementary school. Given the lack of materials for FLES and the enduring and somewhat misguided notion that elementary students need only develop comprehension skills, literacy development lags behind when compared to the development of listening and speaking skills. The lack of literacy instruction becomes especially acute in extended K–5 (kindergarten to grade 5) foreign language programs that anticipate the requirement for literacy ability as students move to middle school and high school. In these extended programs, such as the program we report on in this study, instruction is differentiated across the years, requiring students to possess literacy skills to participate in content-enriched or content-based foreign language programs in the later years of instruction. If students do not experience literacy in a foreign language from a young age, their ability to cope with more demanding curricular content is seriously compromised. Additionally, learners grow in foreign language literacy across the years in much the same way as they do in their first language when, for example, they have access to print materials, adult–child interactive book reading, and opportunities to create texts with invented spellings (Sulzby & Teale, 1991; Cecil & Gipe, 2003).

The purpose of this chapter is to report on a two-year long research project on curricular reform with a group of elementary school Spanish teachers, which culminated with the introduction of literacy into the K–5 curriculum. The research reported here examines the work of one researcher with a group of six FLES teachers of Spanish, and it presents successes and challenges in implementing a curricular innovation dealing with the introduction of literacy from kindergarten to grade 5. The model of instruction adopted for this innovation was based on the work of Adair-Hauck et al. (1994) and Adair-Hauck and Donato (2002) and involved the use of stories, folktales, and legends as starting points and core materials for FLES language lessons. This model was ideally suited for elementary school since stories remain an integral part of the language arts curriculum, capture the interest and imagination of children, and reflect the target language culture. Additionally, after stories are told and discussed, literacy activities involving reading, retellings, and creative writing are easily implemented as extension activities to the storytelling event. Thus, in this curricular project, language learning moved from discrete skill-based learning that emphasizes listening and speaking comprehension to an integrated approach in which all modes of communication – interpersonal, interpretive, and presentational – were present in the unit of study.

One area of focus of this research consists of describing the complex process of curricular innovation. Based on the work of Markee (1997) and others, our findings highlight the importance of dialogue as a critical tool in establishing mutual understanding and a shared vision. Within this dialogue, the roles of participants, the decision-making process, and the nature of the innovation are forged and enacted. Moreover, innovative curricular projects are affected positively or negatively by a host of factors, such as the teachers' beliefs about learning and teaching, administrative attitudes, institutional support, language planning factors, and historical and economic conditions (Markee, 1997; Holliday, 1994). In each school context, the interplay of many of these factors explains initial resistance by some teachers to curricular change and the eventual exploration and evaluation of the newly introduced literacy practices. What is striking in our research is that, for these teachers, a central concern and an important factor in facilitating progress was coming to terms with the concept of literacy itself. Here, historical understandings, beliefs about language learning, and previous language planning factors had an impact on the shape and trajectory of the innovation.

The Spanish Program: Background

The Spanish FLES program started in 1995 as an initiative of a District Superintendent in the state of Pennsylvania (Tucker et al., 2001).[1] A Foreign Language Program Committee was created as a mechanism for making decisions and providing feedback, and consisted of the school superintendent, the principals (at elementary, intermediate, middle, and high school), each school's director of instruction, the Spanish teachers, and Tucker and Donato – faculty members at two universities in the Pittsburgh area. After considering various factors, including the results of a community survey, the Committee chose Spanish and decided to make its study (for 20 minutes, 5 days a week) compulsory for all children from kindergarten onwards. The implementation of a Spanish content-based FLES program in September 1996 for all kindergarten children in the district was proposed to the School Board. The proposal included the extension of the program with the systematic introduction of new cohorts of kindergarten youngsters in subsequent years.

Currently, Spanish is taught in grades K–6, as shown in Table 4.1. There are 10–11 sections per grade. The total number of students per grade is approximately 250, with a distribution of 24 students per classroom. The presence of students of Hispanic background is very small, with perhaps one or two Hispanic descendants per grade. In grades K–5, six teachers are

Table 4.1 Overview of the Spanish Program

Grades in which Spanish is taught	K–6
Number of sections per grade	10 to 11
Number of students per classroom	max. 24
Number of teachers hired in grades K–5	6
Number of teachers hired in grade 6	2
Time allocated for Spanish in grades K–5	20 minutes x 5 days
Time allocated for Spanish in grade 6–8	40 minutes x 5 days
Total number of school facilities: Primary school (K–2); Intermediate school (3–5); Middle school (6–8); High school (9–12)	4
Number of facilities where content-based Spanish program is currently being taught[2]	3

responsible for delivering Spanish, one per level. This practice changes in grades 6 to 8. At the middle school the program has become a content-based program in which two teachers at each grade level integrate the teaching of Spanish with mathematics, science, social studies, and language arts in four 9-week blocks. In grades K–5, Spanish is taught for 20 minutes every day, while in grade 6 the time allocated doubles to 40 minutes a day. Thus, one of the goals of the K–5 program is to prepare the students to participate in a more academically oriented content-based program at grade 6. At this level, Spanish equals in importance and time allocation the other 'core' subjects such as Reading, English, Science, and Social Studies. In contrast, in grades K–5, Spanish is considered a 'special' course together with Computers, Library, Music, and Gymnastics.

The Profiles of Spanish Teachers in Grades K–5

The majority of teachers hired for the Spanish program reported that they had two certificates, one in FL (Foreign Language) Teaching and one in Elementary Education. All teachers graduated from universities located in the State of Pennsylvania. In addition, teachers at all grade levels reported having studied abroad in a Spanish-speaking country for at least two months. In particular, Spanish teachers in grades 3–5 reported that they had traveled to different countries in Central America on several occasions.

With respect to teachers' background in teaching Spanish as an FL, the teacher with the most years of experience in the Spanish program was Liliana,[3] the grade 2 teacher for the 2001–2002 school year. She was hired in the summer of 1996 and taught Spanish in grades K–2 throughout these years. The second most experienced teacher was Mia, the Spanish teacher in grade 3. After graduation in 1994, Mia taught at a variety of schools and levels until she was hired by the school district in the summer of 1999. The Spanish teachers in grades K–1 reported having four years of experience in FL teaching. Except for Norah, the Spanish teacher in grade 4, all teachers reported that they had graduated in the previous decade. These teachers were in their late twenties or early thirties. In contrast, Norah, who was in her mid-forties, graduated in 1971. After graduation, she earned a Masters in Teaching from a university in the Pittsburgh area, and went on to teach Spanish for two years at high school level in a public school in that area. For family reasons, Norah stopped teaching for a long period, until she was hired to teach grade 4 in the Spanish program in the summer of 2000. Finally, Olivia, the grade 5 teacher was hired in the summer of 2001. She has a certificate in FL Teaching and an undergraduate concentration in Latin American Studies. In addition, she received a Masters in Teaching Foreign Languages from a university in the Pittsburgh area in May 2001. Olivia had one year of FL teaching experience when she was hired by the district.

Challenges of the Spanish Program

As we mentioned above, at the beginning of the Spanish program, the FL Committee attended to numerous priorities such as selecting the language of instruction and the instructional model for instruction, hiring qualified teachers, and designing curricula, among others. In turn, teachers devoted most of their time to engaging young monolingual children in learning a foreign language and in designing adequate assessment tools for student evaluation. Motivated by the imminent expansion of the program to higher levels in the curriculum during the 2000–2001 school year, the Spanish teachers in grades K–4 and the principal of the intermediate school raised concerns about the development of literacy at the upper levels. In other words, the literacy component became a priority in grades K–5 because it was felt that students must be well prepared for a more academic language program in terms of content and time in grade 6.

During the first year of the project, data were collected on: a) a revision of the K–5 Spanish curricula, b) classroom observations conducted in grades K–4 during the 2000–2001 school year, and c) personal communication with the Spanish teachers in grades K–5. These data revealed that the Spanish program faced four challenges related to the development of Spanish literacy in grades 3–4:

(1) Across levels, the Spanish curricula did not contain explicit objectives for Spanish literacy. It was observed that students were given little opportunity to read in the target language. In the majority of observed lessons, students received only Spanish oral input. Occasionally, students in grades 1–4 were requested to read aloud words or sentences introduced by the teachers. According to the teachers, no reading comprehension was promoted at any level. Reading in Spanish was understood as 'reading aloud,' not individually but as a group.

(2) The Spanish in grades 2–4 revealed no activities to enhance creative writing in Spanish through activities in which students are guided to construct meaning by creating written texts (Hornberger & Skilton-Sylvester, 2000). According to Spanish teachers in grades 2–4, writing activities were limited to fill-in-the-blank exercises and picture descriptions using short phrases, a practice that showed no continuity in the implementation of Spanish writing in grades 2–4. It is also clear that at the upper levels literacy activities were not demanding or challenging.

(3) The grade 5 curriculum contained many literacy activities, but the lack of literacy activities in grades 3–4 led to the belief that the task of acquiring Spanish literacy is a difficult one for children and, thus, student outcomes at this grade level may be lower than expected. In addition, this grade level is crucial, considering that students need to

be prepared for a more academically challenging content-based program.
(4) Teachers were used to introducing the language from the parts to the whole. Teachers first introduced vocabulary, then moved on to phrases and sentences, and finally, introduced the students to the whole text. These practices conflict with the assumptions of teaching a FL in context (Goodman, 1986; Fountas & Hannigan, 1989; Hudelson, 1994; Skilton-Sylvester, 1998; Adair-Hauck & Donato, 2002).

The Action Plan

Concerns raised by the Spanish teachers in grades K–4 and by the principal of the intermediate school about Spanish literacy development in grades 3–4 motivated the development of a procedure for working collaboratively with the Spanish teachers over the course of the 2001–2002 school year. This procedure led to curricular discussion, innovation, and reform. During that school year, the Spanish teachers were expected to discuss and determine goals for Spanish literacy in grades K–5 and to implement these goals. At the first meeting, Olivia, a new faculty member, suggested using an innovative FL method called PACE (Presentation, Attention, Co-construction, and Extension) for implementing Spanish literacy in grades K–5. She reported using PACE for her lessons.

This model was developed by Adair-Hauck and Donato (Adair-Hauck *et al.*, 1994) for implementing standard-based FL instruction. PACE is grounded in both Vygotskyan psycholinguistics and a story-telling approach. The PACE model is consistent with theories that underscore the importance of meaning-making, authentic context, and connected discourse in L2 development. Thus, it embraces a content-based instruction (CBI) approach. This model stresses the importance of whole discourse as a starting point in second language (L2) development. Unlike bottom-up processing models, which fragment the language system by encouraging students to learn grammar rules and vocabulary before using them to communicate, the PACE model encourages students to use language communicatively from the very beginning of the lesson. With PACE, the teacher may also focus on literacy development by engaging students in creative writing projects or in reading comprehension activities. Unlike other models, this model acknowledges the role of the teacher in negotiating new language vocabulary, forms, and explanations. In conclusion, Olivia's initiative was supported because: (1) PACE is consistent with latest findings in the research on FL teaching; (2) the method promotes literacy development; (3) the method is appropriate for content-based instruction; and (4) the initiative came from within the Spanish program.

Expectations for Teachers' Performance

Aside from discussing and determining Spanish literacy goals, the Spanish teachers were expected to implement PACE once during the school year. In grades K–5, a unit lesson can span three to four weeks for a daily 20-minute class. Thus, the implementation of PACE for a single lesson was expected to be time-consuming for teachers because they would need to design new activities and prepare new materials. Finally, we presumed that some parts of the PACE model might be perceived as challenging for teachers. As the Spanish teachers reported being accustomed to introducing stories and other *realia* to their students going from the parts to the whole, we expected that PACE would be perceived as very different in that respect since this method advocates the presentation of texts from the whole to the parts.

Data Collection and Data Analysis

In what follows, we document the process of curricular reform of the literacy component in a FLES Spanish program. Data were drawn from multiple sources such as documents, various perspectives on the curricular innovation by the teachers, and classroom observations. By combining multiple sources, our aim was to add rigor to our qualitative approach. As stated by Denzin and Lincoln (2002: 5), 'the use of multiple methods, or triangulation, reflects an attempt to secure an in-depth understanding of the phenomenon in question.' The study was limited to grades 3–4 because the grade 5 teacher, Olivia, had introduced PACE to her fellow teachers.

Our data came from eight sources: (1) transcripts and notes from regular monthly meetings with the Spanish teachers; (2) copies of a teacher's notes of the meetings; (3) teachers' checklists and questionnaires (see Appendices A and B at the end of this chapter); (4) transcripts and notes of individual interviews with the K–5 Spanish teachers and administrators; (5) transcripts and notes of classroom observations in grades 3–4; (6) copies of teachers' relevant lesson plans (2000–2001; 2001–2002) in grades 3–4; (7) teachers' student reports; (8) K–5 Spanish curricula (September, 2001; June, 2002).

Data gathered were examined in order to find evidence of changes in the curricula. These data were in turn compared to the teachers' lesson plans (2001–2002) and to portions of the Spanish curricula in grades 3–4 (Domínguez, 2002). A copy of the data analysis was given to all the Spanish teachers for their review and comments. This practice allowed the researcher to address ethical concerns by letting each teacher corroborate the researcher's interpretation of the data. The purpose was to avoid gaps and misunderstandings and to add triangulation to the data analysis. Norah, the grade 4 teacher, had no comments on the draft, but Mia and

Olivia, the teachers for grades 3 and 5, respectively, agreed that the researcher's interpretation '... was an accurate description of what we did and what happened.'

Findings: Writing Goals for the K–5 Spanish Literacy Curricula

Writing the Spanish literacy goals was a lengthy and complex process. The teachers were provided with a summary of the researcher's classroom observations (2000–2001) of student outcomes in grades K–5 regarding speaking, listening, reading, and writing in Spanish. This line of action turned out to be a simple and easy way to facilitate discussion among the teachers. The procedure provided multiple perspectives on classroom activities, and it enriched the teachers' understanding of the need for the innovation. The teachers were also provided with a copy of the National Standards for FL. The teachers discussed their expectations concerning students' reading and writing at each level. Mia posed the following questions: 'What do we understand by writing?' 'Does it mean correct grammar and spelling?' 'Is it creative writing?' With these questions in mind, the group started discussing the concepts of reading and writing. From the discussion, it emerged that the teachers would shift gradually from reading to students to letting students read texts appropriate to their age by themselves with the teacher's assistance. As for writing, the teachers agreed that, in contrast to what they had been doing, they needed to favor creative writing in the classroom rather than fill-in-the-blank exercises. The teachers understood that creative writing involved letting students create their own texts as long as they had access to resources and support materials (such as dictionaries, word banks, and vocabulary lists) for them to accomplish the task successfully. Then each teacher wrote a first draft of the Spanish literacy goal at her level, and this was discussed at the next meeting. After extensive discussion and revisions, the group presented these goals to the FL committee.

Finally, feasibility was another important component that came up during the discussion of goals for Spanish literacy. The grade 2 teacher commented that feasibility was always a top priority for the group when it came to making decisions. This piece of data confirms that the feasibility of an innovation is an important factor in the teacher's decision to try it (Markee, 1997). Regarding our expectations for teachers' performance during the innovation process, the Spanish teachers accomplished their first challenge successfully and they set goals for Spanish literacy looking for progress throughout the K–5 curricula. In addition, these goals were consistent with current thinking regarding the acquisition of literacy in general.

The Implementation of PACE in Grades 3 to 4

The Spanish teachers for grades 3 and 4 each implemented two PACE lessons during the 2001–2002 school year. Norah's first attempt at implementing PACE failed. She interrupted the PACE lesson shortly after starting because she did not understand how to continue implementing it. Feedback from the group provided suggestions such as activities for the attention and co-construction phases, which led to a successful second attempt. Mia, the Spanish teacher in grade 3, implemented the PACE model successfully twice during the year, which exceeded the expectations for PACE implementation established by the group. Later, Olivia added that Mia was an active participant in FL meetings, showed a willingness to collaborate with others, and asked for feedback before implementing lessons; in a word, she was 'confident.'

During her first interview, Mia spoke positively about the PACE model. She mentioned that 'it helps the students to put together sentences' and remarked that 'most of the students were able to compare sentences easily.' This statement supports data drawn from Mia's report of the evaluation of students' writing for the first PACE lesson. In her report, Mia stated that:

> the majority of students did better [than in the past] when writing their journals by using the PACE model. I found that each step was a building block toward better formation of ideas and sentence structure.

According to data gathered from the questionnaire, checklist, and interview, Norah also saw PACE as a method that facilitates literacy. Norah marked in her checklist that PACE was a way to reinforce both reading and writing. Data from Norah's student report points in the same direction. Part of a transcript of a group meeting describes this view of PACE reinforcing reading and writing:

Researcher: Compared to your last year's lesson in terms of the results for reading and writing, what do you think?
Norah: Last year they had just a little paragraph to read, they had to fill in the blanks that's all they had ... , this year I think they learned it quicker...
Researcher: Maybe you give them more room to be creative. Maybe that's one thing you want to consider, the kids respond as much as we ask them to do.
Norah: Yes!

Norah liked 'the flow' and 'variety' that PACE introduces into the lesson and the fact that it provides direction for the teaching of grammar. In her questionnaire, she wrote: '[PACE] gave me a newer way to track a lesson.' Norah also commented positively on PACE in her student report:

PACE gave the students more variety in the lesson, therefore I believe it held their interest more than a conventional lesson. There was a better and more meaningful 'flow' to the lesson, especially regarding the grammar aspect. Comparing and contrasting the verb forms provided them with a more concrete understanding of a difficult concept. When they wrote their own travel scenarios, I believe that they wrote them faster than they normally would have. They had 6 scenarios as models, which really helped them, perhaps unconsciously, to form their sentences for their paragraph. We practiced a lot but it was not repetitious and boring. The PACE lesson was sprinkled with a variety of great teaching methods. It was a smoother learning experience for the students.

Positive reactions from Norah's checklist pointed in the same direction. Norah remarked: 'I observed good results in terms of students' oral outcomes' and 'I observed good results in terms of students' written outcomes.' She added: 'They seemed to be able to write quicker and better.' Data from the transcript of a meeting corroborated these statements. In her interview, Norah expressed the view that the PACE method facilitated her students' writing process:

> ... [the lesson] was easier [for them], they could write it quicker this way because they had so many models, they had so many resources I think ... but ... there were still errors ... but the [writing of the] sentences came easier to them ...

The positive experience of the second attempt led Norah to conclude that curricular innovation requires time and multiple opportunities to experiment with innovation during instruction. Trying PACE twice during the academic year was not enough for her to become familiar with it, and she reported that she will probably use PACE for teaching the same lesson and others in future. These data are confirmed by similar data drawn from the interview with this teacher:

Researcher: Is there any other lesson you are thinking of doing with PACE?
Norah: After PACE I have to rethink everything, my lessons are going forward even though all my lesson plans were done last year, I don't even work with them anymore 'cause I know they are old ... I'll never forget PACE now ... it's not like this one time and I don't want to talk about PACE anymore now I'm more comfortable with it ...

After implementing PACE, the Spanish teachers in grades 3–4 declared that they would continue using this method in the future. In brief, both teachers responded positively to the challenges of the implementation of PACE.

Sustainability of Changes in the Spanish Curricula for Grades 3 to 4

Evidence pointing to the sustainability of PACE comes from the revisions made by Mia and Norah to their lesson plans as well as their planned course of study (see Appendix C). Both Mia and Norah included the revised objectives of the PACE lessons they implemented in these new versions as well as the activities they conducted during those PACE lessons. Activities described in the new version of the curriculum reflect the PACE philosophy of teaching a foreign language from the whole to the parts. It is important to note that the new versions are far more 'teacher friendly' than the previous ones. At both grade levels, the new versions include objectives related to student outcomes in reading, writing, speaking, and listening as well as grammatical objectives. These data lead us to conclude that the use of PACE had a positive impact on the practices of grade 3–4 Spanish literacy teachers.

Conclusions

In this chapter, we have described the development and implementation of a curricular reform project designed to infuse the teaching of literacy across the elementary grades of a relatively new district-wide Spanish as a Foreign Language program we have been involved with since its inception in 1995. The results of the ongoing work reported here are fully consonant with other experiences we have had with personnel in the School District. The following themes came up regularly during our informal discussions with school board personnel as well as during our systematic interviewing of all of the various stakeholders in the district – the superintendent, school board members, parents, principals, regular classroom teachers, and Spanish teachers. All participants routinely expressed enthusiasm for the program, which they considered to be a success. Over time several overarching and consistent themes emerged, which are also relevant to the present investigation and to the introduction of literacy activities across the FL curriculum.

Articulating a shared vision

The superintendent wanted a foreign language program for this school district 'because of a sense that American education was behind [the rest of the world] with regard to exposure to foreign languages.' From the time he first proposed the idea of a foreign language program as part of the district's plans, his vision resonated positively throughout the committee overseeing implementation of the program, and all participants (including the teachers with whom we worked in this study) embraced the idea of working to implement the best possible Spanish language program. More importantly, all of the participating teachers came to feel that they were important 'stakeholders' in this program and in its success.

Empowerment

In other words, there was a unanimous feeling of ownership for the program among all levels of school district personnel. This empowerment felt by teachers, department heads, principals, and others was attributed to the superintendent's strong leadership.

Teacher support

Another central thread woven throughout the various interviews that we conducted was that of support *from* and *for* the Spanish teachers. For example, care was taken throughout the life of the program to provide assistance to the teachers through continuing linkage with university partners and the systematic provision of in-service training.

Positive concerns for the future

The final theme reflects a realization that issues of articulation from elementary school to middle school and from middle school to high school will be critical if the district is to have a coherent and viable foreign language program across 13 years of instruction. This helps, we believe, to explain the willingness of district officers to participate actively in this project in order to infuse the teaching of literacy throughout the intermediate curriculum, a development that should better prepare students for the linguistic and academic challenges that they will face at the middle and senior high school levels, where Spanish will become a core subject used to provide instruction in social studies, science, and mathematics.

By telling the story of one school district's experience with curricular reform for its FLES program, we hope to have described at least partially several of the key elements involved in the development of successful educational innovation. The direction and decisions of this district rested on the concerns of several important constituents and reflect Markee's (1997) observation that innovative projects are affected, positively or negatively, by complex sociocultural variables such as cultural beliefs, political climate, historical and economic conditions, administrative attitudes, institutional support, and technological, sociolinguistic, and language planning factors. When viewed globally, the themes of vision, planning, empowerment, support, and future concerns described above reflect all of the sociocultural variables listed by Markee and attest to their importance as well as to the need to acknowledge and address these factors openly when designing and implementing new programs. Others in the process of contemplating the development of a program such as the one presented here or in monitoring and evaluating current FLES programs might be well advised to benchmark successes and failures against these themes.

Notes

1. Before 1995, the school district had an FL program in high school only.
2. Spanish is also taught in high school, but it is not a content-based FL program.
3. All names have been changed to preserve anonymity.

Appendix A: Checklist for Spanish Teachers

Please, think about the time you were planning and conducting your PACE lesson. The following is a list of several statements. Check those that, in your opinion, apply to your experience.

While planning my PACE lesson...

( ) It took me a while to decide what unit I was going to do with PACE
( ) It took me a while to decide the lesson objective
( ) I relied greatly on other teachers' past experiences as guidance for developing my lesson plan
( ) I didn't pay much attention to other teachers' experiences with PACE for developing my lesson plan
( ) I asked some questions about PACE of my fellow colleagues in our meetings

While doing my PACE lesson...

( ) I found that the presentation phase was easy to deal with.
( ) I found that the presentation phase demanded more work than I expected initially.
( ) I asked my colleagues and Rocío questions for clarification purposes.
( ) I found that the co-construction and the attention phases were easy to deal with.
( ) I found that the co-construction and the attention phases implied some procedures I was not entirely aware of before.
( ) I had more questions on how to conduct the _____ phase.
( ) I felt confident but I also asked for feedback from my colleagues and/or Rocío.
( ) I felt very confident about what I was doing and didn't ask for feedback.
( ) I felt _____ throughout the whole process.
( ) I think I did well coping with the 'newness' of this method.
( ) I tried to see this experience as an experiment (I made minor changes from class to class for fine-tuning).

When correcting my students' projects...

( ) I could observe good results in terms of students' oral outcomes.
( ) I couldn't observe any major differences in students' oral outcomes compared to those from last year.
( ) I could observe good results in terms of students' written outcomes (please explain briefly and provide an example).
( ) I couldn't observe any major differences in students' written outcomes compared to those from last year.

Documenting Curricular Reform

In conclusion...

( ) I think that trying PACE once this year was enough for me to become familiar with this technique.
( ) I think PACE pretty much resembles my usual teaching practices.
( ) I think PACE resembles my usual teaching practices in some ways.
( ) PACE was completely new to me as far as my teaching practices are concerned.
( ) I may use PACE for teaching the same lesson next year.
( ) I don't think I will use PACE again.
( ) I think what I have learned from PACE is another way. to teach grammar
( ) I think what I have learned from PACE is a way to reinforce both reading and writing.
( ) I think my teaching practices have expanded after using PACE.
( ) Some of my ideas about how to teach reading and writing in Spanish have changed a bit after using PACE.
( ) I don't think I have learned much from using PACE.

Appendix B: Questionnaire for Spanish Teachers

Querida profesora:

The purpose of this questionnaire is to get feedback from you about the areas where you struggle the most when designing and implementing a PACE activity. Please take your time to respond. The questionnaire is anonymous.

I will summarize the information you provide together with the feedback from the other *profesoras*. This will be a subject for further discussion in our meetings.

¡Muchas gracias por tomarse el tiempo para responder al cuestionario!

(1) Please state your instructional objectives for the lesson.
(2) Were the texts used in the PACE activity difficult to find/make? Please explain why.
(3) Were the visuals used in the presentation phase difficult to find/make? If so, please explain the reason(s).
(4) Did you struggle when planning TPR activities for the presentation? If so, please give details.
(5) Was it difficult to guide students' attention during the lesson? Why?
(6) Please describe briefly how you focused the children's attention on the linguistic features? What 'hints' or 'helping questions' did you ask them?
(7) What extension activities did you design?
(8) In general, did the extension activities work? What worked and what didn't? Do you have an idea of why it didn't work?
(9) In your opinion, what is the most difficult part of using the PACE model?
(10) How much did you have to adapt the model to your own purposes?
(11) Is your teaching style very different from the one required in this model? Please explain the differences.
(12) Do you see any advantages in using the model?
(13) Do you see any disadvantages in using the model?
(14) What is your final conclusion about the PACE model?

Appendix C: Planned Course of Study from Grades 3 and 4

Grade 3

School Year 2000–2001

(5) Students will be able to comprehend and use vocabulary related to architecture:
  (5.1) Students will use a variety of activities such as songs, charades, pictures, vocabulary games, and worksheets.
(6) Students will be able compare and contrast architecture in the US and Spain:
  (6.1) Students will use a variety of materials such as video, visuals, and books.

School Year 2001–2002

(8) Students will be able to recognize and identify different buildings and locations in Spanish:
  (8a) Students will identify different buildings and locations through TPR activities using flashcards and visuals.
  (8b) Students will identify buildings and locations through a TPR activity in a city on the board.
  (8c) Students will identify different buildings and locations through a listening comprehension worksheet
(9) Students will be able tcomprehend a teacher-created story using vocabulary related to buildings about a trip to Spain.
  (9a) Students will recognize different buildings through a teacher-created story.
  (9b) Students will create a graphic organizer based on the story.
  (9c) Students will retell the story through cue cards
(10) Students will be able to identify, use correctly, and compare all the different forms of the verb 'to go' (*ir*) in the story 'A Trip to Spain.'
  (10a) Students will find all the subjects and verbs in the story, circle them, and discuss why they are different.
  (10b) Students will create a subject and verb chart with the verbs from the story.
(11) Students will be able to write and use correct grammar.
  (11a) Students will write and illustrate a journal about a trip to Spain.

Documenting Curricular Reform

Grade 4

School Year 2000–2001

(1) Students will be able to identify roles and develop the responsibilities of a travel team (navigator, payload specialist, interpreter, travel agent)
   (1a) Develop prepositions, such as *in front of, behind, below, above, next to, close to, for, from* (NAVIGATOR).
   (1b) Develop travel vocabulary, such as *passport, tickets, plane, airport, suitcase, accommodation, family hotel*, etc. and action verbs related to travel, such as: *flying, packing, taking a bus, taking a trip*, etc. (TRAVEL AGENT).
   (1c) Express greetings and questions related to costs, bank, money exchange, etc. (INTERPRETER).
   (1d) Acquire vocabulary related to clothing, food, hygiene, etc. (PAYLOAD SPECIALIST).
   (1e) Acquire map-reading skills, such as locating Costa Rica, choose groups and assign roles, brainstorm responsibilities, take part in games, songs, visuals, and TPR to acquire new vocabulary.

School Year 2001–2002

(1) Students will be able to talk and write about a trip to a specific destination of their choice.
   (1a) Students will review prior knowledge (family members, months, weather, money).
   (1b) Using manipulatives and flashcards, the teacher will introduce new vocabulary.
   (1c) Students will listen to six different places read to them by the teacher (Mexico, España, Florida, Costa Rica, California, Kennywood).
   (1d) Students will be engaged in different TPR activities while listening to the six scenarios read first by the teacher and then by other students.

(2) Students will be able to compare and contrast the meaning and form of the 1st person singular and 1st person plural of the verb *ir* (to go) and *necesitar* (to need).
   (2a) With the help of an overhead projector, teacher and students will go through one scenario identifying and circling the verbs.
   (2b) Students will be engaged in a discussion about similarities and differences in the meaning and form of these verbs.
   (2c) Students will summarize information from the six scenarios on working sheets containing guide questions.
   (2d) Following the guide questions, students will write their own scenario.

Chapter 5
Research Perspectives on Non-native English-speaking Educators

LIA D. KAMHI-STEIN

Introduction

In the first issue of the newsletter published by the Caucus of Non-native English Speakers in the TESOL organization, Kaplan (1999: 5) wrote the following: 'The terms *native speaker* and *non-native speaker* obviously and pointlessly dichotomize the world neatly into "us" and "them," but beyond that, they are fairly useless.' While I agree with Kaplan that the dichotomy is fairly useless, it is a reality that, as noted by Pasternak and Bailey (2004: 156), 'teachers who are perceived as speaking a language other than English as their mother tongue – regardless of their actual proficiency with English – are typically labeled as "non-native" English speakers.'

Non-native English-speaking (NNES) teachers constitute up to 80% of English teachers around the world (Canagarajah, 1999). However, it is only recently that NNES educators have become more visible as they have begun to raise their concerns in relation to issues of professionalism in English language teaching (ELT) (Braine, 1996, 1999a; Medgyes, 1994). This chapter takes the position that, given that most English teachers in the world are non-native English speakers, there is a need to understand how factors such as NNES educators' perceptions of themselves as well as others' attitudes toward them (including those of language learners and administrators) may affect their instructional practices and contribute to their success (or failure) as educators.

The goal of this chapter is to review the literature on NNES educators, with the emphasis on research relevant to instructional issues. The chapter begins with a discussion of the 'native' and 'non-native' labels and presents a summary of research focusing on the labels as they relate to NNES educators. Next, the chapter reviews research on how NNES educators are perceived, including the perceptions they hold of themselves and the perceptions others hold of them as ELT professionals. It concludes by identifying future research directions.

To Label or Not to Label

The term 'native speaker' (NES) is commonly used to refer to people 'who learned a language in a natural setting from childhood as first or sole language' (Kachru & Nelson, 1996: 81). Within the ELT (English Language Teaching) field, the notion that the native speaker of English is the ideal teacher was a tenet formulated at the Commonwealth Conference on the Teaching of English as a Second Language, held in Makerere, Uganda in 1961 (Phillipson, 1992). The tenet supports the assumptions that NES teachers are (1) better linguistic models; (2) have the ability to use language more fluently and idiomatically; (3) are aware of the cultural connotations of the language; and (4) can rely on intuition to make accurate linguistic judgments. Phillipson (1992) calls the tenet 'the native speaker fallacy' and questions the assumptions on which it is based since non-native speakers can, through professional training, acquire the features attributed to native speakers. Researchers such as Canagarajah (1999) and Thomas (1999) also question the tenet because it assumes that, in Canagarajah's words (1999: 4), 'periphery teachers,' that is, teachers from post-colonial settings, are 'second best, if not expendable for teaching English' (Thomas, 1999: 126).

Other researchers also question the validity of the NES construct and, by extension, challenge the notion that the native speaker is the ideal English teacher (e.g. Amin, 1997, 1999, 2001; Kachru, 1992; Kaplan, 1999; Kramsch, 1998a; Nayar, 1994; Paikeday, 1985; Pasternak & Bailey, 2004). For example, Kramsch (1998a: 79–80) argues that the 'native speaker' construct is an abstraction 'based on arbitrarily selected features of pronunciation, grammar, lexicon, as well as on stereotypical features of appearance and demeanor,' and that the construct relies on the assumption that native speakers are monolingual and monocultural and speak only a standard variety of the language. However, this assumption is not supported by reality, since most people speak more than one language or varieties of a language and participate in more than just one culture and subculture. Kaplan (1999) questions the validity of the construct on similar grounds. The construct, he writes, 'creates an impression that linguistic unity exists, when global reality reflects vast linguistic diversity' (Kaplan, 1999: 5) and terms such as 'native speakers' or 'non-native speakers' serve the purpose only of separating people into different camps, a point also made by Bhatt (2001), Kachru and Nelson (1996), and others. Further criticizing this notion, Amin (2001: 90) argues that the NES construct 'is not only about language competence but is deeply embedded in discourses of racism and colonialism.'

Despite this apparent unity of views, the literature on NNES educators presents a range of perspectives on the NES/NNES dichotomy. One position, advanced by Medgyes (1994) and labeled the 'noninterface position' by Liu (1999: 86) views the dichotomy as useful since it reflects the idea that native and non-native speakers 'are two different species' (Medgyes, 2001: 434) in that membership of one group excludes membership of the other and that differences in pedagogical practices can be attributed to the teachers' NES or NNES status. Cook (1999) also views native and non-native speakers as different in terms of their knowledge of their second language (L2), their first language (L1), and in some of their cognitive processes. For Cook (1990: 185), however, 'L2 speakers should be considered as speakers in their own right, not as approximations to monolingual native speakers.' Another position, advanced by Davies (1991, 1995, 2002, 2003), argues that the NES construct is a myth, but we need this myth as a model and a goal. Davies (2003: 210) notes that, though with difficulty, an L2 learner 'can become a native speaker of a target language.' However, the fundamental difference between native and non-native speakers is one of power that has to be taken by those secure enough in their own identity.

A third position sees the labels as problematic in that they place emphasis on the biological rather than the social factors that affect the L2 learning process (e.g. Kachru & Nelson, 1996; Kaplan, 1999; Liu, 1999; Nayar, 1994). They disregard the role that language plays as a symbol of social identification (Rampton, 1990) and have no relevance in multilingual or multicultural communities, where the teacher of English is perceived as an 'intercultural speaker' (Kramsch, 1998b; Velasco-Martin, 2004).

Advocates of this view also argue that in the ELT field, the debate over the NES/NNES construct has been 'overly simplistic and unhelpful' (Pasternak & Bailey, 2004: 155) in that it has treated NES and NNES teachers as having absolute characteristics. They further argue that the discussion as it relates to NES and NNES educators needs to focus on issues of professionalism and to address the interplay between '[language] proficiency and professional development, viewing these constructs as continua rather than categorical absolutes' (Pasternak & Bailey, 2004: 155).

A question that has only recently been raised in the literature refers to the factors that contribute to educators' self-identification as native or non-native speakers. Liu (1999) argues that research in this area is needed since it would help to explain the extent to which the labels affect not only NNES educators' self-image but also their instructional practices and, ultimately, their students' development. In one such study focusing on English as a foreign language (EFL) teachers in Israel, Inbar (2001) found that the two best predictors of the teachers' self-identification as native or non-native English speakers were 'having spoken English from the age of 0 to 6' and 'others' perception of the teachers as native English speakers.' Results also showed that differences in the teachers' perceptions of their pedagogical practices could be attributed to factors other than NES/NNES background, including personal and professional factors. Results further showed that teachers who identified themselves as NES educators reported being more confident as English users and teachers of culture. In contrast, teachers who viewed themselves as NNES educators reported having better relations with students and feeling more confident in using the L1 as a pedagogical tool.

In a related study, Liu (1999) investigated how seven NNS educators who had learned English in a variety of settings (in the US, in bilingual settings, and in EFL settings) differed in their definition of the term 'NNES professional.' Results showed that several factors contributed to this variation, including language learning sequence, language competence, cultural affiliation, perceived dual identities, and the setting in which they had learned English. According to Liu, the label 'NNES professional' is problematic because it perpetuates the perception in the job market that NNES educators are less competent than their NES counterparts, while failing to capture the range of language learning experiences of all ELT educators. Liu concludes that:

> ... rather than reducing the rich complexity involved in being a speaker of a language to an NES/NNES dichotomy and letting this dichotomy override qualifications to teach ESL/EFL, we as TESOL [Teachers of English to Speakers of Other Languages] educators should shift our focus to the importance of being a TESOL professional and consider whether an individual has received adequate professional training to teach ESOL. (Liu, 1999: 101)

The notion that the NES/NNES labels can be misleading because they reduce or minimize the experiences of educators is also supported by Hansen (2004). In a literacy autobiography, Hansen describes her own experience as a member of an invisible minority: a white woman who emigrated from Denmark to the US at age 10 and perceives herself to be a non-native speaker of English. Hansen argues that invisible minority non-native English speakers are usually perceived to be native English speakers. Their proficiency in English is not questioned, and their L2 learning experiences go unnoticed. On the other hand, in the case of visible minority non-native English speakers, it is their L2 learning experiences that may be visible, and their proficiency in English and their ability to teach that may often be questioned. Hansen (2004: 55) agrees with Liu that there is a need to hire and evaluate educators 'by virtue of what they can do, by their professionalism and teaching ability.'

Self-perceptions of Non-native English-speaking Educators

Teachers' self-perceptions and beliefs play an important role in influencing their instructional practices (Richards & Lockhart, 1994; Samimy & Brutt-Griffler, 1999). Beginning with the seminal work of Medgyes (1983,

1986, 1992, 1994; see also Arva & Medgyes, 2000; Reves & Medgyes, 1994), there has been substantial research dealing with NNES educators and their self-image, with emphasis on the relationship between educators' self-perceptions about their language skills and their instructional practices. More recently, research has focused on the role of race in relation to NNES educators' self-perceptions as classroom teachers. This section synthesizes this research by looking at four specific areas:

(1) the relationship between NNES educators' perceptions of their language proficiency and their instructional practices;
(2) the role that NNES educators play in the L2 classroom;
(3) the relationship between language proficiency and professionalism;
(4) the role of race and language status in relation to the 'ideal English teacher.'

Discussions of NNES educators have been heavily influenced by two different views regarding the extent to which NNES educators' perceptions of their language proficiency and their non-native status affect their instructional practices. The first view (Medgyes, 1994: 40) posits that NNES teachers suffer from an 'inferiority complex' that results from a 'linguistic deficit' (Medgyes, 1994: 33) and that differences in the instructional behaviors of NES and NNES teachers can be attributed to this deficit. Medgyes' position draws at least in part on research by Reves and Medgyes (1994) that focuses on the perceived differences in the instructional practices of NES and NNES teachers in Europe, Africa, and Latin America. Reves and Medgyes (1994) found that these perceptions differed in four areas: (1) their perceived use of English (with NES teachers speaking 'better' English, using 'real' language, etc.); (2) their general teaching practices (with NES teachers being more flexible and innovative, etc.); (3) their approaches to L2 teaching (with NES teachers having fewer insights into the L2 learning process, focusing on fluency, etc.); and (4) their attitudes toward teaching culture (with NES teachers supplying more cultural information). Reves and Medgyes (1994) concluded that the discrepancy in language proficiency between NES and NNES teachers accounted for most of these differences.[1]

The second view holds that, while NNS educators are aware of their linguistic difficulties, they have positive self-perceptions and do not perceive these difficulties as negatively affecting their instructional practices. Two studies supporting this position (Kamhi-Stein et al., 1998; Samimy & Brutt-Griffler, 1999) focused on the self-perceptions of NNES teachers-in-preparation. These studies showed that, while NNES educators were aware of their language difficulties, they did not perceive their instructional practices as being negatively affected by such difficulties and instead perceived themselves to be successful teachers. Contributing to the positive self-perceptions of the teachers-in-preparation were factors such as teaching experience (Kamhi-Stein et al., 1998; see also Brinton, 2004 and Seidlhofer, 1999 for similar findings), program objectives, students' age and level of proficiency, and the teachers' personality and professional preparation (Samimy & Brutt-Griffler, 1999). Also contributing to the NNES educators' success as teachers is personal experience of ESL, which Maum (2003: vii) sees as 'a crosscultural and language learning experience similar to that experienced by the students.' In her investigation of NES and NNES adult ESL teachers, Maum concluded that having gone through the ESL experience led NNES teachers to focus their teaching on crosscultural communication issues to help students in their adjustment process. Maum's conclusions support Auerbach's (1993) view that the immigrant experience of many NNES teachers provides them with a critical understanding of the struggles that their students go through, and that it is this very experience that allows teachers and students to make connections that NES teachers may miss (see also Ellis, 2002 for a discussion of this idea).

The second area of interest in relation to the self-perceptions of NNES educators focuses on the role that these educators play in the L2 classroom. Two views, both focusing on the EFL context, have been advanced. The first, proposed by Medgyes (1983, 1994), could be understood to support the notion of 'language as problem.' In this view, when teaching in the L2 classroom, NNES educators have to leave their L1 behaviors behind and 'pretend' they are someone different. For Medgyes (1994), the 'double role' that NNES educators have to play in the EFL classroom seems to create a conflict in the teachers' minds since they have to 'play the role' of someone they are not. The second, more current, view could be understood to support the notion of 'language as resource.' This view, best reflected by Seidlhofer (1999), posits that the 'double role' that NNES teachers have to play has a positive connotation since it is perceived to add 'value' to NNES teachers. For Seidlhofer (1999:235), NNES teachers are 'double agents' in that sharing their students' L1 and culture *and* being knowledgeable about the target language (TL) puts them in the position of being mediators between languages and cultures.

The third area of interest in relation to NNES educators' self-perceptions concerns the relationship between teacher proficiency in English and issues of professionalism. Work in this area, best reflected by Bailey (2002) and Pasternak and Bailey (2004), argues that, rather than viewing NES and NNES educators as belonging in one or the other camp, English proficiency and professionalism need to be viewed as continua. According to Pasternak and Bailey, the reason for this is that viewing NES and NNES educators as having discrete qualities (and weaknesses) disregards three facts: (1) teachers can be proficient in the TL regardless of whether they are native or non-native speakers; (2) proficiency in the TL is only 'one element of professionalism' (Pasternak & Bailey, 2004: 161); and (3) teacher preparation is a key element contributing to professionalism.

Supporting the notion that English proficiency and professionalism need to be viewed as continua is a study by Kamhi-Stein *et al.* (2001) that focuses on the self-perceptions of NES and NNES educators teaching K–12 (kindergarten to grade 12) in California. This study showed that NES and NNES teachers, most of whom had lived in the US for more than 10 years, were characterized by a complex set of similarities and differences. The study also showed that viewing NES and NNES educators as belonging to two separate categories and as having absolute characteristics is unrealistic since several factors (e.g. professional preparation, length of residence in a particular country, and teaching assignments) may help make the two groups of educators more similar than dissimilar.

The last area of interest dealing with NNES educators' self-perceptions has emerged only recently and addresses the role of race and language status in relation to issues of credibility. Several researchers have argued that visible-minority NNES teachers working in an ESL setting often experience their students' initial mistrust because they are perceived to be 'outsiders' or 'less able' than white teachers despite their professional qualifications and skills (Amin, 1997, 2001; Braine, 1999b; Ding, 2000; Kamhi-Stein, 1999; Thomas, 1999). Teachers may then react in a variety of ways. They may be affected to the point of becoming less effective than white teachers. They may need to invest a great deal of time and energy until they can establish themselves as authentic educators in the eyes of their students. Or they may build effective pedagogies that draw on their NNES status. These pedagogies may include creating learning communities, disrupting NES myths of birth and intuition, and promoting anti-racist materials (Amin, 2001), enriching the cultural experiences of students by bringing into the classroom topics of cultural diversity and diverse value systems (Ding, 2000; Hansen, 2004; Liu, 2001), sharing their own learning strategies (de Oliveira & Richardson, 2001; Ellis, 2002; Liu, 2001), or helping students become intercultural speakers by learning how to play the role of intermediaries between the TL culture and the L1 culture (Velasco-Martin, 2004).

Others' Perceptions of Non-native English-speaking Educators

In the past few years, attention has started to be paid to how NNES educators are perceived by language learners and program administrators. As noted by Braine (2004: 19), studies designed to investigate the perceptions of language learners are needed since these are 'the most affected by the NES/NNES dichotomy.' Also needed is research focusing on program administrators since their beliefs about and attitudes toward NNES educators ultimately affect their hiring practices and decisions. Research on students' perceptions about NNES educators has focused on two areas: teacher accentedness and pedagogical skills. Studies that have explored how teacher accentedness in English affects students' perceptions about teachers lead to three conclusions.

First, exposure to and familiarity with particular NNES teachers may play a more important role in the development of students' attitudes toward the teachers than does the teachers' accentedness in English. In an investigation of the attitudes of college-level ESL students toward teacher accentedness, Liang (2002) found that the students had very positive attitudes toward the most recent NNES teachers they had had in their country of origin. In another investigation that focused on the perceptions that students enrolled in an intensive English-program (IEP) had of NNES teachers from Japan, Argentina, Ecuador, and Switzerland, Moussu (2002) found that, after being their students for one quarter, the students' attitudes toward their NNES teachers uniformly improved. Finally, Kelch and Santana-Williamson (2002) found that intermediate-level ESL students' familiarity with a particular variety of English led them to have more positive perceptions of the teachers who spoke that variety. Specifically, students gave more favorable ratings to the teachers who spoke varieties of English they were accustomed to.

The second conclusion in relation to teacher accentedness is that, while students may not be capable of distinguishing between the accents of NES and NNES teachers with 'a high degree of accuracy' (Kelch & Santana-Williamson, 2002: 62), there is a correlation between a teacher's degree of accentedness in English or the students' perception of the teacher's status as NES or NNES and the students' attitudes toward the teacher who exhibits the accent. Liang (2002) shows that, the stronger the teachers' accent in English, the less positive are the students' perceptions about those teachers' professional qualities. Similarly, Kelch and Santana-Williamson (2002) show that the students' attitudes correlated with their perceptions of whether or not the teacher was a native speaker, and that students attributed more favorable professional characteristics (i.e. a higher level of education and training or greater teaching experience and excellence in teaching) to teachers who they perceived to be native speakers.

The third conclusion is that language learners do not necessarily perceive accentedness to be a criterion for the 'ideal' English teacher. Liang (2002) shows that the characteristics found to contribute to the 'ideal' teacher were related to professionalism and personality (e.g. being interesting, being prepared, being professional, and being qualified). Support for this idea is further provided by Moussu (2002). She showed that most of the students in her study already had positive attitudes toward their NNES teachers at the beginning of the quarter: they felt that they could learn English just as well from NNES teachers as they could from NES teachers (69%), they expressed admiration and respect for their NNES teachers (79%), and they expected to have a positive experience in the classes taught by their NNES teachers (84%).

Turning now to students' perceptions of NNES teachers' pedagogical skills as reported in the work of Cheung (2002), Mahboob (2004), Moussu (2002), Kelch and Santana-Williamson (2002), and Lasagabaster and Sierra (2002), five generalizations seem appropriate.

(1) Both NES and NNES educators are perceived to be good teachers, each with their unique strengths, and students, regardless of the setting in which they are studying, feel that they can learn English just as well from either group. Both ESL and EFL students have been found to have positive attitudes toward their NNES teachers, high expectations for their teachers, and confidence in their teachers' ability to teach. Moreover, the strengths that characterize NNES educators are directly related to their status as non-native speakers and include their empathy, their ability to understand their students' needs and to teach learning strategies, and their ability to better relate to their students and to provide more emotional support than their NES counterparts.

(2) There is some support for the idea that ESL and EFL students prefer to study listening, pronunciation, and speaking with NES rather than NNES teachers. As noted by Mahboob, language learners seem to believe that, to acquire a 'true' and 'correct' pronunciation, they need to be exposed to native speaker models. However, Kelch and Santana-Williamson (2002) show that students are not always capable of distinguishing a native from a non-native speaker; nor are they capable of distinguishing between different varieties of English (Shim, 2002). It could therefore be argued that language learners believe that there is one 'ideal native speaker' and disregard the fact there are many varieties of English.

(3) ESL and EFL learners perceive NES teachers as being more knowledgeable than their NNES counterparts in the area of the target language (TL) culture. The students' perceptions of NNES teachers' knowledge of the TL culture corroborate what NNES educators have to say about themselves, namely that their knowledge of the culture is not as comprehensive as that of their NES peers (e.g. Inbar, 2001; Kamhi-Stein et al., 1998; Reves & Medgyes, 1994).

(4) ESL and EFL students favor NNES educators in the area of grammar teaching, and language learners find their NNES teachers able to answer grammar questions in more specific ways than their NES counterparts.

(5) While there is support for the idea that NNES teachers are favored as reading and writing teachers, research results are somewhat mixed. For example, Lasagabaster and Sierra (2002) found that EFL students were somewhat neutral in their preference for NES or NNES teachers in the area of reading. Kelch and Santana-Williamson (2002) found no preference for NES teachers in the area of writing. Mahboob's (2004) findings were stronger in that the ESL students in his investigation considered NNES educators to be better at teaching literacy skills. Students were aware that literacy skills and oral skills are different in nature and that regardless of language background, reading and writing skills require studying.[3]

As noted above, research has also begun to focus on the attitudes of administrators toward NNES educators. Mahboob *et al.* (2004) investigated the weight that IEP administrators give to various hiring criteria and the degree to which NNES teachers are represented in such programs. The study showed that most of the 118 program administrators who participated in the study considered NES status to be an important hiring criterion (60% of the respondents considered the criterion at least 'somewhat important') and that the presence or absence of NNES educators in a given IEP could be explained by three hiring criteria found to be statistically significant: NES status, recommendation, and teaching experience. The finding that NES status was considered to be an important criterion for hiring could be explained by Kaplan's (1999) view that program administrators in the US may simply be under the impression that students expect to be taught by native English speakers. At the same time, the results of the study suggest that program administrators are not aware of – or choose to disregard – TESOL's (1991) statement strongly condemning hiring practices solely based on NES/NNES status.

Looking to the Future

The last few years have seen substantial growth in research focusing on issues related to NNES educators. The review of the research presented here shows that this work has gone through three phases, each reflecting a different area of interest. The first phase focused on the self-perceptions of NNES educators. This research investigated NNES educators' perceptions of their language difficulties in relation to their perceived instructional practices and provided information on how self-image can affect teachers' perceptions of teaching and learning. The second phase explored the role of race and language status in relation to issues of credibility. This work, in the form of qualitative studies and autobiographical narratives, mainly focused on visible minority NNES educators and how their minority status may affect their students' perceptions of their 'authenticity' (or lack thereof) as ELT educators. It could be argued that research on NNES educators is currently going through a third phase, and that two distinct strands are now receiving attention. The first comprises research dealing with the NNES label. Work carried out so far suggests that the label is problematic in that it does not capture the range of language learning experiences of NNES educators. Further work on the NNES label would help to clarify its complexities, particularly in relation to visible and invisible minority NNES educators and their classrooms. The second strand of research explores others' perceptions of NNES educators, although research in this area is, again, at a preliminary stage. So far, work in this area has explored two topics. The first is that of ESL/EFL students' perceptions of teacher accentedness and pedagogical skills, including the extent to which time with and exposure to NNES teachers affect students' attitudes toward NNES teachers. The second topic is the hiring criteria of college-level ESL program administrators. Though both research areas look promising, more work remains to be done. Replications and extensions of some of the studies reviewed above (in different instructional settings and with different student and teacher populations) would help to develop a better understanding of the factors affecting students' and administrators' attitudes toward NNES educators and of how students' and administrators' attitudes toward NNES educators develop over time.

While there has been considerable growth in research focusing on NNES educators, future studies need to take into account two factors that have so far received only cursory attention. First, future investigations would benefit from not treating NES and NNES educators as having absolute characteristics and from taking into account potential individual differences among NES and NNES educators with respect to their language proficiency, professional preparation, and the settings in which they teach. Second, future research should move beyond issues of self-perceptions of language proficiency and instead deal with NNES educators' levels of English language competence in relation to curriculum delivery (in different language settings and at different instructional levels). At present, this type of research is in progress, funded by the TESOL International Research Foundation (TIRF).

NNES educators and issues related to professionalism have become a legitimate research topic. Research addressing the above factors and exploring topics such as the NNES educator label, hiring criteria in various settings and for different levels of instruction, attitudes of students and administrators toward NNES educators, and models of effective language teacher preparation are critical to developing a better understanding of a group of educators that constitutes the vast majority of English teachers around the world.

Notes

1. It should be noted that a follow-up study by Arva and Medgyes (2000), designed to investigate the actual teaching behaviors of NES and NNES educators in Hungary, provided only partial support for Reves and Medgyes' (1994) findings. However, the fact that the two groups of teachers in the Arva and Medgyes (2000) study differed in terms of their professional preparation, experience, and English and Hungarian language competence made comparisons difficult.
2. These generalizations should be treated with caution, for several reasons. First, the number of studies in this area is still limited. Second, these investigations focus on student populations studying in different settings (ESL and EFL) and, possibly, for different purposes. Finally, the studies differ in their instrumentation.
3. Clearly, much of this work is tentative, and further research is needed in order to corroborate these conclusions.

Part 3
English for Academic Purposes

Part 3
Introduction

DWIGHT ATKINSON

Without question, Robert Kaplan has had a powerful influence on English for Academic Purposes (EAP). There was even a time, according to Ann Johns (this volume), when many in the profession thought that:

good writing is about structure. At the text level, students need to learn the discourse patterns (or 'modes') of the target language. If students can prepare an effective comparison/contrast, cause/effect, exemplification (etc.) essay, then they can write. Thus, there is a generalized writing ability, realized through the discourse patterns.

Kaplan's special contribution was of course the claim that preferred expository discourse patterns vary crossculturally – a claim that has since spawned virtual cottage industries of research and critique. But Kaplan also contributed in other areas; on the teaching front, for example, he introduced various approaches to formulating academic essays (e.g. Kaplan, 1971, 1980b).

But this may seem like ancient history. Certainly, as Johns shows in Chapter 7, EAP is now a different and more complex field. The interesting thing is that Kaplan is still contributing to EAP, and his contributions have continued to be controversial. In a series of recent articles with Vaidehi Ramanathan (Ramanathan & Kaplan, 1996a, 1996b, 2000), for instance, he has argued that all university writing should be taught in an English for Special Purposes (ESP) framework, and that the concept of critical thinking – widely considered central to academic modes of thought – is problematic.

But to view Kaplan's influence on EAP merely in terms of his own writings would be to grossly underestimate it. In fact, he has made (and continues to make) an equally powerful but quite different contribution through his attentive mentorship of graduate students, junior colleagues, and indeed individuals the world over who have no particular connection to him, at least originally. One fact about this aspect of Kaplan's career – less well-known because less public – is that, although he certainly has strong views, he has been particularly undogmatic and open-minded in his mentoring practices. Thus, between 1987–1993, when I studied with him, Kaplan advisees were writing dissertations on (among others) the consumption of Spanish-language advertising in Mexican-American communities, workplace education, Mexican-American literacy, interaction and miscommunication in a university computer lab, graffiti as a signifying practice in minority communities, the educational life history of a Mexican-American child, frequency and functions of linguistic features in university ESL students' pre-academic writing, and the history of scientific discourse. In only the last case am I able to connect any of these topics even indirectly with strands in Kaplan's own research. In any case, this list clearly indicates that his advisees were working on topics emerging from their own concerns and situations, and that (although he could be intimidating at first) Kaplan has worn the mantle of advisor lightly and well. There will never be a 'Kaplan School' of EAP (or language planning or contrastive rhetoric or anything else). In its stead exists a sizeable cadre of scholars whose self-motivation, independence, and indeed strong wills were carefully mentored and patiently nurtured.

The open-ended and ecumenical nature of Kaplan's mentoring is strongly reflected in the four chapters featured in this section of the present volume. Dana Ferris, one of Kaplan's doctoral advisees from the early '90s, starts things off with a lively and free-wheeling discussion of the different 'collars' worn by applied linguists – from bluest blue to whitest white. For Ferris, blue collar applied linguists are those who work on real-world problems in ESL settings, in what seems close (in my view) to an action-research model, if the scope of action research can be extended beyond single classrooms (e.g. Kemmis & McTaggart, 2000). White collar applied linguists, on the other hand, are those who engage with social theory – still problem-oriented in many cases, but without the narrow and concrete focus of blue collar work. What is especially interesting about Ferris's chapter is that, in a processual and dialectical manner, she manages to gradually break down and move beyond this dichotomy, ending up in a quite different place from where she began. And she does so in a truly 'blue collar' way, by reflecting on her own changing experience as a researcher over the course of her (very active) career. There are few discussions in applied linguistics that so engagingly and effectively bridge the theory–practice gap.

Ann Johns, the second contributor to this section, was, like Ferris, a doctoral advisee of Kaplan's, but she did her doctorate in the middle stages of a long and active career. Johns is therefore both Kaplan's student *and* his near-contemporary. In her chapter (Chapter 7), Johns uses her lengthy experience in EAP to great advantage, providing a historically informed but up-to-date account of the teaching of academic literacy to US undergraduates. She begins by posing four questions: (1) What theoretical and pedagogical frameworks should inform undergraduate literacy instruction? (2) What should the content of such courses be? (3) What are the purposes of undergraduate literacy instruction? and (4) What is the place of contrastive rhetoric in all this? Johns then takes us on a historical tour of the field, showing in a notably fair-minded way the strengths and weaknesses of past answers to these questions. Next, she introduces and describes three areas of current EAP research that can help us answer her questions anew: the social construction of texts, academic literacy contexts, and multi-literacies. She follows this with a series of 'applications' – descriptions of concrete situations in which rhetorical consciousness-raising (Sengupta, 1999) was fostered and engaged in. Johns concludes by summarizing current answers to the four major questions stated at the beginning of her chapter.

The next contributor to this section, Joy Reid, was never a doctoral advisee of Kaplan, at least formally. Instead, she and Kaplan have been long-term associates in various settings, including the TESOL organization, of which both are past presidents. It is notable, however, that Reid regards Kaplan as her mentor in the sense that, often from afar, he actively advised and supported her own PhD work, which, like Johns', was completed in mid-career. In her chapter (Chapter 8), Reid engages with a question of great current relevance in the US and perhaps in all modern societies that have had large influxes of immigrants in the past quarter century: the language problems of US-born ('Generation 1.5-and-later') writers of academic English. While virtually all novice academic writers are likely to have at least some problems in this regard – they are, after all, acquiring a new social language (Gee, 1996) – the group that Reid focuses on has its own special issues. These include the apparent imperviousness of their non-native-like grammars to traditional forms of grammar instruction, a problem of considerable concern to university writing teachers. Reid attributes this problem to the fact that such students tend to be 'ear' learners – unlike international students. They have learned their English largely in informal, oral-language contexts. After identifying categories of the non-target-like forms these students, Reid goes on to make a number of innovative suggestions for their remediation, given that more traditional approaches don't seem to work. Reid then concludes by calling for further research and development regarding instruction in this area.

The final contributor to this section, Cheryl Zimmerman, adds yet another dimension to the range of Kaplan mentees represented here. Zimmerman was a doctoral student in the School of Education at the University of Southern California, whereas Kaplan was a professor in the Linguistics Department. Her advisor of record was the late David Eskey, a longtime Kaplan associate. Perhaps for this reason, Zimmerman reports having found herself advised by committee, with Eskey and Kaplan playing different but complementary roles. Of Kaplan she states: 'He met with me weekly for a year, and showed me how the discerning writer works through every step of the research writing process' (personal communication). Zimmerman has since put what Kaplan taught her to good use, making important contributions to the fast-growing area of L2 vocabulary research (e.g. Zimmerman, 1997; Schmitt & Zimmerman, 2002). Here, she provides an empirical study of teacher responses to lexical anomalies (i.e. lexical combination errors that show incomplete understanding of semantic restrictions on particular words and phrases). Zimmerman's participants were a group of experienced ESL teachers, none of whom had had formal instruction in vocabulary teaching. They were asked to categorize and explain the same set of English sentences containing lexical anomalies. Zimmerman found that the teachers were not, in general, very accurate in classifying the anomalies in terms corresponding to their analysis from a vocabulary research perspective. They were, on the other hand, more successful in providing explanations and examples that captured some of the items' problematic characteristics. However, much of what is most interesting in Zimmerman's study comes in the details – e.g. the different levels of accuracy with which participants categorized different types of anomalies.

The field of EAP is evolving and growing rapidly at the start of the 21st century. Long considered (at least partly) a subfield of ESP, and perhaps limited to some degree by a US post-secondary focus, it is now beginning to come into its own. Among other signs of this development is the appearance of a new international journal, *The Journal of English for Academic Purposes*. There is no doubt in my mind that, as this field changes and develops, Robert Kaplan will continue to contribute signally to it, both through his own original work and the work of those he mentored so well.

Chapter 6
Reflections of a 'Blue Collar Linguist:' Analysis of Written Discourse, Classroom Research, and EAP Pedagogy

DANA R. FERRIS

In 1988, as a graduate student in applied linguistics at the University of Southern California (USC), I was fortunate to have the opportunity to take a course entitled Analysis of Written Discourse from Professor Robert B. Kaplan. My classmates and I were even more fortunate in that we had available as our primary text the recently-published collection entitled *Writing Across Languages: Analysis of L2 Text* (Connor & Kaplan, 1987). Just how unique this opportunity was is much more apparent to me today, as I observe that (1) such courses are still extremely rare in academic institutions; (2) the Connor/Kaplan volume was a ground-breaking pacesetter for subsequent explorations and discussions; and (3) the analysis of written discourse has grown and evolved dramatically in recent years.

One of my classmates back in 1988 was Dwight Atkinson, who is also a co-editor of this volume. He and I have reminisced over the years about 'the box in Bob's office' – Kaplan's personal collection of papers and dissertations on written discourse analysis, which prior to the publication of the Connor/Kaplan book was the only major resource available for students in this class. More importantly, we have reminisced about how inspirational and significant Bob's course was in shaping our thinking and the future course of our scholarly careers. In my own case, I was so gripped by what I learned there that I completely changed direction (and dissertation advisors) in my doctoral studies. By the time I graduated in 1991, I had completed two major text analysis projects (Ferris, 1991, 1993, 1994a, 1994b) by using or adapting several different research models to analyze the writing of ESL university students.

Despite our shared origins, however, Dwight and I have engaged in diverging scholarly pursuits since those days. While still pursuing questions related to second language writing, Dwight has focused on qualitative explorations, theoretical discussions, and critical reflections on the state of second language writing research (e.g. his contribution to Santos *et al.*, 2000). In contrast, I have focused my research exclusively on classroom-based projects that address some very specific ESL writers' problems (a word I use intentionally and to which I will return later in this chapter) – with the exception of my most recent research project, which I describe near the end of this chapter. While Dwight and I still like and respect each other, I sometimes feel that we do not quite 'get' each other. In microcosm, our divergent paths from common roots illustrate the divide I have observed between 'theorists' and 'practitioners,' or, as the title of this chapter suggests, between 'white collar' and 'blue collar' (applied) linguists. Both trends, it should be noted, were modeled for us in Bob's work, and I have observed the divide and believe it exists, if subconsciously, in the minds of others as well. Over time I have learned to question and reject such rigid distinctions and to believe that many of us (starting with myself) could benefit by working harder at understanding, appreciating, and even intentionally entering the world of scholars whose intellectual choices have been different from ours. In this chapter, I will examine some of the distinctions I have observed by discussing my own continuum of research approaches and by weaving in a personal narrative about the evolution of my philosophical and practical orientations toward research over the years since I left Bob Kaplan's classroom.

Applied Linguists and Their Collars

I started referring jokingly to myself as a 'blue collar linguist' some years ago, primarily as a defense mechanism. I had published a number of articles, including reports on the text analysis studies I had completed in graduate school and specific classroom research projects I had undertaken after graduation. Some mentors and peers who had appreciated my earlier efforts expressed disappointment in the decidedly hands-on turn my work had taken and criticized it, though not in these exact words, as being too narrowly focused on the classroom and not concerned enough with building or adding to more broadly based-theoretical models. I felt like an under-achiever who had failed to live up to my potential and found myself justifying my postdoctoral work by explaining that my institution, being primarily dedicated to teaching rather than to research, expects its faculty to engage in scholarly work with direct applications to the classroom. Indeed, in order to compete for scarce research funding, we must explicitly and convincingly make a connection in our proposal between the project and our current and future teaching. While these are legitimate realities for me, the unvarnished truth is that I focus on extremely practical classroom research because that is what interests me.

My nomenclature has been challenged subsequently by the reading I have done in preparation for writing this chapter. In the first chapter of the recent *Oxford Handbook of Applied Linguistics* (Kaplan, 2002: 10), Bill Grabe defines applied linguistics as 'a practice-driven discipline that addresses language-based problems in real-world contexts.' By that definition, of course, *all* applied linguists are 'blue collar,' and many would attest to feeling marginalized and disrespected by (so-called) theoretical linguists who view the work of the former group as lower in the academic food chain and thus quite uninteresting. I realized, though, that when I refer to myself in this way, I am comparing myself not with theoretical linguists but with other applied linguists. Is there a finer distinction operating at least in my own mind between 'applied (blue collar) applied linguists' and 'theoretical (white collar) applied linguists'?

Analysis of Written Discourse and Its Collars

Rather than discussing this question with regard to all of applied linguistics research – an extremely broad universe of inquiry – I will focus on my own area of specialization, which has been, from the beginning, the analysis of written discourse and in particular its applications to second language writing. As I have thought about this further, I have identified four general categories of second language writing scholars, operating along a continuum that extends from the most theoretical (white collar) to the most practical (blue collar) (see Figure 6.1). At academic conferences I attend, I have sometimes been struck by hearing highly respected second language writing scholars refer to themselves as being 'not practitioners.' Rather, they read and draw extensively from cross-disciplinary sources to

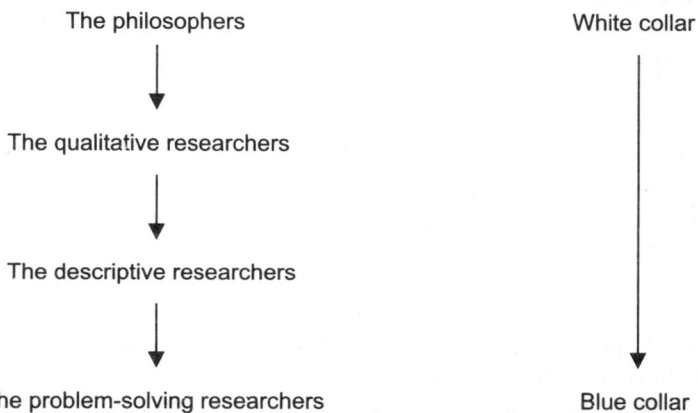

Figure 6.1 Orientations of second language writing researchers

highlight the issues and questions that should shape our thinking about second language writing. These scholars I refer to as the Philosophers.

The next broad category of writing researchers is what I am calling the Qualitative Researchers. As discussed by Duff (2002), most applied linguists now resist a mutually exclusive (sometimes even bordering on hostile) absolute dichotomy between qualitative and quantitative research paradigms, and more and more mixed-paradigm designs are being used. What I mean by qualitative research here, though, is in-depth, richly textured descriptions of writers, their contexts, and their writing processes, utilizing case study and ethnographic techniques such as observation, interview, and stimulated recall. Such research may or may not also involve the analysis of artifacts such as actual texts, and it focuses narrowly on a small number of writers in one specific writing context.

The third category is the group of researchers I am calling the Descriptive Researchers. What distinguishes these from the previous group is that they tend to be primarily or exclusively quantitative in orientation, relying on tools such as large-scale surveys or automatic analysis of sizable corpora for specific linguistic features (for helpful overviews, see Polio, 2003; Silva, 2005). Though such research leans toward the blue collar end of the spectrum because it involves the examination of actual texts (or perhaps the types of texts student writers will need to read or produce for a specific discourse community), it is definitely descriptive in orientation, offering an aerial view of a large number of subject characteristics (in the case of surveys) or textual features in combination with one another (in the case of corpus research). It does not attempt to offer solutions to problems encountered by the writers under investigation, and in fact, the subjects and/or the texts are rarely problematized at all in the design or reporting of these studies.

The Problem-Solving Researchers, in contrast, typically look at texts and their authors, most often (but not always) in real-world classroom contexts, with the specific intent of trying to understand or offer solutions to problems that subjects may face in using the language to meet their practical needs. For instance, in academic contexts, second language writers may have 'problems' meeting institutional requirements – passing their English courses or writing proficiency examinations or writing acceptable papers for their professors – because of 'problems' that are observable in their written products (which may in turn be attributable to 'problems' in their overall second language development and/or in their individual writing processes and practices). The 'problem-solving researchers' – otherwise known as classroom/program/curriculum researchers or action researchers – pose problems as research questions and design studies to help get at the source of the problem as the preliminary step toward proposing or testing possible pedagogical solutions. (While researchers at other points on the blue collar → white collar curriculum certainly could and should also be identified as problem-*posers*, I am distinguishing this group by its primary orientation towards finding applicable answers, or being problem-*solvers*.)

While many scholars regularly and seamlessly cross the amorphous boundaries of the ad hoc categories I have just proposed, many of us – particularly those closer to the ends of the continuum – are fairly bewildered by one another. Obviously, I do not mean that we cannot understand one another on an intellectual level. Rather, we do not grasp *why* others not like us do the things they do. Qualitative researchers look at problem-solvers and think, 'How could they have such tunnel vision that they do not grasp the complex mass of factors operating in the classroom? How can they possibly think that what they have found in a particular setting or group of texts has any meaning outside of that population?' Problem-solvers look at philosophers and think, 'Why do they find it interesting to talk about issues on such an abstract level?' And all three of those groups look at the corpus linguists among the descriptive researchers and think, 'How and why would anyone do that much work, and at the end of the day, how much do those descriptions really teach us?' In my experience, most researchers who are card-carrying members of one of the four groups are respectful of and collegial toward the work of those in other groups. But what we are too polite to say is that we do not really 'get' them.

From Light Blue → Dark Blue → Lighter Blue

My research puts me primarily in the blue collar, problem-solver group. But I did not start there and I have not always stayed there. I began as a purely descriptive researcher who increasingly started focusing my descriptive work on the real-world problems that I was encountering in my own teaching, but who has also learned to value and to incorporate qualitative methodology and to utilize the analyses of the philosophers to extend my own thinking about what questions to ask and about different ways to look at what I find.

As I noted previously, as a graduate student I was captivated with the research models and methods presented in Bob Kaplan's class. The two projects I completed for my qualifying paper and dissertation were purely descriptive – large-scale text analyses that involved applying or adapting several analytic models to groups of student texts. It never for a moment occurred to me to incorporate qualitative methodology into my designs. At that point, I understood qualitative and quantitative paradigms to be fundamentally in conflict and felt I had to choose one or the other. As for being a problem-solver, I was not encouraged to apply the results of my decontextualized descriptive work to the classroom, but rather to think of descriptive work as the basis for testable hypotheses that needed to be investigated before making any pedagogical recommendations.

My early post-graduation work continued to be descriptive and included both text analytic studies (Ferris, 1995a,[1] 1997, 2001; Ferris et al., 1997) and survey research (Ferris, 1995b, 1998; Ferris & Tagg, 1996a, 1996b[2]). However, the immediate difference was that I became a problem-solver rather than a model builder, posing and investigating research questions that arose in my own classes and collecting data from ESL students then in our courses, not simply from my department's examination files (the source of my two major projects completed under Bob Kaplan's supervision at USC). As an illustration of the shift, one of the questions I examined in my dissertation was whether there were differences between students at higher and lower L2 proficiency levels across 62 textual variables, a question arising from a purely descriptive framework (Ferris, 1991, 1994b). In contrast, as a problem-solver I have used text analysis (and other approaches) to investigate questions such as 'How does teacher commentary impact student revision?' (Ferris, 1997) or 'How explicit does error feedback need to be in order to help ESL writers self-edit their texts?' (Ferris & Roberts, 2001).

As I have explained elsewhere (Ferris, 2002, 2005), these particular research questions arose from my own anxieties about the problems facing my students, my need to qualify for research funding from my home institution, and my admitted preference for classroom research. For instance, as a writing teacher trained in the 1980s, I had been taught (following authorities such as Krashen, 1984, and Zamel, 1982, 1985) to de-emphasize grammar and focus on students' ideas and writing processes. Yet the students I taught had persistent and serious language errors that without question were impeding their academic progress and in some cases even preventing them from completing their degrees. Though I do not especially enjoy dealing with student errors in the classroom or studying them empirically, I felt compelled to do so by a sense of responsibility for the welfare of my own students as well as the welfare of the teachers I trained and supervised. Similarly, I began looking at teacher commentary and student revision out of a feeling of dissatisfaction and dissonance with what I found in the available L1/L2 composition literature. Teacher feedback rarely helps students, scholars wrote; in fact, our charge may be to see that it does the least possible harm to them (see, for example, Elbow, 1999; Knoblauch & Brannon, 1981; Leki, 1990). But I had observed my own students making effective revisions and notable progress as writers as they drafted, considered and incorporated feedback, and redrafted. Perhaps, I thought, it is not that teacher (and peer/self) feedback is without merit or potential, but rather that we have not yet arrived at appropriate methods for delivering or studying feedback. And so I became a problem-solver on two distinct levels: responding not only to the problems I observed in the classroom but also to the problem caused by my own cognitive dissonance with what I had learned and read. I was still adapting and developing descriptive text analysis models to pursue these questions, but my light blue collar definitely was beginning to turn a darker shade.

However, I had not finished evolving. As a descriptive researcher turned problem-solver, the more I read, heard, thought, and taught about various research paradigms, the more convinced I became that I was overlooking important information by not including qualitative tools in my research designs. I told my graduate students that viewing qualitative and quantitative approaches as mutually exclusive was an unnecessary and counter-productive way to think, and I needed to start practicing what I preached. As a result, two of my more recent projects, both of which dealt with error feedback in ESL writing classes, combined text analyses, surveys, quasi-experimental features, and qualitative features such as teacher and student interviews and case studies (Ferris, 2002, 2003; Ferris & Roberts, 2001). To be frank, combining these disparate elements made the design, data collection, analysis, and reporting more time-consuming and a lot messier and more slippery – but more interesting, satisfying, and convincing to me and to others.

Tracing my own evolution as a researcher over time has made me aware of how much we in the four groups in Figure 6.1 all need each other, and how we cheat ourselves and our discipline if we do not exert the effort to read, wrestle with, understand, and incorporate one another's insights into our thinking and into our work. In my earlier years, I had little patience for the abstractions of the philosophers, who seemed mainly to be carping that we were asking the wrong questions and investigating them in inappropriate ways. While they were telling us that we were missing the big picture, and even expounded existential and postmodern views that the knowledge we sought was both unattainable and irrelevant, our students had legitimate problems that were affecting their lives. The difference seemed akin to the divide between, say, sociologists and social workers or between educational theorists and schoolteachers. The latter group wonders why the academics take so much time describing larger social dynamics while not trying to solve urgent problems. The former group wonders why the problem-solvers cannot see that there are larger, deeper, more complex issues behind those they face and that their efforts constitute merely short-term band-aid solutions, or a finger in the dyke.

But, in spite of myself, I found my mind being stretched and troubled by the questions and issues raised by the philosophers. Two simple examples should suffice. First, in my early enthusiasm for text analysis, with its quantitative rigor (relatively speaking) and its precision, I failed to appreciate or even consider that there were a variety of individual and contextual factors that shaped the production of the texts I was studying in isolation. Second, I have been influenced, somewhat grudgingly, by the voices of critical researchers, to begin not only trying to *solve* problems but to consider that the *sources* of those problems may be more multifaceted than I had acknowledged. For instance, I would formerly have said simply, 'ESL students cannot pass their writing proficiency examinations because they make too many language errors due to inadequate second language development and poor strategies – so we must find ways to solve this problem pedagogically.' But I have been challenged also to think critically about whether such institutional assessments are fair to students – whether they are evaluated in the most helpful and valid ways, and even whether writing is truly as important in the lives of students as we have always assumed (Leki, 2003).

My most recently completed research project reflects my growing appreciation for the entire white collar → blue collar continuum. It began, as usual, with a problem. As an ESL writing instructor and the coordinator of a large ESL program, I had noticed over the previous couple of years that we were serving two distinct groups of L2 writers, only one of which was doing well. This puzzled me because on the surface the students in the two groups seemed very similar in terms of social and educational demographics. So I had both practical and intellectual problems to solve. Looking at our population a bit more closely, I noticed a general difference: the students in the higher achieving group were far more likely to be second-generation, native-born US citizens, the children of first-generation immigrants; the students in the at-risk group were, in contrast, mostly 'Generation 1.5' students (Harklau et al., 1999; Roberge, 2002b), born in the US or abroad, whose US public school education has been fragmented and whose generally fluent English often exhibits idiosyncratic features. Still, from a practical standpoint, this seemed like a fairly minor distinction. The two groups of students had a lot in common: they were of a similar age, they had received most or all of their schooling in the US, and they had been raised in homes in which the primary language was not English. Influenced by the philosophers, especially sociolinguists and second language acquisition researchers, I began to wonder whether more subtle issues of language ego/identity and sociocultural assimilation patterns were operating. Ultimately, the research questions that guided the project were derived from the white collar end of the spectrum.

Having started from a problem-solving standpoint and then backed up to consider big-picture philosophical issues, I (and two collaborators) then turned to both descriptive and qualitative research techniques to investigate the questions. We utilized surveys (of 200 students in the two groups), text analysis (of 73 essays written by students in the two groups), and in-depth interviews (of four representatives from each group). Interestingly, though the project definitely derived from a problem-solving perspective, the findings and conclusions do not, after all, solve any problems, but rather describe differences between the two groups, posit some explanations for those differences, and suggest some questions for further investigation. Perhaps in one or two studies down the line we may be able to propose and test some pedagogical treatments responsive to the different profiles and needs of the two groups. But we cannot get there without a thoughtful and in-depth look at a range of philosophical, contextual, and practical issues.

Oh, the Farmer and the Cowman should be Friends...[3]

To this point, I have argued primarily from the perspective of a (light- or dark-) blue collar researcher who has realized the need to consider the insights and approaches of lighter-collared colleagues. But I would also suggest that many philosophers and qualitative researchers need to challenge themselves to read with appreciation the empirical work of their more quantitatively minded counterparts, and to consider even participating in larger-scale descriptive research, at least occasionally. Further, L2 writing researchers should not stray too far from L2 writing students, their classrooms, and their texts. A couple of years ago, I found myself teaching an ESL composition class for the first time in eight years. In the interim, I had trained over 100 writing teachers, published articles and a book on teaching ESL composition, and spoken frequently on various writing topics to conference audiences and groups of teachers. To my surprise, I found it humbling and even intimidating to contemplate teaching L2 student writers again. Would the findings of my research be borne out in my own classroom? Had I been training others to do the right things? The experience, happily, proved to be successful, satisfying, and inspiring – but it convinced me of the importance of staying intimately connected with the real and constantly changing world of ESL student writers. If even someone like me – definitely a blue collar researcher – needs to teach or otherwise be closely interacting with students and their texts, how much more do scholars at the opposite end of the continuum?

Arguing that academics need to strive to be not merely, well, 'academic' in their thinking and investigation is hardly a viewpoint that originates with me nor is it unique to our discipline. The divide between the abstract discussions of the philosophers and the hands-on approaches of the problem-solvers is an easy one to focus on. The other divide, of course, is between the two groups in the middle of the continuum, the qualitative group and the descriptive/quantitative group. Unfortunately, the two groups not only view each other with suspicion, but they may also be on the defensive against the verbal arrows of the philosophers and the problem-solvers.

Qualitative researchers in second language writing (and applied linguistics in general) have viewed themselves as an under-represented minority (see Blanton, 2002; Cumming, 2002; Duff, 2002), at least with regard to the representation of their paradigms in applied linguistics journals. It may well be true that statistical studies appear more frequently in print. However, the articles that win awards and garner the most prestige are often either philosophical or qualitative in orientation. They may not be the most frequent, but they appear to carry the most cachet in some circles. Yet qualitative researchers must constantly justify their work to reviewers, editors, and readers on the issues of reliability and generalizability.

Descriptive researchers conducting large-scale quantitative studies have their own biases and burdens. They may give lip-service to qualitatively based values such as 'triangulation' and the 'thick/rich description' that results from ethnographic methods, but they cannot bring themselves to rely on or cite such studies in support of their arguments. Yet their own work is viewed with bewilderment by the white collar scholars and with disdain even from the problem-solvers. So the researchers work incredibly hard at conducting precise, reliable, valid, and *large* descriptive studies and are met with discouraging, even dismissive responses from both ends, the white collar side saying, 'Why is this interesting?' and the blue collar problem-solvers saying, 'How does this help anyone?'

In the end, and based on my more recent experience, I am starting to question the usefulness of the white collar versus blue collar divide – although it may capture certain truths, it clearly limits the ways we can see ourselves. I have described my own background, biases, and evolution as a researcher to remind myself and others that we do need each other and can learn from one another. But I would make the even stronger point that we need to go further than being friendly to each other at conferences and respectful of one another in print (though this would be a good start for some!). Rather, we need to read widely within and across our disciplines, to allow our own questions and analyses to be broadened – and perhaps even, at least sometimes, to cross the boundaries not only in our thinking but also in our practice (research and teaching), becoming blue collar philosophers or white collar problem solvers. This would, after all, be following directly in the footsteps of Bob Kaplan.

Notes

1. In this study, I experimented with action research by relating the textual analysis to a pedagogical treatment. But since there was no control group involved, it was speculative rather than being truly quasi-experimental in nature.
2. These latter three papers, all based on survey research, focused on academic oral/aural skills rather than on writing. I include them to demonstrate my continued devotion to descriptive research.
3. From the musical *Oklahoma!*

Chapter 7
English for Academic Purposes: Issues in Undergraduate Writing and Reading

ANN M. JOHNS

For a very long time, there has been active interest in academic literacy among applied linguists, rhetoricians, and – not incidentally – campus administrators, for at least two reasons: because literacy is seen as central to success in secondary and post-secondary education, and because academic literacy issues are complex, controversial, and daunting. I have been in the literacy business, as a teacher, researcher, and administrator, for almost as long as Bob Kaplan (see Johns, 2002b),[1] and controversies surrounding academic literacy have been raging throughout my professional life. The debate has been especially heated among those of us who teach undergraduates in North America, where most colleges and universities require students to complete a number of 'breadth' (general education) courses before they begin to specialize. However, many of the same issues are now also being raised in European universities (see Björk et al., 2003), where students are usually better prepared to immediately begin their major studies.

In contexts in which academic writing is taught to undergraduates, there are at least four questions that have continued to arise, and they are answerable in a number of ways:

(1) *In what theoretical and pedagogical frameworks should academic writing classes be taught?*
    In this regard, Bob and I have lived through the heydays of the Structuralist and Current-Traditional approaches, during which time Bob wrote his famous 'doodles' article (Kaplan, 1966), as well as through Expressivism, Cognitive Approaches, and the Process Movement. Now, Social Constructionists challenge all of these earlier views.

(2) *What should the content of academic reading and writing classes be?*
    Should our classes be devoted to literature, as English departments often require? Should we attempt to concentrate on topics that interest students? Should we focus on the disciplines of rhetoric/composition,

teaching ethos, pathos, logos, and other issues related to argumentation? Should course content interact with general education or students' majors, or should we teach stand-alone courses?

(3) *What are we educating students for?*
For initiation into the practices of the academy or into professional life? For resistance and critique of the hegemonic practices of our institutions (Benesch, 2001)? For research into literacy values and practices (Johns, 1997)? Or for the students' own enjoyment?

(4) *What is the place of contrastive rhetoric (CR) in our literacy efforts?*
Can we use CR's current insights to understand rhetorical situations? To identify argumentation and/or discourse structures, text styles, and pragmatic features? To work with students' persistent errors?

It would be impossible to cite even a small portion of the literature devoted to these questions and to the arguments that stem from them. But for many of us in the profession, mentored by Bob and others, the issues that these questions raise have provided a lifetime of research, theory, and heated debate at conferences and in print.

After working with two generations of teachers and several generations of students, I am convinced that all practitioners should acknowledge openly – and justify to their students and institutions – their answers to these questions, and my colleagues and I are trying to do just that. After considerable ambivalence and trial and error (see Johns, 2002b), in an attempt to codify what seems to work in a number of academic contexts, I am writing a freshman textbook (Johns, forthcoming) in a series that applies current theory and research as well as insights from years of pedagogical practice. But first, a historical overview.

Some History

Before discussing the present, we need to note that the academic literacy story has been one of increasing complexity over the years. In the good old days, when we were reading Bob's 'doodles' article as gospel, there was only one major college literacy textbook for ESL on the market in North America: Robert Bander's *American English Rhetoric* (1971). At that point, the experts' answers to questions about writing – and reading – were these:

- Good writing is about structure. At the text level, students need to learn the discourse patterns (or 'modes') of the target language. If students can prepare an effective comparison/contrast, cause/effect, exemplification (etc.) essay, then they can write. Thus, there is a generalized writing ability, realized through the discourse patterns.
- At the sentence level, structure (grammar) is also key. Being a good writer means self-correction and production of almost perfect papers.

Students learn how to correct by drilling grammar patterns and completing fill-in-the-blank exercises.

Because classroom teaching based on this structural, drill-based approach is relatively easy, many unschooled writing teachers still follow this rather restricted model. At our local CATESOL (California-TESOL) conferences, for example, presentations on teaching reading and writing using structural templates (the comparison/contrast essay, the cause/effect essay) are common.

During the 60s and 70s, however, learner-centered approaches, driven by the political ideologies of the time (and, of course, by Chomsky's linguistics), encouraged teachers to turn away from the structuralist paradigm. First, there were the Expressivists, those folks in the tie-dyed shirts who told us that nothing should interfere with our students' creativity or with their conversations with the Muse. We were to encourage students to 'journal,' writing fluently without direct correction or focus on form. Not surprisingly, this was the period during which many writing teachers refused to teach grammar explicitly. Presumably, ESL students could learn about structure at the sentence and paragraph levels through osmosis.

Another, more sophisticated, learner-centered approach soon followed. In fact, it was, and continues to be, much more than an approach. It is a movement – devoted to assisting learners to understand and reflect upon their own writing (and reading) processes. In this Process Movement, it is the mind that is central to the development of language. Using oral protocols, literacy researchers studied how students' minds worked as they attempted to complete their written texts. Because this movement was – and remains – so powerful, many teachers felt free to pay little heed to the worlds in which texts are produced or to the audiences who read them. What really matters are students' metacognitive development and text processing. In classes, students select their own motivating topics and write essays using 'the writing process.' Readings are selected for student interest. Text structure and other 'product' elements become non-issues in instruction (see Zamel, 1983) since they inhibit student motivation and creativity.

We certainly must be grateful for the Process Movement. It transformed literacy teaching into a profession, and led to an explosion of research and the development of textbooks that continue to benefit us all. The movement also introduced pedagogies for writing: invention, drafting, and revising texts from the top down, and student reflection, all excellent approaches that should be central to our work. However, teachers who carefully assessed the needs of ESL and bilingual students in their classrooms became dissatisfied. One reason is that in many textbooks and curricular materials the 'Writing Process' rapidly became formalized. In the more routinized classrooms, students followed an identical process as they prepared papers, over and over, in one genre[2] ('the English class essay'): brainstorming a topic, identifying vocabulary, drafting, peer reviewing, redrafting, and editing. For this reason, many American-educated college students can recite the formula for the 'Writing Process' as if there were only one such process instead of many. Thus, students became fully as frustrated with the 'process' formula as when they were told to write comparison-contrast essays using Current–Traditional (Structuralist) templates. In addition, ESL students, many of whom would never again write an English class essay, needed to attempt other types of texts, from a number of genres and for a variety of audiences. Leki and Carson (1997), who investigated the disparities between academic assignments in second/foreign language writing classes and in other classes, found support for variety in the academic literacy classroom. How can students be certain that their writing will evolve into a satisfactory form and style for audiences when the language and conventions sanctioned by these audiences are foreign to them? Australia's Jim Martin (1985: 61) has argued that pure process approaches are demotivating and frustrating for our ESL students, because they 'promote a situation in which only the brightest, middle-class monolingual students will benefit.'

The three literacy approaches discussed so far, Current–Traditional (Structuralist), Expressivist, and Process, continue to thrive in many classrooms throughout the world because our textbooks, our hurried lives, and our insecurities promote them. Of course, there have been modifications over time, since publishers are concerned about selling textbooks. Today, template-driven textbooks mention the writing process, and writing process books make concessions to text structure and audience. Nonetheless, much actually remains the same, though this adherence to past practices is periodically questioned at conferences.

Current Discussion and Research, and Pedagogical Implications

In this section, I will discuss some of the current complicating factors introduced by theory and research:

(1) texts seen as socially constructed through the study of discourse moves, stance, and voice;
(2) related issues stemming from writing in context; and
(3) multiliteracies.

I have chosen these three broad categories because the recent work has been so rich and because each of these topics begins – and sometimes ends – with the social construction of discourses.

Text analysis and social construction

Influenced by systemic functional linguistics, pragmatics, stylistics, and corpus linguistics, many current researchers are treating texts as socially constructed, living documents with which writers, readers, discourse communities, and other texts interact. Though there is much to discuss in terms of current approaches to text analysis, I will touch upon three areas that are particularly valuable for academic literacy teachers: moves analysis, voice, and author's stance – all of which are influenced by and integrated into the rhetorical context in which a text is produced.

Moves analysis

One of the several lasting contributions made by John Swales to the teaching of writing (and reading) has been his 'moves analysis,' an approach to analyzing the functions of various sections of texts. Based on the view that paragraphs and larger discourse chunks serve writers' purposes within a genre, this approach has been remarkably useful, especially for writers in sophisticated genres such as scientific research articles. After studying a large number of these articles, Swales (1990: 141) proposed a template for introductions that consists of three moves (each with submoves), namely: (1) establishing a territory; (2) establishing a niche; and (3) occupying the niche. Of course, there are a number of variations on these moves depending upon the discipline, the writer, the context, and the audience; for, like all elements of expository texts, moves are affected by context. Despite some contextual variation, these three functional moves have become an essential starting place in ESL academic literacy classes throughout the world.

Moves analysis research and teaching has been extended to other sections of research articles (e.g. results and discussions) and to expository genres of all types. One example is the functional 'charting of paragraphs' to assist students in understanding authors' methods for developing an argument with a particular audience.[3] This approach helps the readers to identify the relationships between a text's structure, the community, and the writer's purpose. Thus, the social construction of the text and the interrelationship between readers, writers, and context become more transparent to our students as they analyze texts and prepare to write.

Voice and social construction

Unfortunately, a writer's 'voice' has often been identified as personal and individual, a province for the Expressivists and their Muses. Many North American English teachers admire and reward students with a strong, recognizable personal voice, who project themselves as unique individuals within texts. However, for a number of reasons, including the fact that some of our ESL students may not subscribe to the ideology of individualism, writing with a personal voice can be difficult and even embarrassing (see Matsuda, 2001). After discussing a number of approaches to voice in a special issue of the *Journal of Second Language Writing*, Atkinson argues that voice is:

> ... at least *co-owned*. Like language, 'coming to voice' ... involves not so much learning to express one's 'own' ideas for one's 'own' purposes as learning how to be a person-in-society, basically the only way people can be. It therefore involves a constant negotiation and tension between what one may 'want to do' or say and a social system or technology that allows, or as often as not does not allow, one to say it. (Atkinson, 2001: 121)

In the same volume, Ivanic and Camps (2001) work through some of the complexities of the concept and outline the responsibilities of the ESL instructor in assisting students to both recognize a writer's socially-constructed voice in a text and write in a voice that is appropriate to the text:

> All writing contains 'voice' ... which locates their users culturally and historically. Writers may, through the linguistic and other resources they choose to draw on in their writing, ventriloquate an environmentally aware voice, a progressive-educator voice, a sexist voice, a positivist voice, a self-assured voice, a committed-to-plain English voice, or a combination of an infinite number of such voices. (Ivanic & Camps, 2001: 3)

As I understand it, voice, as discussed above and elsewhere, is somewhat comparable to the classical term *ethos*, 'the character or reputation of the writer' (Crowley & Hawhee, 1999: 371) as realized in discourse. If, as Peter Elbow (1991: 145) has claimed, many academic texts 'should maintain a 'rubber-gloved' quality of voice ... [and] should show a kind of reluctance to touch one's meanings with one's naked fingers,' then students need practice in recognizing and developing the kind of 'rubber-gloved' voice and character that they see in text. This language of distance, of apparent objectivity and critical analysis, gives teachers and students an avenue for studying how writers develop authority in text and develop reputations as scholars. Elbow's comment encourages them to discover voices that portray, first of all, the 'person-in-society' that Atkinson discusses.

Author's stance and social construction

Closely related to voice, and perhaps subsumed under it, is the notion of 'stance.' Through use of their academic voices, skilled writers take stances toward topics and the work of others. Of course, the conventions of a discipline may require that a stance be couched in certain language, particularly if the author is addressing her/his peers or reviewers, as in the hedging of conclusions common in scientific research articles (Hyland, 1994, 1998). In addition, writers within specific disciplinary communities have other stance options available to them, and they can use their knowledge of genre and community to project a stance and evaluate a topic, an issue, or another author's work. Thompson and Hunston (2000: 6ff) classify these stance options into three categories:

(1) 'To express the ... writer's opinion (of something mentioned) and in doing so to reflect the value system of the person and his/her community.' Examples (drawn from an academic corpus) of lexical items whose primary function is evaluation are adjectives (e.g. *obvious, important*), adverbs (e.g. *unfortunately, plainly*), nouns (e.g. *success, likelihood*), and verbs used to quote another author (e.g. *comment, note*).
(2) 'To construct and maintain relations between the writer and reader.' Under this heading, the authors include three possibilities: manipulation (with opinions presented as given in the discourse), hedging (expressing the author's degree of certainty or modifying knowledge claims), and politeness (e.g. Brown & Levinson, 1987).
(3) 'To organize the discourse.' To this purpose, metatextual features are often included to lead the reader through the text (e.g. *first, second, now I will discuss...*), with evaluation sometimes integrated into these discourse signals (e.g. *This is the first part and this is why it is so interesting*).

Thus, though writers may be constrained by their roles vis-à-vis text, audience, genre, and context, they still can effectively take a stance (see the corpus studies in the Thompson and Hunston (2000) volume, e.g. Channell, 2000 and Conrad & Biber, 2000). In academic writing, this can be seen, for example, in the 'attribution' (Hunston 2000: 178) of a statement to someone other than the writer, since so much of academic argumentation is supported by citation (e.g. *Kaplan comments... , Kaplan remarks...*).

Academic literacy in context

Moves, stance, and voice are concepts that are difficult to understand or explain (especially to students). But context is an even more difficult term to explain in our classes. Effective texts are written for specific contexts, for specific situations in which the writer is attempting to get something done. But what is context? What are the central elements of the rhetorical situation that academic writers must be aware of? One researcher who has attempted to dissect the elements of academic contexts is Samraj (2002). In this attempt, Samraj completed extensive ethnographic and analytic studies of two graduate majors in an attempt to discover contextual influences on students' texts. What she found is a multi-layered set of interlocking influences, which she portrays in Figure 7.1.

As Samraj shows, various influences interact with the student's text, including institutional examinations and requirements, disciplinary genres,

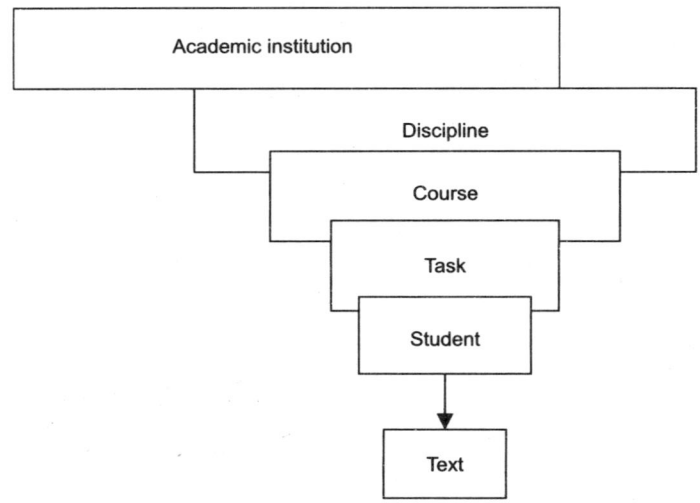

Figure 7.1 Multi-layered set of interlocking influences
Source: Samraj, 2002: 165

the proclivities of the instructor, the task itself, and the student's own interests and stance. We might also want to add government requirements, the student's prior reading, what the student's room-mate told him or her about the course, ... and the list goes on. Despite the sophistication and depth of the Samraj model, it still might be too static to portray real tasks in contexts because so much is going on. In his study of the life of an assignment in a graduate class, Prior (1998) found that assigned tasks evolved as the instructor changed her mind, the students asked for clarification or began to negotiate the task, time got short, and paper length was modified, and so on. Thus, influences on any written text are both synchronic (occurring at a particular moment, such as when the instructor introduces the task) and diachronic (changing over time), at least until the paper is turned in and graded. And even then...

Multiliteracies

Literacy teachers tend to rely on words. We like them, and we assume that our students do too.[4] However, the demands of academic literacy, particularly outside the humanities, are becoming increasingly multimodal. Writers' responsibilities often include producing effective visual representations of their arguments, and other non-linear text such as charts and graphs (see Fahnestock, 2003). Thus, we now turn to the issue of multiliteracies.

In response to the technological revolution that has occurred in the past 30 years or so, the New London Group (Kress, Fairclough, Cope, Kalantzis, and Cazden, among others) met in 1994 to ask this question: 'What constitutes appropriate literacy teaching in the context of ever more critical factors of local diversity and global connectedness?' (Cope & Kalantzis, 2000: 3). In their thought-provoking volume, this group lays out the argument that. as teachers, we should recognize that the 'human mind is embodied, situated, and social' and that an understanding of language should be 'action-oriented and generative,' emphasizing 'the productive and innovative potential of language as meaning-making.' The authors note that many of our students are – or will be – reading or writing multimodal texts that integrate language with one or more of the following: audio design (music, sound effects), spatial design (geographic and architectonic renderings), gestural design (proxemics, kinesthetics), and visual design (colors, perspective, foregrounding and backgrounding). The group suggests three implications for teachers, the first two of which should not be new to readers of this chapter:

(1) We need to seriously view literacy as socially constructed – as taking place within social contexts. This implies that the role of writer, audience (and discourse communities – see Swales, 1990), and the situation are central to the writer's invention and writing process as well as to the text produced.
(2) Writers are constrained in any public literacy act not only by their own purposes but also by the context in which they are attempting to accomplish their ends.
(3) Student literacies should consist of working with several modal designs (see above), only one of which is language.

It is important to mention the visual modality, long ignored in many of the North American writing classes that are often taught by humanities-trained faculty with little interest in the visual. Visual images in academic texts include non-linear text such as charts, graphs, and other non-linguistic representations of information found in books, lectures, or on the Web. Kress and van Leeuwen (1996), among others, have noted the major importance of visual images to literacies, particularly in science and technology and in the professional world. Business and economics professors believe that one of the most basic language practices that students can learn is first to create and then to discuss visual information central to their disciplines (Johns, 1998). In everyday life the 'semiotic landscape is becoming more and more populated with complex social and cultural discourse practices,' and language is becoming 'decentered in terms of meaning making' (Iedema, 2003: 33). As our students read textbooks, research assignments online, attend concerts, or read magazines and newspapers, they must be increasingly aware, and critical of, the visual texts in their lives.

Drawing from a number of theorists, the New London Group proposes a pedagogical approach for the new multiliterate era: one that borrows from and extends much of what we know. They argue that all possible designs should be recognized by teachers, and discussed, critiqued, and practiced by the students. Here are their recommendations (followed by my comments in brackets) regarding how these points relate to the teaching of academic literacies. Students should have:

- *Practice*, in which they play 'multiple and different roles' (Kalantzis & Cope, 2000: 234). [Thus, in academic writing, students take the role of student, expert, peer, critic, etc. These roles can be taken in writing groups as they peer-critique each other's texts, but they can also be diversified as students become experts and report on a researched topic or become critics as they review a book or article. Students need to understand when these roles should be taken and what taking a role implies in terms of stance, voice, genre, and other issues.]
- *Overt instruction*, during which students develop 'a conscious awareness and control over what is being learned' (Kalantzis & Cope, 2000: 243) through working collaboratively with an expert and building upon what the learner already knows. [This, of course, is a Vygotskian principle, implying scaffolded writing instruction. In the Process Approach, teachers generally scaffold by taking students through the writing process itself. From a more socially-oriented viewpoint, scaffolding begins with the analysis of the rhetorical situation, which includes the genre, community and context, and specific audience. The process then relies heavily on the genre identified as appropriate to the situation (see, for example, Bawarshi, 2003).]
- *Critical framing*, during which time 'students stand back from what they are studying and view it critically in relation to its social context' (Kalantzis & Cope, 2000: 246). [Reflection is not new, of course. It is an integral part of portfolio development and assessment in many writing classes, and is often central to the Process Approach. The difference is what is reflected upon. Students can respond in their reflections to questions such as: 'Who is empowered by means of this text?' 'Who is being dominated?' 'How can we read this text to answer the first two questions?' 'How can you, the writer, begin to take power over the text and the situation?']
- *Transformed practice*, in which students try out what they've learned in different contexts. [If one of our pedagogical goals is a degree of mastery in practice, then immersion in a community of learners engaged in authentic versions of such practice is necessary.]

Given these suggestions, how can we assist students to understand the social and ideological nature of discourses, particularly within a democratic and participatory society? For the past 15 years, I have been teaching a group of first-year post-secondary bilingual and ESL students (from immigrant families) in a program called Freshman Success, which was designed by the university to increase student retention. Freshman Success students are enrolled in this class, a linked 'breadth' requirement or major class (e.g. anthropology, biology), a university orientation class, and a study group. One important element of Freshman Success classes is community-based service learning, a component that brings students into direct contact, for purposes of co-writing papers, with new immigrant secondary school students. There are many benefits to this program (see Johns, 2001), the most relevant of which are the students' mentoring and advising of the secondary students, and the process of writing their research paper. In their mentoring work, the university students help to convince immigrant secondary students to consider the possibility of attending university – to view college entrance as an accessible goal. While mentoring, the students begin to work on their research paper, for which sources are interviews with the secondary students. One of our associated breadth/content courses, anthropology, is particularly well-suited to the learning community. Using the concepts highlighted in this course (e.g. adaptation, assimilation) and a relatively standard genre in the social sciences (the IMRD research paper[5] modified for this class), the students draft and redraft their research papers, which are graded (when completed) by both myself and the anthropology instructor. Authentic practice is in play through the interviews and the integration of sources into the final text, both within the context of anthropology and of the secondary school students and situations they studied. All of this makes practice real and, of course, remarkably motivating for all concerned. Throughout the semester, both groups of students have multiliterate experiences: using visual texts from the web and from studies in anthropology to augment their research, discovery, and writing.

Applications

How then can classroom practitioners make use of current literacy research and theory in their pedagogical lives? In response, I will repeat my earlier questions and then supply some answers.

(1) In what theoretical and pedagogical frameworks should academic writing classes be taught?

In response to this first question, it is becoming increasingly clear that the concept of the social construction of texts in their multimodal forms should be central to our teaching. Yet, we cannot ignore earlier approaches that have played important historical roles in our field and still have something important to offer. Below, I suggest how these approaches can be adapted to current pedagogies.

Structuralism/Current-Traditional approaches, which focused on the importance of text structures (comparison/contrast, cause/effect, etc.) used as conceptual tools what rhetoric called 'discourse modes.' As time went on, and it became difficult to find an authentic text that employed one of these text structures exclusively, it was suggested that discourse modes, which appear across genres, should be considered as writer 'strategies,' methods by which the writer achieves his/her purposes in the text (see, e.g. Bhatia, 2001). A well-crafted textbook that embodies this view is Kiniry and Rose (1993), *Critical Strategies for Academic Thinking & Writing*. In it, the authors argue that the strategy chosen at any point in a text (e.g. cause/effect) may vary depending upon the writer's intent, evidence, and other social factors, including the writer's academic discipline. In their excellent volume integrating research and teaching, Grabe and Stoller (2002) point out that reading research supports the role of student understanding of text structures: better readers recognize writers' discourse strategies.

Elements of the Process Movement have also been invaluable to us as practitioners and researchers, revolutionizing classrooms across the world. Invention, drafting, revising, editing, peer reviewing, and reflecting are central to student understanding. The difference, of course, is that reading and writing processes will now be framed and initiated by the writer's purpose and the community-sanctioned genre characteristic of the rhetorical situation. Students should be encouraged to develop an awareness and critique of audience and community, genre, visual elements, and contextual factors as early as the invention stage and to revise their work as that awareness becomes keener (see Bawarshi, 2003). Thus, literacy processes and the students' reflections on the multiple uses of the literacies they control will mirror the elements of the situation in which they are producing their texts.

If text structures are to become strategies and writers' processes are situated within actual rhetorical situations, writing tasks need to begin with rhetorical analyses: of the situation, of the writer's purposes, and of texts from a relevant genre.[6] Students need to understand from the very beginning of a literacy task that though a genre is 'repeated social action' (Miller, 1984: 151) and the organizing principle of a task, no genre is static. Genres evolve and are adapted by writers as situations change. Elements of a genre may be repeated (e.g. the moves in research article introductions), but since there are few, if any, identical rhetorical situations, writers must always be open to revising their notions of a genre in order to produce appropriate texts. Berkenkotter and Huckin (1995) speak of the tension within a particular rhetorical situation between the centripetal forces that contribute to the prototypical elements of a genre and the centrifugal forces that require writers to revise their genre knowledge along with their texts, for a specific rhetorical situation. In a memo-writing task, for example, the centripetal forces are represented in the memo format, while the centrifugal forces (audience and content) will differ widely from those that applied to any memo the students may have written in the past.

Among the questions we can ask students as they study texts from genres (e.g. research articles, timed essay examination prompts, reviews) and begin the task of writing in the genre are:

(1) what does the task look like, what instructions are given, and what is implied?;
(2) what do the writers know about the task from reading the assignment; and
(3) what do they have to find out?

For example, in a Freshman Success class I taught in connection with an introductory geography class, the geography instructor gave the students the following prompt for a take-home examination:

> Illegal international migration between Mexico and the United States has commanded a great deal of attention from policy makers in both countries. A sound policy needs to be grounded in an understanding of the magnitude of the flows as well as the forces that generate this form of migration. In your memo, you are to assume the role of a policy analyst who is responsible for providing this information and a discussion of the impacts of this migration on both countries. Additionally you are to suggest a plan for stemming the migration flow between the two countries. Use your textbook, the web, and library sources for your discussion (American Psychological Assocation style).

Together, the students and I developed a chart for what the writer knows (and doesn't know) from reading the prompt (Table 7.1). This chart was used for the invention stage but it continued to be central to the discussion about the prompt as the students drafted their responses.

Initially, the students worked in groups to complete as many of the 'known' slots as they could. Then, they planned their strategies for immediate research in order to discover the unknowns. This chart and their discussions became central to the invention and revision steps in the writing process, to decisions about what the text should look like (macrostructure) and sound like (language), how the discourse should be framed, and other factors. To answer these questions, the students analyzed examples of positively evaluated student papers written in response to a related prompt for the same class. To complete their 'unknown' slots, they also interviewed the faculty member who gave the assignment.

Table 7.1 Invention chart

		Known	Not known
a	Writer's role	Policy analyst	
b	Audience	Government officials	Which ones?
c	Genre	Memo	
d	Source	Class textbooks, the web, the library	What specific sources under these categories (e.g. the web and the library) will be acceptable?
e	Referencing style	APA	
f	Content	Information about the impact; a plan	
g	Length		How do we ask the paper length question without offending the professor?
h	Course concepts to be integrated		What central concepts are provided by the textbook and lectures?
i	Appropriate language for the role		Can the professor provide an example of good student work so that the language (etc.) can be studied?
j	Use of charts or illustrations		What types of visuals can be used for this genre? What are the characteristics of the language used to discuss these visuals in the text?

(2) What should the content of academic reading and writing classes be?

As can be seen from the above, a writing course should be devoted to developing students' research skills, encouraging them to view purposeful writing (and reading) as situated and genre-driven (see Johns, 1997: Ch. 6). If writers are to achieve their purposes, whether to receive a high score on a paper, to argue a point, or to please their employer, they must investigate a number of situational and textual factors. It goes without saying, then, that the tasks the students research in our literacy classrooms must be varied, and as authentic as possible. Students need to be exposed to, and write in, a variety of genres for a variety of situations. The traditional English class essay following some rigid textual scheme is no longer appropriate.

(3) What are we educating students for?

In response to this question, we can return to the goals of the New London group. If students are to be educated as critical and observant citizens in democratic societies, we need to assist them in researching how writing can be effective in different situations, and how they can make their textual voices heard within academic and political communities. This approach encourages them to be more critical and also to be more analytical readers. By necessity, we are educating students to be multiliterate in their text processing and production of texts.

(4) What is the place of contrastive rhetoric (CR) in the scheme of things?

In response to this final question, effective texts demonstrate a writer's purposes and an understanding of a rhetorical situation and the language and genre associated with those purposes. In CR, there is a growing body of research juxtaposing the work of L1 English speakers with that of L2 English speakers, based upon some of the text features discussed above. The research indicates important differences across writers from different parts of the world. For example, Maier (1992) studied politeness strategies in a variety of L2 learners as they wrote business letters for a particularly difficult situation (a missed job interview). She found that 'although non-native speakers were aware of various types of politeness strategies, their language tended to be less formal and more direct than [that of native speakers]' (Maier, 1992: 189). Mauranen (1993a) examined the metatext (i.e. text about text) in the English writing of Finnish and Anglo-American students. She found that the English native-speaking students used significantly more metatext in their writing than did the Finns, and she hypothesized that the reasons for these differences were based on different notions of politeness: 'The poetic, implicit Finnish rhetoric could be construed as being polite by its treatment of readers as intelligent beings, to whom nothing much needs to be explained. Saying too obvious things is, as we know, patronizing' (Mauranen, 1993a: 17). As these two examples show, the social construction of texts and issues such as voice and stance are very much a part of CR research. As teachers, we need to be sensitive to the possibility of different linguistic and social perceptions among speakers of different languages.

Conclusion

I am well aware that teachers of academic writing throughout the world, who do some of the most important work on our campuses, are unappreciated and undervalued (see Johns, 1997: Ch. 5; and Blythman *et al.*, 2003). I am also aware that a large majority of literacy teachers are tutors, teaching associates, or lecturers – dedicated individuals but without prestige and often with little experience. However, if the teaching of academic literacies is to gain status within our institutions, we must stay current and aware of the shifting nature of text analysis and the demands of multiliteracies.

Practitioners are beginning to receive concrete help from social constructivists (see Paltridge, 2001; Hyland, 2002; Johns, 2002a; Swales & Feak, 1994). But it is a hard sell, particularly to publishers, who know that many teachers have little time to read about the relationship between theory and practice. As I noted at the beginning of this paper, it is so much easier to teach context-free text structures ('the discourse modes') or to keep working through conventionally ritualized writing processes than it is to take on social construction. Perhaps Casanave (2002) has the right idea: we should encourage students to think of each writing task (and their research into rhetorical situations) as a game: there are rules, but they vary, depending upon the team, the situation on the field, and a multiplicity of other factors.[7]

Notes

1. Bob Kaplan was on my dissertation committee, but that was after I had been teaching for a number of years.
2. A 'genre' may be defined as '... complex, evolving mental abstractions held by individuals within communities that share ... rhetorical situations' (Johns, 1997: 22). See also Swales (1990).
3. Thanks to Micah Jendian for this approach.
4. There is growing evidence that many of our students do not like words, or, at least, do not like using them in L2 writing (see Leki, 2003).
5. IMRD = Introduction, Methods, Results, Discussion.
6. See Bawarshi (2003) for an excellent discussion of genre and invention.
7. This is an appropriate moment for the profession to thank Bob Kaplan for his many contributions to, discussions of, and continuing interest in ESL and applied linguistics, to the topics discussed above, and in particular to contrastive rhetoric and discourse analysis. From his students, there should be special thanks. Many of us are grateful for his patience (disguised as gruffness) with our dissertations, and for his fabulous letters of recommendation when we sought jobs. At a TESOL Conference held after Bob retired, he asked at his session, 'Who are all of you people here at 5:30?' And we answered, 'Your students.' Thanks, Bob.

Chapter 8
'Ear' Learners and Error in US College Writing

JOY REID

In 1990, 32 million US residents spoke a language other than English at home, and more than seven million lived in households with no fluent English speaker over 14 years old (Swerdlow, 2001). The number today is much larger. There are currently more immigrant students in US schools than ever before, nearly 5 million students nation-wide. In addition, these students are the fastest growing population segment in primary and secondary schools (Strauss, 2003). For many of them, unfortunately, the outlook is grim. Often they are low-income and marginalized. Many fail to attend college or even to graduate from high school. Their limited educational preparation may prevent them from becoming productive citizens in a country that values education and in which standard English is the language of power. These students are typically under-educated, under-served, under-estimated, under-acculturated, and under-studied. The result: they become a disempowered underclass (Pinzur, 2003; Ruiz-de-Velasco *et al.*, 2001).

As Ferris (2002) and others point out, little empirical research has focused on US resident ESL student writers.[1] While the substantial differences between resident and international student errors have been explained and described, the differences have not been subjected to empirical study (Ferris & Hedgcock, 2005; Leki, 1999b). Of course, these students' writing teachers recognize the differences, but they rarely report their observations in writing (for exceptions, see Muchisky & Tangren, 1999; Hartman & Tarone, 1999). Further, no ESL writing textbooks focusing on the academic needs of resident ESL writers have hitherto been available; grammar handbooks for native English speaking (NES) college students may contain a section designed for ESL students, but the errors considered are often specifically targeted at international students.

In this chapter, I profile the diversity of these students and their common educational disadvantage, with a particular focus on the way they acquire English and the problems that result. I then discuss the types of written language errors made by these students, focusing on how they differ from the more widely studied errors of international ESL students.[2]

First, I need to distinguish between 'generalization' and 'stereotype.' In this chapter I write about two general categories of students: 'ear' learners and 'eye' learners. I discuss these learners as 'typical' in their language problems and solutions. Of course, I am keenly aware that while many stereotypes begin with a grain of truth, there are, statistically speaking, often more differences between people in a single group than there are between two groups of people. Still, the differences exist along continua, and although some students do not fit the descriptions below, many students from different linguistic and cultural backgrounds do. Thus my intention is to clarify needs and behaviors based on general tendencies, not on stereotypes.

Second, this chapter does not discuss Hispanic or African-American students who are third- or fourth- generation (or longer-standing) North Americans and whose spoken English is fluent and without 'foreign' accent. Nor does it consider students who exemplify ESL success stories, those who for a variety of reasons (ranging from being strong auditory learners to having ongoing, effective language support at home and in public schools) have developed proficient English language skills, both written and spoken, and who need only minimal language support in college. Nor does this chapter focus on high school exchange students, whose ESL acquisition and goals parallel those of international students. It does not consider adult education, those English classes open to adults who need to learn survival English to cope in the workplace. Finally, it does not directly address the problems of refugee students external to language learning: little or no education, an education interrupted by war, flight, or stay in refugee camps, or trauma caused by previous experiences or arrival in the US without planning or resources.

Instead, the focus is on those students who are typically second-generation US residents, whose first language is not English but who aspire to attend college. Often these students have had little or no formal education in their first (home) language. They have learned English in the US, primarily by being immersed in the language and culture(s).[3] They have acquired English principally through their *ears*: they listened, took in oral language (from teachers, television, grocery clerks, etc.), and subconsciously began to form vocabulary and syntax rules, learning through trial and error. As a result, their oral skills are relatively fluent but not always accurate (Harklau *et al.*, 1999). Many of these 'ear' learners have had some English language tutoring – often fragmented – in ESL pullout programs when they first entered school.[4] Further, they have been accumulating US culture(s) for some years.

'Ear' Learners and Disadvantage

It is probable that some 'ear' learners do not learn well by hearing/listening and therefore struggle intensely to learn aural English. For them, the language is 'noise' for much longer than it is for learners who prefer auditory acquisition of language. Because ineffective 'ear' learners may never hear, for example, verb endings that native speakers take for granted (e.g. -*ed*, -*ing*), they acquire a reduced form of English that contains some (or many) non-native-like forms, and they simply make the most of their limited skills.[5] They may become relatively successful with oral communication, and they may become proficient in language skills and strategies that fulfill socially situated language expectations. In Cummins' terms (1979, 1996), they have acquired BICS (Basic Interpersonal Communication Skills), but not CALP (Cognitive Academic Language Proficiency).

Often, acquiring English through the ears is a major disadvantage for resident ESL students who wish to enter college. First, their non-academic spoken English is not valued by the school system or by teachers in the system. It follows that if that form of conversational English is seen as worthless, the very identity of the students may be perceived as worthless – even by the students themselves (Cornell, 1995). Further, resident students are often saddled with prior academic experiences that have led to failure, and the fear of failure can interfere with or even negate learning. Another consequence is that these students may have delayed academic acquisition because their English is limited. That is, they have not achieved adequately in the content areas, at least in comparison with their NES peers, and they are therefore underprepared for college work. At the very least, they are inexperienced and/or unsuccessful readers and writers (Blanton, 1999; Hinkel, 2002; Padrón *et al.*, 2000). Finally, in most cases, they lack learning strategies and confidence, and they have little information about college academic culture(s) (Muchisky & Tangren, 1999).

'Ear' Learners vs. 'Eye' Learners

'Ear' learners differ from 'eye' learners, those international students who usually begin to learn English as a foreign language (EFL) in school in their home countries. These 'eye' learners typically enter the US after a significant period of preparation and are supported by families who chose to send them abroad to expand their educational opportunities. Generally, these students are traditionally-aged (that is, 18–20 years old for undergraduates), and they will most likely return to their families and countries following their post-secondary education. Further, international students tend to understand the grammar of English explicitly, and they can often articulate their language problems. They may also be proficient readers of English, though they may have fewer and less developed listening and speaking skills, and their knowledge of US culture(s) may be quite limited (Reid, 1998a).

Both 'ear' and 'eye' learners in the US are learning English as an additional language as young adults. Both need guidance and structure, an organized curriculum, and well-informed teachers who can facilitate their learning. Further, both groups are diverse in language, culture(s), and education. Both also differ in individual aptitudes and personalities, preferred learning styles and strategies, and goals and motivation. Most important, they differ in their language errors, principally because they learn English differently. For that reason, college administrators and ESL/developmental teachers must formulate curriculum for resident 'ear' learners accordingly (Hinkel, 2003b; Murie & Thomson, 2001). In addition, they must recognize the diversity within the resident student group: from traditionally-aged college students to mature students; from foreign high school graduates to those who have been mostly US schooled; from those with extensive formal education in their first language to those with no formal first-language education (Browning et al., 1997). Within this diversity, the following general categories of resident students are present in pre-college language programs:

(1) US-resident ESL students who are fluent and literate in their first language, but who may not have studied English. Acquiring written English will be easier for these 'ear' learners than for students who are semi-literate or illiterate in their first language (Bosher & Rowenkamp, 1992; Ruiz-de-Velasco et al., 2001).

(2) Traditionally-aged students who prepared for emigration to the US by studying English, at least for a time, and who have had some education in their first language as well. These students may also find writing academic English less difficult than students who have not been so privileged (Freeman & Freeman, 2003).

(3) Students who have not attended US high school but who have completed a secondary education in their first language and who aspire to higher education in the US (Olsen & Jaramillo, 1999). These students may differ in age and interests, but they may have learned a substantial part of their English through their 'ears.'

(4) Students who have attended only the last year or two of US high school, along with some classroom study of English prior to arrival, and thus may have learned most of their English through their 'ears.' They may have a combination of international and resident errors that make solutions to writing problems even more complex (Harklau, 1999).

(5) Traditionally-aged students who have attended US public schools for a significant period of time (three years or more) and may even have been born in the US, but whose formal ESL education has been frag-

mented. Orally fluent, many consider English to be their primary language, and they have developed (perhaps unconsciously) idiosyncratic language 'rules,' some of which must be identified and adjusted if these students are to become successful academic writers. These students are popularly called 'Generation 1.5,' a title that originated in an article by Rumbaut and Ima (1988).

Strengths of 'Ear' Learners

It is important to realize that 'ear' learners are not entirely without language and cultural strengths. Typically, they have relatively well-developed English oral fluency, and their listening skills are often of near-native speaker quality, even for the more formal English of the media and public school discourse. Unlike international students, they use phrasal verbs and idioms with ease. They understand reduced forms effortlessly, and they speak in highly complex sentence structures without difficulty. Moreover, most have some familiarity with the US educational system and US academic literacy (Freeman & Freeman, 2003; Harklau, 1999). They recognize classroom behaviors such as group work, conversational turn-taking, student input during classroom discussions, the administrative processes of registration and changing classes, the use of US published textbooks, the use of computers in academic writing, the overall organization of paragraphs and essays, and classroom behaviors such as pre-writing and face-to-face response to the writing of peers.

Another area of knowledge that many ESL residents have control over is what's 'hot' and what's not: They are usually familiar with the slang, body language, music, behaviors, humor, and dress codes of the diverse students in the schools they attend. They can talk about television sitcoms, and they have opinions they can support about MTV programs. Many are members of a cohort – a group of friends who speak their first (community) language and with whom they spend most of their time (Ruiz-de-Velasco et al., 2001; Strauss, 2003).

They also have opinions about ESL courses. Generally, they share a negative attitude towards the typical ESL classes they test into. They believe that the curriculum of these classes focuses on the international students in the class, that these classes are obstructing their educational goals and are not for 'Americans' like themselves, and that they do not belong in classes with students who 'can't even speak English.'

And they may be right (Fu, 1995; Roberge, 2002a): few ESL classes are directed toward resident students. In ESL writing classes, for example, students are often asked to write about cultural features of their 'home country.' Textbooks present grammar with terms and examples that presuppose metalanguage familiar to international 'eye' learners but often seem incomprehensible and unnecessary to resident 'ear' learners (Harklau, 2000; Hinkel, 2002). Teachers speak more slowly and deliberately, and near-native resident student listeners find such speech boring and even patronizing. Readings about American culture(s) seem simplistic to resident learners, and listening to the oral presentations of international students is painful. Moreover, the language problems that resident students have with academic writing are only rarely addressed. Generally, teachers are unprepared even to understand 'ear' learner writing errors (Hinkel, 2002). In fact, the phonetic spellings in the papers of many resident students are often enough to contaminate the content for the teacher/evaluator. The typical, underprepared response of these teachers is to assign grammar exercises (Biber et al., 2002; Byrd, 2002).

Characteristics of 'Ear' Learner English as a Second Dialect

The informal conversational English of 'ear' learners is the foundation for many of their language errors. Characteristics of their speech include: short, simplex phrases rather than long, complex sentences; short versions of questions that may rely on intonation instead of interrogative syntax, heavy use of personal pronouns, frequent use of the (usually simple) present tense, a limited range of academic vocabulary, and a specialized vocabulary used to mark group membership. At least in part because of these language limitations, the academic reading skills of 'ear' learners are often limited.

Research has shown that the popular strategy of guessing from context is ineffective unless the reader understands approximately 95% of the words in the text (Carver, 1994; Hu & Nation, 2000; Nation, 1990, 2001, personal correspondence; Nation & Wang, 1999). For less experienced and less proficient readers who know little about the subject, the percentage rises to 98%. Little wonder that academic vocabulary presents a struggle for resident students.

Consider, for example, the textbook excerpt below, selected (randomly) from a popular college introduction to psychology text (Bernstein et al., 2000). Notice the accumulation of technical vocabulary (underlined), words that many resident students have probably not encountered previously.[6] Notice also in the sample below the density of prepositional phrases, often in sequence (italicized), the use of in-text citations, and the passive voice (boldfaced). (Some words occur in more than one category.)

> The evoked brain potential is a small, temporary change *in voltage on an electroencephalogram* (EEG) that occurs *in response to specific events* (Ruggs & Coles, 1995). Figure 8.4 shows an example. Each peak reflects the firing *of large groups of neurons, within different regions of the brain, at different times during the information-processing sequence.* Thus, the pattern *of the peaks* provides information that is more precise than

overall reaction time. For example, a large positive peak, called P3000, occurs 300–500 milliseconds after a stimulus is presented. The exact timing *of the P300 is affected by factors* that affect the speed *of perceptual processes*, such as the difficulty *of detecting a stimulus*. But the timing *of the P300* is not affected *by factors* – such as changes *in stimulus-response compatibility* – that just alter the speed with which a response is selected and executed (Rugg & Coles, 1995; Siddle *et al.*, 1991). (Bernstein *et al.*, 2000: 253)

The language limitations of resident students in reading are also evident in their writing. First, the unevenness of register, which can range from formal vocabulary to conversational informality and slang in the same sentence, reads like the developmental writing of a native speaker. The examples below (with instances boldfaced) are from academic assignments for first-year composition classes.

- Young **folks** usually get a better **kick out of** trips than older people.
- ... which is imparative **to hang around** a large number of friends.
- ... they will want **to take off ASAP**.
- **Guys** like Neil Bush are destroying the American future.
- ... when you spend time with **a couple** of your close friends and there **kids**.
- Don't ask me **why, Because** this is my personality.
- I don't want them to **worry about a thing**.

But notice that, despite the fact that these students probably have not studied the grammar of English in depth as 'eye' learners often have, the examples above demonstrate complex use of verb forms (*are destroying* and *will want*) and subordinate clauses. Further, these sentences are more fluent and native-like (Sternglass, 1997) than those of many international students.

Second, perhaps the most visible indication of resident writing is that, as their spoken language is translated into writing, residents may display phonetic ('ear' learned) spellings such as *depence on, everwhere, look fullther, iwan, everythings,* and *obstained*. For the academic reader, these errors leap off the page; they demand attention. Although the errors are only one aspect of written academic work, many teacher-evaluators feel obliged to concentrate on them, with the (incorrect) idea that if the students can first learn to control formal features of the language, then they can learn to write (Byrd, 2002; Hartman & Tarone, 1999).

Third, some of the spelling errors made by resident students reflect the morphosyntactic blendings seen in the writing of NES writers rather than the errors international students would typically make. Examples include giving *they're* opinions on things, when *your* having difficulty, and *they made* copies or had the *employee's* do it.

Fourth, 'ear' learners have unconsciously developed language grammar rules as they acquired English, and the results of these rules appear in their writing. These rules may, upon examination, prove to be overgeneralized or false. Moreover, most resident students may not realize, and almost certainly will not be able to articulate, the rule-governedness of their errors. In addition, academic readers may notice only the frequency of errors and fail to realize that the errors are largely systematized and consistent. Thus remediation is doubly difficult: the teacher cannot identify the system present in each resident student's writing, and the student believes there is no system, so there can be no remediation. However, if students can be made aware of their own idiosyncratic rules, they can compare them with those that produce the conventions of standard written English and eventually be able to monitor their own errors (Ferris, 2002, 2003; Sternglass, 1997).

Below is a writing sample from a Vietnamese student, written during her first day in a first-year university composition course in response to an article about students having jobs while in college. Following the sample is my analysis of the errors and comments by the student writer about her 'rules.' (Verb errors are underlined, word choice errors are in italics; other errors such as spelling and punctuation are in square brackets.)

> The main idea<u>s</u> of the Article <u>is</u> saying that working while going to School reduces the G.P.A. of students. Some of the [R]easons *while* students <u>gettings</u> jobs is because of [A]dvertisements and personnal luxuries that the students <u>needed</u> during [S]chool.
>
> What the [A]rticle is saying is true about students getting lower <u>grade</u> in school[,] while working. But if we try to put strict rules on [C]ollege curriculas and <u>stopping</u> [T]elevision advertising, it wouldn't help much[. B]ecause almost all students know what they're doing to themselves. Students are <u>awared</u> of the lower grades they're getting but there <u>are</u> more to it[,] [then] just *because of* [W]ork. I agree[,] that when you get a job, your *hour of studying* <u>reduces</u>. After coming home from work you <u>felt</u> tired and only <u>wanted</u> to put [S]chool *words* aside. I <u>have</u> this experience in the past myself. It <u>does reduced</u> my G.P.A., but I'm not blaming it on T.V. advertising or anything else.

Three general categories of errors stand out. First, there are numerous errors in verb inflection (verb tense or agreement). Some of these errors might occur because the student's first language is not as inflected as English is or does not have auxiliary verbs. In addition, even if the student has been tutored in English, it is quite possible that subject–verb agreement may not be a fully developed concept. It is more likely, however, that many of the student's verb-form errors occur more from 'ear' learning than from first-language transfer. The English verb system is complex: a single sentence, and certainly a single paragraph, may contain several verb forms. Because these students have listened to the language rather than studied it, they may not recognize their errors even when they are identified for them, especially if the errors have not interfered with their ability to communicate orally. Second, the student has made some vocabulary errors and has used some idiomatic expressions (correctly or incorrectly) that indicate her immersion in US culture(s). During a writing conference, this student indicated that she had never noticed the word 'why,' thinking that 'why' and 'while' were the same word ('while') with different meanings ('like lots of English words'). While international students would probably not make this error, the command of idioms displayed by this student goes far beyond that of most international students who have studied English as a foreign language. Finally, when I asked the student about the seemingly arbitrary capitalization in her writing (as in *Article* and *School*, she responded that she had learned that all nouns had to be capitalized. She then stated the (correct) rule about capitalizing the personal pronoun *I*, though she added that she found English capitalization rules peculiar and intimidating because capitalizing *I* made her 'stand out too much' in her writing.

Writing Errors and Grammar Practice of US Residents

In response to the seemingly overwhelming language problems faced by resident student writers, how can writing teachers treat such multiple errors in students' papers? As a beginning, they should understand that:

(1) getting students to do grammar exercises does not necessarily improve their writing;
(2) some syntactic errors are more serious than others;
(3) some errors are more treatable than others (Ferris, 2002, 2003);
(4) for less treatable errors, students should use a NES proofreader.

Grammar errors

The issue of error in student writing has consumed English teachers in L1 and L2 classes for decades.[7] Until quite recently, errors in academic writing were often seen as indicative of a deficit, or deviant, or just plain wrong. However, research has demonstrated that errors are not the result of faulty performance (Selinker, 1972, 1995; James, 1990, 1998; Wolfram & Schilling-Estes, 1998; Gass & Selinker, 2001). Rather, as learners attempt to impose regularity on the language, errors become part of the student's internal grammar, or 'interlanguage.' An interlanguage (also called a 'learner language') contains elements of both the L1 and the L2; it is an intermediate state of the language being acquired and is evidenced by systematicity in the errors. In other words, learning a language is a 'creative process of forming the learner's self-contained linguistic systems' (Brown, 2000: 216), testing language hypotheses and, inevitably, making errors. Naturally, systematicity also marks the interlanguage of resident students, and in particular, their writing. As Shaughnessy (1977) found in her seminal studies of immigrant/resident students, many of the errors in typical 'developmental' student essays were reiterations of a few consistent errors. Two decades later, Sternglass (1997) reported that second-dialect or second-language writers' errors are often based on misunderstood, misapplied, or incorrect but systematic rules. These findings support the view that 'ear' learners as well as 'eye' learners communicate in individual yet systematic interlanguages.

ESL resident writers are not native speakers, although many regard English as their 'first language,' perhaps because it is the language in which they are most literate. However, given the characteristics of resident writers exemplified in the student samples above, we might describe the errors in their writing as belonging more in a second dialect than in a second language – errors that stem from oral language but spring from systematic rules that result in frequent but consistent writing errors concerning inflection, word form, and spelling. That is, the forms of ESL resident student writers may more closely resemble the forms found in second dialects such as African-American Vernacular English than those found in the interlanguage of international students. Or they may be a mixture of both types. Certainly research in this area is needed.

More recent research in L2 acquisition suggests that the habituated errors of 'ear' learners also occur in school immersion programs such as French immersion programs in Canada in which accuracy is not automatically developed in the second language, even when students are instructed in it (Long, 1991; Swain, 2000). Indeed, after more than 20 years of research with English-speaking students in these classes, Swain (1998) describes these L2 speakers in language that resembles the description of ESL resident writers presented here:

> ... immersion students are able to understand much of what they hear and read even at early grade levels. And although they are well able to get their meaning across in their second language, even at intermediate and higher grade levels, they often do so with non-target-like morphology and syntax. (Swain, 1998: 65)

Grammar practice and errors

It may seem self-evident that students who make frequent grammar errors in their writing should study and practice grammar in order to improve their writing. However, long-standing research on developmental NES students has not demonstrated that remedial grammar study (such as workbook exercises or, for L2 students, oral language drills) transfers to students' writing (Hartwell, 1985; Hendrickson, 1978; Lalande, 1982; Semke, 1984). On the contrary, as early as 1963 in a landmark research review (albeit in a somewhat different context), Braddock et al. (1963: 37–38) concluded that 'the teaching of formal grammar has a negligible or, because it usually displaces some instruction and practice in composition, even a harmful effect on the improvement of writing.' Although the issue remains controversial, studying grammar structures, especially in developmental workbook settings or decontextualized drills, may at best help the writing of only a few L2 EAP writers.

One reason may be that, even for a single habituated error, remediation is time-consuming and difficult, and takes high levels of ongoing motivation and self-monitoring. For a resident writer whose work is filled with errors, the prospects of ever writing standard English prose must seem unattainable. Even the most motivated student is faced with overwhelming barriers, including the accumulation of errors, identifying and adjusting the interlanguage rules responsible for the many errors they may not even realize they make, and the constant monitoring for grammatical structures, many of which are impossible to avoid in academic writing.

Error Gravity

Research on error gravity reports the judgments of post-secondary academic faculty in English departments and other departments across the curriculum (Johnson, 1985; Santos, 1988; Vann et al., 1984; Vann et al., 1991). These faculty were asked to read examples of student errors and to rank them in terms of how serious they believed each error to be. Results showed that ESL error types that interfere with comprehension are labeled as more 'grievous' than those that do not. These errors included word order, verb tense, and word choice. Of these, word order is rarely a problem for resident students, perhaps because they have been speaking fluent, relatively successful English for some time.

Error gravity research in ESL lists the following as less serious errors: article errors, incorrect preposition choice, lack of pronoun agreement, comma splices, and spelling errors (Vann et al., 1984). As the student samples above suggest, resident writers make many of these errors, often persistently and frequently (Frodesen & Starna, 1999; Valdes, 1992). Teacher-evaluators are greatly irritated by the less grievous errors, yet comprehension is generally possible provided the reader does not allow the errors to contaminate the content (Hartman & Tarone, 1999; Muchisky & Tangren, 1999; Rusikoff, 1994).

Treatable errors

To treat ESL resident writer errors, teachers must first recognize the level of difficulty that students experience in learning and remediating specific English language structures, especially if their unconscious language rules are habituated. Students may be able to identify, correct, and monitor some of their errors with relative ease. Other errors may take a lifetime to remediate. For example, article and preposition errors are difficult for many resident writers to remediate because (1) these linguistic features may not occur – or at least not in such numbers – in their first language, (2) the rules governing the use of these features in English may be complex or especially arbitrary and idiomatic, and (3) 'ear' learners may not have recognized differences in the use of these features between English and their first language. In other words, some errors are more treatable than others (Ferris, 2002, 2003).

Strategies for solutions

One solution is to help students not only to identify and correct their errors but also to prioritize them, based on the concept of error gravity. Typically, resident student writing will contain phonetic spellings, incorrect or missing verb endings and verb agreement problems, and often a sprinkling of inappropriately informal idioms. By dividing students' errors into these broad categories, and later perhaps into subcategories, the process of remediation seems more attainable. In addition, students can take the responsibility for what they should remediate immediately. Some may decide to concentrate on learning about verbs in academic writing or on developing strategies for monitoring for verb agreement errors. Others may identify prepositions they misuse and that occur frequently in academic writing, and devise strategies for learning them. Fortunately, pedagogical materials and resources for resident writers are finally becoming available for both students (e.g. Byrd et al., in press) and teachers (Gregory & Chapman, 2003; Ferris, 2003; Ferris & Hedgcock, 2005; Hinkel, 1999, 2002; Linfante, 2002; Murie & Thomson, 2001; Reid, 2005).

Another student-based strategy for identifying and correcting errors involves a listener; that is, reading their writing aloud seems to help US-resident students hear errors in that they often unconsciously correct some of their errors as they read. But the readers may not hear their corrections; a teacher in conference with the student or a NES peer can do that for the reader.

More generally, interaction with peers, particularly NES writers, can be a powerful and empowering experience for resident writers (Adamson, 1998; Hartman & Tarone, 1999). Peer tutors and NES friends can serve as editors and language informants. For this strategy to succeed, teachers must first accept the fact that a NES peer can become a valuable resource for a US resident student without interfering with resident student learning, appropriating resident writing, or being a source of cheating for the resident student. The NES peer can proofread for less treatable second-language errors and suggest correct usage, thereby allowing the resident student the confidence and time to focus on content and organization. It is imperative, however, that students do not expect a NES proofreader to write or rewrite their papers; indeed, the NES editor should *never* use a writing instrument. As Bean (2001: 59) states, 'To change, we do not need grammar lessons so much as behavior modification, perhaps by enlisting ... a friend to stop us ... [from] social embarrassment.'

Conclusion

It is unlikely that US-resident students deliberately turn in papers laden with errors or set out to irritate their academic readers. Indeed, many spend much more time and energy on the language than on the content of their written assignments in their best efforts to avoid error. For many US resident writers, the task of avoiding error seems overwhelming; in fact, it *is* overwhelming. Resident students are not by nature lazy, unmotivated, language deficient, or cognitively limited. Rather, these students are struggling with a second dialect (i.e. standard English), and they have very few linguistic resources and prior knowledge to aid them in their struggle. They need skills and strategies that will allow them to work toward effective academic writing. They need additional linguistic information, careful analysis of their writing weaknesses by professionals, and consistent support.

Further research into immigrant student errors and error gravity is essential to developing appropriate approaches and curricula for these students. For example, in what ways are resident student writer errors systematic, rule-governed, and amenable to being categorized? Are immigrant student writer errors closer to NES second dialect forms than they are to international student L2 errors? Are some resident errors more offensive to academic evaluators than others? If so, can these errors be prioritized so that students can work through a logical plan of remediation? Does a focus on grammatical structures in writing classes help or hinder US resident writers? Is it possible to set up programs in which these students can find resources and support for their academic writing throughout their college careers? In particular, do the written errors of these students decrease over a college career in which their academic writing is both frequent and well-supported (Sternglass, 1997)?

Finally, teachers and students who embark on a plan for identifying and correcting standard English errors must expect that improvement in resident students' writing will be neither quick nor easy; in fact, writing development in the second dialect (i.e. standard English) should continue to occur throughout a student's college career.

The time, effort, understanding, energy, and patience spent preparing US resident students for their futures are important, not only for the student but also for the college and the community, even the country. These students are not worthless; they are priceless. No community can afford to lose a generation of potentially productive citizens.

Acknowledgement

Many years ago I approached Bob Kaplan after a paper he gave with Shirley Ostler about contrastive rhetoric. 'You're right,' I said to him. 'I know,' he replied. Later, he and Bill Grabe mentored me through my dissertation, a computer discourse analysis of student writing. I continue to believe that Bob is right, and that he is a wonderful mentor. I hope this chapter, which is about contrastive discourse though from a somewhat different angle, will continue his faith in me.

Notes

1. These students are identified by multiple acronyms and labels: LEP (limited English proficiency); ELL (English language learners); functional bilinguals; ESL (English as a second language); Generation 1.5 (between the first and second generation immigrants); immigrant students; language minority students; L2 (second language). For the purpose of this article, the label 'US residents' encompasses the diverse group of students I am discussing.
2. While this chapter focuses on students in the US, their profiles and language problems appear to apply in substantial ways to immigrants in other countries, from post-colonial Europe to post-apartheid South Africa (Harklau, 2003) and present-day India (Atkinson, 2003).
3. I offer the plural alternative for the word 'culture(s)' throughout this chapter because, of course, culture is not uniform. By 'culture(s),' I mean the amalgam of cultures and subcultures of the individual involved.
4. 'Ear learner' is not an empirical term but rather a description that accurately covers the way most US-resident students learn English as a second language.
5. Conversely, some of the resident-student success stories may be the consequence of a related talent in an auditory learner; learning style research indicates that students who prefer 'ear' learning often have correlating abilities in music and mathematics (Gifted Development Center, 2003; Learner, 2003; Reid, 1995, 1998b).
6. A check of the Web Vocabulary Profiler (Cobb, 2003) reveals that 15 of the underlined words in this sample appear in Coxhead's (2000) Academic Word List while the other eight are too infrequently used to be included.
7. Surprisingly, students' frequency of error has not risen appreciably at least since 1917 (Connors & Lundsford, 1988).

Chapter 9
Teachers' Perceptions of Lexical Anomalies: A Pilot Study

CHERYL BOYD ZIMMERMAN

It can be argued that language is lexically driven and that lexical knowledge is central to communicative competence. However, many second language (L2) teachers have had little or no formal training in either the teaching of vocabulary or the handling of everyday questions from students about words. How does this phenomenon play out in the language classroom, and especially in the English for Academic Purposes (EAP) classroom? Specifically, how do native speakers of English respond to the lexical anomalies produced by language learners in their academic writing when they have little formal training and few formal constructs to rely on?

Lexical anomalies are inaccurate or inappropriate usages of words based on a speech community's standard of use. They may occur when words are combined in ways unlikely to occur in the production of native speakers (e.g. *The weather is attractive* or *Student records are annihilated after five years*), or when language conventions are not known (e.g. *Least but not last, I'd like to thank my friend Trang*). A teacher's response to lexical anomalies becomes relevant in the classroom when learners want information and feedback about the use of English words, but their teachers find it dificult to introspect and describe their own intuitive judgments about word use. Native or proficient speakers are not typically attuned to the semantic and syntactic properties of words. Knowledge of subtle semantic distinctions are part of a speaker's *implicit* knowledge of language, but it is usually not identifiable *explicitly* (Bauer, 1983; Tobin, 1993). The ability to 'explain' meaning is an uncommon skill.

In fact, there is no reason why language users should be especially attuned to the semantic properties of words. We do not generally communicate with isolated words. Most words do not bear messages on their own. They do not, of themselves, 'make sense.' Taken singly, most words are not true or false, beautiful, appropriate, paradoxical, or original. Most linguistic items must occur minimally in the context of a phrase to show such properties. Words contribute, via their own semantic properties, to the meanings of more complex units, but individually they do not occasion our most vivid and direct experiences of language (Cruse, 1986: 9).

This pilot study examines teachers' perceptions of the semantic and syntactic constraints that govern word use and their strategies for explaining lexical anomalies. While most masters programs in the teaching of English to speakers of other languages require courses and provide training in the teaching of grammar, reading, oral language, and composition, it is less common to hear of courses related to the teaching and learning of vocabulary. Typically, L2 teachers have very little exposure to theories of L2 vocabulary acquisition or to the various properties that govern word use and word learning. Which lexical features are familiar to teachers and how do they identify them? When formal categories are used (e.g. 'error of collocation,' or 'error of connotation,' etc.), do some lexical anomalies stand out as more difficult to identify and describe than others? Is there consensus among teachers on the terminology used to describe these features in their explanations, and if not, what insights might be gained from responses given? What is the role of alternative wordings offered by teachers? The goal of this study is not to investigate the features of accurate categorization of lexical anomalies, but rather to investigate how native or proficient speakers of English perceive certain anomalies, and how they choose to address them as part of language instruction.

Background

Linguistics and language teaching

Since Charles Fries introduced the Audiolingual approach to second language teaching in the 1940s, language instruction programs have focused less on language as an intellectual activity (language as an object) and more on language in use, or language as a tool (Kaplan, 1997b). More recently, a growing emphasis on communicative competence and authentic language use has led to important changes in the demands placed on language teachers. Whereas in traditional education models the teacher's role is to transmit knowledge, in communicative models the teacher is an 'active participant in the construction of meaning' (Crandall, 2000: 35). The focus in applied linguistics and teacher-training has shifted from a focus on structural and functional linguistics to a 'genuine problem-solving enterprise' based on a growing interest in addressing 'real world, language-based problems' (Grabe, 2002: 4). One aspect of this new role is the need for teachers to be prepared to work with authentic language and to spontaneously respond to learners' language.

The question of how teachers should be prepared for this task has been hotly debated. Though some may posit that training in formal linguistics is the best source of language information for L2 teachers, Widdowson

(2000b) argues against this notion, suggesting that language as the object of study for the linguist and for the language teacher are not the same object. Linguists and educators, Widdowson argues, operate in separate domains, though he adds that the applied linguist should act as mediator between the two. In practice, the role of mediator between linguistics and L2 pedagogy has been assumed by applied linguists who have historically trained L2 teachers in many Masters in Teaching English to Speakers of Other Languages (MA-TESOL) programs. However, there has been considerable debate and some change in the conceptualization of what teacher trainees need to know. In many current programs there is less focus on language training and more on pedagogy (see Crandall, 2000; Freeman & Johnson, 1998; Ramanathan *et al.*, 2001). Crandall describes a recent change in language teacher education programs that she considers to be a reflection of trends in general teacher education:

> Until recently, applied linguistics ... formed the core of language teacher education ... However, during the last decade, general educational theory and practice have exerted a much more powerful influence on the direction of the education of both preservice and inservice language teacher education, resulting in a greater focus on: (1) practical experiences ... ; (2) classroom-centered or teacher research ... ; and (3) teacher beliefs and teacher cognition in language education ... (Crandall: 2000: 34)

In the current educational climate, the focus in teacher training programs in general and language education in particular has shifted from content to pedagogy (Borg, 1994, 1996; Johnston & Goettsch, 2000), or has redefined content to include both pedagogical content and disciplinary content (Shulman, 1987). Shulman (1986: 6) has highlighted this trend in education by referring to content as the 'missing paradigm,' and he has initiated numerous investigations of the sources of teachers' knowledge and the processes of pedagogical reasoning and action, investigating such questions as the source of teacher explanations and how teachers deal with problems of misunderstanding. Though Shulman's questions exceed the scope of the current study, they speak to the same concern that is central here: when teachers have gaps in content knowledge in areas in which they teach, what information and strategies do they rely on?

This historical shift toward a broader definition of content has a variety of explanations and some advantages for both teachers and learners (see Freeman & Johnson, 1998). Nevertheless, while the focus in teacher training has shifted away from language preparation, the demands of the classroom have not lessened, and teachers are often left facing many language-based questions they are unprepared to analyze and respond to.

Lexical knowledge and lexical analysis

Though vocabulary acquisition is subject to some regularities, vocabulary is not a rule-governed system (Laufer, 1990) and the field of L2 vocabulary acquisition has not produced models that provide detailed insights into the many factors involved (Kroll & Dijkstra, 2002; Meara, 1997). As a result, lexical generalizations are difficult to make and word use is difficult to explain.

The lexical errors that L2 learners often find most problematic (and the anomalies investigated in this study) are seemingly subtle. They occur frequently in the speech and writing of L2 *learners*, yet are not typically addressed in exams or course materials. A sentence such as *The weather is attractive* is understandable, but attractive probably would not be used by a native speaker of English to describe *weather*, at least not in this context. Errors such as this represent what researchers consider learners' partial control (Bialystok & Sharwood-Smith, 1985) or partial word knowledge (Palmberg, 1987), demonstrating that word knowledge is not an all-or-nothing proposition; rather, it has many dimensions and it develops over time. Nation's (1990, 2001) widely accepted approach to what it means to know a word, for example, represents word knowledge as a taxonomy of components including form (e.g. pronunciation, spelling), meaning (e.g. underlying concept, particular instantiations, associations), and use (e.g. collocations, grammatical constraints, register). Taxonomies such as this allow us to analyze the anomalous *The weather is atttractive* and see that the user appears to know the form and meaning of each word but has combined the two in a way that does not sound like the English of a native speaker. This illustrates the enormity of the word-learning task. The intermediate or advanced L2 learner must acquire not only thousands of words but also a great deal of information about each one. Acquiring the wide variety of features needed for both *receptive* knowledge of a word (required for reading and listening) and *productive* knowledge (required for writing and speaking) is a daunting task, even if the receptive lexicon exceeds in size the productive lexicon.

This study investigates teachers' reactions to some of the subtle lexical features that are problematic for L2 learners, especially in the EAP context. This investigation of how teachers describe errors and how they identify patterns for generalization was prompted by the frequency of lexical errors in the academic writing of L2 students. These errors are first described below under the categories of Collocations, Language Conventions/Set Phrases, and Meaning (Connotations and Degree).

Collocations

Vocabulary is made up not only of single-word units but also of patterns of words that frequently occur together. Collocations are words that often co-occur (e.g. *take a nap, by the way, communicate with*), and knowledge of these recurring combinations is critical to word knowledge (Nation, 1990, 2001). Errors of collocation occur frequently in L2 production, perhaps in part because learners are led to assume that the lexicon is an open system that allows for an infinite combination of words (Seal, 1991). There are few 'rules' governing collocation, and it is difficult to group items by their collocational properties or to teach them systematically (Schmitt, 2000). Nevertheless, collocational knowledge is critical, and the notion of collocation provides a useful framework for expanding one's productive vocabulary.

Language Conventions/Set Phrases

Related to the notion of collocation are 'lexical phrases' (Nattinger & DeCarrico, 1992) or 'fixed expressions' (Singleton, 2000). These pre-fabricated units of two or more words occur in the speech of native speakers for a wide variety of discourse functions ranging from inquiring (e.g. *What's the matter?*) to advising (e.g. *Look before you leap*) to signaling a transition (e.g. *Last but not least*). In addition, they vary in form and in semantic transparency. Researchers often reserve the term 'idiom' for those lexical phrases that are least semantically transparent (e.g. *bite the dust* gives little hint of the meaning of *die*) and that collocate with little variation (e.g. to *kick the bucket* may be altered to *kicked the bucket* but not to *the bucket has been kicked*) (McCarthy, 1990; Nattinger & DeCarrico, 1992). Nattinger and DeCarrico also stress that idioms are but one kind of lexical phrase and that there are many other formulaic fixed phrases that serve important roles in language use and teaching.[1]

Research has shown that fixed phrases and ritualized language play a key role in the language use of native speakers (Pawley & Syder, 1983; Sinclair, 1991; Singleton, 2000). Schmitt (2000: 78) suggests that one of the most important new trends in vocabulary study is the realization that 'words act less as individual units and more as part of lexical phrases in interconnected discourse.'

Meaning (Connotation and Degree)

There are principles that guide the native speaker's choice of specific words according to their meanings. However, meaning is elusive and difficult to categorize. The relationship between a word and its referent is never neat or predictable, but neither is it random or haphazard.[2] One category used to describe the relationship between sets of lexical items, in this case graded according to the property of size, is seen in the set *minuscule, tiny, small, big, huge,* and *gigantic*. Referred to as 'grade-terms' (or, in this study, 'degree terms') and found most frequently in adjectival forms, these sets of words have rather vague boundaries, but the vagueness becomes 'less marked when the terms are explicitly contrasted with one another' (Cruse, 1986: 194). Though rarely discussed in the literature, errors of this sort are problematic for language learners and frequently seen in L2 production, including in academic writing.

However, researchers must reach beyond core meaning in order to describe the features of word meaning that are less salient but still essential for practical use. Nation (2001) represents this distinction between a word's core meaning and these additional features by breaking down the aspect of meaning into 'underlying concept,' 'particular instantiations,' and 'associations.' McCarthy (1990: 47) uses the terms 'basic cognitive domains' for universal and fundamental qualities including dimensions such as the knowledge that a *cup* is normally solid and compact, and 'abstract cognitive domains' for 'schematic representations of particular entities' such as the knowledge that a *cup* is probably used for tea but not for beer. Each of these views implies that, although the basic concept of many words may be universal, the additional features of word meaning often differ from culture to culture, often causing particular difficulty with translation and learning.

It should be pointed out that it is impossible to completely disentangle semantics from grammar, at least partly because many grammatical elements are themselves bearers of meaning (Cruse, 1986). This difficulty accounts for some of the problems that native or proficient speakers encounter when trying to explain anomalous sentences. Teachers are left with a difficult task. What, then, will they do when they are faced with lexical anomalies that they would never create themselves and lack the metalinguistic knowledge needed to explain? What do their responses tell us about how to prepare language teachers to address the lexical needs of their students?

The Study

Participants

Fourteen native English-speaking teachers of English as a second language (ESL) participated in the study. Native speakers of English were used in order to control for L1–L2 differences in language proficiency. Nine of the teachers had more than 15 years of teaching experience, and only one participant had less than 8 years of experience. All of them had taught in both intensive English and adult education programs, and 12 of the 14 teachers had also taught in either community college or college/university programs in the US. All had experience of teaching a vocabulary class, but none had taken a class in the teaching of vocabulary. An informal survey asking the teachers what they considered most helpful in preparing to teach vocabulary revealed that only two respondents identified their own study of another language as most helpful, while others mentioned additional items, namely textbooks, teaching experience, curiosity about words, and the dictionary.

Procedure

It is widely believed that the best way to tap people's semantic knowledge is 'to elicit intuitions *about* meaning rather than *of* meaning' (Cruse, 1986: 10). That is, the average native speaker of English knows much more about a word than s/he can explain, so it makes sense to tap into those intuitions rather than to elicit full definitions of words. In addition, semantic knowledge of words is best investigated with words in meaningful contexts (Nagy, 1997). For these reasons, this study used contextualized lexical items and informants were asked to comment on their impressions of these items and their strategies for explaining them to students. The participants completed a questionnaire in which they were asked to respond to lexical anomalies in each of 12 sentences drawn from student academic writing (see Appendix). First, the participants were invited to decide whether or not the sentences were anomalous and, if they were, if the anomaly could be categorized in terms of generalizable lexical patterns? That is, could the participants ascribe a name to the type of anomaly that was represented? Second, respondents were asked to briefly describe the explanation they would give to any students who had made such errors. The directions urged participants to write a brief, natural response that reflected what they would tell a student, not all they knew about a word.

In order to best examine the information captured by teachers in their analyses and descriptions of anomalous sentences, several criteria were followed. First, anomalous lexical choices were identified and selected from L2 student writing assignments. Second, the concept of 'accurate category' was introduced, broadly defined as identifying a category with informative or instructive explanatory value (e.g. 'culturally inappropriate' or 'faulty collocation' provide greater information value about an anomaly than the broader 'wrong word' label). It was not expected that all of the semantic and syntactic rules that govern the use of the word would be captured by the chosen category, nor was it expected that the teachers would respond with a pre-determined set of categories. Rather, the category labels were judged in light of their value in identifying a generalizable lexical pattern or in explaining at least one significant feature of the word that might have the potential to guide a student toward a more appropriate use of that word. For example, in the case of the anomalous use of *incurable* in *The mechanic told me to sell this car because it was incurable*, categories offered by the participants and considered accurate included 'animate word used for inanimate thing,' 'organic/inorganic,' and 'faulty collocation.' Unacceptable or inaccurate categories (that did not suggest a pattern of use) included 'wrong implication,' 'word choice,' and 'lexical error.' As a result of this broad definition, several different terms were judged as 'accurate' for each category.[3]

As well as investigating the terminology used to identify lexical categories or lexical features, participants' responses were examined for explanatory information in the form of elaborations or suggestions. That is, after the participants named or categorized an anomaly, what additional information did they choose to add? Whether or not accurate categories were known, could teachers provide explanations about patterns of lexical use? To answer such questions, instructions on the questionnaire were worded to encourage teachers to write brief explanations that duplicated the terminology they would use with a student (see the Appendix at the end of this chapter). The explanations were expected to provide insights into teachers' word knowledge and their ability to provide learners with effective lexical instruction.

Results

As shown in Table 9.1, most respondents relied upon a combination of categories and explanations. In general, teachers were more informative in their explanations than in their categorizations. Some teachers focused their attention on the meaning of the sentence while others focused on the meaning of the anomalous word. For example, in the sentence *The weather was so attractive that we hated to stay inside*, some teachers gave advice about how to describe *weather* while others focused on an appropriate context for the word *attractive*. Although respondents offered many comments that showed insight into language (e.g. 'This is an old fashioned usage for this word') and sensitivity to the intricacies of the language learning process (e.g. 'I would use humor to explain this one'), there was, as expected, little consensus regarding the terminology used either in categorization or explanation. Many respondents found it difficult to identify lexical patterns or to generalize about lexical errors.

Use of categories

Considerable latitude was given in the terms accepted as 'accurate categories.' For example, the category of 'idiom' was used to categorize the anomaly *least but not last* by 8 of the 14 teachers and was used to categorize the phrase *my view of point* by 4 of the teachers. Given how ESL textbooks vary in their use of the term 'idiom,' these categorizations were considered accurate. Since there was no finite set of categories and teachers were left to their own devices, it is not surprising that, for the reasons mentioned above, only 30.4% of the items were categorized accurately (see Table 9.1). Additionally, 33.3% of all responses included no categories while 36.3%

Table 9.1 Summary of categories and explanations

	No or inaccurate category	Accurate category	Accurate explanation	Inaccurate explanation	No or inaccurate category with accurate explanation
Lexical phrases (n = 28)	11 39.30%	17 60.70%	17 60.70%	11 39.30%	2 7.10%
Positive/negative connotations (n = 28)	19 67.90%	9 32.10%	24 85.70%	4 14.30%	16 57.10%
Specific connotations (n = 28)	19 67.90%	9 32.10%	18 64.30%	10 35.70%	12 42.90%
General collocations (n = 28)	21 75.00%	7 25.00%	10 35.70%	18 64.30%	7 25.00%
Animate / inanimate collocations (n = 28)	22 78.60%	6 21.40%	22 78.60%	6 21.40%	16 57.10%
Degree (n = 28)	25 89.30%	3 10.70%	10 35.70%	18 64.30%	8 28.60%
Totals (n = 168)	117 69.60%	51 30.40%	101 60.10%	67 39.90%	61 36.30%

were inaccurately categorized (collectively totaling 69.6%). While 9 of the 14 teachers provided accurate categories for less than a third of the 12 items, only three teachers identified more than 58% of the categories with accuracy.

Many of the categories used by respondents were so general that they failed to distinguish one type of anomaly from another. Terms such as 'word choice,' 'lexical error,' 'usage,' 'wrong word,' and 'inappropriate usage' were used to refer to every category. Three teachers each used one category accurately and then categorized all the other errors under a broad heading. For example, one of them used the 'connotation' category accurately, then labeled all the other items as 'lexical errors.' Another informant used 'set expression' accurately, then labeled all the other errors as 'word choice' errors. The strategies used by these three teachers suggest that uninformative, general labels for error types may be used as a default when more specific terms are not known.

Use of explanations

The respondents provided considerably more information through the use of explanations than they did through categories. Explanations were considered 'accurate' when they included at least one informative feature that might guide students to appropriate word use. While less than a third of responses included accurate categories, 60% of the responses contained accurate explanations. In the category of positive/negative connotations, for example, while only 32.1% of the responses were accurately categorized, 85.7% of the explanations contained words such as 'positive,' 'negative,' 'harmful,' or 'good v. evil.' Similarly, in the category of 'animate/inanimate' collocations, only 21.4% of the responses were accurately categorized while 78.6% contained information related to animacy or inanimacy (e.g. 'This adjective is used for people, not things;' 'Used for diseases or illnesses;' or 'Used for humans, not machines'). Overall, of the responses that were either not categorized at all or categorized inaccurately, 36.3% were followed by accurate explanations.

It was of interest to ascertain which types of lexical errors were most difficult to either categorize or explain. Whether category names were known or not, the categories fell into a particular pattern of difficulty for respondents to identify, as seen in Table 9.2. Lexical phrases and connotations were most frequently categorized or explained accurately while feedback about errors of collocation and degree was least frequently accurate. Respondents identified the subcategory of animate/inanimate collocations with far more accuracy than general collocations. Thus, even though animacy is not considered a category in this analysis, it should be acknowledged as a lexical pattern that the respondents in this study were able to identify. In contrast, animacy was also applied inaccurately to explain *exposed military honors, struck by happy events, slight crimes,* and *attractive weather.* The lexical feature referred to here as 'degree' was accurately categorized and accurately explained in the fewest number of responses, with only 10.7% of the respondents able to categorize the anomaly and only 35.7% able to explain it accurately.

In addition to the overly general categories and explanations that have already been mentioned (e.g. 'wrong word'), there were other inaccurate explanations. The term 'idiom' was used 13 times; 8 of the 14 teachers used the term at least once. It was most often used in reference to the lexical phrases *point of view* or *last but not least,* while three respondents identified only one of these lexical phrases as an idiom and identified the other differently (e.g. as a 'phrasal form'). 'Idiom' was also used to refer to the compound noun *streetwalker.* This label seems to be overused by teachers to describe a wide variety of features of meaning, collocation, and convention.

Table 9.2 Categories (listed from most accurately to least accurately identified)

		Accurate category	Accurate explanation	Inaccurate category / inaccurate explanation
1	Lexical phrases ($n = 28$)	60.70%	60.70%	7.10%
2	Connotations (total) ($n = 56$)	32.10%	75.00%	5.40%
2a	Positive/negative connotations	32.10%	85.70%	0.00%
2b	Specific connotations	32.10%	64.30%	10.70%
3	Collocations (total) ($n = 56$)	23.20%	57.20%	17.80%
3a	Animate/inanimate collocations	21.40%	78.60%	3.60%
3b	General collocations	25.00%	35.70%	32.10%
4	Degree ($n = 28$)	10.70%	35.70%	32.10%

The largest number of inaccurate explanations were given in response to the sentence *The weather was so attractive that we hated to stay inside*. Rather than describing the principle of collocation, some respondents tried to explain why certain words did not belong together: 'We don't usually use *attractive* when it calls attention to itself' and '*Attractive* means nice to look at, but we don't just look at the weather.' An attempt to explain another error of collocation (i.e. *slight crimes*) seemed to reflect a similar attempt to attribute the error to a detailed breakdown of the word's meaning: '*Slight* means a partial amount of something, but you can't have a partial amount of a crime' and 'A crime is a crime. When you break the law it is not slight; it is usually a bad thing. *Slight* means ever so small.' Several teachers extended the principle of animacy to explain cases in which it was not relevant: 'Only people or animals are annihilated'[4] and 'Only a person can influence.'

Use of alternative wordings

Although the questionnaire did not ask respondents to provide alternative wordings for anomalous word choices, 42.9% of the explanations did so. For example, in response to the sentence, *The mechanic told me to sell this car because it was incurable*, teachers responded with replacements for *incurable* such as *beyond repair* or *irreparable*. Two respondents suggested replacements without explanations in all of their responses while most respondents used alternative wordings to supplement an explanation and give information about a pattern of use (e.g. 'This applies to diseases; try *impossible to fix*').

Discussion

Overall, the respondents in this study did not generalize about lexical categories with much consensus. However, many explanations and suggestions contained useful information about lexical patterns, especially in particular categories. On the other hand, inconsistencies and inaccuracies reveal gaps in the formal lexical knowledge of the teachers.

The categories that appeared most familiar to the respondents were 'lexical phrases,' 'connotations' and 'animacy/inanimacy.' The explanatory terms used with the most frequency were 'idiom' and 'connotation.' Although it could be argued that the term 'idiom' was used too broadly by many of the teachers (i.e. to describe lexical phrases, other multiword units, and single-word expressions), the underlying concept was used accurately and indeed reflected explanations given in some (though not all) ESL textbooks.

Similarly, the categories that stood out as most difficult to identify were 'collocation' and 'degree,' and these two terms were used infrequently. The concept of collocation was not mentioned in 89.3% of the explanations in which it would have been relevant. Though collocation is a well-established notion in lexical research, these data support the suggestion that lexical research has not 'trickled down to the practicing language teacher' (Seal, 1991: 298). Indeed, collocation may be particularly difficult for native speakers to explain because it is part of the 'shadowy area between grammar and meaning' (Nation, 1990: 38). It has also been suggested that the difficulty may be that native speakers store and process lexical items as much by collocations as by single words, whereas language learners appear to be joining lexical items based on their knowledge of individual words (Seal, 1991). The data collected here supports the hypothesis that the unconscious process of collocation is difficult for teachers to identify and describe.

It was not surprising to find that participants' attempts to identify the category referred to here as 'degree' included only two terms that provided any lexical information ('question of degree' and 'major/minor'); the respondents' inventory of terms appears most limited in this category. In addition, 89.3% of the responses to the two sentences in this category were either inaccurately categorized or not categorized at all. The error reflected in the sentence, *Student records are annihilated after three years* suggests that the learner is not aware of the distribution of a graded set of words that share a core meaning (e.g. *erase, delete, destroy, annihilate*). Errors of this type (related to the untidy distinction between words due to specificity or degree) are frequent in L2 writing. Although they are difficult to categorize, teachers should prepare to identify this pattern of use in a way that students can understand.

In their responses to anomalies related to word meaning, 6 of the 14 teachers used the term 'connotation' accurately and even more respondents referred accurately to the 'positive' or 'negative' feelings words evoke. There were many insightful comments suggesting that teachers understand that word meaning includes more than a word's core meaning (e.g. in reference to the sentence, *The reporters exposed the candidate's list of military honors,* one teacher explained: '*Exposed* has a negative feeling. Using this verb makes it seem like the honors had some scandal attached to them').

The role played by teachers' suggestions is also of interest to this investigation. Most teachers offered alternative wordings to supplement explanations. In fact, two teachers consistently provided alternative wordings only. Although further study would be needed to understand the teachers' motives for doing this, it appears that some teachers consider suggesting alternatives to be sufficient. Although alternative wordings are a clear source of information about a specific item, without explanation they have no generalization value.

Conclusion

The purpose of this study was to investigate how native speakers of English perceive certain lexical anomalies, and how they choose to address them as part of language instruction. Additional research is needed to better understand the extent of the teachers' knowledge and the reasons for their responses, with the use of follow-up interviews a likely methodology for doing this. In addition, it would be useful to observe teachers and to note their word-correction strategies. It would not be possible to control for the types of errors that occur with this method, but the spontaneous responses of teachers would be more likely to be representative of classroom reality.

Although the data gathered here provide some insights into teachers' responses to lexical anomalies, there are several practical limitations to this study. First, in light of the lack of consensus in the literature about terminology for lexical categories, it might have been advisable to disregard the option of 'categorizing' the errors and to examine only the explanations. In addition, it was difficult to untangle the effects of ESL materials that may have been used, differences in pre- and post-service training, and time limitations on busy teachers, who for this reason may have described their responses with varying accuracy when they responded to the prompts given in the questionnaire.

This pilot study raises several issues about the lexical judgments of and vocabulary instruction by L2 teachers. First, it appears that, though teachers tend to lack formal lexical terminology, their explanations reveal an ability to recognize some generalizable tendencies in the areas of lexical phrases (referred to by many respondents as 'idioms'), positive or negative connotations, and animacy/inanimacy. The respondents' explanations reveal considerable insight into what limits students' accurate word use in these categories. In contrast, the lexical features of collocation and degree were less frequently identified. Second, it appears that, when teachers lack formal terminology, they offer alternative wordings and try to make generalizations about these wordings, but their generalizations vary in accuracy. In addition, the results of this study offer some insight into the strategies that teachers use to deal with what they do not know about words. For example, many respondents illustrated word meaning by showing the relations between two or more words and by giving accurate explanations or offering suggestions even with inaccurate categorizations. Finally, it should be noted that, even though the experienced teachers in this study were often able to respond to anomalies with helpful information, experience alone does not bring about consistency or consensus in the terminology used to describe lexical features. As a result, learners may receive inconsistent or even contradictory information from their teachers. Teachers need greater awareness of lexical patterns, relevant terminology, and the basic principles that govern word use. Teacher-training communities should be aware of teachers' needs for the conceptual framework and formal terminology required to explain the language they know implicitly. If lexical knowledge is central to communicative competence, teachers should be prepared to foster it with skill.

Acknowledgement

I wish to thank Margaret Plenert for her insightful and resourceful assistance at all stages of this project.

Notes

1. Language users, and indeed ESL materials textbook developers, extend the use of the term 'idiom' much more loosely and with little consensus. For example, while some texts include only examples that 'have special meanings which are different from the usual meanings of the words (e.g. *feeling blue, yellow journalism, high time*)' (Richek, 2000: 41), others extend their definitions to include phrasal verbs (e.g. *drop by, fall through, count out*) (Broukal, 1995; Goldman, 1981), frequently used prepositional phrases (e.g. *ahead of time, at the most, on the whole*)

(Reeves, 1975), and compound words (e.g. *bookworm, copycat*) and single-word expressions (e.g. *chicken, baloney, fishy*) (Broukal, 1994). Classroom materials, therefore, cloud the distinction between these items, often referred to collectively as 'informal usage' (*Longman Advanced American Dictionary*, 2000; *Oxford Advanced Learner's Dictionary*, 1995).

2. For example, many words operate over continuous scales based on various properties, such as a temporal sequence (e.g. *baby, child, adolescent*), in which a continuous property increases with time (in this example, *maturity*).
3. For example, terminology accepted as accurate for lexical phrases included 'set expression' or 'phrase,' and 'idiomatic word order.' For connotations, accepted terminology included 'culturally inappropriate,' 'slang/colloquial,' and 'negative v. positive.' For collocations, accurate terminology included 'major/ minor' and 'animate/inanimate.'
4. Though the concept of animacy may explain some misuses of this word, inanimate objects can be annihilated (e.g. cities, rain forests, planets). The problem with the sentence concerning 'annihilating student records' has more to do with the degree or range of meaning than with animacy.

Appendix: ESL Instructor Questionnaire

This survey is designed to help us better understand a fundamental part of the ESL teaching task: how do teachers explain lexical anomalies to students? This is not a test; rather we see it as a reflection of a skill that you use in the classroom daily.

Directions: (no names please)

(1) Read each of the following sentences, which were produced by high-intermediate to advanced level ESL students. If a sentence has no error, indicate OK and pass on to the next one.
(2) If a sentence has a lexical anomaly, answer **two (2)** questions:
   (a) Can the anomaly be categorized? If so, how would you categorize it?
   (b) How would you explain the error to a student? Please try to duplicate the terminology you would use with a student. Keep your explanation brief.
We are interested in the type of natural response you might use in the classroom or in response to a student's question. Do not spend more than a few minutes on each question. Your answers should reflect what you tell a student, not all you know about a word.

Sentences:

(1) The mechanic told me to sell this car because it was incurable.
(2) The reporters exposed the candidate's list of military honors.
(3) The price of a book influences how much sales tax you pay.
(4) While she waited for her friend, she went streetwalking and looked in the shop windows.
(5) Least but not last, I'd like to thank my friend Trang.
(6) The family was struck by a series of very happy events.
(7) He has been accused of some slight crimes.
(8) They were singing a gay song.
(9) The weather was so attractive that we hated to stay inside.
(10) Student records are annihilated after five years.
(11) My view of point has changed considerably since I came to the US.
(12) The lawn mower was disabled.

Part 4
Contrastive Discourse Analysis

Part 4
Introduction

WILLIAM GRABE

Bob Kaplan has made many contributions to applied linguistics, English studies, writing research, and educational practices. One of his best-known contributions is the contrastive rhetoric hypothesis, though he prefers to call it the contrastive rhetoric notion, pointing out that it is not sufficiently theorized to merit the status of hypothesis (but see Chu *et al.*, 2002, for a clear example of experimental support). In the early 1960s, Kaplan witnessed first hand the rapid surge of international students coming to study at US universities. One of the outcomes of this increased enrollment was the rapid growth of intensive English programs at universities. A second outcome was the concern raised by university faculties that these students had great difficulties in writing assignments in their courses.

Kaplan explored the writing difficulties of these students, and observed that students from different languages seemed to write in ways directed by the rhetorical and cultural patterns of their first language (L1). From this initial work, Kaplan proposed an early version of the contrastive rhetoric hypothesis with the argument that different languages imposed a cultural logic on the writing of ESL (English as a second language) students (Kaplan, 1966, 1972). Kaplan's 1966 article, infamously labeled as the 'doodles' article, suggested in a visual manner the diverse composing preferences of writers from different L1s.

By the mid 1980s, Kaplan had modified his position on the contrastive rhetoric hypothesis considerably (though critics seemed to prefer the early 1960s version, citing it far more often than later writings). In several articles, Kaplan (1987, 1988) argued that the notion of contrastive rhetoric is as likely, if not more likely, to reflect cultural and educational training factors as it is to reflect linguistically guided preferences from the L1. Thus, the educational socialization of students in writing practices in their L1 is likely to remain with them as they learn to write in the L2. While such preferences can be overcome with extended writing instruction, the L1 influence tends to remain strong. Research in the 1980s by a growing number of scholars also extended the contrastive rhetoric notion to more direct comparisons of writing in two different languages and the examination of writing across cultures in specific genres. No longer was the notion of contrastive rhetoric limited to the study of ESL students writing in US tertiary institutions.

In the 1990s, in a series of articles, Kaplan further refined his position. He applauded and supported the many studies in contrastive rhetoric that examined writing across two L1s, that compared students' writing in their L1 and in their L2 and compared the writing of specific genres across two L1s, both within and outside academic settings, and that called for further study of the concept of "evidence" in written discourse cross-linguistically (Grabe & Kaplan, 1996; Kaplan 1997a, 2000, 2001). Throughout his career, the notion of contrastive rhetoric has evolved and so has Kaplan's own position on this notion.

The notion of contrastive rhetoric has taken on a remarkable life of its own. When one considers that Kaplan's original proposal appeared only 15 years after Whorf's (1956) own writings and the Whorfian hypothesis, and when one sees the interest that this notion continues to generate today, it is clear that contrastive rhetoric raises fundamental issues in cross-cultural communication. Kaplan's joining of culture, language, and rhetoric was remarkably innovative at the time, anticipating other serious applied linguistic attempts at discourse analyses by more than 10 years. Given the complexity of the issues surrounding the contrastive rhetoric proposal, it is also not surprising that Kaplan would evolve in his own thinking on this notion, especially in light of its now almost 40-year history. (It is worth noting also the changing, and revived, perspectives on the Whorfian hypothesis: Bowerman & Levinson, 2001; Gumperz & Levinson, 1996.)

The extent to which contrastive rhetoric has grown beyond the early arguments by Kaplan is also indicated by the many articles written on contrastive rhetoric by scholars from around the world (see Connor, 1996, 2002, 2003; Mauranen, 1993b). Connor, in particular, has pointed out that the study of genres cross-linguistically needs to be explored across multiple genres and also with respect to changes in specific genres diachronically. Such orientations reveal how genres in different cultures may change in response to pressures from other genres or from the same genre in another language (e.g. the impact of English-based science research articles on similar articles in another language).

In the four contributions to this section, contrastive rhetoric is further exemplified through innovative extensions and detailed analyses. The four contributions together stretch the notion of contrastive rhetoric considerably from its earlier uses, and that is welcomed. Kaplan has always been a strong proponent of exploring ideas, expanding the scope of inquiry, and finding new ways to conceptualize continuing issues and questions. In Chapter 10, Connor and Moreno propose a theoretical framework for future contrastive rhetoric research. Drawing on concepts from corpus development, they propose a series of text-collection guidelines that would eventually lead to a principled sampling of cross-cultural texts and a corpus of a wide range of texts. This corpus could then be a significant resource for contrastive rhetoric research and provide opportunities for analyses across multiple types of texts and multiple languages.

The next chapter (Chapter 11), by Daubney-Davis and Patthey-Chavez, examines the narrative writing of two groups of 7th grade students, Mexican-American students and African-American students. This study extends contrastive rhetoric both by exploring the narrative writing of language and dialect minority students in secondary school and by analyzing texts for stylistic features of the narratives. The students in this study were from the same school and thus had received the same instruction from teachers. They had also been in the same school in previous years, and their educational experiences were parallel. Daubney-Davis and Patthey-Chavez found that both Mexican-American students and African-American students wrote in very similar ways as far as writing conventions and syntactic structures were concerned. However, the two groups of students produced types of narrative development that appeared to be consistently different from one another. Daubney-Davis and Patthey-Chavez argue that the narrative genre provides a good site for exploring culturally distinct influences on writing, particular for minority secondary school students.

Chapter 12, by Hinkel, explores the concept of evidence in L2 student writing in a university setting. In particular, Hinkel operationalizes the concept of evidence in writing by exploring the use of examples in writing and the linguistic features associated with examples (e.g. first person pronouns, past tense). Her argument focuses on the emphasis given to examples as a type of evidence in composition courses and the disjunct between using examples in composition course assignments and the lack of 'examples as evidence' expected in student writing in other disciplines. She argues persuasively that many L2 students from Chinese, Japanese, and Korean backgrounds are already well versed in the concept of 'examples as evidence' since that rhetorical strategy is emphasized in the academic writing of their L1 cultures. As a result, they use examples, and linguistic features of examples, at significantly higher frequencies than do writers who are native speakers. Hinkel concludes by suggesting that composition courses in the US might better serve L2 students from certain cultures by focusing on other ways to present evidence in academic writing.

The final chapter (Chapter 13), by Poole, also explores language use cross-culturally in the classroom, though, in this case, the focus is on patterns of spoken turn-taking in various classroom settings. Poole extends the notion of contrastive rhetoric into patterns of spoken interaction between teachers and students and analyzes how turn-taking processes vary in culturally distinct classroom settings. Much as in contrastive rhetoric analyses of written texts, Poole argues that students who come from educational environments privileging one specific set of interactional patterns may have difficulty learning in classroom contexts in which turn-taking involves somewhat different interactional patterns. Poole concludes that teachers of L2 students from diverse backgrounds should become more aware of the multiple ways in which students are socialized into classroom interactional practices.

The four chapters in this section together offer interesting new perspectives on the contrastive rhetoric hypothesis while still highlighting the main themes that have fascinated so many over the past 40 years. Perhaps the greatest strength of the contrastive rhetoric notion is that it is organic: it grows and evolves in natural ways in response to new research methods, new ways to collect data, and new theoretical insights.

Chapter 10
Tertium Comparationis: A Vital Component in Contrastive Rhetoric Research

ULLA M. CONNOR AND ANA I. MORENO

Contrastive rhetoric has had a significant impact on the teaching of second-language writing, and thousands of English teachers around the world are thankful to Bob Kaplan for starting the field. Contrastive rhetoric is premised on the insight that, to the degree that language and writing are cultural phenomena, different cultures have different rhetorical tendencies. Furthermore, the linguistic patterns and rhetorical conventions of the first language (L1) often transfer to writing in the second language (L2). Kaplan's research was pioneering in calling attention to cultural differences in the writing of students of English as a second language (ESL) and English as a foreign language (EFL). This focus on writing was especially welcome for ESL instruction as the emphasis on oral language skills had dominated ESL contexts in the US and elsewhere.

The past 35-plus years since Kaplan's seminal article (Kaplan, 1966) have produced an impressive set of studies conducted in both ESL and EFL settings (for recent reviews see Connor, 1996, 2002.) Significant changes have taken place in contrastive rhetoric research in terms of what kind of writing has been studied and how it has been studied. There has been an increase in the types of written texts considered the purview of second language writing instruction around the world, and thus also the object of contrastive rhetoric research. The student essay, required still in the majority of school and college classes, is no longer the only type of writing taught in ESL and EFL classes. Other genres, such as the academic research article, research report, and grant proposal, are considered important in today's ESL instruction. While linguistic text analysis was the tool of choice in the first two decades of contrastive rhetoric research, writing and its study are today increasingly regarded as socially situated, with each situation requiring special consideration to audience, purpose, and level of expertise. Thus, the expectations and norms of discourse communities or communities of practice (cultural and disciplinary) will help shape the writing practices of these communities.

Both of these reasons – proliferation of writing types or genres and consideration of the social context – are placing new demands on the research methods of L2 writing cross-culturally. Traditional text analyses (e.g. analyses of cohesion, coherence, and textual superstructures) have been supplemented with 'genre analyses' specific to genres such as research articles, book reviews, job applications, and grant proposals (see Bhatia, 1993; Connor, 2000; Swales, 1990). In addition, the study of the social context has called for ethnography and case study approaches to be added to the analysis of texts.

Hyland (2000) advocates a methodology for investigating academic writing that considers writing as the outcome of social interactions. He suggests that ethnography can provide valuable understandings about the ways writers negotiate their immediate situations. To achieve this, Hyland advocates the use of a large number of texts to gain insights into the core values and beliefs of the communities of writers, and he stresses the need to examine 'what is conventional and typical in the behavior of skilled writers as they construct the meaning potential of their texts, constrained by the sense of a reader's expectation' (Hyland 2000: 136).

Given that cross-cultural analysis needs large-scale textual analyses of written genres for baseline comparisons, it is important that we compare elements that can in fact be compared. In this chapter, we propose a new agenda for contrastive rhetoric research using well-designed corpora that can be analyzed rigorously and then compared with equivalent English corpora. In such studies, the concept of *tertium comparationis* or common platform of comparison is important at all levels of research: in identifying texts for corpora, in selecting textual concepts to be studied in the corpora, and in identifying linguistic features that are used to realize these concepts. Common ground needs to exist on the conceptual level as much as on the explicit linguistic feature level for the juxtaposition of any two corpora. There needs to be an adequate match before mapping from one to the other can take place. This kind of rigorous corpus building is needed so that we can have good baseline descriptions of rhetorics and genres within cultures and languages for comparison and contrast purposes.

Using a study by Moreno (1998), we explain how such genre-specific corpus studies with appropriate *tertia comparationis* can be designed and conducted from corpus collection to final analysis and interpretation. The research method we advocate for these studies can be best described as quantitative descriptive research as opposed to reflective inquiry, prediction and classification studies, sampling surveys, case studies and ethnographies, and quasi- and true experiments (Connor, 1996). The method is different from most of the early contrastive studies (e.g. Kaplan, 1966), which relied on texts produced in English as a second language with no comparable L1 corpora.

The method consists of six phases:

(1) independent description of two comparable parallel corpora of expert L1 texts;
(2) identification of comparable textual concepts (e.g. coherence relations, premise-conclusion);
(3) operationalization of the textual concepts into linguistic features appropriate to each language;
(4) quantitative text analyses;
(5) juxtaposition of the analyzed corpora;
(6) explanation of similarities and differences using contextual information about the languages and cultures in question.

Before explaining the concept of *tertium comparationis* and describing how it was used in Moreno's (1998) contrastive study, however, we will briefly discuss types of corpora used in contrastive writing studies, and also give some background to the concept from the fields of contrastive analysis and translation studies.

Corpus Types in Contrastive Studies

Corpus linguistics is having a beneficial effect on contrastive studies, especially because it forces us to pay attention to corpus design. According to Johansson (1998: 3), 'a computer corpus is a body of texts put together in a principled way and prepared for computer processing.' Johansson writes about the importance of corpora for contrastive research and translation studies, and he classifies types of corpora as follows: *parallel corpora* of comparable original texts in two or more languages, *translation corpora* of original texts and their translations, and finally *learner corpora* containing language by learners of a particular target language. In contrastive rhetorical studies, learner corpora have been the most common. Learner corpora allow for the examination of interlanguage errors when they are used for comparison with native language writing in the target language, as in the *International Corpus of Learner English* project (Granger, 1996). Kaplan's (1966) work relied on a learner corpus of ESL students' writing; no comparable native speaker corpus was employed, nor was a comparison made between the learners' L2 texts and the L1 texts of the same students.

As the study of contrastive rhetoric has advanced, there has been growth in the use of comparable corpora. It is understood that apples should not be compared with oranges, nor student writing in an L2 with expert writing in the target language or the learner's L1. It is commonly agreed in contrastive rhetoric research that any attempt to determine whether the expression of a given text-rhetorical constant in language A is similar or different from its expression in language B must begin by comparing how competent speakers of both languages express it. Accordingly, Reid (1988: 19) argues that texts written by nonnative speakers – whether L2 texts or translations – do not constitute 'a sufficient data sample for valid analysis because they use second language texts to investigate first language rhetorical patterns.' The major reason is that in both cases it is mere speculation that the rhetorical conventions of the L1 may have been transferred or translated into the L2 texts. Thus, contrastive rhetoric studies should attempt to describe and explain differences or similarities in text-patterns across cultures on the basis of comparable parallel corpora of texts, written independently by expert speakers of each particular language/writing culture. Applying appropriate *tertia comparationis* at the design and analysis stages of contrastive rhetoric research will help us build comparable corpora that can provide baseline data for meaningful cultural comparisons.

Tertium Comparationis in Contrastive Analysis and Translation Studies

In contrastive analysis, it is important to compare items that are comparable. The contrastive analyst James writes:

> The first thing we do is make sure that we are comparing like with like: this means that the two (or more) entities to be compared, while differing in some respect, must share certain attributes. This requirement is especially strong when we are contrasting, i.e. looking for differences – since it is only against a background of sameness that differences are significant. We shall call this sameness the *constant* and the differences *variables*. (James, 1980: 169)

In translation theory this factor of sameness has been referred to as *equivalence* or *tertium comparationis* (Chesterman, 1998). *Tertia comparationis* can be placed at any level of textual organisation, from microlinguistic levels (i.e. phonological, lexical, or syntactic levels) to macrolinguistic levels (i.e. textual).

A useful guide to how contrastivists have understood the notions of equivalence is the work of Krzeszowski (1990). He adopts a taxonomic view of this concept and considers various types of equivalence: statistical equivalence, translation equivalence, system equivalence, semanto-syntactic equivalence, rule equivalence, substantive equivalence, and pragmatic equivalence (for discussions of these different conceptions and how they have evolved over time, see Chesterman, 1998; Moreno, 1996).

It is clear from contrastive analysis and translation theory that the concept of equivalence or *tertium comparationis* is a relative one and that the original idea of *identity* is giving way to the idea of *maximum similarity*. In addition, judgments about what constitutes maximum similarity and how it is to be measured depend on the assessors. Thus, definitions of equivalence (or maximum similarity) will be relative to the theoretical framework in which they are made.

Tertium Comparationis in Contrastive Rhetoric Studies

Tertia comparationis should be defined on the basis of concepts that are comparable cross-culturally and can be established at a variety of levels of analysis. This will imply defining the criteria of comparability (or prototypical features) that will make it possible to establish the constants of the comparison at two major phases of the research: (1) choosing the primary data and (2) establishing comparable textual concepts as constants. Establishing adequate *tertia comparationis* at these two levels will allow contrasts at subsequent levels of the research, namely, at the explicit textual levels.

Selecting primary data for comparison

In quantitative descriptive studies, large data sets are needed. In Kaplan's early study (1966), more than 600 essays were included. Collecting large numbers of texts is important because in descriptive studies it is not possible to manipulate the variables. When texts are collected, they are already products. All the possible variables affecting the production process (i.e. the model, the author, the purpose, the setting, the topic, etc.) are already fixed and cannot be changed. If you change one, you get a different text. All variables, except the independent variables under investigation, need to be constant.

One of the greatest difficulties in the comparison of texts across cultures is the selection of the appropriate texts for comparison. In the study this chapter builds on, Moreno was interested in comparing the use of premise–conclusion signalling devices between Spanish and English. Typical signals of this kind of coherence relation are connectives such as *therefore* and *as a consequence* as well as expressions such as *the results indicate that*. An example from Moreno's corpus shows a premise-conclusion relation between two sentences (not a condition in all premise–conclusion expressions because often causal relations are implicit or span many sentences):

> The average profitability of US industry is higher than that in Japan and Germany, yet American shareholders have consistently achieved no better or lower returns than Japanese (and recently German shareholders). There is thus no simple connection between average corporate returns on investment and long-term shareholder returns, as much conventional wisdom about shareholder value seems to suggest. (Moreno, 1998: 555)

Naturally, Moreno wanted to generalize the results of her research as much as possible. Yet, to control for context, she decided on the genre of the academic research paper. To define the similarity constraint, Moreno argued, following Widdowson (1979), that there is a universal rhetoric of scientific exposition that is structured according to a certain discourse pattern that 'with some tolerance for individual stylistic variation, imposes a conformity on members of the scientific community no matter what language they happen to use' (Widdowson, 1979: 61). So the prototypical feature of *text form* = *scientific exposition* plus the prototypical feature of *genre* = *research article* were the first *tertia comparationis*. On this basis, Moreno chose 36 research articles in each language following conventional sampling procedures.

In addition to establishing a similarity constraint on the basis of the *genre*, Moreno conjectured that the *subject matter* (or *topic*) factor (directly related to a specific academic discipline) might also affect the expression of the phenomenon under comparison. She therefore decided that the two samples of research articles should be balanced in terms of subject matter. Accordingly, the resulting sample in each language/writing culture consisted of 18 research articles about marketing-management and 18 research articles about finance/economics. Thus the prototypical feature *subject-matter* = *business and economics* was used as her second *tertium comparationis* for the design of her corpus in the sense that the two independent samples were made up similarly in this respect.

Thirdly, all research articles in the corpus were assumed to have been written in Spanish or English by expert members of the corresponding academic disciplines as they had been published in some of the most widely-read academic journals on business and economics. This similarity constraint involved the application of another *tertium comparationis* to the selection of Moreno's corpus, that is, the prototypical feature *level of expertise* = *expert writer*.

Finally, although Moreno was looking at the expression of a given text-rhetorical variable in textual material included within the boundaries of complete texts (i.e. a further *tertium comparationis*), she predicted that not all sections of the research article could be considered homogeneous in terms of the frequency of occurrence of the phenomena under comparison. This variability could be due to the text type predominating in each section of the article (see Werlich, 1976). In order to control for this text-rhetorical variable, Moreno decided to balance her two independent corpora on the basis of similarity perceived in relation to the prototypical feature *global superstructure* (see van Dijk & Kintsch, 1983: 54). Thus, 11 research articles in each corpus followed the overall pattern of *Introduction-Procedure-Discussion* and 25 research articles in each corpus showed more variable superstructures: *Problem-Analysis-Solution*; *Situation-Explanation*; *Situation-Analysis-Forecast* and *Problem-Solution-Evaluation*. Table 10.1 includes a list of the similarity constraints in the study.

Table 10.1 Similarity constraints in Moreno's Spanish-English corpus

Tertium comparationis	Value of prototypical feature perceived as constant across both corpora	No of texts in each independent corpus
Text form	Scientific exposition	36
Genre	Research article	36
Mode	Written language	36
Participants: • Writers • Targeted readers	• Researchers, professors and professionals in business and economics • Researchers, professors, advanced students, top executives, politicians	36
Situational variety	Formal	36
Dialectal variety	Standard	36
Tone	Serious	36
Channel	Graphical substance	36
Format features: • Length • Intertextuality • Visual features	• 2000–16,000 words of core text • References to other texts • Graphs, tables, drawings, footnotes, appendixes, typographical distinctions to indicate sections	36
Point of view	Objective	36
Global communicative event	Sharing results from research	36
Setting	Office, library, etc.	36
General purpose of communication	• Writer's viewpoint: To persuade the readers to share the writer's viewpoint • Reader's viewpoint: To improve one's knowledge about a given field of research	36
Global rhetorical strategy	Demonstrating a theory Discussing the advantages of: • Applying a given model • A given business practice Analyzing the reasons for a given situation Proving the accuracy of a prediction Evaluating the solution given to a situation	36
Overall subject matter or topic	Business and economics	36
Academic discipline	• Marketing/management • Economics/finance	18 18

Table 10.1 *continued*

Tertium comparationis	Value of prototypical feature perceived as constant across both corpora	No of texts in each independent corpus
Level of Expertise	Expert writers	36
Textual unit of analysis	Complete texts	36
Global superstructure	Introduction-procedure-discussion	11
	More variable superstructures • Problem-Analysis-Solution • Situation-Explanation • Situation-Analysis-Forecast • Problem-Solution-Evaluation	25
Predominant text types (depending on the focus of each section in the superstructure of the article)	Argumentation Exposition Description	36

Adapted from Moreno, 1996: 162

Establishing textual constants for qualitative equivalence

Having established similarity constraints for the design of the comparable parallel corpora, Moreno's study assumed that both Spanish and English language users employ the conceptual category of premise–conclusion to interpret and express coherence relations. This category is situated on the plane of suprapropositional meaning and allows for the interpretation of discourse segments above and beyond the semantic interpretation. This conceptual category is functional or pragma-discursive since it is defined contextually and is independent of concrete textual realizations.

Finally, after pragma-discursive equivalence (or similarity) was established as the qualitative *tertium comparationis* or prototype that helped to define the constants at linguistic levels of analysis, Moreno proposed the next concept, that of statistical equivalence. According to Krzeszowski (1981), qualitative contrastive analyses alone cannot produce useful results. Instead, they must be reinforced with quantitative contrastive analyses that investigate the relative frequencies of equivalent phenomena. Originally proposed by Becka (1978) for stylistic contrastive analyses, statistical equivalence allows the researcher to determine the equivalence of two groups of phenomena belonging to the same qualitative category if their relative frequencies do not display statistically significant differences.

Moreno's contrastive examination showed that both language groups seemed to make the premise-conclusion pattern explicit with similar frequency. So, the phenomena under comparison displayed not only qualitative but also statistical equivalence.

Deciding on textual variables

Once the constants have been established on the basis of similarity judgments in relation to given qualitative categories (such as *coherence relation = premise–conclusion*) at a given level of analysis (e.g. *discourse coherence*), it is important to decide carefully which explicit textual variables to use in the subsequent quantitative analysis.

It must be stressed that the variables should be formulated according to a common theoretical framework that provides appropriate objective tools for analyzing textual material from the two languages. This is a difficult stage in contrastive rhetoric research because the descriptions of similar phenomena available in the two languages are likely to have used different theoretical frameworks, and may not be compatible. So, the task of the researcher is to choose or design tailor-made tools to apply to the analysis of the two rhetorical systems independently. In her study, Moreno built up an elaborate taxonomy of premise–conclusion signaling devices. Instead of relying on pre-existing taxonomies of coherence, she developed a system specifically for the study of premise–conclusion at the intersentential level of texts. Four levels of similarity constraints or *tertia comparationis* were established, dealing with issues such as the directionality of the causal relation (anaphoric or cataphoric), whether the expression is modified (i.e. hedged) or not, etc. The taxonomy was used to classify every case of premise–conclusion signalling device in the two comparable corpora. In this way, it was possible to juxtapose phenomena meeting the same criteria in order to search for similarities and differences.

The application of Moreno's contrastive model led to the determination of one area of great similarity between the Anglo-American and the Spanish writing cultures. Contrary to initial expectations, the use of signalling devices to express premise-conclusion in the particular rhetorical context of the research article proved to be very similar in both languages; that is, the same qualitative categories were identified after the analysis of the two corpora. Moreover, those strategies appeared similarly distributed, showing no statistically significant differences except in the distribution of integrated anaphoric signals. In other words, the two writing cultures used similar textual strategies to express premise-conclusion both qualitatively and quantitatively at the textual level. However, there were differences on the interpersonal plane, pointing to different conceptions of what is an appropriate rhetorical attitude and interactive tenor for offering claims to the academic community. Overall, Spanish academics seemed to hedge their conclusions less frequently than English academics, suggesting that Spanish writers tend to show greater conviction and confidence in expressing their claims.

Conclusion: Toward a Model of Contrastive Rhetoric Research Methodology

Moreno's (1998) cross-cultural study of premise–conclusion in research articles has been used in this chapter to demonstrate the importance of the concept of *tertium comparationis* in empirical contrastive rhetoric studies. In Moreno's study, the relational category of premise–conclusion was chosen as the conceptual category, which was studied in two comparable parallel corpora. Explicit textual variables were chosen and applied to the two corpora independently, and quantitative analyses were compared to establish similarities and differences between the two languages. Equivalences (or *tertia comparationis*) were created at a variety of levels including selecting data, establishing qualitative textual constants, and determining the explicit taxonomy for quantitative textual analysis. These strict *tertia comparationis* allowed Moreno to juxtapose taxonomies and contrast the quantitative results for comparable qualitative categories. After interpreting quantitative similarities and differences through statistical analysis, Moreno was able to draw conclusions about the comparative results.

Equally strict *tertia comparationis* should apply in other contrastive studies. Following Moreno's other work (1996, 1997), which dealt with other relational categories such as cause–effect, we could compare other relational categories such as concession, enumeration, and opposition, until we cover all possible explicit coherence relations. We would then be contributing substantially to the descriptive characterisation of genres across languages. In addition, we could study rhetorical features such as audience awareness in texts across cultures. Similarly, other genres could be chosen for comparison, including the grant proposal or the application letter.

On the level of design, one implication for further contrastive analyses in this area of rhetoric is that their *tertia comparationis* should be based on functional meaning rather than on formal criteria. For example, if Moreno had restricted the comparison of premise–conclusion metatext to only connectives – a formal criterion – she would have left out of the analysis almost 50% of the resources available in each language to express a broadly similar functional–relational category.

On the level of methodology, Moreno's approach could be used to match comparable corpora in other genres. For instance, matching two corpora of grant proposals from two languages for contrastive research could be justified on the basis that both sets of texts are judged as similar in relation to the prototypical features included in the following definition: global units (*tertium comparationis* 1) belonging to the grant proposal genre (*tertium comparationis* 2) with the global communicative purpose of applying for funds to carry out research (*tertium comparationis* 3) (see Connor & Mauranen, 1999).

Another possible application would consist of matching two sets of 'moves' in comparable cross-cultural corpora. For example, one could compare closing evaluations in book reviews from two languages on the basis that both sets of textual units are judged as similar in relation to the prototypical features contained in the following definition: move units (*tertium comparationis* 1) belonging to the book review genre (*tertium comparationis* 2) with the purpose of evaluating the reviewed book in order to recommend it or not (*tertium comparationis* 3) (see Motta-Roth, 1998). Similarity constraints would be defined in two comparable corpora in relation to the global communicative purpose (*tertium comparationis* 3) of a given textual unit (*tertium comparationis* 1) belonging to a particular genre (*tertium comparationis* 2) if those *tertia comparationis* were considered relevant in shaping the type of rhetorical phenomena under comparison, including their frequency of occurrence.

To sum up, the approach to contrastive rhetoric methodology we propose for parallel corpora would consist of the following steps:

(1) Formulating clear hypotheses about the relationship between writing cultures and how textual meanings are expressed.
(2) Defining the population of expert L1 texts that can be considered comparable and specifying the basis for the similarity constraints.
(3) Selecting a representative sample of the population in each writing culture being compared.
(4) Identifying comparable textual units, e.g. (a) moves such as *establishing the territory* or *creating a niche*; (b) discourse functions such as *defining* or *evaluating*; (c) pragmatic functions such as *requesting* or *apologizing*; and (d) relational functions (i.e. coherence relations such as *cause-effect* or *claim-support*).
(5) Validating those units of analysis as functional or pragma-discursive units recognizable by language users in each culture either through literature review or further research (e.g. through interviews with L1 informants). This verification would allow the researcher to propose these units as language/textual universals, which can be taken as qualitative constants for the two languages compared and allow juxtaposition of comparable rhetorical phenomena.
(6) Quantifying the occurrence of these textual universals in each corpus. This step would allow the researcher to propose categories as quantitative constants if they occur with similar frequency in both languages.
(7) Devising objective criteria to describe the textual realizations of the universals proposed in the two languages. This phase would imply

designing specific criteria that do not privilege one language over the other. In other words, the criteria should not be biased toward any particular descriptive model of one of the languages compared.
(8) Applying the devised analytical criteria to the description of the two corpora independently.
(9) Juxtaposing the taxonomies.
(10) Contrasting the quantitative results for each comparable qualitative category.
(11) Interpreting the significance of quantitative similarities and differences through statistical analysis.
(12) Drawing conclusions about the relationship between writing cultures and how textual meanings are expressed on the basis of the comparative results.

The methodology discussed in this chapter applies to contrastive studies using parallel corpora in any two languages. Such parallel corpora are needed if there is no previous empirical research or proven theory concerning similarities and differences in linguistic/rhetorical structures in a given genre between the two languages and cultures. That was the case in Moreno's study. However, when such baseline comparisons are available, it is also possible for contrastive rhetoricians to design studies using translation and learner corpora, and the work of Krzeszowski (1990) and Chesterman (1998) is especially helpful in formulating appropriate *tertia comparationis*. Clearly, *tertia comparationis* are still needed for many languages and genres.

Acknowledgement

Ana Moreno's contribution to this chapter is part of a research project financed by the Spanish Ministry of Science and Technology (Plan Nacional de I+D+I (2000–2003), Ref: BFF2001–0112), entitled 'Contrastive Analysis and Specialized English Spanish Translation: Applications and Tools (ACTRES).'

Chapter 11
Structure and Style in the Narrative Writings of Mexican-American and African-American Adolescents

ANN DAUBNEY-DAVIS AND GENEVIEVE PATTHEY-CHAVEZ

While a number of cross-cultural discourse studies have examined the language and literacy uses of both African-American and Mexican-American children (Ball, 1992; Edelsky, 1986; Heath, 1983; Michaels, 1981; Vasquez *et al.*, 1994), far less attention has been paid to the evolution of their language use in adolescence. This remains the case despite the fact that many of these adolescents are educationally at-risk and despite explanations of academic underachievement that stress discontinuities between home cultures and the mainstream American culture dominant in school (for an exception, see Montaño-Harmon, 1988). Very few (if any) studies compare the written discourse of African-American and Mexican-American students who share the same classrooms. Yet such studies would be important with respect to theories of minority school achievement (Banks, 1995; Heath, 1995) and practical educational issues since this situation is a common one in many American cities.

This study explores the structure and discourse features of the narrative writing of a group of urban Mexican-American and African-American 7th graders. Through a contrastive examination of their written stories and their classroom environment and discourse patterns, three points are made:

(1) commonly-used frameworks for narrative analysis must invoke a theory of literary style if they are to produce valid representations and conceptualizations of older children's written narrative;
(2) an understanding of the role of convention, structure, and style in narrative discourse can be used to highlight contrasts in the classroom writing of these students; and
(3) these contrasts, based only partially in culture, need to be examined further in light of the classroom discourse of these students and their teachers. The methodology involves comparing the written texts of Mexican-American 7th graders with those of their African-American

classmates, using a social and cognitive approach to text analysis and carrying out extended observations of the students in their classroom.

Why Narrative?

The importance of expository writing in later schooling is a cultural artifact, and hardly up for negotiation (Applebee, 1981), though it is not without its critics (DiPardo, 1990; Hymes & Cazden, 1980). The present study, however, privileges narrative writing. The chosen writing task was meant to be typical of the classroom – not typical of an achievement test. It was meant to be something that was conceptually familiar and could come from self-selected content and without much outside help. Written narrative is familiar to 7th graders: creative writing and writing about personal experience or about characters in literature are familiar writing experiences for students of this age, and all are narrative, or predominantly so. In addition, the writing task needs to be seen as an important activity. Despite our cultural bias toward expository writing during the educational process, we are not so narrowly biased against narrative in other contexts. Admittedly, as students progress to high school, personal narrative is demoted as exposition is elevated in status (Applebee, 1981; DiPardo, 1990). However, narrative skill, if not the school-sponsored practice of it, remains a significant writing activity in the 'real world' of reports, plans, explanations, complaints, and presentations. Moreover, it frequently forms an important component of successful expository writing, and it remains a path through which children reach other knowledge, including expository knowledge.

The bias in school curricula and in writing research toward exposition and away from narration has led us to ignore the intellectual and artistic development of many young writers. Yet written narration is a fertile genre for research because it is, as Jacobs (1985) puts it, the 'perfect game.' It is easy to learn, but hard to play. Exposition, on the other hand, is both hard to learn *and* hard to play. Researching only the expository writing of traditionally lower-achieving groups thus leaves out those writers who lack expository knowledge and practice. Narration is a skill that everyone brings to school, albeit with important cultural variations. In addition, narrative is not just a reflective discourse instrument, but an organic, culture-forming one. Through the telling of narrative, we continually reflect and shape our discourse community as well as our membership of it (Ochs, 1988; Scollon & Scollon, 1981). Researchers of expository writing eschew narrative *because* of its universality; it is seen as less taxing cognitively, a strategy fallen back upon to avoid the expository (Bereiter & Scardamalia, 1987). However, it could be argued that this very universal quality also makes narration a genre in which young writers can develop, not only narrative skills (such as audience sensitivity and the evaluation of experience), but also an individual persona, including writing skill and style. What makes narration especially interesting is how some young writers go beyond its basic requirements.

Our work follows applied linguistic research on narrative in that it examines multiple dimensions in narrative writing (focusing on structure, convention, and style) and acknowledges the social and cognitive underpinnings of each. A purely cognitively-based model of narrative is inadequate for dealing with variation in spoken and written narrative (Dyson, 1989; Freedman, 1987; Hicks, 1990; Peterson & McCabe, 1983; Tannen, 1982). Instead, the issues of convention and creativity need to be examined from both cognitive and social perspectives in order to say something useful about the nature of, and the processes involved in, writing narrative in school settings.

The Contrastive Framework

The comparison of narrative writing by Mexican-American and African-American 7th graders situates this work in a contrastive framework. The contrastive premise proposes that primary discourse patterns and literacy practices influence the school writing of children and their literacy education in general (Heath, 1983; Michaels, 1981). An inherent challenge for work in this framework is to guard against reducing culture to a group-level variable, thereby disguising within-group variation or masking important similarities across groups (Atkinson, 1999; Reese, 2002). Cross-cultural researchers caution against stereotyping and argue for a view of culture as dynamic and continuously constructed by members, not as collections of fixed traits or attributes passed down from one generation to another (Banks, 1995; Scollon & Scollon, 1981). Nevertheless, cross-cultural research is often transformed into collections of group characteristics that in turn feed back into essentialist and usually negative stereotypes of 'others' already in circulation (Borofsky, 1994; García, 1995). Our results provide ample evidence against such distortions of cross-cultural work, and bring into focus the formative cross-cultural influence of school as an institution, an influence that has already been noted nationally (Eckert, 1989; Patthey-Chavez, 1993) and internationally (Alexander, 2000).

The study of children's writing can reveal both home and school influences on different levels. One is the morphemic/syntactic level, not of great interest to the text linguist. Another involves the text-forming features of cohesion and coherence. Yet another is the significance and location of literacy for the writer and her primary discourse community as compared to her secondary one, that is, the literary community of school and mainstream society at large. There are also the features of genre, for example, what a good story is like for a certain discourse community. The use of genre, writing conventions, original or inventive language, and other narrative elements in a student's writing provides clues about the writer's position with respect to the writing task and perhaps her involvement or interest in school tasks in general. This orientation rests entirely within the realm of contrastive rhetoric studies, broadly conceived.

Contrastive Studies

Montaño-Harmon's 1988 study of expository writing among 9th grade Mexican-Americans remains one of the few that have examined the writings of Mexican-American adolescents. She concluded that their writing style could be distinguished from that of Mexican adolescents, both for those in Mexican schools and those who had recently moved from Mexico and were in the middle of an ESL program. Other studies of Mexican-American language and literacy socialization have focused on younger children, as have most ethnographic studies of African-American children, at the expense of the later development of more mature forms and genres. Still, language and literacy socialization research has led to some important insights about the preferences of each group. It has also led to an important model of literacy practices and preferences usually taken for granted in mainstream US society.

Scollon and Scollon (1981) were perhaps the first to elaborate a model of what they termed 'essayist' literacy in contrast to a different pattern of language use in evidence among Athabaskan Indian groups in Alaska. They found the function and form of self-display crucial in forming early and distinct orientations toward literacy, and characterized essayist literacy, the mainstream form taught in US schools, in the following manner:

> The ideal essayist text is an explicit, decontextualized presentation of a view of the world that fictionalizes both author and audience. There is a high level of new information and the internal structure is cohesive and clearly bounded. (Scollon & Scollon, 1981: 52)

This crucial emphasis on self-display was found to be dispreferred by Athabaskans, to whom Anglo-English speakers appeared to be '[talking] like a book' in a relentless monologue. Because of the difference in the role of self-display between Anglo-English speakers and Athabaskans, especially in situations where an individual is a novice, young, or an outsider, communications between the two could become strained and, in the case of school, educationally challenging.

In a review of language-socialization fieldwork done among Mexican-American and Chinese-American families, Heath (1986) contrasted the extent to which children were included in adult talk and in interactions outside of the family, the explicitness demanded of the child in family talk, how children's questions were tolerated, and the function of American middle-class family discourse patterns such as recounting the day at school, reading stories, and discussing future plans. According to Heath (see also Vasquez *et al.*, 1994), the Mexican-American families provided rich verbal environments for children, surrounding them constantly with many adult figures as well as other children. However, children were seldom asked to perform prototypical school tasks such as repeating facts and foretelling plans. Another school genre, recounting information or an event to a listener who already knows the information, was also rare in the Mexican-American data, as was explaining the steps an individual would take to do something (i.e. event-casting). Further, children did not tend to initiate conversations with elders. While stories were important and common in family and group gatherings, they were rarely addressed directly to children. Young children were not initiated into storytelling through guided practice and display of their abilities. Instruction happened more by way of example and observation than by verbal plans and recitation of known information. In addition, story books specifically for children were not common in the homes of the families observed.[1]

In contrast, ethnographic studies of African-American communities find 'display' texts – using Pratt's (1977) term – to be a feature of the discourse community. In the context of narrative, at least, exaggeration and personal success are likely features. Self-aggrandizement in narrative is not only condoned, but expected (Gilmore, 1986; Heath, 1983; Kochman, 1981; Labov, 1972b). A long and distinguished history of oratory in African-American culture (Delpit, 1995; Smitherman, 1977) finds itself reflected in the spoken word performances of adolescent gatherings, where narrative skill and verbal felicity are highly valued. It is true that, in the early school years, the 'topic-associating' style of African-American children with its reduced need for tight cohesive marking and its non-linear qualities, often challenge audiences with more mainstream expectations (Cazden, 1988; Michaels, 1981). However, as Heath (1995) has pointed out repeatedly, the same features that challenge elementary school teachers are highly rated in contemporary literature as 'experimental' and 'avant-garde.'

In summary, discourse-level differences may well lead to contrasts and potential conflicts between primary (home) and secondary (school) discourses, not just at the sentence level but at the textual level as well. While classroom research has demonstrated some effects of these differences for early primary school, little discourse-level research has been done on writing, especially in the case of urban minorities such as Mexican-Americans and African-Americans. Comparative studies of school writing are one way of looking at differences, and schools with mixed minority groups matched for socioeconomic status (SES) provide an opportunity to do this. The aim of the present work is to examine older children's classroom writing in detail, to see if suggested contrasts are borne out in a community of Mexican-American and African-American students, and to understand these data in light of the school community in which they were produced.

Method

Setting

Student writings were collected in five 7th grade classrooms in an urban middle school in a large metropolitan area. The community was mainly working class and low-income. According to a grant application written by teachers and administrators at the school, more than 55% of the students came from families receiving government assistance, and the school had the highest percentage of 'at-risk' middle-school students in the district. The racial make-up of the student body was 41% Hispanic, 34% African-American, and 15% Caucasian.

Data

Initially, one classroom was observed for one week, at the end of which a personal narrative was written by the students in class.[2] The prompt was: 'Write a story about someone or something that got lost.' These narratives were personal, personal-imaginative, and purely imaginative, since the students were told that they could tell a true story, exaggerate the truth, or make-up the story if they wanted to. The topic was introduced by the researcher (Daubney-Davis) using a prepared protocol, which included the group brainstorming together on the topic. A language use survey was also administered in order to identify Mexican-American and African-American students and to group the former according to their educational history and get a sense of their self-reported use of English and Spanish.[3] The survey was also used to remove any ESL students from this group. On the basis of the survey, a Mexican-American student was defined as (1) having attended US schools since kindergarten, and (2) identifying himself as Mexican, Mexican-American, or Chicano.[4]

Another set of written data was collected 18 months later at the same school. The primary data were again written narratives of personal experience, this time assigned in four 7th grade classrooms by the students' regular teachers. The topic and writing assignment protocol was uniform in principle and agreed upon through extensive discussions with participating teachers. Each teacher led the students through a pre-writing/writing process that extended over part or all of class on three days. The topic was to write a story about 'something really important that happened to you in the past year.'

In addition to obtaining the primary data, the researcher observed and participated in one of the classrooms for 15 weeks. During this period, most of the written work done by the students in this 'focus' class was also collected for later analysis. Given the nature of the school, the students, and the realities of day-to-day life for these 7th graders, it was not surprising that, of the 114 students identified for the study in the four classes, only 70 actually wrote the personal narrative. Following Labov (1972b; see also Labov & Walezky, 1967; Peterson & McCabe, 1983; McCabe & Peterson, 1990), a narrative was defined as a text that minimally included two related past-time events. The definition was expanded somewhat in two ways: (1) to allow for texts that narrated future plans that had not transpired when the text was written, and (2) to include descriptive sequences based on a past event but focusing more on setting and evaluative comment than on telling what happened. Applying these criteria led to further data reduction, with a final data set of 57 narratives, 24 written by Mexican-American students, and 33 by their African-American peers.

Measures

Text length

Measures of text length were selected and adapted from prior discourse analysis of narratives and written language development. First, word counts were generated using each writer's word divisions, even if these were nonstandard (e.g. fusing *kindof* or separating *a nother*). Texts were also divided into clause units, the basic unit of narrative/text analysis. For comparison purposes, all counts were either normed to 100 words of text or converted to a proportional ratio. Because of the unequal sample size for the two groups, simple regressions were used to assess the extent to which any of the discursive variables could be tied to group membership (classified as a dichotomous variable).

Written language conventions and subordination

The extent to which each text adhered to written language conventions was assessed categorially. Five conventions of school writing were noted: paragraph division, indentation of the first line of paragraphs, the provision of a title written at the top of the first page, repetitions of the prompt, and obligatory punctuation. None of these conventional features of writing were discussed specifically in class during the pre-writing process. The students' control of sentence-end punctuation was assessed by setting a criterion of control with two-thirds of obligatory contexts punctuated. Finally, the students' use of subordination was assessed because of prior research linking increased use of subordination to written language development over time (McCutchen & Perfetti, 1982; Tannen, 1982; Peterson & McCabe, 1983).

Cohesion and coherence

Following Halliday and Hasan (1976), a selective analysis of cohesion focused on lexical and phrasal repetition, pronoun anaphora, and syntactic conjunction. Tense-marking was eliminated from this analysis because it could not be determined if tense-shifts reflected a lack of control, common spoken pronunciations for the population, or even a stylistic choice. For repetition, a lexical cohesion total included all lexical and phrasal repetitions.[5] The figure for synonymy for each paper was the sum of all synonymous expressions, excluding the original term in each chain. Personal anaphora included subject and object pronouns (no possessives) and, together with demonstratives, these constituted the total anaphora figure for each text. In addition, any indeterminate or confusing anaphoric reference was noted for qualitative analysis. The conjunction analysis recorded six categories (based on Halliday & Hasan, 1976): (1) additive (e.g. *and, and then, also, plus*; (2) contrastive (e.g. *but, but then, but soon*); (3) temporal (e.g. *after that, then, one day, until now*); (4) cause/result (e.g. *so, so then*); (5) enumerative/general-particular (e.g. *first, the most of it*), and (6) other (e.g. *well*). In addition, a separate count of coordinating conjunctions was recorded for each text.

Strictly speaking, Halliday and Hasan (1976) do not classify subordinating devices as cohesive, since such devices are syntactically motivated, that is, constitutive of a syntactic choice, namely the process of subordination. On the other hand, Halliday and Hasan explain that their category of 'conjunction' is cohesive because its use is a semantically or rhetorically motivated choice. However, these 7th grade writers often used subordinators such as *because* and *after* to orient what otherwise appears to be an independent clause. Further, their logical connectors tended to fall into two categories: coordinating conjunctions and subordinators. The other conjunctions (conjunctive adverbs, e.g. *however, therefore, on the other hand*) were rare, except in the category of time expressions. Categories of subordinating conjunctions were: (1) temporal (e.g. *when, before, after*); (2) causal: (e.g. *because, cause, since*); (3) conditional (e.g. *if*); and (4) contrastive (e.g. *even though*).

The texts were also read for coherence but with a focus only on problematic clausal relations. Examining the full range of categories of logical relations among clauses found in expository writing – namely, additive, contrastive, enumerative, example, detail, and cause–effect (Montaño-Harmon, 1988) – often does not make sense for narrative, where the development is chronological and descriptive and the norms of writer/reader responsibility are often deliberately violated. However, two general categories based on Montaño-Harmon (1988) were used to identify major problems with coherence: logical shifts and deviations. A logical shift is a contradiction of fact that could not otherwise be explained. A deviation refers to a clause or clauses that deviate from the narrative, are tangential to the topic, or miscue the audience. Occurrences of these two types of clausal relations were recorded for each text. Ultimately, both logical shifts and deviations proved to be rare in these data.

Stance marking

Clause-internal stance marking was examined by identifying individual words and phrases that had an evaluative function (Biber & Finegan, 1989). Stance-markers have been grouped into intensifiers (*all*, *big*), qualifiers (*so*, *very*), evidentials (*probably*), affect markers (*nice*), and comparators (*never*, *barely*): these categories were adopted for this analysis. Because stance marking in texts is still an exploratory area, the goal was to find a subset of consistent stance markers. More complete analyses of these subcategories of stance can be found in Biber *et al.* (1998) and Precht (2003).

Narrative structure

The narrative structure analysis followed the models proposed by Labov (1972b; see also Labov & Walezky, 1967; Peterson & McCabe, 1983). Six prototypical elements of narrative (or 'functional categories') were identified: abstract/prologue, orientation, event, evaluation, resolution, and coda. Each text was divided into narrative clauses, defined as all independent clauses, subordinate clauses introduced by subordinate conjunctions, and clauses in either indirect or direct speech. Each clause was then assigned to a functional category and the number of narrative clauses contributing to each of the six functional categories for each text was recorded. Although functional categories are to some extent chronologically ordered, orientation, event, and evaluation can occur at any point in a narrative.

In analyzing the functional structure in narratives, five major categories of phrases and clauses were counted as well as total number of words for each functional category. Table 11.1 provides examples from the students' texts.

Qualitative stylistic analysis

Quantitative comparisons were complemented by a more qualitative analysis of a subset of 17 narratives, 7 written by Mexican-American students and 10 by African-American students. The qualitative analysis focused on stylistic features that could not be readily quantified, though differences in the deployment of key features could be recovered from the quantitative comparisons. The results reported for stylistic analysis are, admittedly, exploratory in nature. However, they provide important insights into student writing variation that is supported by social factors introduced in the review of the literature. The stylistic categories used in this paper (perspective, pattern, and devices) all reflect ways of examining

Table 11.1 Definitions and examples of functional categories of narrative structure

Definitions	Examples
Abstracts: Briefly summarize or introduce the narrative by means of some generalization (a, d) or prologue (b, c).	(a) The last time I felt sad was when my mom got into a accident. (b) I have a sister I never saw before but I knew one day will be the big day to see her. (c) Well I have a story to tell you about my Great grandmother. Here we go. It start like this. (d) Something bad happened to me this year with school. I got an F-U in Math for what reason I really don't know.
Orientation clauses Provide background, describing places, people, or environments away from the narrative time-line. Orientation clauses may use stative verbs or be marked as past perfect or past continuous.	(a) So one day my mom was waiting for a phone call. (b) ... and my mom and dad was in the house sleep. (c) On Friday afternoon I was riding with my mom. We were going to Maple and Orange Blvd. to the gas station. (d) But I had found a jacket on the bus...
Event clauses Tell the event. A clause marking a narrative climax is referred to as the 'high point.' Event clauses following a high point are 'resolution clauses.'	(a) So I got a ladder and I climbed. (b) ... so my mother went to the store and then my sister called and then I got to talk to her. (c) ... all of a sudden this girl stepped into the street and this drunk driver hit her...
Evaluation clauses Mark the significance of events and tell about mental states of narrator or other characters. Such clauses relate mental states, emotions, judgments, speculations, and comments addressed either to narrator (self-address) or to the implied reader (audience-address).	(a) ... and I dont like her at all that much cause she likes to pick on me all the time. (b) My sister never told me until now. (c) It was exciting. (d) The Phoenix Suns were awesome. (e) Well, I'm so sorry that I can't go to summer school. (f) I will never forget her. (g) I was so hurt that my eyes burned.
Codas Provide an ending. Such clauses range from a 'quick-exit' clause (a), to more or less formulaic codas repeating the topic (b), to invoking a genre (c), or to comments on the narrative or a link between the narrative and the present (d).	(a) Well, that's it I got to write. (b) and that was the last time I was SAD. (c) And they lived happily ever after. (d) After that I never ever went back in there again.

the impact of socialization practices of local communities on students who are then expected to perform in way sanctioned by schools (as institutions of the wider culture).

Statistical comparisons

Since most of the variables involved frequency counts, group-differences were explored using statistical analysis. Due to the non-parametric nature of the data and the uneven sample sizes, the analysis proceeded from a discriminant analysis that tested whether all variables distinguished between the two groups to simple regressions and Spearman Rank Correlations for individual variables. Only significant results are reported. The discriminant analysis did not distinguish between groups, indicating that overall, the two groups of writers could not be distinguished according to their language use. Only a few of the variables reliably predicted group-membership.

Results

Similarities: Written language conventions, narrative structure, and lexical evaluation

Few of the discourse variables discriminated reliably between Mexican-American and African-American writers. Where significant differences were found, they are noted throughout the results section. Table 11.2 summarizes the word and clause counts for each data set, and also shows that each group produced narratives of equivalent length with similar standard deviations. Writers from both groups used most written language conventions similarly. They also tended to order their narratives into equivalent functional narrative elements and deployed lexical evaluation elements (e.g. evidentials) at similar rates. Only in the areas of subordination, cohesion, and stylistics did the two groups diverge sufficiently to approach statistical significance. The measures used in our analysis suggest that writers from both groups – who, after all, had attended the same schools – had learned similar lessons about the conventions of writing.

Table 11.2 Mean length of narratives

Measure	Mexican-American		African-American	
	Mean	Std Dev.	Mean	Std Dev.
Words	153	74	143	74
Clauses	18	9.8	16	9.4

Table 11.3 Written language conventions

Convention	Mexican-American		African-American	
	Mean	Std Dev.	Mean	Std Dev.
Paragraph division	0.12	0.34	0.27	0.45
Indentation	0.71	0.46	0.70	0.47
Title	0.71	0.46	0.64	0.49
Prompt-repetition	0.33	0.48	0.33	0.48
Punctuation	0.50	0.51	0.61	0.50
Total conventions	2.38	1.01	2.49	1.25

Counts were standardized to n occurrences per 100 words

Table 11.3 provides an overview of each group's use of five written language conventions: paragraph division, indentations, titles, repetitions of the prompt, and obligatory punctuation. These conventions were coded categorically as present or absent, with the exception of punctuation, which was coded as present when a writer used punctuation in at least two thirds of obligatory contexts. Except for paragraph division, writers from both groups adhered to these conventions at very similar rates, with an overall per-text average of 2.4 for Mexican-Americans and 2.5 for African-Americans. Relatively high standard deviations for both groups also indicate that convention use was uneven across writers. On the whole, writers tended not to indent their paragraphs, but to use titles. Their command of punctuation appears to be emerging, with about half the writers in either group using obligatory punctuation correctly two-thirds or more of the time.

In addition to adhering to written language conventions at similar rates, writers from both groups also tended to organize their narratives in similar ways. They devoted equivalent proportions of their clauses to prologues, orientations, and events. Noticeable differences emerged in the use of evaluation clauses and resolutions, but these were not statistically significant and would not reliably discriminate between the two groups. However, Mexican-American narratives read more like event-reports and tended to group event-clauses whereas African-American narratives alternated between event and evaluation clauses, creating an impression of greater evaluation and stance-marking. These impressionistic differences in emphasis will be explored further in the qualitative analysis. Table 11.4 presents the result of the narrative structure analysis, repeating some examples from Table 11.1 for illustrative purposes.

Despite this emergent difference in their use of evaluation clauses, the students appeared to share similar preferences in their use of lexical or embedded evaluation. Table 11.5 displays each group of writers' mean use

Table 11.4 Narrative structures

Measure	Examples	Mexican-American		African-American	
		Mean	Std Dev.	Mean	Std Dev.
Prologue/ abstract	The last time I felt sad was when my mom got into a accident.	0.09	0.11	0.09	0.08
Orientation	So one day my mom was waiting for a phone call	0.24	0.15	0.24	0.12
Event[a]	...all of a sudden this girl stepped into the street and this drunk driver hit her...	0.28	0.17	0.26	0.2
Evaluation[b]	and I don't like her at all that much cause she like to pick on me...	0.27	0.17	0.34	0.17
Resolution	I will never forget her.	0.06	0.09	0.03	0.06

Counts were converted to a proportional ratio of text.
a = impressionistic emphasis in M-A narratives;
b = impressionistic emphasis in A-A narratives

of intensifiers, qualifiers and evidentials, lexical expressions of affect or causality, and comparative terms, including use of metaphoric language, all of which are examples of lexical stance markers. Both groups use similar rates across all categories, with a cumulative overall frequency of 10.2 for Mexican-Americans and 10.5 for African-Americans. Table 11.5 once again includes earlier examples for illustrative purposes.

Table 11.5 Lexical or embedded stance markers

Measure	Examples	Mexican-American		African-American	
		Mean	Std Dev.	Mean	Std Dev.
Intensifiers	Quantifiers (*all, many, all over*), correlatives (*great big*), repetition (*we got in trouble, big trouble*), onomatopoeia (*It went bam!*), graphics (*It went BAM!*)	1.62	1.35	1.73	1.31
Qualifiers & evidentials	Adverbs (*so very, really*), hedges (*pretty good*), evidentials	1.25	1.36	1.39	1.27
Affect & causal	Mental and emotional states, guesses and judgments (*fortunately, nice, lousy*), compulsion words (*He made me do it*)	5.75	4.33	5.79	2.85
Comparators	Negative comparatives (*no one not, never, nothing*), adverbs (*hardly, barely, almost, nearly*), metaphorical language	2.00	1.75	1.94	1.52

It seems likely that at least some of the similarities in written language use across groups are the result of similar learning experiences. Mexican-American texts were specifically elicited from students who had been educated in the US since kindergarten. For most of them, this US education came from the district that currently served them. The same district had also served most of their African-American peers for most of their schooling. Along with learning the same written language conventions, students from both groups also appeared to have learned a similar prototypical narrative form. Although the similarities in lexical evaluation cannot be tied to schooling quite so readily, they hint at a common vocabulary that could have developed in the common arena of primary school. At the same time, school socializations similarities do not eliminate all group differences. The differences reported below suggest that, underlying the common writing conventions, there remain distinct understandings of how to tell a good story.

Differences: Cohesion and style

Differences between groups did emerge with respect to other linguistic features, specifically with measures of cohesion and style. As shown in Table 11.6, Mexican-Americans consistently used more cohesive features in their narratives than did African-Americans. Their greater use of these features reaches statistical significance with lexical repetition, conjunctions, and subordination. In simple regressions, these three variables discriminated reliably between groups ($F=13.4$ and $p<0.01$ for lexical repetition; $F=7.7$ and $p<0.01$ for use of all conjunctions; $F=4.6$ and $p<0.05$ for use of subordination). Only one feature is used more frequently by African-Americans than by their Mexican-American peers: the switch to the historical present for a 'surprise ending.' Six of the African-American writers used such a device compared to only one Mexican-American writer. As already indicated above, though logical shifts were monitored, they only occurred in three of the 57 narratives, two written by Mexican-American students and one written by an African-American student.

Differences between groups in the use of cohesion are consistent with findings from ethnographic research to date. Michaels' early research (1981) identified what she termed a 'topic-associating' style among African-American children, and Cazden (1988) later established that 'topic-associating' narratives are heard differently by European-American and African-American listeners. The former have trouble following the thread of the stories, and often qualify them as 'incoherent.' The latter, on the other hand, have no trouble understanding the stories. Such differences are consistent with different requirements for cohesive marking, with African-Americans requiring fewer cohesive cues than members of other groups. It

Structure and Style in Narrative Writings

Table 11.6 Cohesion and coherence

Measure	Examples	Mexican-American		African-American	
		Mean	Std Dev.	Mean	Std Dev.
Lexical repetition*	Lexical and phrasal repetition	11.96	4.92	7.76	3.74
Anaphora	Personal anaphora including subject and object pronouns, demonstratives	7.38	3.60	6.52	3.83
Conjunction*	Additive (*and, and then, also, plus*), temporal-spatial (*after that, then, one day, until now*), contrastive (*but, but then, but soon*), cause-result (*so, so then*), enumerative/general/particular (*first, the most of it*)	7.37	3.08	5.24	2.72
Historical present	'Surprise ending'	0.04	0.20	0.21	0.42
Topic logical shift	Tangential material	0.08	0.28	0.03	0.17
Subordination*	Subclauses	3.17	3.35	1.79	1.31

Counts standardized to n occurrences per 100 words; * = $p<0.05$

therefore makes senses that African-American adolescents would use fewer cohesive cues in their narratives.

The analysis thus far may be broadly conceptualized using a linear approach to narrative in that it examined specific aspects of textuality (Halliday & Hasan, 1989): a definition of 'minimal narrative' based on chronological sequence and cohesion from one clause to another. However, the narrative writing of adolescent students necessarily include social markers in their writing that cannot be reduced to easily to lexico-syntactic features. If one considers the progressive construction of a narrative by the audience/reader, other dimensions of language use come to attention. In particular, stylistic devices such as explicit expressions of stance and the use of literary-poetic patterns and devices assume some prominence. African-American writers used consistently more of these stylistic features than their Mexican-American peers.

Table 11.7 presents exploratory feature counts for such expressions of style as sarcasm, addressing the reader, patterned repetition,[6] and imagery. While such categories will be open to greater variation and interpretation with respect to feature counts, they nonetheless provide an important alternative lens for analyzing students' constructions of stories. The overall use

Table 11.7 Stylistic analysis

Measure	Examples	Mexican-American		African-American	
		Mean	Std Dev.	Mean	Std Dev.
Perspective	stance (familiarity vs. formality), engagement, attitude (sarcasm)	0.29	0.46	0.39	0.50
Pattern	repetition, parallels, alliteration, rhyme and rhythm	0.25	0.46	0.36	0.49
Devices	simile, exaggeration/hyperbole, genre display or borrowing	0.33	0.48	0.36	0.49

Counts were converted to indicate per text averages for each group

of these features distinguishes the two groups of writers, with African-Americans more likely to incorporate them into their narratives than Mexican-Americans. This difference is particularly true for our first two measures, 'indicating perspective' and 'applying a pattern,' with approximately one out of three African-American writers making use of these stylistic devices compared to one out of four Mexican-American writers.

Though these results are exploratory, they represent a useful way to identify stylistic aspects of students' narrative writing. Our findings are consistent with earlier descriptions of language use by each group. Given the long tradition of oratory and the high value placed on engaging storytelling in the African-American community, greater stylistic marking by African-American adolescents would be expected. However, two points need to be made. First, standard deviations for all measures are high for both groups, indicating uneven distributions. That is, it appears that the majority of the stylistic features are found in some narratives from each group while none was used in other narratives in each group. Second, in general, no obvious 'ESL effect' was found in the writing of the bilingual Mexican-Americans. At least as measured in this study, their command of the language appeared on a par with that of their African-American peers.

The picture that emerges from the analysis undertaken thus far indicates that narratives from both groups of writers have many features in common. Divergences appear to be matters of style, in keeping with findings from language socialization research to date. To provide a richer description of both divergences and commonalities, we now explore representative narratives in greater detail.

Qualitative analyses: Reporting vs. commenting on events and the importance of stance in storytelling

While our analysis of narrative elements revealed no significant differences between groups overall, the two sets of narratives did leave us with distinct impressions. Narratives by African-American writers suggested

Structure and Style in Narrative Writings 181

Table 11.8 Reports of traumatic events from 7th grade

Narrative 1 (B7)	Narrative 2 (B23)	Narrative 3 (B11)
My Boogie board One day I was going to the beach and my boogie board was on the roof. So I got a ladder and I climbed. Then when I got up and I saw boogie board at the other side of the house. So I went. Then I got closer and I slipped and fell off the roof and broke my arm and I had to go the hospital. Then nobody went to the beach. And I got a cast. Then the next weekend I got to go to the beach. (89)	When I was little I got bit by a dog at the age of ten I was play and the dog was run at me and I run from the dog and I turned a round and the dog jump on me and bit me in chest and I bit the dog and hurt the dog in the chest when he was on me and I yelled and my mom and dad was in the house sleep and my mom and dad did not hear me so I hit the dog and it fell and I went over the rail and went in the house and went to the hospital and clean me up. the End. (116)	Something bad happened to me this year with school. I got an F - U in Math for what reason I really don't know. Maybe because I was absent and didnt do make up work, but I took all of the test that she gave. But I passed all the other classes but Math. That was my first F in my entire life and I almost cried but I held it in. My parents were angry. I was so mad because I always get a B in Math and that's one of my favorite classes and I was so hurt that my eyes burned. After that I hardly talk to my teacher. (111)

greater evaluation and more commentary on reported events than those of their Mexican-American peers, who seemed to stick to the reporting task without further elaboration. These differences could be likened to stylistic choices, an area where other measures did detect differences between groups, and are best illustrated with actual narratives.

The three narratives in Table 11.8 all report somewhat traumatic events in the lives of the narrators using roughly equivalent text lengths.[7] Narratives 1 and 2 do so with a minimum of evaluation, both at the lexical/ embedded level and in terms of dedicated clauses. In Narrative 1, a Mexican-American writer reports on events leading to a broken arm. He uses the evaluatives *got to* and *had to* and dedicates one of his 13 clauses to evaluation. In Narrative 2, an African-American writer describes a mutual exchange of bites with a dog, using the lexically evaluative *hurt* and dedicating one of his 15 clauses to evaluation. In contrast, the African-American author of Narrative 3 interspersed her report with an abundance of lexical stance markers (*bad, reason, really, don't know, maybe, all, entire, almost, cried, held it in, angry, so, mad, favorite, hurt, my eyes burned, hardly*) and dedicated more than half her 15 clauses to expressing her disappointment. Of partic-

Table 11.9 Two stories told with and without stylistic elaboration

Narrative 4 (B22)	Narrative 5 (7.6)
On June 26, 1987 I went to Mexico I went to visit my grandmother. I was at the back yard playing with my cousin hide and seek I was hiding on some bushes when I felt that something grabbing my shoulder when I turned around to see what it was it was my grandmothers sister but my grandmother's sister was dead. I ran away from her but she wanted me to go with her I ran with my mom and I was crying and I told my mom what I saw and my grandmother told us that her sister had died there seven years ago. After that I never ever went back in there again. (113)	LOST Dear Diary, Where did go? What could it have happen? Who stole it? How did it leave? Where is it? Those were the thoughts in mind when I couldn't find my 'Lucky Charm.' Now where could I look? How about in my room on my key chain. It's not there. Ah! That's where it has always been. I knew it. Then darkness came over my whole room 'My Big Brother!' He walked in shouting about how he knew what I was looking for. I asked, but he didn't respond. So I asked him again. He said my panty hose. I said yes. Then he said 'No you're not you're looking for your lucky key.' He was right that was exactly what I was looking for. How did he know? What did he do with it? I didn't even know that was missing I said loud. Where is it! Where is it? I shouted loud as I could. Then he ran and while he was running my key fell out I felt more lucky just looking at it. So I picked it up and put it in my pocket and the rest of the day was terrific Love, The End! Janey P.S. I never Lost it again (209)

ular note is her adroit reporting of the trauma's origin as *an F – U in Math*, a faithful rendering of the facts that communicates all the necessary emotion.

Two final examples in Table 11.9 illustrate different styles of storytelling. Both Narrative 4 and Narrative 5 begin with an identifiable opening, build to a climax and a resolution, and include embedded evaluations. Beyond that, they diverge fairly dramatically. Whereas Narrative 4 presents its ghost story without much adornment, Narrative 5 is studded with features that call attention to the writer's persona. The African-American author of 'Lost' uses genre-borrowing, casting the narrative in the form of a letter complete with closing and postscript. There are questions and comments addressed to the reader, a humorous presentation of the evil but buffoonish brother easily tricked into telling the truth, and a notable and dramatic metaphor (*darkness came over my room*). The 12-year old author also knows how to wield dialogue and how to cut between direct and reported speech for dramatic effect. These techniques utilize the potential of narrative fiction to show rather than tell and thus to involve the reader. The writer asserts her individuality as a story writer by playing with conventions, and she succeeds in telling an engaging story. In contrast, though Narrative 4's ghost story brims with potential drama, its Mexican-American author keeps to reporting events with no dialogue, no metaphors, and no shifts in narrative perspective.

As our results in Table 11.7 demonstrate, it is by no means the case that only African-American authors engaged in the kinds of hybrid text construction put to such good effect in 'Lost.' In fact, each data-set included at least one report-like narrative (similar to Narratives 1 and 2 above) at one extreme, and at least one richly structured, evaluated, and stylistically distinguished narrative (like Narrative 5) at the other. Moreover, the most evaluated text was written by a Mexican-American and the least evaluated text by an African-American. Nevertheless, more Mexican-American writers stayed with a report-like and rather conventional narrative style, and more African-Americans felt free to incorporate the kinds of literary techniques on display in 'Lost.'

Conclusion

Our texts and their analyses support a social-affective rather than an individual cognitive view of adolescent narrative writing. Pratt's (1977) forceful argument in favor of a Labovian, that is, context-based approach to the study of literary stylistics can be applied to the pre-literary efforts of middle school writers. As a theory of story in context, the approach encourages multidimensional explorations grounded in actual language use, and it has allowed us to consider such elements of linear story construction as narrative structure and cohesive marking as well as less linear qualities such as expressions of affect and stance and the emergence of style. Our data suggest an alternative to the 'story grammar' approach adopted by developmental studies of children's narratives. The same data make us wary of group-level distinctions and generalizations despite the instructive light cast on some of our results by prior cross-cultural studies. (Note that the large majority of features examined pointed to similarities across groups.) Let us begin with the more linguistic issues brought into focus by this analysis, and subsequently return to the cultural ones.

Since development was not an issue and indeed most of our narratives were complete in Peterson and McCabe's (1983) sense, we were able to see beyond the discrete measures of text form pursued in the psycholinguistic literature regarding the role of elements of narrative structure as well as the different effects brought about by different executions in actual storytelling. Stylistic display, as defined here, may be integral to narrative development at this stage, and is perhaps integral to adolescents' sociolinguistic development as a whole. Both Kamberelis (1999) and Wollman-Bonilla (2000) found emergent genre awareness in very young students (kindergarten through 2nd grade for Kamberelis, and 1st grade for Wollman-Bonilla), and Critical Discourse analysts have long argued that schools are a key arena for the development of multiple discourse fluencies as students grow older (Christie, 1989; Martin, 1993). Indeed, where but in school would many writers like ours get much access to 'genres of power' such as essayist literacy or science writing, which 'must first be learned' (Christie, 1989: 163)? We may add that students must also be practiced to achieve the mastery on display in 'Lost,' and that schools have a critical role to play in providing that necessary practice. The more strictly cognitive concerns of much prior narrative analysis lead to overly narrow models of narrative development. While understanding that stylistic variation is nothing if not challenging, the methods employed here were conservative, presented in some detail, and productive in their results. For ultimately, what distinguished the more report-like texture of many Mexican-American narratives from the more expressive and persona-driven texture of many African-American texts was style. And given the roots of style in the overlapping discourse communities of each group of writers, this of course brings us back to culture.

In much of cross-cultural discourse analysis, in particular for school discourse, the gestalt has been a home–school contrast through which the features of home-based discourses are seen as being in conflict with school discourses for some students, and in harmony for others. This home–school contrast is then often used to explain the academic troubles that persistently and disproportionately afflict African-Americans and Mexican-Americans. That is, group-level academic differences are attributed directly to ethnically-based discourses: students write the way they do because they are reflecting home discourses. Our findings cast some doubt on this dichotomy.

First, demographic realities in the setting for this study present different and much more complex experiences for the home and school language socialization of our adolescent writers. Both bilingual Mexican-Americans and bi-dialectal African-Americans learned how to read and write in standard English. According to our measures, they acquired equivalent competence in written language conventions, produced writings of equivalent lengths, and achieved equivalent levels of linguistic complexity. If one were to focus squarely on the features of their writing, both groups exhibit elements that are valued by the literary community and that are distinctive and stylistic. Yet, neither group appears to be very successful in school. The writings in our data suggest a power grasped, if temporarily: a power to invent with language in school, to exercise creative license, to break rules in order to write a "good story." Perhaps the time has come for schools to work with that kind of energy. In recent years, ethnographic researchers have increasingly turned to the classroom to examine the acquisition of literacy *in situ*, one could say in its natural habitat, but so far, they have not ventured beyond the elementary setting (Dyson, 1989; Kamberelis, 1999; Lensmire, 1994; Orellana, 1995; Patthey-Chavez & Clare, 1996; Wollman-Bonilla, 2000). It is hoped that our work will help both researchers and educators to examine the continued teaching and learning of literacy as it diversifies into literacies rooted in different genres and traditions in secondary school.[8]

Notes

1. Ainsworth's (1981) findings regarding the personal narratives of adult Mexican immigrants to the US also stress recurrent themes of cooperation, support, and humility rather than self-display, heroism, or self-aggrandizement.
2. At this point, the students were familiar with the researcher who, at the beginning of the week, had been introduced as 'a USC student who is studying how young people learn to write in school.' During the course of the week, the class had done their normal language arts work with their teacher, completed a language use survey as well as another brief writing exercise, and had had a discussion with the researcher about the history of English in America.
3. Of course, not all people fit neatly into ethnographic categories. If the student could say that she identified with one group, she was placed in that group. Those few students who could not identify with one group or who reported that they were half African-American and half Mexican-American were removed from the writing analysis portion of the study.
4. The term 'Mexican' typically refers to a person of immigrant descent with strong roots in Mexico; 'Mexican-American' refers to individuals with stronger on the US side: 'Chicano' refers to a resident of California with more distant Mexican descent. However, perceptions vary, and the terms frequently overlap.
5. This excluded self-reference (repetitions of *I*).
6. The category of patterned repetitions refers to rhythmic repetitions that draw explicit attention to the language, as in rap.
7. All narratives were transcribed as close to the handwritten original as possible, preserving original spellings and line breaks.
8. That hope is what originally inspired Ann Daubney-Davis to undertake her doctoral work, though sadly she did not live to see it to publication.

Chapter 12
Functions of Personal Examples and Narratives in L1 and L2 Academic Prose

ELI HINKEL

Introduction

Since the appearance of Kaplan's (1966) seminal paper on cross-cultural variation in rhetoric and discourse, a large body of work has emerged to identify specific differences across rhetorical traditions and their manifestations in text. In the past several decades, much has been learned, for instance, about how native (NS) and non-native (NNS) speakers of English organize written discourse and what specific features of text they employ in their writing. The study discussed in this paper represents one more attempt at an analysis of contextual uses of exemplification in formal essays written by NS and NNS university students.

In written prose, exemplification can take many forms, and examples can range from very short phrases to lengthy narratives or stories to illustrate, for example, particular events or complex social, economic, or political issues and developments. Various types of illustrative examples are discussed in practically all writing guides and composition textbooks, and providing examples to clarify and explain a particular point is a useful means of elaboration in many (if not all) rhetorical traditions.

In Anglo-American (and Aristotelian) rhetoric, examples are often considered to be a desirable practice. However, developing the writer's argument rather than exemplifying it represents the main purpose of writing (Hacker, 2000). On the other hand, in other rhetorical traditions such as Chinese, Japanese, or Korean, for purposes of persuasion, exemplification is often seen as a prominent means of making a point because a well-chosen and relevant example can be 'by far more powerful than argument' (Oliver, 1972: 177). One of the reasons that in classical Chinese rhetoric examples are seen as more persuasive than overt argumentation is that the audience may be induced by an indirect suggestion to 'arrive for themselves at the right conclusions' (Oliver, 1972) without being told what to think. Most importantly, experiential examples are a highly valued means of conveying the writer's sincerity, which is intended to convince the reader. Studies of rhetoric and discourse in diverse rhetorical traditions have long noted that what constitutes evidence and how evidence can be made convincing differs across cultures and genres (Kaplan, 1991; 2000). As Kaplan (2005) indicates, a number of conventions determine what evidence is acceptable in various discourse communities and how it is to be employed in writing. He also points out that, while evidence in the form of data and facts is highly valued in Anglo-American academic discourse, it is looked down upon as trivial in the Chinese rhetorical tradition, which prefers a suggestive style.

Hvitfeld (1992) and Fox (1994) report that many Asian students narrated personal stories and presented lengthy personal conversations in lieu of evidence in their formal essays and research papers. Hvitfeld and Fox further explain that for many NNS writers, the idea of truth results from everyday experience, and personal examples can be just as valid as the factual information and data extracted from published sources. Hvitfeld also notes that ESL (English as a second language) students from China, Japan, and Korea demonstrate greater personal involvement with examples and text through the use of first person references and extensive narrations of their experiences. According to Hvitfeld's (1992) findings, NNS students often produce highly personal argument support when they are not certain of the forms that academic rhetorical support and examples should take.

In her study of ESL writing at the university level, Dong (1998) similarly found that Chinese and Korean speakers frequently transfer strategies from L1 (first language) discourse paradigms for providing rhetorical evidence and proof in academic discourse. She notes that providing various types of examples as evidence in academic writing is not only a prevalent strategy for thesis support but also a means of establishing solidarity with the reader to create common ground and develop rapport with the goal of persuasion. Dong reports her students' observations regarding the similarities in constructing academic discourse in their L1s and in English because in the construction of academic discourse relying on personal experience in exemplification is appropriate in both discourse traditions. However, Dong indicates that Chinese and Korean university students often comment on the confusion they experience regarding the types of examples that can be used in academic writing in English.

Exemplification in Non-Anglo-American Rhetorical Traditions

Chinese rhetoric, based on Confucian and Taoist principles, is also closely followed in classical rhetorical practices prevalent in Japanese and Korean written discourse (Taylor, 1995). In all three traditions, contextually relevant examples can serve several important functions, including providing persuasive factual data and evidence to convey the writer's main points and/or narrating illustrative stories ('reasoning by analogy': Hall & Ames, 1987) for explication of and support for the validity of one's claim. Hall and Ames (1998: 137–138) point out that analogical reasoning and positive and negative 'exemplars' represent one of the pivotal elements of argument in the Chinese rhetorical tradition, when the writer 'seeks to establish similarities and differences among paradigmatic situations' that serve as resources for 'practical proposals.'

Another purpose of exemplification in Confucian and Taoist rhetoric is to establish the dual and reciprocal responsibility of the writer and the audience for finding a solution to a particular problem and thus to improve society to the general advantage of the community as a whole (Hall & Ames, 1987, 1998; Jensen, 1987; Maynard, 1998). In this way, rhetorical exemplification seeks to bring together the knowledge, experience, and intellectual resources of the writer and the reader in order to advance society by means of combining their cumulative expertise. An important additional function of examples in Confucian and Taoist rhetoric is to lend authority and credibility to a writer's position by representing ideas as not necessarily his or her own, but as rooted in real-life experience and social practice.

According to Chinese classics, evidential information and experiential knowledge in support of the writer's position attain the highest degree of validity and trustworthiness when they come from within the writer, and acquiring knowledge and experience within oneself represents a key characteristic of wisdom. Chuang Tzu (Merton, 1965: 239) explains that one's inner resources are far more important than external knowledge: 'Cherish that which is within you, and shut off that which is' outside because external information may simply be distracting without being productive.

In classical Chinese rhetoric, the four-part *qi-cheng-zhuan-he* and the classical 'eight-legged' *ba gu wen* essay paradigms are expected to contain evidence, reasoning, and 'the proof or the evidence' (Kirkpatrick, 1997). Evidential information takes the form of examples that can be derived from the writer's own knowledge and experience to benefit the community and the collective sense of self (Bodde, 1991). The organization and wording of the essay can adhere to two basic types of reasoning, both of which are based on exemplification: 'inductive, which proceeds from example(s) to a conclusion, and deductive, which proceeds from "the truth" or conclusion to the examples' (Kirkpatrick, 1997: 241).

Similarly, in Japanese written discourse, several rhetorical patterns of idea organization can be identified to include three-, four-, or five-part organizational formats, which are typically inductive (Maynard, 1997, 1998). According to Maynard (1997: 159), in the *ki-shoo-ten-ketsu* 'organizational structure for expository (and other) writing,' the topic and subtopics require the writer to provide evidence for the validity of a position, and the evidence often takes the form of concrete examples. Furthermore, examples can also be employed in support of definitions, explanations, problem statements, or as 'data leading to evidence' (Maynard, 1998: 55). The author explains that in formal writing, examples, including 'wrong examples' or 'pointing out mistakes' represent the pivotal element of a clear and 'explicit presentation of thoughts' (Maynard, 1998: 60). This use of examples is expected in most essays even at the level of high school writing instruction. Because the purpose of writing is to explain the writer's own thoughts and opinions, the examples provided in evidence can be derived from the writer's personal experiences, observations, or narratives.

In the Korean rhetorical tradition, the classical model of evidentiality by example and analogy in story forms in also expected to be derived from direct experience and knowledge to bring together the writer and the reader as a collective social whole (Oliver, 1972; Hwang, 1987).

Exemplification in Academic Writing in English

It is important to note at the outset that types of writing in English usually referred to as 'academic writing' can vary a great deal (Grabe & Kaplan, 1996; Kaplan, 1983, 1988). For instance, published research articles, academic books, or student papers and assignments written in university settings may all be described as 'academic' despite the fact that published works and written student assignments clearly employ different discourse, textual, and rhetorical features, such as persuasion techniques.

In English academic prose, for example, providing examples has the somewhat limited function of clarifying and supporting the writer's position in argumentative writing or of supplying detailed information in expository texts in order to enhance textual clarity. The uses of clarifying and supporting examples represent one of the features that differ substantially between, for example, student papers and published articles. In addition, important divergences have been noted across various types of student writing, such as that produced in English composition and other courses in such disciplines as sociology, history, or psychology (Hinkel, 2001, 2002, 2003a, 2003b).

The current methodology ubiquitously found in composition instruction for NS and NNS students alike encourages academic writers to employ examples, including personal ones, to support their position and argumentation. For example, instructional texts such as Beason and Lester (2000) indicate that to explain their ideas clearly in writing and to address the expectations of the audience, well-developed compositions should rely on the writer's own experiences because readers may have had similar experiences and would thus be able to relate to the writer's point of view. In general, in composition teaching, providing extended examples as rhetorical support for the thesis is considered to be a highly appropriate technique and is promoted in many writing guides and instructional texts (e.g. Holten & Marasco, 1998; Lunsford, 2001; Reid, 2000; Smoke, 1999.) Hacker (2000: 40) states that giving examples represents the most common pattern of topic development, and that these 'are appropriate whenever the reader might be tempted to ask, "*For example?*".' In Hacker's view, '[i]llustrations are extended examples, frequently presented in story form ... [and] they can be a vivid and effective means of developing a point.' Similarly, Connelly (2000: 80–81) strongly advocates using personal examples, observations, and experiences as advantageous to the writer because they have an evidential function in academic discourse: 'Personal observations, accounts of your own life can be convincing support.' According to Connelly, the advantages of including personal stories and experiences in academic texts also lie in their authoritative function: 'Personal experiences can be emotionally powerful and commanding because the writer is the sole authority and expert ... Individual accounts can humanize abstract issues and personalize objective facts and statistics' (2000: 80–81).

In the teaching of L2 (second language) academic writing, instructors and writing guides consistently point out that in compositions and other types of academic writing, examples need to be representative of general points and ideas discussed in support of the writer's thesis. The types of examples included as rhetorical support and illustrations of a point also need to be interesting and varied and include materials such as relevant facts, statistics, descriptive details, and useful explanations (Leki, 1999a; Raimes, 1999; Smalley *et al.*, 2000). Practically all instructional texts provide examples of examples that can be appropriately employed as evidence in compositions and academic writing.

By contrast, studies of academic prose written in the disciplines other than composition conducted since the 1960s have found examples to be relatively rare. Personal examples are particularly uncommon (Swales & Feak, 1994), because academic writing outside of composition courses is rarely concerned with the writer's own knowledge and experiences. In fact, Swales' (1990) analysis of written academic genres found that academic texts are often expected to project objectivity in presenting information and depersonalize text by various lexical and syntactic means.

An extensive analysis of a corpus of written English carried out by Biber *et al.* (1999) found that in academic prose, the frequency rates of explicit example markers, such as *for example, for instance,* and *e.g.*, were extremely low (0.09%). Biber *et al.* point out that, in most cases, these common example markers are stylistically interchangeable and that the discourse functions of exemplification in academic writing are predominantly limited to adding specific support for more general claims, providing concrete examples of technical terms, and illustrating background information rather than main ideas. Biber *et al.* (1999) also point out that reference to personal knowledge and experiences (as marked by first person pronouns) is also rare in formal academic writing (i.e. occurrences of first person pronouns, for instance, are limited to the rate of 0.65%, or 6.5 per 1000 words). Similarly, third person pronouns of all types (excluding non-referential *it* in *it*-cleft constructions) are encountered at the rate of 0.9% (9 occurrences per 1000 words). On the whole, in written academic discourse in English, exemplification seems to play a relatively minor role compared to the prominence it receives in composition instruction and textbooks.

The Study

The purpose of this study is to examine the types and discourse functions of marked examples in NS and NNS academic essays at the university level in a corpus of L1 and L2 student writing (444 essays; 124,063 words). The NNS writers in this study were L1 speakers of Chinese, Japanese and Korean. Specifically, the study focuses on the frequency rates of exemplification markers, first and third person pronouns, and occurrences of past tense verbs. By analyzing these features together, the study attempts to determine whether NS and NNS student writers differ in their use of examples in the argumentation/exposition essays that are commonly required in diagnostic tests of writing skills in universities. In this way, the study attempts to determine whether contextual uses of examples were similarly employed to support the writer's position in argumentation essays. In particular, the study addresses the median frequency rates of overt exemplification markers ((*as*) *an example, for example, e.g., for instance, in my/our/his /her/their example, like, such as...*), first and third person pronouns (excluding non-referential *it*), and occurrences of past tense verbs.

Subjects

The essays included in the data were written during 50-minute placement and diagnostic tests, administered to NS and NNS students alike in four US universities. All students had been admitted to various degree programs and were enrolled in mainstream classes. The NNS students had achieved a relatively high level of English language proficiency; their TOEFL (Test of English as a Foreign Language) scores ranged from 543 to 627 with a mean of 597). Of the NNS students, 82% were holders of US associate degrees earned in various community colleges, and were admitted as transfers at the junior level in four-year comprehensive universities. These individuals had received at least three years of ESL and composition instruction in the US, having completed at least a year in academic intensive programs followed by two years of community college training. Among the other NNS writers, 9% consisted of first-year students who were graduates of US high schools. The other 9% consisted of graduate students who had similarly completed their ESL studies in US English for Academic Purposes (EAP) programs and had resided in English-speaking environments for periods between 19 and 28 months.

In total, essays from 317 NNS students were analyzed in the study: 112 speakers of Chinese, 108 of Japanese, and 97 of Korean. There were also 127 NS students in the study. All NS students were enrolled in required first-year composition classes. These students were all graduates of US suburban high schools from three states representing the east and west coasts as well as the Midwest.

Procedures

The essays were written in response to one of three prompts:

Prompt 1:
Some people believe that when parents make their children's lives too easy, they can actually harm their children instead. Explain your views on this issue. Use detailed reasons and examples.

Prompt 2:
Many people believe that grades do not encourage learning. Do you agree or disagree with this opinion? Be sure to explain your answer using specific reasons and examples.

Prompt 3:
Many educators believe that parents should help to form their children's opinions. Others feel that children should be allowed to develop their own opinions. Explain your views on this issue. Use detailed reasons and examples.

Table 12.1 Distribution of student essays by prompt

L1 Group	Prompt 1 Parents	Prompt 2 Grades	Prompt 3 Opinion
NS	44	36	47
Chinese	39	39	34
Japanese	32	35	41
Korean	32	33	32
Totals	147	143	154

Of the total, 147 essays were written on Prompt 1, 143 on Prompt 2, and 154 on Prompt 3. The distribution across the three prompts was proximate for all student groups, as presented in Table 12.1.

Analysis

To determine whether NS and NNS students employed exemplification markers, first and third person pronouns, and past tense verbs in similar ways in their writing, the number of words in each of the 444 essays was counted, followed by a count of the occurrences of each of the markers, pronouns, and past tenses. For example, NS essay #1 for Prompt 1 consisted of 250 words and included one exemplification marker (*for example*). To determine the percentage rate of exemplification markers used in this essay, a computation was performed (1/250 = 0.4%) and then repeated for the 30 occurrences of first person pronouns in the essay (30/250 = 12%). The computations were performed separately for exemplification markers, first person pronouns, third person pronouns, and past tense verbs in each of the NS and NNS essays.

Because the numbers of essays written to each prompt by each L1 group of students were proximate, the analysis of example use in students' texts was carried out based on pooled data for all essays combined. Non-parametric statistical comparisons of the NS and NNS data were employed because the majority of the percentage rates were not normally distributed. The Mann-Whitney U Test was selected as a conservative measure of differences between the NS and NNS data, as this test compares two sets of data based on their ranks below and above the median. The percentage rates of example use in essays written to the same prompt by NS students were compared first with the Chinese-speaking group, then with the Japanese-speaking group, and finally with the Korean-speaking group.

Results and Discussion

The results of the data analysis are presented in Table 12.2. The data demonstrate that NNS students in all L1 groups used example markers at rates significantly higher than those identified in the essays of NS writers. Specifically, in the essays of speakers of Chinese, Japanese, and Korean the median frequency rates of example marker clustered around 0.48–0.57%, versus 0.25% in NS students' texts.

Excerpts 1 and 2 below illustrate this finding.[1] In the relatively short Excerpt 1, the NNS writer employs three example markers, although only the first seems to be followed by additional information to support the writer's position. It is interesting to note that information supplied by the writer is almost entirely autobiographical and is based on personal experiential knowledge without generalizations.

Table 12.2 Median frequency rates and ranges (%) for exemplification markers, pronouns, and past tense verbs in NS and NNS academic essays

Markers/L1s	S	CH	JP	KR
Example markers	0.25	0.50**	0.48**	0.57**
Range	2.08	3.03	2.63	2.86
First person pronouns	1.74	3.24*	3.69*	4.55**
Range	14.35	17.65	15.63	13.68
Third person pronouns	4.44	5.50**	6.28**	6.19**
Range	18.27	24.34	19.08	19.05
Past tense verbs	1.51	3.53**	2.96**	3.70**
Range	10.95	14.37	13.02	11.4

** 2-tailed $p \leq 0.05$; * 1-tailed $p \leq 0.05$

Excerpt 1 *(Prompt 3)*:
Older and wiser adults should help young people for form their opinions. For example, for me, the people who had the greatest influence on my life are my family. My parents are the ones who instilled the moral value that I possess today. I grew up in a city called Nagoya. My parents were very ancient descent, and they raised me according to the important values. They cared about my education and taught me everything I know. For instance, I was taught the old rule of 'do unto others as you would want them to do onto you.' My parents helped me grow up and respect others. I was taught that family is the most important, and my parents brought up me and my siblings with care. My mother took care of us every day, and my father was the head of the family. My parents did and still do some type of effect on my life, but other people also did. For example, my best friend formed my opinion about fashion, my taste of food, and even my taste of girlfriends. However, my friend's opinion was only a little part of my life, compared to my parents. (Japanese)

In many essays, NNS writers included extended examples that consisted of narratives of their past experiences in lieu of developing their arguments. In Excerpt 2, the writer does not actually argue for his position, which is explicitly stated at the outset (*grades do not encourage learning*), but instead exemplifies it by means of a personal story (also highly marked by first person pronoun use). He narrates his own positive experience in an academic course and compares his position with that of other students who became confused by the disparity between the instructor's light-hearted attitude and their own low grades. At the same time, the writer's narrative seeks to present a balanced perspective to explain that what seems to be beneficial for some individuals may not be for others.

Excerpt 2 *(Prompt 2)*:
As an engineering student, my course materials are often dry and not so interesting, and the grades that I get are not very high because when I am bored with a class, I don't study. I believe that grades definitely do not encourage learning. For example, I took my second series of mechanical courses. The instructor in that course was the main reason that my boring college life became bright, and in his course I got good grades. He was never extremely humorous, but he was sort of funny and I studied more in his class than I did in my first mechanical class. But I know that some students didn't like his grading because I talked to some other classmates at that time I took my mechanic course. For example, these classmates thought that the instructor's grading was unfair because he joked all the time. These classmates thought that if he joked, then he didn't have to give low grades. (Chinese)

The interesting divergences between the median frequency rates of other features of text in NNS and NS prose, however, extend to third person pronouns, as well as first person pronouns. Specifically, the frequency rates of these two types of personal pronouns in the NNS essays were significantly higher than those in NS prose. In light of the finding that many L2 writers referred to their own and third party experiences in place of argumentation, this finding is not particularly surprising. The text in Excerpt 3 recounts two third-party experiences that serve as analogies:

Excerpt 3 *(Prompt 2)*:
I believe that grades are not important for students to encourage their skills of learning. Today, many schools grade students only the score of exams. Therefore, they only make an effort to get good scores and grades. My friend's case is a good example. When she was a high school student in Japan, she only studied textbooks and just memorized many words that were expected to be in the exam just one night before the exam. After the exam, she forgot almost all what she studied. Other students always do this too.

In addition, grades disregard what students felt. For example, my brother. When he was a junior high student, he had an exam of art class. The question was 'What do you feel about the picture?' It looked dark and sad, and my brother answered he felt lonely and cold. However, the answer was strong and bright. He had to answer the question not about his feeling but what the teacher expected to answer. In this way, students don't like to see their grades because sometimes no matter how much they studied, they couldn't get good grades in some classes, like when the teacher expects only one answer. (Japanese)

Past tense verbs were also used with significantly greater frequency in NNS writing. In many NS and NNS academic essays, the types of examples included in the text determine the type of text that students compose: lengthy narrations of past personal experiences presented as examples can and often do become a writer's entire essay. In NNS prose, however, the preponderance of past-time narratives recounted in the first or third person helps explain the significantly higher median rates of occurrence of past tense verbs relative to those identified in NS texts. The text in Excerpt 4 consists of a student's entire essay:

Excerpt 4 *(Prompt 1):*
My hometown is a small village in China. A great number of parents to work all the day in the fields in order to support their kids' education. The children stay in school most of the time. Their parents do the laundry, housework, help the kids with homework, and pretty much anything for their kids. For example, my parents did the same thing for me too. It seemed to me that I was the queen in my family, and my parents were my servers. They cooked wonderful meals for me, cleaned the house, and gave me money for anything I wanted. They worked hard to give me anything I asked, and I thought that this was a normal life for all the kids. My parents already planned everything for me even my future job. I lived in such a condition for 18 years. I live in America today. I finally realized that my parents made my life too easy, but they actually harmed me instead. For example, I didn't have an opportunity to learn to become responsible for others and myself. I expected everything to be the best. I had no experience in working, socializing with others. In my case, I didn't know how to do anything, such as cook or do laundry. So, I believe that when parents make their children's lives too easy, they can actually harm their children instead. (Chinese)

Excerpt 5 presents a clear contrast with Excerpt 4 in that first-year students appear to have little trouble following the conventions of written academic discourse that call for generalizable arguments and less personal exemplification.

Excerpt 5 *(Prompt 1):*
A parent probably wants to let their child enjoy their childhood with games and learning new knowledge. But what is the knowledge that is taught? When the term 'easy' is used to describe parenting, the word shelter comes to mind. Easy life shelters a child from the world's reality. The child will become so dependent on their parents to take

care of a situation and even his own basic needs, leaving a child defenseless. One of the greatest attributes a parent has is to share the difficulties of life with their children. It is a knowledge of survival that parents need to teach their children. Parents have the responsibility to raise their children and not live their lives for them. (native speaker)

The text in Excerpt 5 argues for essentially the same position as the text in Excerpt 4, and there is little doubt that the quality of writing in both excerpts is similar (i.e. first-year NS students in this study were novice writers whose writing required improvement). However, in Excerpt 5, the NS writer includes no personal examples or past-time narratives. Instead, the argument is structured around generalizable (though rather trivial) points, as is usually expected in formal compositions (Hacker, 2000). On the whole, many NS essays included a preponderance of generalizations while few NNS compositions were similarly constructed. Jensen (1987: 223) indicates that in classical Chinese rhetoric, overt argument is 'heavily deprecated' because it is seen as contentious and rather pointless. Similarly, generalizations are almost always seen as untruthful, at least to some degree: general statements cannot apply to every situation or individual and, hence, little can be learned from them (as in the case of Excerpt 5). On the other hand, a truthful and sincere narrative, as in Excerpt 4, can become a useful example that has the goal of educating the reader by means of analogical reasoning (Hall & Ames, 1998). From a broader perspective, the dual responsibility of the writer and the reader to combine their knowledge for the benefit of the community as a whole is accomplished to a greater extent by direct and personal exemplification than by vague generalizations that can easily be disputed (Oliver, 1972).

Excerpts 6 and 7 show that NS writers do use examples. In these two excerpts, NS writers discuss whether or not grades encourage learning in general terms, and they present brief examples that are intended to illustrate the writer's point while being varied, as is expected within the conventions of student compositions in English (Leki, 1999a; Lunsford & Connors, 1997; Raimes, 1999). A few important characteristics of NS examples should be noted because they are distinct from those identified in the essays of L2 writers. In NS prose, many examples are not explicitly marked by means of example markers and, as is reflected in Table 12.2, significantly fewer contain past-time narratives of personal or third-party experiences.

Excerpt 6 *(Prompt 2):*
The grading system does a great job promoting education and setting a universal standard for knowledge. Patients who come to see their doctors would like to know that the doctor has passed his medical classes and exam with an A, or at least a 3.75 GPA. If the grading system

did not exist, patients may find that the doctor's best friend gave him the job because he sounded professional on an oral evaluation.

During a child's life, self-esteem is an influential factor. Without it, he or she may actually become as worthless as he or she feels. The grading system gives children a boost. Little Tommy is going to come home with an A on a science text and think that he is on top of the world. (native speaker)

In Excerpt 6, the writer presents two examples of the benefits of the grading system, and although both of these are relatively specific, they are generalized sufficiently broadly to be applicable to practically all patients or children.

The writer of Excerpt 7 also includes an example constructed similarly to those in Excerpt 6. Again, the example is one that is generalizable, partly because it is written in the plural and partly because it represents what is seen as a commonly held view.

Excerpt 7 *(Prompt 2)*:
The many children who go to school everyday would never put forth effort unless grades are handed out. The grading system pushes the child day-to-day to excel in school for that A. If it isn't an A that the child strives for, then it is a B or C. Particularly, when children are young, they are not interested in boring reading or math – they just want to play on the playground with their friends. If they didn't have to worry about grades, most children between the ages of 5 and 10 would fail at the level of elementary school because they are too young to know that they need to learn the basics. It is safe to say that without grades, any elementary schooling would fail. (native speaker)

Although NS and NNS examples are similarly extended and detailed (Beason & Lester, 2000), the linguistic features and rhetorical functions of exemplification provided by speakers of English and by speakers of Chinese, Japanese, and Korean differ substantially. While NS writers cited specific information, their compositions did not refer to specific individuals to whom the information applied directly or to situations in which particular events actually occurred. On the other hand, NNS writers provided narratives about specific persons (e.g. themselves or others) or events/situations and presented particular experiences, most of which, however, are limited to one specific individual or occurrences of specific events. Thus, readers of such narrated experiences are expected to generalize for themselves and to arrive at their own appropriate conclusions (Oliver, 1972).

Conclusion

This analysis of a small corpus of NS and NNS academic essays shows that academically advanced and proficient NNS students employ exemplification markers at rates of approximately twice those identified in the essays of NS writers. Another important difference between the features of written discourse in the NS essays and those of the speakers of Chinese, Japanese, and Korean lies in the types of examples provided to achieve their rhetorical and persuasive goals. The findings of this study demonstrate that NNS prose relies much more on extended past-time narratives and recounted first- and third-party personal experiences. By contrast, NS texts included shorter, generalizable, and impersonal references to experiences and situations applicable to entire groups of individuals, such as parents, students, or children. Due predominantly to these divergences in the types of exemplification, past tense verbs and first and third person pronouns were employed at significantly higher median frequency rates in the texts written by speakers of Chinese, Japanese, and Korean than in those of native speakers.

As Kaplan's (1991, 2000, 2005) extensive work has emphasized, the types and persuasive purposes of evidence differ across cultures and rhetorical traditions. Kaplan has also underscored that what is considered acceptable (or unacceptable) evidence in various written genres is highly conventionalized not only across cultures but also within rhetorical paradigms across different genres. His analyses of discourse and texts produced in divergent discourse communities that include speakers of the same language have shown that the types of evidence, such as data and facts, widely expected in formal and published writing in English is crucially distinct from that acceptable in other written genres such as student compositions.

Although in Anglo-American formal written discourse in various academic disciplines, including humanities, personalized examples are hardly ever used, composition instruction for college and university students actively advocates employing personal examples and narratives as evidence and to give rhetorical support in argumentative writing. For this reason, in NNS prose, the prevalence of past-time personal narratives and anecdotal recounts of experiences may not be particularly surprising: advanced L2 writers, such as those whose essays were included in this study, simply write the way they were taught to write in the many composition courses they have taken in US colleges and universities. The extensive use of personal examples in NNS prose may be further exacerbated by L1 to L2 transfer of discourse paradigms that value what Kaplan (2000, 2005) calls 'suggestive style,' illustrative stories, and analogical reasoning (Hall & Ames, 1987, 1998).

An important issue arises with regard to how NNS students learn what is regarded as appropriate evidence and proof (Kaplan, 2005) when they receive academic writing and composition instruction that advocates personal examples and detailed narratives in lieu of evidence and rhetorical support. If in composition and writing instruction the writer's own experience and authority are considered to be necessary and sufficient evidence for producing an academic essay, personal examples appear to have taken the place of evidence conventionally expected in formal academic writing. Furthermore, in light of the similarity between the types of appropriate and acceptable evidence and rhetorical support in many non-Anglo-American discourse traditions and L2 composition instruction, it is easy to see how the NNS writers' L1-based approaches to writing formal essays in English can only be compounded by the approach widely adopted in writing instruction. The point of fact is that speakers of Chinese, Japanese, and Korean need little additional instruction in employing personal examples in their academic writing in English because, based on the findings of this study, they have already attained that skill.

Note
1. All excerpts from student writings are reproduced here verbatim.

Chapter 13
Cross-cultural Variation in Classroom Turn-taking Practices

DEBORAH POOLE

The past decade has witnessed increased interest in classroom discourse as it relates to second language (L2) learning (e.g. Duff, 1995; Hall & Walsh, 2002; Koshik, 2002; Sullivan, 2000). Much of this work represents a departure from previous L2 classroom-based research, which was largely concerned with input and interactional modifications that might influence second language acquisition (SLA). In contrast, the more recent studies focus on describing the classroom as a social context in its own right and tend to be linked to classroom discourse research conducted in first language (L1) classrooms as much as (or more than) to work in SLA. One focus has been a re-evaluation of the role of initiation-reply-evaluation (IRE) sequences, the widely documented tripartite sequences that constitute most teacher-fronted classroom interaction (e.g. Cazden 1987; Lemke, 1990; Griffin & Humphrey, 1978; Mehan 1979; Poole, 1990; Sinclair & Coulthard, 1975).[1] Collectively, as detailed by Hall and Walsh (2000), this work shows how the teacher, especially through the third turn of the IRE, can influence the extent and nature of student participation. Their review of a number of recent studies points to the considerable variation that can result within IRE sequences (e.g. Consolo, 2000; Boxer & Cortes-Conde, 2000; Boyd & Maloof, 2000; Hall, 1998; Nassaji & Wells, 2000).

The aim of this chapter is to further investigate such variation by focusing on turn-taking patterns that are relevant to second language instructional contexts. Turn-taking, or the means by which teachers and students take, hold, and relinquish the speaking floor, is fundamental to all classroom interaction and is key to understanding participation phenomena both within and beyond IRE-based interaction. In the second language context especially, where students and teachers are often from different cultural backgrounds, knowledge of turn-taking routines in other cultural contexts can deepen teachers' understanding of student expectations vis-à-vis their classroom speaking roles. Even in the foreign language context, knowledge of turn-taking practices typically associated with the target language culture could, without implying a need to change interactional patterns appropriate to a given setting, provide important background information.²

Background

Prior classroom discourse studies that considered turn-taking practices have typically identified three procedures through which students are allocated turns by the teacher. In Mehan's (1979) seminal US-based account (see Cazden, 1988; Griffin & Humphrey, 1978; Lemke, 1990; Sinclair & Coulthard, 1975), these have been labeled as follows:

(1) *nomination*, where the teacher calls on or otherwise indicates (through gaze or gesture) an individual student;
(2) *invitation to bid* (for the right to reply), where the teacher signals that students should raise their hands (in an effort to be nominated); and
(3) *invitation to reply*, where a teacher initiation dictates that any student may self-select or respond at will.

Each of these 'turn-allocation procedures' (Mehan, 1979) constitutes a means of shifting from a teacher initiation move to a student reply within an IRE sequence and, as such, is characteristic of much teacher-fronted classroom activity. These procedures have been repeatedly identified through analyses of naturally occurring classroom interaction across a variety of contexts.

Griffin and Humphrey (1978) proposed that, of the three, nomination and invitation to bid are preferred because they facilitate the maintenance of social order and ensure an equal distribution of turns. Lemke (1990) similarly proposed that nomination and invitation to bid serve the interest of teacher control. He also suggested that invitations to reply may be infrequent in some classes because of prohibitions against 'calling out' or responding without being explicitly recognized. Mehan (1979), however, argued that the specific procedure employed usually depends on the goals of a given activity. To account for student turns occurring in the absence of teacher initiation, Griffin and Humphrey (1978) added a fourth category, 'turn not assigned.' Mehan also considered a category of student initiations, but noted that when successful (i.e. ratified and expanded on), these occurred *between* rather than *within* IRE sequences and 'topically related sets,' the larger organizational units of classroom talk within which consecutive IRE sequences tend to occur.

The classroom categories outlined here contrast with features of turn-taking in casual or face-to-face interaction outlined in the classic conversation analysis account (Sacks *et al.*, 1974). Specifically, in conversation, any participant potentially has the right to construct a first pair-part or initiating move, to select him- or herself as next speaker if the current speaker does not designate someone else, and to select another participant as next speaker when he or she is the current speaker. In contrast, teachers have both initiation and speaker-selection rights in classroom interaction, while student roles with respect to either are often quite limited.

Two additional features of the classroom paradigm are important to note, as they are relevant to some of the findings documented below. First, in Mehan's (1979) account, invitation to reply is responded to in some instances by one or more individuals, often in overlap, while in other cases the class responds in chorus. Griffin and Humphrey (1978) demonstrate that either an individual or chorus response is possible, though neither they nor Mehan quantify the difference.[3] The second feature involves what Mehan (1979: 62–63) termed 'extended sequences,' which occur when students respond incorrectly or inadequately to an initiation. On such occasions, evaluation moves tend to be postponed, as teachers rephrase or break down the original initiation to a simpler form to provide the student with additional chances to respond correctly. The result is typically a longer sequence with two or more initiation–reply pairs preceding the ultimate evaluation (see Griffin & Humphrey, 1978).

A final point concerns the fact that classroom turn-taking is co-constructed through participation of both teacher and students. For the analyst, this means that determining the type of turn-allocation in the absence of an explicit teacher directive requires access to the subsequent student response(s). For example, a bare question (i.e. without clear indication of turn-allocation procedure) in one class may be responded to with student hand-raising; in another class, the same question may be followed by multiple overlapping answers; in yet another a single student may respond without first being acknowledged. Most often, teachers and students together develop an interactional routine such that explicit directions (e.g. 'raise your hand' or 'answer all together') are assumed and become unnecessary. In some cases, however, the teacher may intend one type but be responded to with another. The methodological issue, then, is that the student response must be considered together with teacher elicitation in order to assess which turn-allocation procedure has occurred (c.f. Griffin & Humphrey, 1978). In some instances, that determination may be a consequence of student uptake rather than teacher intent, while in others it may be a broader combination of the two.

A Cross-cultural Perspective

The classroom accounts cited above are all based in English-speaking contexts, largely in the US,[4] so that understanding their relevance for a language teaching perspective seems to beg for comparisons with other cultural settings. In response, this chapter will focus on turn-taking procedures reported from a variety of contexts where different turn-taking patterns may pertain or be more frequent. The purpose is to bring together a body of work that, when considered collectively, suggests that turn-taking practices are linked to their sociocultural context in ways that are relevant to the language classroom.

This approach seeks to complement two major research strands within applied linguistics that have focused on cross-cultural research vis-à-vis L2 learning: contrastive rhetoric and interlanguage pragmatics. Contrastive rhetoric, the more influential (and controversial) of the two, has to date fostered the broadest and most in-depth cross-cultural research for L2 learning purposes. As is well known, contrastive rhetoric takes a cross-cultural approach to discourse and organizational features of written language (e.g. Connor, 1996, 2002; Connor & Kaplan, 1987; Kaplan, 1988; Panetta, 2001). Interlanguage pragmatics represents a more recent body of work (Blum-Kulka *et al.*, 1989; Kasper & Blum-Kulka, 1993; Kasper & Schmidt, 1996) that focuses on spoken language pragmatics, especially speech acts, in L2 development. Each of these approaches investigates, through comparative analysis, ways in which sociolinguistic or discourse level phenomena characteristics of learners' target and first languages may impact L2 development and use (see Boxer, 2002). Moreover, neither is focused principally on grammatical or sentence level phenomena, and both consider how language use and broader cultural phenomena might be linked.

By documenting the characteristics of turn-taking routines in a variety of classroom environments, this chapter aims to contribute to the cross-cultural research agenda represented in these two approaches and to consider how turn-taking variation might affect the L2 pedagogical setting. Moreover, though beyond the scope of the present chapter, an eventual goal is to link interactional findings such as those summarized below with contrastive rhetoric or interlanguage pragmatics analyses from similar cultural contexts. Such connections would provide a means of considering whether underlying commonalities exist across the spoken and written modes (Scollon, 1997) or between classroom interactional sequences and non-classroom speech acts.

At this point, it is important to acknowledge that cross-cultural research as it relates to L2 teaching and learning has not always been viewed favorably. It has been claimed, for example, that such work, especially that undertaken in the name of contrastive rhetoric, may privilege the discourse practices of the Western or English-speaking world and lead to stereotyping that in turn can limit teacher perceptions of student ability. In response, this chapter will draw on the language socialization perspective articulated by Schieffelin and Ochs (1986) (see also Ochs, 1986, 1988; Scollon

& Scollon, 1981), which echoes dimensions of both contrastive rhetoric and interlanguage pragmatics while indirectly addressing these issues.

Language socialization theory views interactional practices as culturally-embedded phenomena through which members of a social group create, reflect, and sustain orientations toward a given context and its constitutive social roles. In this view, expert–novice interaction constitutes a display to the novice of expected ways of thinking and behaving. As such, interactional patterns represent tendencies rather than absolutes, and the ways novices react to and appropriate these patterns may differ. Crucially, individuals encounter many contexts of secondary socialization across their lifespan. In such contexts, new ways of interacting and using language are displayed to and appropriated by novices as they adapt to the language demands of new situations. However, as in primary socialization, the extent to which the novice appropriates new language practices will vary across individuals. Further, as Ochs (1986) has noted, it is crucial in cross-cultural research not to assume or claim mutually-exclusive patterns of language use, where, for example, culture A does x while culture B does not. Rather, variation between cultures is more likely to be found in the distribution and frequency of given phenomena, a point Kaplan (1987) also makes with respect to rhetorical modes across languages.

Taking this perspective as one through which to interpret the turn-taking data described below, the intent is to consider cross-cultural comparisons as a way to dispel stereotypes by expanding and deepening our collective understanding of how a common classroom occurrence can vary. In particular, the discussion below intends to counteract impressionistic viewpoints by documenting the often complex details of classroom interaction based on empirical work across several cultural contexts. The settings reported here are not primarily language-teaching ones, but together they suggest the range of possible turn-taking experiences students may have prior to their encounters with the L2 classroom.

Classroom Turn-taking across Cultural Settings

A Puerto-Rican and Anglo-American comparison

An important study that considered early on whether the standard turn-allocation categories described above could account for non-English speaking environments was McCollum's (1989) comparative analysis of interaction in two 3rd grade classes, a Spanish-medium class in Puerto Rico, and an English-medium (Anglo-American) class in Chicago. In McCollum's data, nomination accounted for most (62%) of the teacher's turn-allocation utterances in the Anglo-American classroom and was thus consistent with the findings of Mehan (1979) and others mentioned above. In the Puerto Rican class, however, invitation to reply, where students responded at will without having to be acknowledged or nominated, was the dominant strategy and accounted for 62% of the teacher's turn-allocation moves. McCollum (1989: 142) noted that the interaction 'resembled the "give and take" of everyday conversation much more than in the English-speaking class,' and that the teacher 'achieved this, in part, by using the invitation to reply procedure most frequently.' Moreover, these invitations to reply were followed by single, consecutive or overlapping responses rather than choral ones. The Puerto Rican class was also marked by more student initiations, with 38% of all initiation moves made by students, in contrast to 9% in the Anglo-American data. In addition student initiations in the Puerto Rican data were recognized and incorporated by the teacher in a wider range of sequential positions than those identified by Mehan. McCollum concluded that, although Mehan's paradigm could readily describe turn-allocation in both classes, it more readily accounted for the Anglo-American class in terms of student initiations. She proposed that interaction in the Puerto Rican class signaled a different sort of social relationship that favoured student participation and could be more fully explained through an additional theoretical perspective. The Puerto Rican interaction, she argued, was more aligned with the notions of responsive teaching and instructional conversation proposed by Tharp and Gallimore (1988; see Goldenberg & Patthey-Chavez, 1995), while the Anglo-American class reflected what they termed the 'recitation' script.

TEFL lessons in a Taiwanese middle school

In contrast to McCollum's findings, Chen's (1998) analysis of TEFL (Teaching English as a Foreign Language) lessons in three first-year middle-school classes in Taiwan documented only choral responses to the teachers' apparent invitations to reply. In Chen's account, all elicitations that could be interpreted as invitations to reply were responded to in chorus, often in the absence of an explicit teacher directive. This indicates that the choice for students to respond individually was not an option as it was in the accounts of Mehan (1979) and Griffin and Humphrey (1978). The unison response, Chen argued, retained the orderly presentation of bidding or nomination, even though many students were speaking at once,· as in Example 1 (Chen, 1998: 41).

Example 1
T: How to spell brother?
Ss: b-r-o-t-h-e-r
T: Okay, b-r-o-t-h-e-r

Chen's study also showed that most of the choral elicitations asked students to repeat after the teacher rather than respond to a question, often

Cross-cultural Variation in Classroom Turn-taking Practices 207

by reading aloud from the blackboard or textbook, as seen in Example 2 (Chen, 1998: 49).

Example 2

T: hao, nian yi ci. In the kitchen.
 okay read one time[5]
 Okay, read it once. *In the kitchen.*
Ss: In the kitchen.

An additional observation was the tendency for the teacher to speak together with the students during the choral reply, so that they were provided (through written support, as above, or the teacher's joint oral response) with ready access to the answers they needed to give.

Choral elicitations in Chen's study accounted for 78% of all teacher elicitations (359 out of 461), so that choral responses represented the main way students were expected to speak. Virtually all of the remaining turn-allocation moves (22%) were nomination utterances, which selected individual students to respond. In these classes, nominated students were required to stand before answering, though the directive to stand up was not always explicit. In some instances, individual nominations led to long, extended sequences that singled out a student who could not supply a desired response. A number of nominations were also achieved when the teacher called on students by class number rather than by name, as in Example 3 (Chen, 1998: 34).

Example 3

T: Uh (.) women qing ge tongxue lai make a sentence. Number one
 we ask CL classmate come
 (.) stand up please.
 Uh, let's ask a student to make a sentence. Number one, stand up please.
 ((S1 stands up))
S1: Where is John.
T: Where is John. Okay.
 ((S1 sits down))

This study also included classroom data from one 3rd year TEFL lesson, where students were two years older. Interestingly, the chorusing so common in the first-year classes did not occur; in fact, there was very little student speaking at all, and most of what did occur was the result of individual nomination. In some instances the teacher seemed to try invitations to reply, but the students did not answer them, so she then resorted to nominations.

Finally, Chen linked the patterns of turn-allocation in her data to broad cultural perspectives, including the authority invested in (and expected of) the teacher role and the Confucian value of group orientation to learning. The first was especially apparent in the asymmetrical features of individual nomination sequences, while the second was consistent with the role of chorusing in the first-year classes.

Choral elicitations in a South African math class

Chorusing also played an important role in Chick's (1988, 1996a) analysis of interactional data in several math lessons recorded near the end of the apartheid era in the KwaZulu region of South Africa. This account was initially offered to counter L2 pedagogical perspectives that, in Chick's view, tended to evaluate traditional pedagogical practices too critically when they diverged from the ideals of communicative language teaching principles. As in Chen's account, students often responded to teacher initiations in chorus. Chick also noted that teacher questions that evoked a choral response could typically be answered with ease. His account diverges from Chen's, however, in that a sequence of several choral elicitations tended to be followed by nominations where individual students were asked to respond to the questions the class had already answered. Chick first interpreted the sequence of chorusing followed by individual nomination as a face-saving strategy consistent with Zulu cultural norms in that the teacher did not put students in the position of losing face by being singled out to speak about what they may not know. He also pointed out the need to understand the locally relevant, situated reasons for practices such as chorusing.

Subsequently, Chick (1996b) expanded his analysis to consider the broader social and political context of the interaction. He ultimately interpreted the interaction described above as a form of 'safe-talk' where teachers and students, in the face of overwhelming oppression, colluded to mask both lack of proficiency in English (a second language for both teacher and students) and the extent to which mastery of the curriculum was not occurring. In other words, it became important to see the interactional patterns as reflecting and constituting not only the local context but also the wider political conditions.

In addition, even a cursory comparison of Chick's account with Chen's (1998) illustrates how similarity along one dimension such as chorusing is not necessarily accompanied by similarity along another. Specifically, individual nomination in Chick's account seems designed to avoid any display of student incompetence or lack of knowledge, while in Chen's data some nominated students who failed to respond correctly were engaged in lengthy interactions with the teacher even though they were unable to answer.

Korean language classes in a US-based Korean-American school

Kim (2000) analyzed interaction in a US-based elementary school with the stated goals of encouraging a strong Korean identity among students and providing an educational environment similar to that in Korea. The students are typically the children of Korean immigrants or residents and are bilingual in Korean and English. The school offers a full curriculum (based on the state curriculum of the California Department of Education) with English as the primary medium of instruction. In addition, students study Korean language with a Korean teacher for one class period daily. Kim's work focused on these Korean language lessons in two 2nd grade classes and two upper grade classes (one 4th grade and one 5th).

The most common turn-taking procedure in her data was the invitation to reply followed by one or more individual responses. These represented 48.3% of the total (134 of 278; 44.2% in 2nd grade and 53.5% in 4th/5th grades). Interestingly, the second most frequent response was chorus elicitation, so that rather than collapsing the category of chorus elicitation within invitation to reply (see Mehan, 1979; Griffin & Humphrey, 1978), Kim's analysis distinguished between them. In her corpus, she found the two to be fundamentally different, with chorus elicitations accounting for 43.8% of all elicitations in the 2nd grade classes and 28.3% in the 4th/5th grades, as in Example 4 (Kim, 2000: 42).

Example 4

T: ((pointing to a picture on the board))
 ku   taum pwupwun-ey   yeki mwue-ye-yo?
 that next part-at   here what -is -PE
 Next, what is it?
Ss: ta:li
 leg
 Leg
T: kuleh-ci-yo.   tali -ye-yo.
 right-SEF-PE   leg -is -PE
 Right, isn't it. (It's) a leg.

These elicitations often signaled that students should read aloud together from the textbook or blackboard, a phenomenon also found by Chen (1998), noted in Example 2, and seen here in Example 5 (Kim, 2000: 47).

Example 5

T: yenge-lo   ilk-epo-say-yo.   For each
 English-in read-try-please-PE.
 Read in English. For each.
Ss: For::each exercise below, write the telephone number in Korean. Follow the example.
T: WOW. Nemwu nemwu   cal   ilk-ess-eyo.
    very   very   well   read-PAST-PE
 Wow, (you) read very well.

An important finding from Kim's research was the difficulty the teachers had with getting the older (4th/5th grade) students to comply with the chorusing routine, a phenomenon that probably accounted for the lower proportion of chorusing elicitations in these grades. The teachers of the upper grade classes varied in their response to this resistance, with one tending to ignore it and the other insisting on compliance. The difference between upper and lower grade responses to the chorus elicitations suggests that socialization to US norms and practices had taken hold to a much greater extent among the older students. Additionally, in contrast to other US-based accounts, nomination was relatively rare, representing only 7.1%, of a total of 278 elicitation moves across the entire corpus. Kim suggested that nomination, along with invitation to bid (6.1% of the total), occurred in the lower grades only when the teacher needed to control order and noise.[6]

A US-based Japanese Saturday school

Yamashita's (1993) analysis of interaction in a different heritage setting – a Japanese Saturday school in southern California – documents yet another set of turn-taking routines and expectations. The school has the stated goal of serving Japanese residents of California who wish their children to remain familiar with the practices of Japanese schooling and be able to function well on their return to Japan (where all teachers in the school were trained and certified). The study considered interaction in three 1st grade and two 6th grade classes. In each one, turn-allocation procedures for nomination and invitation to bid (often with no explicit signal for students to raise their hands) were employed regularly and constituted a majority of the initiations in the 1st grade classes. When invitations to reply occurred, the teachers recognized students who raised their hands and ignored those who simply spoke out.

Teachers used two additional turn-related utterance types, both more frequent in the 6th grade classes and both likely contributing to a reduced amount of student talk in the higher grade. The first, seen in Example 6 (Yamashita, 1993: 35), was a confirmation request (highlighted in bold) in the ongoing stream of teacher talk.

Example 6

T: Hai. Mure nagara tobu. Kono 'tobu' wa honto ni sora o tonderu n ja nakute sugoku hayai kara tonderu yooni mieru. Sooyuu koto ne. **Wakatta?**
Yes. (The horses) fly in crowds. This 'fly' doesn't mean that (they) really fly in the sky, but (they) look like they are flying because (they) are very fast. It means so. **Did (you) understand?**[7]

Ss: ((silence; some nod their heads))

T: Hai. Jaa futatsu me no danrakuikimasu.
Yes, then, let's go to the second paragraph.

Here, as elsewhere in Yamashita's corpus, the teacher confirmation request was responded to non-verbally by a few students but did not evoke a verbal turn by students.

A second strategy, seen in Example 7 (Yamashita, 1993: 40), occurred when the teacher posed a question to which she herself provided an answer. Yamashita termed this an 'ostensible question' because the teacher did not appear to expect a student response.

Example 7

T: Un sukeeru no ookii tokoro. Dakara betsu no kotoba de iu to?
Yes a place on a large scale.   So, how do (you) say (it) with another word?
Ss: ((no response))
T: Chikyuu desho?   Soshite hokani- hokano kotoba de ittara nan nano?
The earth, isn't it? And what else   how do (you) say (it) with another word?
Ss: ((no response))
T: Hiroi ne?   Hiroi sekai desu yo.
Wide, isn't it?   The wide world.

With respect to this phenomenon, Yamashita (1993: 43) observed that the teacher did not really intend for the students to answer verbally and thereby display their own academic knowledge. The teacher's questions were thus 'very likely to become merely a part of the teacher's monologue.' Further, even when the students gave incorrect responses, the teacher did not respond with further elicitations to lead to an extended sequence of the type described by Mehan (1979). Instead, she simply answered her own question.

These two moves – confirmation request and ostensible question – together accounted for 30% of all elicitations in the 1st grade classes (80 of 265) but 60% in the 6th grade (142 of 238), where the interaction was more heavily dominated by monologic teacher turns and where there was much less spoken student participation. Yamashita also noted that when an actual response was desired, the teachers typically repeated or paraphrased the initial question as a signal for students to respond. In some instances, especially in 1st grade, this led to overlap where students answered the question simultaneously with the teacher's repetition, as in Example 8 (Yamashita, 1993: 52).

Example 8

T: Hai. Ookina ookina kabu ni narimashita. Tsugi wa nani kashira? Tsugi wa doo narimasu ka?

Yes. A big big turnip grew. What is next? What happens next?
[
S: Kabu o-
A turnip-
T: Ojiisan ga kabu o nukoo to shimasu ne. Hai e o kakimashoo.
The grandfather tries to pull out the turnip, doesn't he? Yes, let's draw a picture.

Yamashita's study included comparative data from a Japanese language class (taught by a Japanese instructor) at a local community college. She found that the same kind of overlap was common; the American students responded as soon as the question was first asked, while the Japanese teachers repeated the questions without waiting for a student response, as in Example 9 (Yamashita, 1993: 56).

Example 9

T: Hai jaa ichi ban. Yamada-san wa sensei desu ka? Sensei desu ka?
Yes, then, number one. Is Mr. Yamada a teacher? A teacher?
[
Ss: iie
No
T: iie sensei ja arimasen. (1.2)   Nan desu ka?
No, (he) is not a teacher. (1.2)   What is he?

Yamashita (1993: 62) concluded that in this context, 'the invitation to reply procedure did not seem to exist,' at least from the teachers' perspective. When students did respond without first being recognized, the teachers tended to ignore their responses, calling instead on those who raised their hands. Those invitations to reply that are noted in her account (5% of the total in 6th grade, and 9.8% in 1st grade) represent instances where student and teacher utterances overlapped (as in Examples 8 and 9 above), or where students responded but were ignored in favor of those who raised their hands. In other words, although the students occasionally treated teacher initiations as invitations to reply, the teachers' responses indicated they were not intended as such.

Turn-taking characteristics in the Japanese context

Several studies of classroom interaction in Japan have documented further variation in classroom turn-taking phenomena. For example, one study of *kotae-awase* ('going over the exercise') in Japanese junior high school classes (Ikeno, 1998) found that students exercised control over the turn-taking system through a practice unlike others described in this chapter. In Ikeno's account, which analyzed seven *kotae-awase* events in five classes, nomination and invitation to bid were the predominant turn-taking procedures (78% and 16%, respectively, or 54 and 11 of 69), while invitation to reply was quite rare (4 of 69, or 6%). However, when students in the *kotaeawase* event did not know the answer to an item or question or felt unprepared to answer, one option they could exercise was to say *wakarimasen* (literally, '[I] cannot tell' or, more freely, 'I don't know'). According to Ikeno (1998: 43), '*wakarimasen* means that (the student) cannot display the correct answer to a question. Stating *wakarimasen* functions to acknowledge a student's own fault in order to terminate a turn.' In sequences such as Example 10 (Ikeno, 1998: 43), students could use *wakarimasen* to avoid being nominated in subsequent turns.

Example 10

T: 4-ban   mekishiko nado   no ijuumin   no hito,
   4-number Mexico   etc.   PT immigrant PT person
   supeingo   -kei   no hito o   nan   to   ii   masu ka?
   Spanish language -origin PT person O what PT call AUX PT
   Number four. Immigrants from Mexico, etc., people who speak Spanish, how do we call them?
T: ((calling student's name)) Nakamura.
   (1.0)
T: Nakamura.
S: hai.
   yes
   Yes.
T: Nante   ii   masu   ka?
   what   call   AUX   PART
   How do (we) call (immigrants from Mexico)?
S: Wakari   mas   –en
   can tell   AUX   not
   (I) cannot tell (how we call them).
T: hisupanikku   to   ii   masu.
   Hispanic   PART call AUX
   (We) call (them) Hispanic.

In such instances, the student could effectively end the sequence so that further initiations would not occur.

Previous analyses by Anderson (1995) and Cook (1999) have also considered interaction in Japanese classrooms; their work documents a four-part rather than three-part sequence: initiation-presentation-reaction-evaluation (or IPRxE). In these accounts, after one student offers a response to a teacher initiation, one or more students reacts to the first student, typically commenting on how that student responded. While Cook interprets the sequence of presentation-reaction turns as a means through which Japanese students are socialized to the importance of listening to others (see Clancy, 1986), Anderson claims that a multi-party participant structure underlies the sequence, in contrast to the fundamentally dyadic nature of IRE-based interaction. Specifically, while the reaction turn is often initiated explicitly by the teacher, in some instances the reacting student simply interprets the first student's response as a turn-allocation signal in itself, and speaks without waiting to be called on or given the floor by the teacher. Cook (personal communication) notes that this second practice tends to occur as a routine in some classes. From the perspective of classroom turn-taking more generally, it is noteworthy that one student may react to another student without an intervening teacher initiation. This recalls Cazden's (1988) discussion of variation in classroom interaction, which notes the difficulty in most IRE-based interaction of achieving consecutive student turns where one student responds to the previous student turn rather than simply adding another response to the teacher's initiation, as more typically occurs.

Summary and Discussion

Turn-taking variation across contexts

When considered together, the accounts of turn-taking reported here present a complex picture of similarities and differences across the various contexts investigated. Together, they illustrate the importance, noted by Ochs (1986), of stressing distribution and frequency in cross-cultural research without assuming or claiming categorical differences. Each of these studies reports occurrences of at least two of the three basic turn-allocation procedures initially described by Mehan (1979), although which two and in what proportion vary from study to study, as do specific characteristics of the procedures themselves. For example, every study found instances of nomination of individual students. However, the frequencies differed considerably, as illustrated in Table 13.1.[8]

As seen here, nominations were common in some instances, but infrequent in others. The quantitative information does not tell the entire story, however. Chen's study (1998), for example, is the only one that reports that students were required to stand before responding to a nomination. In addition, both Chen (1998) and Chick (1996a) (who does not quantify his findings) report individual nominations in the context of choral elicitations, but characterize them differently. Chick reports that, when individuals were nominated in the Zulu context, they were usually asked to respond to the same question the class had already answered in chorus. This ensured that respondents would not lose face and avoided revealing any failure to master the prescribed curriculum. In contrast, nominations in Chen's TEFL data seemed to challenge the students. In some instances the teachers

Cross-cultural Variation in Classroom Turn-taking Practices 215

Table 13.1 Nominations as percentages of turn-allocation moves

Source and setting	Nominations
Chen, 1998: Middle school TEFL lessons, Taiwan	22%
Ikeno, 1998: Junior high school classes, Japan	78%
Yamashita, 1993: Japanese Saturday school, Southern California	31.3% (1st grade) 22.3% (6th grade)
Kim, 2000: Korean-American school, Southern California	6.5% (2nd grade) 8.2% (4th/5th grade)
McCollum, 1989: 3rd grade classes, Puerto Rico, Chicago	34% (Puerto Rico) 62% (Chicago)

exhorted them to work or study harder, and in others individuals were repeatedly asked questions they could not answer. The contrast is perhaps unexpected in light of the similarities in chorusing routines in the two settings, where the answers needed by students could be readily accessed in context, possibly a common feature of choral responses, since the same phenomenon was also observed by Kim (2000).

Invitation to reply was also documented in most of the contexts reported here, if choral elicitations are included. However, these studies suggest a different relationship of choral elicitation to invitation to reply from that noted by Mehan (1979) and by Griffin and Humphrey (1978), who found that chorusing was an optional response to invitation to reply. However, several settings reported here (Chen, 1998; Chick, 1996a; Kim, 2000) suggest that chorus elicitations are distinct from those invitations to reply that elicit one or more individual responses. For example, Chen reports only chorus elicitations, but no other invitations to reply. Conversely, McCollum (1989) documented a large number of invitations to reply but no choral responses to them. Yamashita (1993) reported neither type, noting that for the teachers in her corpus, the invitation to reply did not seem to be an option for eliciting student talk. In Ikeno's (1998) corpus, only a few instances of invitation to reply occurred, none of which were chorus elicitations. Table 13.2 summarizes these results, which suggest that chorus elicitation, although similar in form to invitation to reply, may be perceived and treated as distinct by classroom participants in some contexts.

As seen in Table 13.2, only one study (Kim, 2000) among these five documented both chorus elicitations and invitations to reply (followed by single or multiple, but not simultaneous responses). Moreover, she did not find the two response-types to be alternatives for one another (Mehan, 1979; Griffin & Humphrey, 1978), as evidenced by sequences where the teacher insisted that a reluctant class produce a choral answer.

Invitations to bid as a percentage of turn allocation moves also provide

Table 13.2 Invitations to reply and chorus elicitations as percentages of turn-allocation moves

Source and setting	Choral response	Individual responses(s)
Chen, 1998: Middle school TEFL lessons, Taiwan	78%	
Ikeno, 1998: Junior high school classes, Japan		6%
Yamashita, 1993: Japanese Saturday school, Southern California		9.8%[8] (1st grade) 5% (6th grade)
Kim, 2000: Korean-American school, Southern California	43.8% (2nd grade) 28.3% (4th/5th grades)	44.2% (2nd grade) 56.1% (4th/5th grades)
McCollum, 1989: 3rd grade classes, Puerto Rico, Chicago		62% (Puerto Rico) 24% (Chicago)

revealing information (Table 13.3). Interestingly, invitation to bid followed by student handraising was relatively infrequent across all the contexts considered here, with 28.7% in Yamashita's (1993) 1st grade data being the highest percentage reported. Even in Mehan's account, only 8.5% of all turn-allocation procedures consisted of invitations to bid. Hence, although invitation to bid is often thought to be a primary means of maintaining social order in classroom interaction, these consistently low frequencies across diverse contexts suggest that it may be a dispreferred one.

An important finding across the three settings where more than one grade level was considered (Chen, 1998; Kim, 2000; Yamashita, 1993) was the difference in turn-taking patterns between the two age groups. In Chen's analysis, older students did not respond in chorus, but the younger ones did so almost exclusively. In both Yamashita's and Chen's accounts, the older students generally engaged in much less turn-taking with the teacher. In Kim's data, the older students in some cases actively resisted attempts by the teacher to elicit responses in chorus, though the younger students chorused enthusiastically. These three studies, especially when taken together, are indicative of the kind of variation that can characterize specific sociocultural settings as well as individual developmental experiences.

Implications for the second language classroom

The variation seen across these settings suggests ways in which different expectations regarding turn-taking can influence the L2 classroom, especially in contexts where teacher and students have interactional histories that might lead to non-congruent expectations. An example was seen in

Table 13.3 Invitations to bid as percentages of turn-allocation moves

Source and setting	Invitations to bid
Chen, 1998: Middle school TEFL lessons, Taiwan	0.4%
Ikeno, 1998: Junior high school classes, Japan	16%
Yamashita, 1993: Japanese Saturday school, Southern California	28.7% (1st grade) 13% (6th grade)
Kim, 2000: Korean-American school, Southern California	5.5% (2nd grade) 7.4% (4th/5th grades)
McCollum, 1989: 3rd grade classes, Puerto Rico, Chicago	2% (3rd grade, Puerto Rico) 11% (3rd grade, Chicago)
Mehan, 1979: Combined 1st–3rd grades, San Diego, California	8.5%

Yamashita's (1993) report of overlapping utterances from teachers and students in a college Japanese language class (see Example 9 above) where the teacher asked a question twice, indicating that an answer was actually expected. However, the American students' answers overlapped with the teacher's repetition of the question in what they probably expected to be the reply slot of an IRE sequence.

Some of the turn-taking phenomena described above suggest further ways in which L2 classroom interaction might lead to a form of 'cross-talk' (Chick, 1996b; Gumperz, 1983; Scollon & Scollon, 1981) or interactional encounters where the assumptions and expectations of teacher and students may differ. Students with early experiences in contexts such as those analyzed by Chen (1998) or Yamashita (1993) – where students expect to respond in chorus, raise their hands, or be nominated – may be reluctant to volunteer a response to a teacher's invitation to reply. It could even be argued that such differences in expectations and histories are the source of a common perception among native English speaking ESL/EFL teachers that certain groups of students are 'quiet' or unwilling to 'participate' in class. The accounts reported here, however, suggest that nominations (where volunteering is not required) could be a more familiar and unambiguous signal to speak in class. They also suggest that more student-centered participant structures such as small group work, where a less asymmetrical social context exists and interaction is student-initiated, may be a more comfortable context in which students might volunteer a turn. At a minimum, language teachers who understand some of the possible turn-taking experiences through which their students have been educated will have a knowledge base from which to make their own interactional choices in the classroom. McCollum's (1989) study of turn-allocation, in fact, was motivated by just such a desire to inform North American teachers of Puerto Rican students so that the two groups might interact more effectively. In a personal account, McCollum reported how the motivation for her study grew from her own experiences of cross-talk in a Puerto Rican school:

> I initially felt that my interaction with the students was getting in the way of learning. I seemed unable to produce behaviors that the students expected and my actions did not bring expected responses from them ... Later as a teacher in Chicago...colleagues who had never taught Puerto Rican students before voiced frustrations about their inability to give lessons where student–teacher communication was in 'sync.' (McCollum, 1989: 134)

In many instances, ESL/EFL and other L2 teachers react similarly; together with their students, they are often acutely aware of the relevance of cross-cultural phenomena to interactional expectations in the language classroom. At times, however, the sources and effects of such phenomena are viewed more impressionistically than empirically. The studies reported here represent efforts towards a more grounded basis from which to consider the interactional complexities in the L2 teaching/learning experience. They also suggest possibilities for comparative analyses of other features of classroom discourse. With respect to cross-cultural research more generally, they contribute to the broader effort toward understanding how different sociolinguistic expectations – whether related to turn-taking, written text structure, apology behavior, or the wide range of language practices still to be investigated – might affect the language learning experience.

Notes

1. An IRE sequence typically includes a teacher initiation move, a student reply, and a confirming or disconfirming teacher evaluation, e.g.:
   Initiation   →   T: Who was President during most of the depression?
   Reply   →   S: Roosevelt
   Evaluation   →   T: Right
   In Sinclair and Coulthard's (1975) account, the third term is labeled, perhaps more accurately, 'feedback,' with the sequence becoming 'IRF.'
2. Other approaches to turn-taking are also relevant and warrant further investigation. For example, turn-taking patterns can be analyzed in order to compare and evaluate participation in different types of small group or pair activities.
3. My own study of middle school classroom interaction (Poole, 1992) found multiple invitations to reply that elicited either individual or overlapping responses, but none that elicited chorusing, suggesting that the option to respond in chorus or individually claimed by Mehan and Griffin and Humphrey varies according to context.

4. The exception is Sinclair and Coulthard's (1975) work, which is based on UK classrooms. Their analysis, a major account that preceded Mehan's, is quite similar. In this chapter, I rely heavily on the Mehan account to provide an easier comparison with the studies reviewed, whose analyses were largely based on his work.
5. The following transcription conventions are followed throughout this chapter: underlining indicates a gloss (literal translation); (.) indicates a pause, with timing optional, e.g. (1.2); ((...)) indicates extralinguistic information; :: indicates lengthening of the preceding sound; [indicates an overlap.
6. This recalls Griffin and Humphrey's (1978) claim that nomination and invitation to bid were a means of maintaining social order; though, in contrast to Kim's (2000) account, this point was used to explain the predominance of both procedures in their data.
7. Yamashita's transcript data does not include literal translations.
8. Not all of the studies reported here provided the frequency data; the tables summarize those that did.
9. The individual responses occurred when the students treated the teacher's elicitations as invitations to reply. However, the teacher's tendency to ignore or overlap with these responses suggested that the teacher did not intend them to be invitations to reply.

Part 5
Language Policy and Planning

Part 5
Introduction

WILLIAM G. EGGINGTON

It is generally acknowledged that language policy and planning has been an academic discipline for only about 40 years. Robert Kaplan has made major contributions to this field almost from its inception, culminating in the publication of *Language Planning: From Practice to Theory* (Kaplan & Baldauf, 1997) and the establishment of the journal *Current Issues in Language Planning* (Multilingual Matters). These efforts have helped discipline the discipline' during a time when the field has been called upon to apply its accumulated expertise to a wide and vital range of language policy development and language planning needs.

In the last section of the final chapter of *Language Planning: From Practice to Theory*, Kaplan and Baldauf review the major practice-derived theoretical constructs developed in the book. These constructs include a need to acknowledge that:

(1) Corpus and status planning are not separate activities; they are intertwined practices.
(2) Language policy involves far more than macro-level general national language policy; micro language planning activities are 'occurring more frequently and with increasingly greater impact' (Kaplan & Baldauf, 1997: 320).
(3) The one nation/one language notion is a myth.
(4) Any language planning activity is embedded within a series of immediate and interconnected eco-systems.
(5) Language planning is a multidimensional activity that requires academic and community input where the communities represented must include all speakers of the languages involved in the language planning activity.
(6) Language planning must not be left to the education sector alone, nor should a language planning activity begin with the education sector. Rather, any language planning activity must include the totality of the ecosystem within which that activity is embedded.
(7) Any language planning activity must centrally derive its authority

from the community(ies) of speakers' (Kaplan & Baldauf, 1997: 322) affected by the planning activity within a bottom-up framework.
(8) Successful language planning requires a continuing process of implementation, evaluation, revision, and implementation.

It may be that these theoretical constructs, derived from practice, form the foundation for future language planning practice. Indeed, many of these constructs are partially reflected in the following chapters of the present book.

The period enveloping Kaplan's language planning contributions has also witnessed the development of economic, technological, and cultural globalization which, in turn, has fostered the equally remarkable international spread of English to the point where it is now seen as the world's language of wider communication. Consequently, much language policy and planning effort in many nations is directed at either fostering the spread of English and/or hindering the erosion of threatened languages by English (Fishman, 2001). In response to the need to address the linguistic consequences of globalization, language planning, once a secondary subdiscipline of sociolinguistics, has now emerged as a vital field garnering the ideological concerns and empirical resources of many government and non-government agencies as personnel in these agencies deal with desired or non-desired, planned or unplanned language shift within their realm of responsibility.

The four chapters contained in this section offer a sampling of the richness of the field. They either directly of indirectly address the practice-derived theoretical constructs reviewed above, and a number of them address a language planning response to the spread of English.

Richard Baldauf's chapter 'Micro Language Planning' (Chapter 14) obviously addresses Construct 2 (micro language planning) by attempting to place the construct within an established language planning framework. Baldauf questions whether the framework (or elements of it) are relevant for small-scale situations, and he devotes the remainder of the chapter to reviewing a number of published examples of micro-planning. He concludes by suggesting that because micro language planning approaches seem to offer successful outcomes, closer attention needs to be paid to this developing area. Indeed, it may be that a consequence of the globalization factor mentioned above is that the frequency and fluidity of localized language-related 'problems' requiring immediate attention by language planners will create a demand for the development of a range of micro language planning procedural models. This will then enable language planners to offer quick and practical solutions to immediate local needs.

Constructs 1 (corpus and status planning), 4 (the ecosystemic nature of language planning), 5 (the multidimensional nature of language planning),

Language Policy and Planning: Introduction 225

and 7 (bottom-up planning) are reflected in Chapter 15, 'The Englishization of Spanish in Mexico, by Baumgardner. He provides examples of direct borrowings, calques and 'pseudo-anglicisms' from English into Mexican Spanish. Baumgardner then describes efforts to prevent English intrusion, thus revealing the relationship between corpus planning and status planning (Construct 1). He shows how the Mexican Academy of Language (modeled after Spain's Royal Spanish Academy) has long been struggling against Anglicisms in its attempt to keep the language 'pure.' He notes that the Academy lacks general respect and support from large segments of the Mexican populace, and he details recent efforts to circumvent the Academy by establishing the Commission for the Defense of the Spanish Language, whose primary function was to defend Mexican Spanish from English intrusion. However, the authority of the commission seems to have been confined to a narrow set of political elites, and neither it nor the Academy have been able to significantly retard the on-going intrusion of English into Mexican Spanish. Contributing factors in their ineffectiveness may be their inability to address the entire ecosystem that is at the foundation of English borrowings (Construct 4). In addition, it appears that the Academy and the Commission followed top-down language planning models and did not derive their authority from the community of speakers, who seem quite content to continue to import anglicisms into Mexican Spanish. These less-than-stellar achievements can be attributed to a failure of these institutions to consider Constructs 5 and 7.

Lo Bianco's contribution (Chapter 16) tangentially addresses Construct 7 (bottom-up planning) but then moves into an extended elaboration of language planning's ecosystem as well as the multi-dimensional nature of language planning (Constructs 4 and 5). Lo Bianco asserts that the academic and scholarly dimension of language planning, tied as it is to its origins as an applied linguistics subfield, is limited in scope in that it relies too heavily on rational approaches. Instead, Lo Bianco argues for an expansion of the scope of language planning to include discourse – an analysis of the politics of language including the analysis of performative speech and writing and, in particular, the language of processes of language policy making. He elaborates this call for the inclusion of discourse in language planning by discussing discourse with respect to corpus, status, acquisition, usage, and esteem planning. Lo Bianco concludes with a suggestion that language planning studies need to include policy analysis that theorizes power.

In Chapter 17, on foreign language policy in Hungary, Medgyes first discusses the language situation in Hungary, drawing attention to the one nation, one language myth (Construct 3). He then describes changes in foreign language teaching and learning in Hungary since the demise of the Soviet Union, paying particular attention to the rise of English and (to a lesser extent), German as desired foreign languages. The major portion of his chapter is devoted to a description of the 'World-Language' program inaugurated by the Hungarian Ministry of Education in 2003, a language-in-education planning approach aimed at fostering the acquisition of German, English, or French in elementary school. As such, Medgyes is addressing Construct 6 (language-in-education policy) by pointing out that the policy came about because of a broader desire for Hungary to meet European Union multilingual expectations. However, in a discussion of the policy, Medgyes suggests that this admirable language-in-education plan could be weakened because it has not been part of a comprehensive language policy for the nation (Construct 6). For example, Medgyes points out that the policy has been attacked by those of a more nationalist bent, who worry that it is part of a larger conspiracy to marginalize and eventually eliminate the Hungarian language. Time will reveal if more attention should have been paid to placing the language-in-education policy under the broad umbrella of a national language policy.

In 1986, I was involved in the organization of a conference on Australian Aboriginal language teaching as part of the pre-conference schedule for the 8th World Congress of Applied Linguistics to be held in Sydney in August 1987. We wanted the conference to be more than a group of non-Aboriginal people talking about Aboriginal people and their languages. So, we involved many Aboriginal leaders and teachers in the planning and implementation phases. At their request, the conference was held at Batchelor College, an Aboriginal teacher educator college located in the Northern Territory of Australia on the fringes of Australia's outback. We invited Dr Kaplan as one of the major speakers to the conference. After visiting an Aboriginal community, Dr Kaplan completed his paper, a document that contained many helpful insights and suggestions toward fostering first language and English language planning in the Australian Aboriginal context (Kaplan 1990). At the conclusion of the conference, the Aboriginal organizers had planned a ceremony. They invited representatives from all racial, ethnic, and national groups to the stage. One by one, these representatives stepped to the front of the stage, held up a hand, and stated in their language: 'Here is my hand. If you cut it, it will bleed red blood' (signifying the universality and equality of all humankind). How fitting that Dr. Kaplan was chosen to perform this ritual.

Chapter 14
Micro Language Planning

RICHARD B. BALDAUF JR

Introduction

In an overview of the field of language policy and planning, Kaplan and Baldauf (1997: 52) suggest that language planning occurs at several levels, the macro, the meso, and the micro. Although they provide several examples of micro level planning, such as a company requiring business translation in North America (Kaplan & Baldauf, 1997: 254ff), this application of the principles of language policy and planning to micro situations is not a significant focus of the volume, nor is it developed in any detail. As Kaplan and Baldauf indicate in their introductory chapter, when applied linguists think of language planning, they normally think in terms of large-scale, usually national, planning, often undertaken by governments and meant to influence ways of speaking or writing within a society. Davies (1999: 123), in a review of the volume, argues that Kaplan and Baldauf have been less convincing about the centrality of applied linguistics to language policy and planning, and he suggests that they try to 'claim too much: language planning is best restricted to governmental activity, difficult as that may be to encompass.'

Governmental activity is, of course, precisely where early language planning studies and practice have their roots, in macro sociolinguistics and related disciplines (see, for example, the Ford Foundation East African Studies: Fox, 1975; Fishman, 1974; Rubin & Jernudd, 1971), and it continues to be the site of most language policy and planning studies and critiques. Furthermore, government officials are often the prime actors in language planning activities (Baldauf & Kaplan, 2003). But the question still remains: is language policy and planning activity, almost by definition, restricted to large-scale (macro) governmental activity, or can the frameworks that have been developed be applied differentially but in an equally valid manner to micro situations? And if such applications are possible, is the resultant work still language policy and planning, or does it then fall into some other subfield of applied linguistics or of some other branch of linguistics, such as sociolinguistics?

There has been some discussion of, but little specific scholarly work on, the idea that language planning can (and does) occur at the micro level (i.e. language planning for businesses, educational bodies and other organizations), and the extent to which many of the same issues that can be found in the policy and planning frameworks and literature are relevant to the micro level. It is perhaps particularly appropriate to explore this question in a volume dedicated to the scholarship of Robert Kaplan, because he and some of his students have provided some of the most well-formed examples of what might be seen as the beginnings of a micro language planning genre.

To put this question in context, it is necessary to examine briefly what is meant by language planning and how the macro models and frameworks that have been developed might relate to micro studies, and then to review the available literature on micro studies to understand more clearly what has already been done or what might be done.

A Language Planning Framework

Some brief definitions

Traditionally, language planning has been seen as the deliberate, future-oriented, systematic change of language code and use, most visibly undertaken by government in a community of speakers. Language planning is directed by, or leads to, the promulgation of a language policy (or policies), by government or some other authoritative body or person. Language policies are bodies of ideas, laws, regulations, rules, and practices intended to achieve some planned language change (Kaplan & Baldauf, 1997: 3). Language policy may be realized in formal (overt) language planning documents and pronouncements (e.g. constitutions, legislation, policy statements) that are either symbolic or substantive in form, in informal statements of intent (e.g. in the discourse of language, politics, and society), or it may be left unstated (covert). While the distinction between language policy (the plan) and language planning (the implementation of the plan) is an important one for users, in the literature the two terms have frequently been used interchangeably.

A framework for language planning goals

Over the roughly 35 years that language planning has been developing as a field, a number of language planners have put forward their ideas about what might constitute a model for it (e.g. Ferguson, 1968b; Neustupný, 1974; Fishman, 1974; Haugen, 1983; Cooper, 1989; Haarmann, 1990), while others (e.g. Annamalai & Rubin, 1980; Nahir, 1984; Bentahila & Davies, 1993) have contributed to our understanding of the field by concentrating on defining the nature of language planning goals. Hornberger (1994) has explicitly brought these two strands together in a single framework, while Kaplan and Baldauf (1997) have argued that any such framework should be situated within an ecological context. Kaplan and Baldauf (2003) have developed a revised and expanded framework with illustrative examples of each of the goals, drawn from polities in the Pacific basin. An alternative conceptualization to this framework has different foci (i.e. language management), but can be seen as a complementary approach (see, for example, Neustupný & Nekvapil, 2003).

This evolving framework reflects the changes that have occurred in language planning itself, which was an outgrowth of the positivistic economic and social science paradigms that dominated the first three decades after World War II. Since the 1990s, critical approaches to the discipline as well as a broadening context for it have taken on greater importance (for a historical overview, see Ricento, 2000a) as those involved have confronted issues such as language ecology (e.g. Kaplan & Baldauf, 1997; Mühlhäusler, 2000), language rights (e.g. May, 2001, 2003, 2005), and the place of English and languages other than English (e.g. Pennycook, 1998; Ricento, 2000b; Maurais & Morris, 2003).

The framework set out in Table 14.1 suggests that the practice of overt (explicit, planned) or covert (implicit, unplanned) language policy and planning (Baldauf, 1994; Eggington, 2002) may consist of four types: status planning (about society; see van Els, 2005), corpus planning (about language; see Liddicoat, 2005), language-in-education (acquisition) planning (about learning; see Baldauf & Kaplan, 2005), and prestige planning (about image; see Ager, 2005).

Each of these four types of language planning can be realized from two approaches: a policy approach (with an emphasis on form: basic language and policy decisions and their implementation) or a cultivation approach (with an emphasis on the functional extension of language development and use). Together, these eight perspectives can be best understood through the goals that planners set out to achieve. But no matter how useful these perspectives may be for mapping out the discipline, most of these goals are not independent of each other; for example, policy-planning goals normally need cultivation-planning support. In addition, a particular language planning problem may have a number of different goals, some of which may even be contradictory; for example, the widespread introduction of a strong foreign language (like English) may potentially conflict in the school curriculum with goals related to local or regional language maintenance. Nor are goals normally implemented in isolation but as part of a broader (even if covert or unstated) set of objectives. Thus, while it may be pedagogically convenient to move progressively through the framework, in practice goals are often tackled independently.

Table 14.1 A framework for language planning goals

Approaches Types (overt – covert)	Policy planning (form) Goals	Cultivation planning (function) Goals

1. Status planning
(about society)
	Status standardization
	• Officialization
	• Nationalization
	• Proscription
		Status planning
		• Revival
		  • restoration
		  • revitalization
		  reversal
		• Maintenance
		• Interlingual communication
		  • international
		  intranational
		• Spread

2. Corpus planning
(about language)
	Standardization
	• Corpus
	  • graphization
	  grammatication
	  lexication
	• Auxiliary code
	  • graphization
	  grammatication
	  lexication
		Corpus elaboration
		• Lexical modernization
		• Stylistic modernization
		• Renovation
		  • purification
		  reform
		  stylistic simplification
		  terminological
		  unification
		• Internationalization

3. Language-in- education planning (about learning)	Policy development • Access policy • Personnel policy • Curriculum policy • Methods and materials policy • Resourcing policy • Community policy • Evaluation policy	Acquisition planning • Reacquisition • Maintenance • Foreign/Second language • Shift
4. Prestige planning (about image)	Language promotion • Official/government • Institutional • Pressure group • Individual	Intellectualization • Language of science • Language of professions • Language of high culture

Source: Kaplan & Baldauf, 2003: 202

Micro Language Planning

Having briefly outlined how macro language policy and planning can be conceived, the question is whether the framework or elements of the framework are relevant for small scale or micro situations (remembering that the framework is meant to be used selectively). First, it may be useful to clarify what is *not* being talked about when micro language planning and policy is discussed. Most people would acknowledge that 'the impact of language planning and policy depends heavily on meso and micro level involvement and support' (Kaplan & Baldauf, 2003: 201), and a number of studies have looked at micro support for implementation of macro language planning and policy. However, these are matters of scale in policy implementation, not exemplars of micro language policy and planning, because the fundamental planning is conceptualized and carried out at the macro level. Rather, micro planning refers to cases where businesses, institutions, groups, or individuals create a plan to utilize and develop their language resources, one that is not directly the result of some larger macro policy but is a response to their own needs, language problems, or requirement for language management. Such micro planning can be contrasted with micro implementation of macro planning, some examples of which are examined in the next section.

Micro implementation of macro policy

As an indication of how terminology has changed or has been used differently at different times, McConnell (1977a; 1977b) characterized language planning as descriptive of macro situations while language management represented the micro planning that was occurring in Canada/Quebec in the 1970s. However, as Neustupný and Nekvapil (2003) explain in their study of language management in the Czech Republic, language management may either be 'organized' (involving multiple participants and ideologies in the management process), or 'simple' (dealing with often specific individual problems). This difference highlights the fact that various frameworks view language policy and planning as working from the macro to the micro. Some examples of studies that incorporate micro examination of macro policy include the following:

- Breen (2002) provides a micro educational example with a clear national policy basis. The macro policy context is the Australian government's idealistic policy in the 1990s to increase access to second language teaching in primary schools. However, the meso and micro implementation of that policy is dependent on the Australian States, which control education and ultimately schools. Thus, specific policy development and implementation occurs at the State and school levels, and makes only general reference to national initiatives. The study examines Western Australian primary teachers with some proficiency in relevant languages who were then provided with professional development in language methodology with the goal of implementing second language study in their schools. Breen examines how this micro implementation of policy affected teachers' professional identity and their on-going social relationships with others in their work context. The tensions revealed by these teachers in their new roles have implications for the implementation of language policy in schools more generally.

- **Blachford** (2000) examined the nature and characteristics of Chinese language policies and their impact on the 90 million people from the 55 ethnic groups that make up the national minorities of China. These policy making and implementation processes were examined to see how they related to micro policy goals and micro implementations through a complex bureaucratic structure. To illuminate the macro processes, several minority groups and their languages and educational situations were closely examined, using a case study methodology.
- **DeLorme** (1999), in a study in Kazakhstan, used an ethnographic case from a Kazakh-medium school to collect micro level data that shows attempts by the Kazakh ruling elite and Kazakh language medium school administrators to restore ethnic national consciousness, consolidate the Kazakh's political power, and implement Kazakh as the official language. This policy and planning had to be undertaken in a way that did not antagonize the large Russian- speaking minority, or Russia itself.
- **Corvalán** (1998) critically analyzed the history and current state of school-based bilingual education in Paraguay, examining both the micro and macro dimensions of linguistic policies. These school programs included both Guaraní and Spanish-only speakers. Corvalán argued that policies must not only cater for these minority groups at the general macro level but also contribute to more micro level decisions such as student classification, teacher training, language of instruction, and teaching the other language as a second language.
- **Kuo and Jernudd** (1993) linked macro-level language planning in Singapore, which was centered on government programs that tried to foster national consolidation through socio-ethnic and economic development, with micro language planning, which focused on individual conduct in discourse and group behavior in communication. They argued that these macro and micro language policy and planning methods were complementary in encouraging a new Singaporean identity that contributes to economic, social, and cultural advancement through greater communicative integration. Kuo and Jernudd suggest that a greater micro level emphasis is needed (i.e. greater attention to individual language and discourse patterns) if a balanced approach to nation building is to occur.
- **Tandefelt** (1992) used a historical case study (1880–1980) of a community in Vanda in Finland to elucidate the on-going language shift

occurring from Swedish to Finnish in the community. Both macro and micro level language developments were examined. Interviews across three generations revealed the Fennicization process (that is, making the society more Finnish) that has been occurring.
- **Tollefson** (1981a) used examples from Yugoslavia and the Soviet Union to distinguish between centralized (macro) and decentralized (micro) language planning.

These examples indicate that micro language planning typically refers to the use of micro situational analysis or methodology (e.g. case studies) to examine macro issues arising from the language problems to be found in nation states or, in Tollefson's case, to the shift from top-down to bottom-up state planning. Although most of the studies are evaluative, there is little or no suggestion that micro level policy should be developed or that planning should extend beyond what is required to implement macro policy. Rather, it is the impact of macro-polity policy (or the lack thereof) on micro situations that is being examined.

Micro examples in the literature

By definition, micro language policy should originate from the micro and not from the macro level, but it is difficult to identify studies of this type in the literature. Perhaps such work is not currently valued because it does not belong to an 'authentic' research genre; or perhaps business and other micro sites are less open to public scrutiny (and therefore academic analysis) than governmental entities; or perhaps such work is published in business-related journals under different headings. Studies that are found relate to education and schooling, business (specifically banking), community language needs, methodology and theory, and law and translation, indicating that there is a range of possible sites for micro policy and planning. Examples of such studies include the following:

- **Mac Giolla Chriost** (2002) drew on micro developments in Wales and used them as the basis for suggesting that progress in planning for Irish in Northern Ireland may depend on the use of micro language planning, since at the polity level, Irish could be either a divisive or a unifying factor. Although Irish was more strongly associated with (and better known by) Catholics than Protestants, attitudes toward it were generally positive among both groups. There also seemed to be a more general revival of the language among the young and the upwardly mobile. Given the dangers of the language issue becoming embroiled in politics at the macro policy level, Mac Giolla Chriost suggests that progress in language planning needs to occur at the micro level and be locally based and tailored to specific community needs.

- **Yoshimitsu** (2000) examined some language planning and policy strategies behind an attempt at language maintenance by bilingual Japanese children in Melbourne whose parents are of Japanese background. This micro level study showed that children's background (sojourner vs. permanent resident in Australia) was the key variable affecting the maintenance process, and that micro level maintenance was the result of a combined effort by both parents and children.
- **Corson's** (1999) book provides an excellent starting point for anyone concerned with developing school-based (micro) language planning and policy. It provides a detailed discussion and a set of questions for micro language planners interested in developing school-based policy in L1, L2, literacy, oracy, and bilingual or multilingual education programs.
- **Nahir** (1998), looking back over the revival of Hebrew a century ago, argued that the shift to Hebrew that occurred within communities and families was a case of micro language planning in which potential speakers constituted the language planning agents. This was the case because there was no macro language planning and policy body involved.
- **Jones** (1996), in a community-oriented study, compared the results of the findings of two methodologically identical micro studies of different Breton-speaking communities in France. These micro-level to micro-level comparisons show that replication and comparative methodology can be used to verify language trends in speech communities as a whole and to reveal localized aspects that might otherwise escape the attention of language planners.
- **Kaplan** *et al.* (1995) and **Touchstone** *et al.* (1996) conducted two related studies on the banking sector in Los Angeles. In the first study they looked at written business communication from bank branches located in identifiable ethnic communities – Japanese, Chinese, and Hispanic. The purpose was to determine the banks' commitment to multilingualism and to analyze their specific attempts to reach out to non-English speaking communities. The second study focused on similar material that related to home loans made to the Hispanic community, which had a lower percentage of bank home loans than other communities and a higher use of non-bank sources of funding. Both studies found three types of language problems with bank materials: (1) translation errors, (2) translation misfit, and (3) translation omission. In both studies, the authors concluded that the substantial failure on the part of Los Angeles banks to cater for their non-English speaking clients could have economic consequences. In response,

they recommend that banks should apply language-planning efforts more uniformly and strategically.

- **Skilton** (1992) examined language acquisition planning and a class action law suit filed on behalf of Asian students in Philadelphia related to meeting their linguistic and academic needs. Both micro and macro perspectives were examined in an attempt to understand the complexities of the situation and the effectiveness of implementing such programs.
- **Kerpan** (1991) pointed out that business translators spend about 45% of their time on terminological research and that this involves standardization at the micro and macro levels. Poorly-researched terminological usage results in mediocre translation. Managers generally have little understanding of the effort involved in providing accurate texts or of the micro level language planning that results from terminological work.
- **Tollefson** (1981b) was one of the first scholars to argue that the second language acquisition (SLA) process can be analyzed as a series of policy level decisions that involve both macro and micro level policy goals and implementation decisions. Tollefson has subsequently gone on to edit several books that provide examples of a wide range of studies of school-based language policy and planning decisions from around the world.
- **Kaplan** (1980c) examined the needs for language instruction among migrant workers in New Zealand by administering a multilingual questionnaire to 291 executives, workers, officials, and teachers. Based on this research, Kaplan offered 30 recommendations on migrant and industrial language training, the preparation of teachers and materials, and language planning and research. He emphasized that these recommendations were not a blueprint but rather provided in a systematic manner a set of options. While many of these options were not new, in the past they had not been implemented because of (1) inadequate resources, (2) inadequate background preparation, and (3) inadequate planning. Arising from this was the challenge for New Zealanders to make choices that would work for and belong to them.
- **Other micro language planning studies** have appeared in the journal *Forensic Linguistics* and in the literature on language in the law more generally (e.g. Dumas & Short, 1998), although such studies often relate to the absence of such planning. There is also some additional micro material related to translation, but much of this work has no specific planning focus and was not written using this genre as a framework.

While these studies provide evaluative examples of micro language policy and planning situations, except for Kaplan's (1980) study, none are descriptive of the development of micro policies or their implementation (planning). While it is undoubtedly the case that the (macro) language policy and planning literature is predominantly descriptive or evaluative, there are studies of policy development and the planning process as well as documents that set out policy decisions and their implementation.[1] Such studies seem to be absent in the case of micro planning, perhaps because such documents, at least in business, may contain confidential commercial information.[2] This raises the question of what such micro planning documents might look like.

Postgraduate responses to the micro language policy and planning challenge

Given the paucity of published micro literature, it is worth examining some of the ideas that postgraduate students have had about how the frameworks and models of macro language planning might be applied to micro situations. The examples in Table 14.2 arose out of questions that postgraduate students enrolled in a Language Policy and Planning course had about its relevance to them and out of a pedagogical decision to put the question back to them to answer. If, as their textbook suggests (Kaplan & Baldauf, 1997), language planning and policy is the premier example of applied linguistics, how could they apply what they had studied in a relevant manner? After all, it seemed unlikely that they would be involved in drawing up a new language policy for Mexico, China, or South Africa. Furthermore, unlike those who have been involved with language planning and policy at a macro level, the students came to this problem with no presuppositions about whether such a task would be possible, so it is interesting to see how they approached the problem.

As Table 14.2 demonstrates, the range of situations postgraduates came up with is broad, and the quality of some of their thinking is instructive.

Many of the problems and the solutions listed in Table 14.2 are based on situations the postgraduates had encountered in their working lives. The students were able to translate what they had learned about macro language policy and planning to micro situations of their own choosing. In these projects there were examples of:

- status planning goals: choosing which languages would be needed for what purposes;
- corpus planning goals: developing appropriate materials to support planning decisions;
- language-in-education planning goals: (re)training for staff in a range of language skills;

Table 14.2 Postgraduate micro language problems and their solutions[3]

Project title	Problem	Solution
Asia Pacific Customer Call Center, Telecom (Australia/Japan)	English/Japanese bilingual staff hired to provide help desk enquiries for Japanese customers lack concepts in communication technology, technical vocabulary, and customer service for Japanese	Go beyond answering telephones in Japanese. Provide training in technology, technical Japanese, and culture; improve product quality; recognize non-confrontational nature of Japanese interaction.
Language Policy for a University Interpreting Program (Australia)	University Interpreting/Translating course not professionally accredited, hence not attracting enough students.	Create community orientation; draw on language skills; meet NAATI (National Association of Australian Translators and Interpreters) requirements.
Language Policy for a Duty Free Store (Australia)	Duty free staff hired because of Japanese fluency (largest group, biggest spenders); visitor profile is changing to Australians, Koreans, Chinese.	Get visitor data; support additional language fluency by holding classes; standardize language and sales techniques.
Intellectual Property Protection Center (China)	Trade mark infringement and investigation, often by overseas companies.	Develop multilingual competence in Mandarin, English, and Japanese.
Singing Department at an Australian University	Opera students need Italian, German, French language skills; Bachelor of Music students don't, now taught together.	Create separate groups; provide intensive coaching; optional tutorials; reading courses; extra-curricular activities; mentoring.
Language Policy for a Japanese School's English Department (Japan)	English is isolated in the classroom, undermining a teaching program aimed at excellence.	Create an English staff and resource room; motivate use English outside of class; change community attitudes.
Language Policy for an After Hours English Language School (Taiwan)	Problems with teaching approach, curriculum, staffing; need to meet increasing student numbers.	Full-time coordinator; train teaching assistants; teachers meetings; F/T foreign teacher; set up local curriculum materials; activity-based learning.
Policy Suggestions for Radio Television Hong Kong (RTHK)	Radio and TV channels provide Mandarin, Cantonese, and English services; other groups not being served.	New 'international channel,' with different languages and language teaching in Cantonese and Putonghua (Mandarin).

Table 14.2 *continued*

Project title	Problem	Solution
Language Policy for a Church, Australia	Is the church meeting the needs of its non-English speaking parishioners, who see themselves as less involved.	Prestige and inclusiveness planning; include non-English music, prayers, signage, nametags, rites for non-English speaking backgrounds in newsletter, etc.
Manufacturing Infant Products (Taiwan)	Chinese workers use English to communicate with 90% of customers; 70% from US, UK, Australia.	Provide staff with LSP (Language for Specific Purposes) to improve communication and cultural skills.
Listening and Speaking Skills for a Primary School (China)	No training in listening and speaking skills.	Develop speaking and listening activities across the curriculum.
Micro Language Policy for Journalism Society at University (China)	Student newspaper is in Chinese, but this is a foreign languages university; create language experience for student staff and readers.	Increase newspaper size (4 to 8 pages) and include English, Russian, Japanese, Korean, French, and German pages.
Language Policy for a Provincial Administrative College (China)	English teaching is inappropriate; civil servants need higher level training for cultural and communicative English skills.	Assess student needs; provide more communicative materials, flexible delivery, and tutorial support.

- prestige planning goals: giving specific languages greater status in particular situations.

Policy positions and decisions were developed and planning processes suggested to meet a variety of goals. These postgraduate projects provide hypothetical examples of micro planning in action.

Summary and Conclusions

In this chapter, I have raised the question of whether micro language planning is a genre that should be explored and developed as a way of analyzing and solving small-scale language problems. While there have been significant developments in the understanding of macro language policy and planning (i.e. at the polity level), much less attention has been paid to micro developments, either in relation to macro planning implementation or in genuine micro level analysis and action. However, neophytes examining the possible use of micro language planning found it a useful concept for solving language problems in business and education. Perhaps micro language planning deserves wider consideration.

Notes
1. The polity studies published in *Current Issues in Language Planning* provide examples of this genre, as do monographs such as Kaplan and Baldauf (2003), Heugh (2003), and Ho and Wong (2000).
2. There is, of course, literature related to business and technology that would be useful for those planning for this sector (e.g. Ulijn & Strother, 1995), but these sources are not in themselves micro language planning documents.
3. The projects listed here were completed in 2002 by Rebecca Conopilia, Margaret Fourer, Scott Lambert, Li Wei, Bonnieanna Mitchell, Stacey Prentice, Shu-Chen Huang, Sum Angel Lam, Donna Toulmin, Tung Chang Lee, Wang Min, Xuesong Wu, Zhang Jie, and Zhao Sumin, respectively. I have modified some of the titles to make the entities being discussed less identifiable. In previous years, students had studied a policy for setting up language programs in a new school in the US, a language policy for a real estate agency in a Korean-Chinese suburb of Sydney, and a policy for staff development in a small computer software firm seeking to export to the US and China.

Chapter 15
The Englishization of Spanish in Mexico

ROBERT J. BAUMGARDNER

In a 1996 essay by José G. Moreno de Alba entitled *Seudoanglicismos* [Pseudoanglicisms], the renowned Mexican linguist discusses the English borrowing *smoking*, a shortening of the compound *smoking jacket* (Moreno de Alba, 1996). The terms *smoking jacket* and *tuxedo* (or *dinner jacket* in British usage) denote different types of attire in English; however, the borrowing for *tuxedo* in Spanish (originally from French) not only shortened *smoking jacket* to *smoking* (or *esmoking*) but also underwent semantic shift from *smoking jacket* to *tuxedo*, with the English term originally designating an ornamental jacket used at home for smoking (Rodríguez González & Lillo Baudes, 1997). The different usages are made clear in the following *Oxford English Dictionary* citation:

> Guests wore tuxedos if they were American males and black dinner jackets if ... European (... except for the odd Italian in tobacco brown *smoking*). (Simpson & Weiner, 1989: xv, 805)

Moreno de Alba's point of course is that a *tuxedo* in Spanish (as well as in French and Italian) is a *smoking*, a word that does not exist in English with that particular meaning. An electronic search of the Infosel database of *El Norte* newspaper (Monterrey)[1] shows that *smoking* was used in 28 articles in 1997, the plural *smokings* in five articles, and the variants *smokin* in one, *esmoquin* in four and *esmoquins* in one. An example from *El Norte* reads:

> Hace 5 años, detectando una necesidad de mercado, José Alvarado Acosta inició la fabricación de fajas y corbata de moño para smoking, ya que era muy difícil conseguirlos en la ciudad a un precio adecuado. [Five years ago, detecting a need in the market, José Alvarado Acosta started producing cummerbunds and bow ties for tuxedos, since it was very difficult to buy them in the city at a reasonable price.] (*El Norte*, July 28, 1997, *Reporte InfoSel*: 14)

Clearly, *smoking* is an established borrowing in Mexican Spanish. Moreno de Alba (1996) is more concerned, however, about another type of pseudoanglicism, namely the use in Peninsular Spanish of Anglicisms that are totally nonexistent in English. He is thankful in particular that two words have not made it into Mexican Spanish: *footing* (meaning *jogging*), and *autostop* (meaning *hitchhiking* – in Mexican Spanish *aventón*). *Footing* is yet another case of semantic shift, a process often associated with borrowing (Bookless, 1982, 1984). The resultant shift in the meaning of this word (originally borrowed from French) is related to the English word *footing*, which, among its many meanings, is 'the act of one who moves on foot, as in walking or dancing' (Costello, 1995: 519), or *jogging* in Spain. Just as well, Moreno de Alba notes, that this Peninsular Spanish borrowing does not yet appear in the official dictionary of the Spanish Academy.

Five years later, in fact, the word did appear in the revered dictionary. DRAE (2001: 1075) lists *footing* as a French borrowing that has undergone semantic shift from the English word *footing*, or *position*. An electronic search of the *El Norte* (Monterrey) and *Reforma* (Mexico City) databases indeed reveals that *footing* meaning *jogging* is not a Mexican usage, occurring only once during 1997 in *Reforma* and twice in *El Norte*:

> Clinton, que llegó el pasado 17 de agosto a la isla de Martha's Vineyard, ha consagrado hasta ahora la mayor parte de su tiempo al descanso. El golf, el footing, los paseos en barco, la lectura y las partidas de scrabble con su esposa Hillary son algunas de sus actividades lúdicas.
> [Clinton, who arrived the past 17th of August on the island of Martha's Vineyard, has up until now devoted most of his time to resting. Golf, jogging, boat rides, and games of Scrabble with his wife Hillary are some of his pastimes.] (*El Norte*, August 26, 1997: 12)

While the English lexical item *jogging* appears in neither Lara (1996) nor Gómez de Silva (2001) as a borrowing in Mexican Spanish, it occurs frequently (in 18 articles) in *Reforma*, though only three times in *El Norte*, as in:

> Según la misma fuente una mañana del invierno 1994–95, ambos personajes se encontraron en la calle mientras hacían jogging.
> [According to the same source, one morning in the winter of 1994–95 both people met in the street while jogging.] (*Reforma* September 25, 1997, *Nacional*: 12)

Thus, it appears that the use of the English borrowing 'jogging' is more widespread in the central, Mexico City area than in Northern Mexico, where *correr* or *trotar* are more widely used.

The case of Peninsular Spanish *autostop* is different from *footing* and in many ways is more interesting since *autostop* was, according to Moreno de Alba (1996), created in French by the combination of French *auto* and English *stop*, and then subsequently borrowed in Iberian Spanish. *Autostop* is found in the *Diccionario de la Lengua Española* (DRAE, 1992) and both *autostop* and *autoestop* are found in DRAE (2001). The interesting thing about *autostop*, of course, is that it is not an English word at all. A search of the 1997 *El Norte* and *Reforma* databases confirms that *autostop* is not Mexican Spanish either, occurring only once in *El Norte* (obviously from a Spanish source) and not at all in *Reforma*:

> Los cuerpos mutilados de las tres adolescentes Myriam, Antonia y Desiré, originarias del pueblo de Alcasser, en los alrededores de Valencia, fueron encontrados en enero de 1993, dos meses después de su desaparición, cuando hacían autostop para ir a una discoteca.
> [The mutilated corpses of the three adolescents Myriam, Antonia and Desiré, originally from the village of Alcasser near Valencia, were found in January of 1993, two months after their disappearance, while they were hitchhiking to go to a discotheque.]. (*El Norte*, September 6, 1997: 10)

The Mexican equivalent of Peninsular Spanish *autostop*, namely *aventón*, is worth further exploration. Moreno de Alba (1996) does not discuss the origin of the term, which, in addition to *hitchhiking* means *shove/push* in Mexican Spanish (Lara, 1996). Gomez de Silva's *Diccionario Breve de Mexicanismos* (2001) defines *aventón* as *transporte gratuito* (free transport/ ride). Neither Lara nor Gomez de Silva list the word as related to English *hitchhiking* or *ride*, i.e. a calque (an expression introduced into one language by translating it from another language). Smead and Clegg (1996), however, feel that the word may indeed be an English calque, though this depends on whether or not the term *aventón* has borrowed the English semantics of *ride*. It is possible, they add,

> that such a shift in meaning is due entirely to the workings of processes like internal semantic extension without any language or cultural contact. However, given the fact that the semantic fields pertaining to the automobile have incorporated numerous Anglicisms, it may well be a calque... (Smead & Clegg, 1996: 125)

In Northern Mexico, the direct English borrowing *raid* or *raite* (ride) is used alongside *aventón*. For example, an article in *El Norte* entitled *Empiezan su jornada con el aventón* [They begin their day hitchhiking] begins:

> Para decenas de maestras en Puebla, llegar a sus lugares de trabajo de *raid* no es sólo una aventura; sus ingresos les impiden pagar los boletos de transporte...
> [For dozens of teachers in Puebla hitchhiking to work is not an adventure; their salaries prevent them from buying bus tickets...] (*El Norte*, November 8, 1997, *Los Estados*: 6)

Similarly:

> Regresamos caminando al pueblo, con la niña muerta en brazos. Nadie nos quiso dar raite.
> [We returned on foot to the village, with the dead girl in our arms. Nobody wanted to give us a ride.] (*El Norte*, September 21, 1997, *Nacional*: 4)

A search for *aventón* shows that it occurred in 34 articles in *El Norte* in 1997 while *raid* (and its variations) occurred in 32. In *Reforma* for the same year, *raid* occurred only once while *aventón* occurred 30 times. The use of *raid* seems to be more widespread in Northern Mexico, in stiff competition with *aventón*. Both *raid* and *aventón* are found in the *Diccionario Breve de Mexicanismos* (Gómez de Silva, 2001) while only *aventón* is found in Lara (1996).

World Spanishes nowadays borrow English lexis either directly (*jogging*) or as translations or calques (*aventón*), but they also use English words alone or in combination with their own words to create new 'English' words. While *footing* and *autostop* may not have made their way yet into Mexican Spanish, numerous other such word-formations have. Moreno de Alba clearly has a preference for one type over the other:

> Habría que preguntarse qué resulta menos malo, si tomar la voz inglesa, sin mayores modificaciones – fonéticas, morfológicas y ortográficas – (o con sólo aquellas que el carácter del español exija), o inventarse terminajos calcados del inglés. Si el español mismo se muestra incapaz de tener sus propias designaciones, más convendría, creo yo, tomar las voces inglesas directamente, y no adoptar estas curiosas invenciones seudoinglesas del francés contemporáneo.
> [One has to ask oneself which is the lesser of two evils – to take the English word, without major phonetic, morphological, or orthographic modifications, or to invent calqued terminology from English. If Spanish is incapable of forming its own words, it would be better, I believe, to borrow English words directly and not to take those curious pseudo-English inventions from contemporary French.] (Moreno de Alba, 1996: 315)

English Borrowing in Spanish: A Brief History

Mexico's concern with English borrowings in Spanish did not reach critical mass until the middle of the 20th century. Until then, '... almost all English words borrowed by Spanish were of British English origin, and were usually transmitted through writing, often via French' (Penny, 1991: 230). Alatorre (1989) supports this position and gives examples of the few words borrowed from English, including *rosbif, dandy, club, vagón, tranvía* (tramway), *túnel, drenaje* (drainage), *yate* (yacht), *confort, mitin* (meeting), and *líder* (leader).

Some English words also reached Spanish directly, e.g. *lord, suicidio* (18th century); *cheque, club, organismo, turista* (19th century); *comité, interviú, racial* (20th century), etc... (Patterson & Urrutibéheity, 1975). But without a doubt, up until the middle of the 20th century, the principal source languages for borrowing in Mexican Spanish were French and Amerindian languages. After World War II, however, contemporary Mexican Spanish began to experience an unprecedented influx of Anglicisms from the US, whereas previously English words had often entered Mexican Spanish through Castilian Spanish. In their seminal history of Mexico *The Course of Mexican History*, Meyer *et al.* (2003) characterize the sociopolitical/linguistic context of that time in the following way:

> United States cultural influences overwhelmed Mexico in the post-war period, occasionally for the better but generally for the worse. If anything, these new cultural inroads were more pervasive than those of the French during the late Porfiriato [the 1884–1911 Porfirio Díaz presidency] ... To the chagrin of those who prized traditional Hispanic values, advertisements and commercials assumed a distinct United States flavor, and hundreds of Anglicisms invaded the language. Somehow *el jit, el jonron, el extra inin* seemed more palatable, and certainly more understandable, than *okay, bay-bay, chance, jipi, biznes,* and *parquear*. Nobody could explain why Mexican teenagers in Gap jeans began calling up their *suiti* for a date. Linguistic syncretism bequeathed its share of amusing redundancies, such as the cocktail lounge that displayed a sign reading '4:00–5:00, La Hora de Happy Hour' and the tourist restaurant whose menu proudly advertised 'Chili con Carne with Meat.' Quick lunches (*quik lonches*) and the coffee break (*kofi breik*) replaced heavy noon meals and afternoon siestas; beer supplanted pulque as the favorite alcoholic drink of the lower classes, while Scotch whiskey took the place of cognac among the middle and upper classes. For the first time, Halloween, complete with plastic pumpkins and trick-or-treating, began to displace Mexico's traditional celebration of the Day of the Dead, and hand-carved folk toys lost favor to imported Tortugas Ninja [Ninja Turtles]. (Meyer *et al.*, 2003: 707)

Today, the influence of English is far greater than that of French earlier. As Alatorre notes:

> Vistas las cosas desde la perspectiva de nuestra lengua (que es también la de muchas otras lenguas), el papel de difusor que durante más de dos siglos tuvo el francés le pertenece hoy al ingles.
> [Seeing things from the viewpoint of our language (which is also that of

many other languages), the role of disseminator, which for more than two centuries belonged to French, today belongs to English.] (Alatorre, 1989: 311)

More specifically, Alatorre points out:

La influencia del inglés es hoy abrumadoramente mayor que la que tuvo el francés en su punto culminante, y cubre una variedad mucho más amplia de terrenos. Basta pensar en el vocabulario de los deportes, del cine y la televisión, de la vivienda, de las técnicas productivas y administrativas, de la economía y el comercio, de la aviación y el automovilismo, de la informática ... Generalizando tal vez un poco, cabe decir que todas las conquistas científicas de hoy (en física, química, matemáticas, biología, medicina, etc.) llegan a los países de lengua española con un vocabulario originalmente acuñado en ingles. [The influence of English today is overwhelmingly greater than that of French at its peak, and encompasses a greater variety of domains. Just think of the lexicon of sports, cinema, television, housing, productive and administrative technology, the economy and commerce, aviation and the automobile industry, [and] computer science ... Perhaps generalizing somewhat, it is possible to say that all of today's scientific discoveries (in physics, chemistry, mathematics, biology, medicine, etc.) arrive in Spanish-speaking countries with a vocabulary originally coined in English.] (Alatorre, 1989: 312)

Efforts to Stop English Borrowings

Some two hundred years after the 1512 *leyes de Burgos* (Laws of Burgos) called for the promulgation of Catholicism through the medium of the Spanish language in the Americas, Phillip V in 1713 called for the establishment of the *Real Academia de la Lengua Española* (Royal Spanish Academy), a move motivated by the growing political and linguistic clout of Castile in early 18th century Spain. Modeled on the French Academy (founded in 1635), the Royal Spanish Academy (RAE) had (and continues to have) as its goal the preservation of the 'beauty' and 'purity' of the Spanish language ('*Limpia, fija y da esplendor*' [It cleans, fixes and gives splendor]). As Kaplan and Baldauf note:

National language academies ... serve to assure certain kinds of standardization, as they are often responsible for the production of dictionaries and sometimes of standard grammars ... Such organizations are almost always concerned with language purity as well as with the standardization of the language. That is, they seek to keep the standard (authorized) version of the language free of foreign language influences or to integrate such usages appropriately into the language. (Kaplan & Baldauf, 1997: 66)

The Royal Spanish Academy began establishing affiliate academies in Latin America, starting in Colombia in 1871. Four years later in 1875 both the *Academia Mexicana de la Lengua* (Mexican Academy of Language) as well as the Ecuadorian Academy were established. Since its inception, one of the concerns of the Mexican Academy has been in the area of borrowing, primarily borrowings from indigenous Mexican languages. As Guitarte and Torres Quintero comment:

> In the beginning the Spanish Academy was decidedly purist for reasons of national defense and because of the conviction that the Spanish language was sufficient to express all that one might want to say. The Latin American academies supported these ideas, although national honor caused them to compromise with regard to the native vocabulary, which was tolerated much more than similar phenomena pertinent to morphology and syntax. (Guitarte & Torres Quintero, 1968: 596)

Another of the Mexican Academy's concerns over the years has been with French, and later US English borrowings (see Huacuja, 1960; Carreño, 1967a, 1967b; Alcalá, 1968). The Academy, report Kaplan and Baldauf (1997: 67), 'has been particularly concerned in recent years with the flood of American English words and with coinage of mixed origin ... ' Regarding English borrowings, Guitarte and Torres Quintero (1968) opine:

> The traditional aim of 'purity of language' which reached its apogee in the fight against Gallicisms is continued today in the aim of 'defense of the language.' And this defense, first of all, is against Anglicisms, considered to be one of the greatest threats to the denaturalization and fragmentation of the Spanish language. This is the case above all in Spanish America, where in many places the influence of English is felt, for obvious reasons, with an enslaving force. The Spanish American academies have intensified their efforts in this difficult struggle against Anglicisms because they consider them to be dangerous for the fundamental unity of the language. (Guitarte & Torres Quintero, 1968: 597)

In certain quarters in Mexico, however, the Mexican Academy – like the Spanish Academy for that matter – is held in very low esteem (Lara, 1993), and it was probably for this reason that the *Comisión Para La Defensa del Idioma Español* [Commission for the Defense of the Spanish Language] was formed in 1981. As Alatorre notes:

> Como es natural, los puristas de hoy están poniendo el grito en el cielo. Uno de esos gritos, muy resonante, se escuchó en México a comienzos de los ochentas. Lo notable es que no brotó de la Academia, sino del

mismísimo presidente de la República.
[As one might expect, the purists are screaming to high heavens. One of these screams was heard very clearly in Mexico at the beginning of the eighties. And notably, it did not emanate from the Academy, but from the very President of the Republic.] (Alatorre, 1989: 315)

On August 11, 1981, President José López Portillo signed a decree that gave birth to the Commission. Less than two years later this Commission, little-known outside of Mexico, was no longer functioning. During its short tenure, however, it was relatively productive, and its publications included works on status, corpus, and language-in-education planning.

One of the Commission's principal concerns – in fact, some say, its *raison d'être* – was English borrowings: the Mexican language and culture were being invaded by a force that regarded itself as superior and manifested itself in loans from science and technology, mass communication, and advertising (*Qué es...*, 1982). There can be no doubt that the Commission was concerned about the penetration of US language and culture into Mexico at the expense of the home language and culture. The Commission pointed out that, while other Spanish-speaking countries (e.g. Chile, Colombia, the Dominican Republic) had taken steps to curb this linguistic and cultural invasion, it was Mexico's responsibility to defend the Spanish language since it is the world's largest Spanish-speaking country; other countries, such as France, Switzerland, and Canada, cited the Commission, had also taken similar steps. The Commission was composed of eight sub-commissions within the Departments of *Gobernación* (Interior), Commerce, Communication and Transport, Tourism, and Public Education. The subcommission on language included the Mexican Academy. Alone it seems, the Academy lacked clout; the Commission could help to strengthen its voice.

The Commission's battle against Anglicisms was fought on three fronts – published literature, a radio campaign, and a television campaign. The published literature ran the gamut from articles on borrowings by noted Mexican linguists (e.g. Juan M. Lope Blanche and Luis Fernando Lara) who cautioned against over-reaction to borrowings and 'language mavens' (Pinker, 1994) such as Pedro Gringoire (1982, n.d.), who had choice descriptions for certain borrowings such as *chance* (*anglicismo insufrible* [insufferable Anglicism], n.d.: 73), *fólder* (*craso anglicismo* [crass Anglicism], n.d.: 107), and *gangsterismo* (*¡horroroso híbrido!* [horrible hybrid!], n.d.: p. 109). The television campaign (Lara, 1993) included six short scenes about

(1) a Mexican boy with his father and other townspeople in Acapulco who could not find their way because the signs in the city were written in English;
(2) a young man declaring his love for his girlfriend in vernacular Spanish, with the girlfriend rejecting him because of his speech;

(3) a group of high society ladies having a conversation filled with Anglicisms;
(4) a director filming a scene and giving directions to his crew in cinematic jargon filled with Anglicisms;
(5) a worker in a mechanic's shop asking another worker for tools using very few words;
(6) children frightened at Christmas time by the laughs of Santa Claus in a store window surrounded by 'Merry Christmas' signs, with the children preferring to go to a traditional Mexican Christmas festival.

These scenes were aimed at discouraging not only the use of Anglicisms (1, 3, 4, and 6) but also the use of vernacular Mexican Spanish (2) and informal spoken Mexican Spanish (5), the point here certainly being that the mechanic was not using 'complete sentences.'

In 1982 the Presidency of José López Portillo came to an end with the election of Miguel de la Madrid. In the first months of 1983, the work of the Commission ceased. Lara (1993) cites economic and other reasons for its disappearance (some did not approve of the Commission's criticisms of Spanish usage). The fears of many of those who lamented its birth had, according to Lara (1993), finally been laid to rest, and those who approved of the work of the commission found other venues to express their unhappiness with English borrowings in Mexican Spanish.

English Borrowings in Mexican Spanish Today

To understand fully the impact of US English on Mexican Spanish today it is necessary to look beyond the 2000-mile shared border between Mexico and the US to the world at large. Certainly the proximity of Mexico to the US has an influence on English borrowings in the Spanish of Mexico (as well as on Spanish borrowings in US English). However, the importance of English in the world today must also be taken into account. In her plenary address to the 9th Annual Conference of the International Association of World Englishes, Margie Berns (2002) listed countries in Kachru's (1995) Expanding Circle in which English is neither native (as in the Inner Circle) nor indigenized (as in the Outer Circle) but where it has had influence on the official/national language of those countries. The list, culled from the journals *World Englishes* and *English Today*, consisted of Albania, Brazil, Bulgaria, China, Cyprus, Denmark, Egypt, Estonia, Finland, France, Germany, Hungary, Italy, Japan, Jordan, Mexico, Saudi Arabia, South Korea, Spain, Sweden, Switzerland, Taiwan, and Tunisia. At the same conference, papers were delivered on the influence of English in Costa Rica, Ecuador, Lithuania, Macedonia, Moldova, Thailand, Turkey, and Uzbekistan. Mexico, it appears, is among a growing number of Expanding Circle countries whose languages and cultures have been influenced by English. Proximity is no longer of prime importance.

In his extensive studies of the far-reaching effect of English in the world, Kachru (1995) has shown how the influence of English has produced what he terms 'nativization' and 'Englishization.' These two processes have developed, as it were, two faces of English, one showing what contact has formally done to various varieties of English – see, for example, Kachru (1983) for Indian English and Baumgardner (1993) for Pakistani English – and the second showing what impact the English language and literature have had on other languages of the world (see Baumgardner, 1997, for Mexican Spanish). According to Kachru, where English and the other language are in contact, Englishization manifests itself in three different ways: in loan words, loan shifts (or calques), and hybridization. Present-day Mexican Spanish is replete with each of these word-formation processes. English loans range from older, established borrowings such as *lord, club, récord*, and *boicot* to more recent borrowings from US English such as *rockanrol, backpack*, and *backstage*. The extent of recent English borrowings can be seen in the following list of words taken from *El Norte* for the year 1995 (numbers in parentheses indicate the number of articles in which the word appeared during that year):

- Automotive: *cab forward* (7), *camper* (14), *cruise control* (7), *dragster* (57), *fuel injection* (10), *overdrive* (21)
- Cuisine: *brunch* (29), *corn flakes* (9), *queso* (cheese) *cottage* (10), *gravy* (22), *hot cakes* (20), *prime rib* (4), *rib-eye* (16), *T-bone* (12)
- Entertainment: *backstage* (6), *grunge* (10), *Latin lover* (7), *new age* (pop) (28), *stand-by* (24), *talk-show* (10), *rocanrol* (rock and roll) (39)
- Fashion: *baby-dolls* (5), *backpack* (21), *flats* (13), *halter* (8), *jeans* (116), *lipstick* (23), *stretch* (14), *top-model* (18)
- Sports: *balk* (7), *down-hill* (15), *dragster* (59), *funny car* (49), *infield* (39), *muster* (60), *quarterback* (10), *touchdown* (26)

Included in the category of borrowings are also lexical items that have undergone grammatical or semantic shift. For example, the English verb *relax* is used in Spanish both as a noun, as in

En estos momentos busco sólo relax y tiempo libre.
[At those times I only look for relaxation and free time.] (*El Norte*, December 2, 1994, *Deportiva*: 5)

and an adjective, as in

... en un momento que se encuentre muy relax, de preferencia fin de semana.

[... at a time when you feel very relaxed, preferably on the weekend]. (*El Norte*, July 20, 1996, *Moda*: 21)

Neither of these usages is known in English-speaking countries. In fact, *relax* as an adjective appears to be Mexican usage, with only the nominal form found in Peninsular Spanish (Rodríguez González & Lillo Baudes, 1997).

Other borrowings have also undergone semantic shift; a *socket* in Mexican Spanish is a plug in US English, a *boiler* is a hot-water heater found in homes, not in factories, and *happy* means tipsy:

> Parece ser que en el festejo todos se la están pasando muy pero muy bien, ya que el jueves la pachanga comenzó a las 10:00 horas y terminó alrededor de las 11:30, tiempo durante el cual a los invitados se les ofreció una 'copita' de buen vino y todos salieron bien happy.
> [It appears that everybody was enjoying the celebration, since Thursday the party started at 10:00 and ended somewhere around 11:30, a time during which he offered the guests a glass of good wine and everyone left very tipsy.] (*El Norte* April 30, 1994, *Moda*: 14)

This particular shift appears to come from the borrowed compound *happy hour*:

> ... Lo que pasa es que por decreto y a partir de diciembre, en todo el Estado de Texas quedaron prohibidas las 'happy hours'... 'No happy hours: No happy mexicans.' ¡Ah, raza! ...
> [What is happening is that by decree beginning in December happy hours will be prohibited in the state of Texas. 'No happy hours; no happy Mexicans.' Oh! Mexican People!] (*El Norte* December 27, 1994, *Internacional*: 6)

None of these shifts (*socket, boiler,* or *happy*) appears in Rodríguez González and Lillo Baudes (1997).

Kachru's second category, loan shifts or calques, includes Spanish lexical items such as *aventón* for hitchhiking (see previous discussion), *ratón* (computer mouse), *pizza personal* (personal pizza), *control remoto* (remote control), *la punta del iceberg* (the tip of the iceberg), and *hora feliz* (happy hour), all of which are both a borrowing and a calque. Hybrid word formations (many of which are used in other World Spanishes) include:

Periphrastic compounds:
- clip de video, jack de audífonos, luz de stop, roster de playoffs, switch de reset.

Nominal suffixes:
- –azgo: *liderazgo;*
- –(e)ador: *bateador, entrevistador, sandblasteador;*

- –aje: *drenaje, porcentaje, reportaje;*
- –azo: *flashazo, golazo, pistoletazo;*
- –ción: *dolarización, filmación, vulcanización;*
- –dura: *ponchadura;*
- –eo: *catcheo, flirteo, goleo;*
- –era/o: *beisbolero, golero, rocanrolero;*
- –ería: *coctelería, hamburgesería, lonchería;*
- –ismo: *alcoholismo, esnobismo, snobismo;*
- –ista: *basquetbolista, esnobista, lobbista.*

Adjectival suffixes:
- –esa: *lideresa;*
- –iano: *hertziano;*
- –il: *reporteril;*
- –ístico: *beisbolístico, futbolístico, turístico;*

Prefixes:
- des–: *desdolarización;*
- re–: *remodelar, remixear, remasterizar;*

Infinitive verb endings:
- –ar/–ear: *boicotear, escanear, filmar; surfear;*
- –izar: *estandarizar, monitorizar, vulcanizar.*

Clippings:
- *bull* (bulldozer), *fut* (football), *heavy* (metal), *refri* (refrigerator), *tóper* (Tupperware).

Blends:
- *cantabar, rediqueta, Mexicatessen, servicar, SouBeerNir.*

The last two categories (clippings and blends) are especially interesting. As in the case of *autostop*, clippings of this type are used in Mexican and other varieties of Spanish but are unknown in that particular form in the native variety of English that the word was borrowed from. The blends, like compounds and the products of affixation, are hybrids composed of Spanish and English elements; however, because of the clipped elements in the blends, their meanings are not always as transparent as those of words in other categories. *Rediqueta* is English netiquette (net + etiquette) plus Spanish *red* for *network* (rules of politeness for the Internet), and *Mexicatessen* is a delicatessen Mexican style. A *servicar*, or Spanish *servir* (*to serve*) plus English *car* (pluralized as either *servicares* or *servicars*) is known in Texas as a *beer barn*, i.e. a drive-through liquor store in the shape of a barn. For example, a headline in the *Local* section of *El Norte* in June 1997 read:

Critican construcción de servicar.
[Construction of beer barn criticized.] (*El Norte*, June 21, 1997: 9)

Or from the *Local* section of *El Norte* in August the same year:

> Dado que el negocio Garabatal es un servicar y cuenta con un permiso con el giro de minisuper, puede estar abierto las 24 horas...
> [Given that Garabatal is a beer barn and has permission to operate as a mini-supermarket, it can remain open 24 hours a day...] (August 26, 1997: 3)

The word occurred in 23 articles in *El Norte* in 1997 but did not occur in *Reforma*, showing that it is a Northern Mexican phenomenon.

Another Spanish-English hybrid is *cantabar*, consisting of *cantar* (*to sing*) plus *bar*, or a bar with karaoke. G.L. Othón, in his lively column *Sugerencias del Gourmet* [The Gourmet's Suggestions] in the *Buena Mesa* section of *El Norte* wrote:

> Igual fenómeno ocurre en la zona de la Colonia Country, por la Avenida Revolución, donde se amontonan restaurantes, cantabares, hamburgueserías, taquerías, pizzerías y todo tipo de empresas gastronómicas exitosas...
> [The same phenomenon is occurring in the suburb Contry along Revolution Avenue, where restaurants, karaoke bars, hamburger establishments, taquerias, pizzerias, and all types of successful eateries are opening...] (*El Norte*, June 20, 1997: 2)

The hybrid *cantabar* occurred twice in *El Norte* 1997 and not at all in *Reforma*, though there are numerous *cantabares* in both Monterrey and Mexico City that advertise in newspapers. Electronic databases, therefore, do not accurately reflect the number of times a lexical item appears in newspapers since such databases contain only text, not advertisements or visuals.

The last word among blends is *SouBeerNir*, which was the name of a shop in Monterrey, and a good example of bilingual (or for that matter trilingual) creativity in Mexican Spanish. *SouBeerNir* sold products related to Mexican beer (coasters, T-shirts, mugs, etc.), all with the logos of different Mexican beers (*Tecate, Dos Equis, Carta Blanca,* etc.). The word is based on the French borrowing in Spanish (and English) *souvenir*. The word *SouBeerNir* is formed by deleting the '*ve*' from *souvenir* and inserting the English word *beer*. What results is a word that sounds something like the way a Mexican-Spanish speaker would pronounce the French borrowing *souvenir*, since the orthographic *v* in Mexican Spanish is pronounced as a phonetic *b*. The genius of the name is that it contains the English word 'beer' and sounds almost like the products sold in the store; no doubt it was aimed at English-speaking customers. When languages become creative with borrowed words, they take part in the 'acculturation of English in "un-English" sociocultural and linguistic contexts' (Kachru, 1995: 243), a phenomenon that has been documented in un-English contexts throughout the world.

Conclusion

Is Mexican Spanish in danger of being 'contaminated' by English? All languages borrow (see Baumgardner (1997) on why Mexican Spanish borrows from US English). So exactly how many English borrowings would it take to do irreparable harm to Spanish? Did the some 4000 words borrowed into Spanish from Arabic from the 8th to the 13th centuries damage the language? Alatorre (1989: 316), in fact, calls them '... una de sus bellezas' [one of its beauties]. As regards the number of English borrowings in Spanish, a close examination is indeed surprising. Luis Fernando Lara, director of the *Diccionario del Español Usual en México* (Lara, 1996) and editor of the *Diccionario Fundamental del Español de México* (Lara, 1982), sheds some much-needed light on this topic when he writes:

> Although the vast majority of words in standard Mexican Spanish are of Spanish origin, a small fraction of the lexicon is composed of words from foreign languages, particularly French and English ... If during the 19th century Gallicism was considered the accursed manifestation of foreign influence over the Spanish language, this role is now played by borrowings from English. Due to the United States' considerable economic and political influence, Anglo-American culture also has considerable influence in contemporary Mexico. Anglicisms can be found everywhere in Mexican Spanish, although the absolute number is probably negligible (Lara, 1997: 876).

This position is supported by the fact that, out of 14,000 entries in Lara's (1996) dictionary, fewer than 2% (0.018) are English borrowings. This trend holds for other dictionaries of Mexican Spanish: of the 30,550 entries in Santamaría's *Diccionario de Mejicanismos* (1974), 1.6% are English borrowings and at least 20 % are of Aztec (Nahuatl) origin (Cotton & Sharp, 1988). In Gómez de Silva's (2001) recent *Diccionairo Breve de Mexicanismos*, a compilation of 95 previously published works on Mexicanisms since 1761 including Santamaría (1974) and containing 77,000 entries, less than 1% (0.003) are noted as coming from English, while words of French origin are even fewer (.001). The Amerindian (especially Aztec) influence is far greater.

In a recent article in the *New York Times* on the growing importance of the Internet in Latin America, Sam Dillon (2003) reported on the characteristics of *chatear* for *to chat* and *clickear* for *to click* and on attitudes toward this latest contact zone between English and Spanish. José Carreño Carlón, Director of the Department of Communication at Iberoamerican University in Mexico City, told Dillon:

> This was a hard-fought battle from the 60s through the 80s, but the nationalists and purists are in retreat, especially because in the cybernetic world many English words have no easy equivalent. (Dillon, 2003)

In the same source, Tarsicio Herrera Zapién, Secretary of the Mexican Academy, expressed a similar opinion, saying that the Academy no longer fought the 'purity' battle, which in fact had been abandoned by the Mexican people. Added Herrera Zapién: 'We can't legislate how people speak; we simply catalog Mexican usages.' Needless to say, the descriptivism expressed by Herrera Zapién is not embraced by all – recall Moreno de Alba (1996) and Gringoire (1982, n.d.). There are, however, voices that rise above the prescriptive din:

> Hay en nuestro mundo muchas cosas de que alarmarse. Entre ellas no está la lengua española en cuanto tal (y en toda la diversidad de sus realizaciones).
> [There are many things in our world to get alarmed about. The Spanish language (in all of its diversity) is not one of them.] (Alatorre, 1989: 318)

Acknowledgement

I would like to thank Dr Georgia Seminet, Assistant Professor of Spanish, Department of Literature and Languages, Texas A&M University-Commerce, for checking my Spanish translations. Any errors that remain are my own. My deep gratitude also goes to Mr Scott Downing of the Interlibrary Loan Department, Gee Library, Texas A&M University-Commerce, for helping me obtain hard-to-find copies of the publications of the Committee for the Defense of the Spanish Language as well as other materials published in Mexico.

Notes

1. Until the year 2000, Infosel México published CD-ROM versions of *El Norte* (Monterrey) and *Reforma* (Mexico City). *El Norte* was available from 1986–2000, and *Reforma* from 1992–2000. These products are no longer available. I would like to thank the Graduate School, Texas A&M University-Commerce, for providing me with funds to purchase some of these CDs.

Chapter 16
Including Discourse in Language Planning Theory

JOSEPH LO BIANCO

Introduction

In a publication honoring Dr Terrence J. Quinn (Candlin & McNamara, 1989), a paper by Robert Kaplan entitled 'Language planning v. planning language' appeared next to a paper of mine entitled 'Science or values: The role of professionals in language policymaking.' Kaplan's paper elaborated a concern that language policymaking ought to adopt systematic and rational approaches, informed by a sociolinguistic survey. He expressed his view that the recently adopted Australian National Policy on Languages (Lo Bianco, 1987) had not proceeded along these lines, and that as a result it constituted a top-down, rather than a bottom-up approach. My paper discussed some specific contributions made by language professionals to development of the recently-endorsed National Policy on Languages, and explored the public policy literature concerning relations between facts and values, seen in this literature as a prevailing dichotomy between technical and political emphases in policy research.

In our recent writing Kaplan and I have both continued to discuss language planning in ways that explore and develop essentially these kinds of dispositions. Kaplan's prolific and admirable work reveals an abiding interest in specifying and rationalizing language policy and planning. It would be fair to say that in my own writing I have expressed skepticism about the real impact of scholarly contributions to language planning. Rather, I have expressed a consequent interest in analyzing the political and ideological dimensions of language policy making. Neither denies the alternative perspective, but each prefers to characterize language planning in a distinctive way. I believe that both emphases are essential to the scholarly conversation about language planning theory and to the analysis of real-world language policy making (Lo Bianco, 2002).

My view is not that systematic processes of language planning are impossible or uninteresting, just that they are uncommon, a view that Kaplan shares (1994). Given that language planning is almost never entrusted to any one professional category of language planners, it is warranted to devote considerable research effort to theorize political dimensions of language planning, in particular to make central within the discipline a theory of power in both its material and symbolic dimensions. As Kaplan and Baldauf (1997) demonstrate, the field is a complex interstitial one, and multiple angles of analysis are required. Power and politics are relatively neglected, however, largely, I feel, because language planning as a scholarly academic discipline, even in recent work, persists in revealing its origins, conceptually and as a discipline, in applied linguistics. The essential point I argue in the present chapter is that one locus for a theory of power in language planning scholarship is to study how authoritative discourse operates to determine which language problems will be elevated for policy attention and which will be relegated to the margins. I call therefore for the addition of an extra field of analysis within language planning research that extends the concepts of language planning analysis to discourse.

Discourse

In a tentative manner in this chapter, I wish to characterize discourse as an element of language planning theory or rather, as an object of research for language planning theories. This proposal aims to articulate a sense of the politics of language, especially the analysis of performative speech and writing, and, in particular, the language of processes of language policy making. The underlying rationale is that if we analyze only policy as text and not policy as discourse (see Ball, 1993, for a distinction between the two), the very political nature of political language may be obscured. Texts of policy may involve simple declarative or propositional content, setting out action, funding, and legislative backup, but they are usually accompanied by talk and writing, especially the notorious 'political promise' in which ideological loading is dominant. Even the declarative language of policy texts is not immune from the performance of language politics, at least to the extent that it nominates some topics or issues as 'problems' requiring treatment in overt processes of policy. It is precisely the process of elevating some issues to the status of 'problem' that is the principal concern. Language planning cannot sensibly be confined to the processes and practices of language change that follow the establishment of language problems as if that process were unproblematic and always neutral.

I do not deny a technical role for a class of professional planners of language or for their techniques and methods. After all, this has been a considerable part of my own work in Australia, Sri Lanka (1999), and Scotland (2001). However the deficiencies of confining definitions of language planning only to that field can be partially overcome by engaging in interdisciplinary analysis of problems and issues of language in society, including overt and technically focused processes of discovery of information as a prelude to action. In doing this we would as language planning scholars seek to move applied and especially sociolinguistic analysis away from forging correlations between phenomena and their linguistic elements, to seeing how sociolinguistics, and indeed language, constitutes social phenomena in processes of performativity. I also believe that Kaplan's (1966) well-known and important work on contrastive rhetoric is sympathetic with this notion, extended here to include the interests expressed by different professional codes and by various politico-ideological formations, as well as by ethno-linguistic groups.

The category of activity that, it is being argued, should be included within new descriptions of language planning is well established, indeed ancient, in other disciplinary areas. Discourse is a focus of literary studies as rhetoric, a focus of political science as persuasion, political language, and propaganda, and it is increasingly understood as argument in policy studies (Majone, 1989; Ball, 1993). Early students of language planning (Dua, 1985, 1986; Nahir, 1984) devoted considerable attention to characterizing language problems, but the focus here is on the processes whereby language problems come to prevail as the focus of attention in policy, such as why and how, for example, Turkish policy makers in the 1920s identified a problem of script, requiring processes of alphabetization reform (Lewis, 1999).

One consequence of these arguments is that 'discourse planning' would come to be recognized as a legitimate category of language planning dealing with both how language planning problems are constructed (thus constituting a data set for analysis), and as a mainstream element of the analysis of language problems that have been made topics of formal policy processes. There are then two aspects to the present argument: first, to include discourse planning within the framework of language planning studies, and secondly, to include the dimension of discourse as a contribution to the understanding of distinctive language problems. Neither methods of analysis nor approaches to discourse are presently found within applied linguistics. Discourse planning and discourse analysis studies seem to range from conversation analysis to critical studies, often inspired by the sociology and historiography of Michel Foucault. These two claims therefore, to include discourse as a component of language planning studies and discourse analysis as a legitimate and prominent part of mainstream language planning scholarship are complementary to the systematic analysis of language planning theory and research.

Before proceeding to describe what an extended field of language policy analysis would look like with these inclusions, I wish to elucidate two kinds of evidence for justifying the proposal: first, the claims of the official English movement in the United States, and second, the 'face value' credibility shortfall of much language policy research work. Before discussing official English and face value, however, I describe the six kinds of activity that constitute language planning theory and scholarship (status, corpus, acquisition, usage, esteem, and discourse), and then report some criticisms of, and allegations against, conventional or classical language planning. I then discuss discourse planning as an additional field for inclusion. Finally, I defend my claim for the inclusion of discourse as a methodological approach for all language policy and planning. My sense that political language – or performative language use in the processes and practices of making language change or resisting change proposed by others – requires the greatest elaboration, and in fact is work in progress, able only to be nominated and briefly described in the present chapter, which should be seen as an instalment for later elaboration.

Status planning

Status planning is perhaps the most well-recognized and long-established activity within language planning, extensively analyzed in Kaplan and Baldauf (1997). Essentially, status planning involves the allocation of status hierarchies to different languages, dialects, or speech forms in a given society or institution. Celebrated cases are the *Loi 101* in Quebec, which regulates the formal relation of French to English; the 1956 *Official Sinhala* Act in Sri Lanka (then Ceylon), which removed English and Tamil from authoritative state functions in that country, and various language laws in other settings and countries around the world. On August 1, 1996, the US House of Representatives adopted the Language of Government Act (the *Bill Emerson English Language Empowerment Act of 1996*, 104–723) by 259 votes to 169, after 15 years of failed attempts at floor action. Although the Bill lapsed in the Senate owing to the adjournment of the 104th Congress, similar measures have now been adopted in many states, claiming Iowa in 2002 as the 24th Official English state, and there are today revived moves for an official English bill in Congress.

The justification for a discourse analytical approach to language planning in general and the inclusion of discourse analysis as a specific field of language planning is highlighted by this very practice of US states proclaiming English official. This is discussed in more detail below; suffice to say here that the weak symbolism of some of these laws and the stronger executive intent and capacity of others requires explanation and understanding that classificatory or taxonomizing practices cannot achieve. Status planning analysis needs to include discourse data centrally within its research for a proper understanding of the phenomenon of official English in settings where the dominant communicative medium is English, and especially when some of the discourse surrounding claims for making English official seeks to 'protect' what is the most powerful language in history. To substantively explain the purposes, effects, circumstances, and local histories of these various laws requires an exploration of the subjectivity of political actors, which, in turn is more amenable to the discursive environment of the problem of status.

Status planning activity generally aims to regulate legal functions among languages or varieties of languages as a correlate of official, formal, and explicit status attributions conducted via unsystematic popular 'policing' of use of languages, though systematic processes of status planning also occur via market-based dictionary standardization. Less formally, juridical processes of this type accompany formal standardization. Language roles, therefore, within language styles as well as across language functions, are shaped by processes of popular talking and writing as well as by legislating and litigating.

Corpus planning

Conventionally next in the analysis of language planning is corpus planning. This is a more linguistically centered practice than status planning, though as most scholars point out, corpus and status planning are in real life often undertaken in tandem. Corpus planning is more technical in content, undertaken more often than status planning by formally trained language specialists, though usually not by specialists trained in language planning as such, and it addresses the determination of norms, script, and other linguistic units, usually for both internal linguistic ends and for wider social ends. Corpus language planning is often also ideological and political. The inevitably cited cases of speech codes and of anti-sexist and anti-racist language support this claim. Here too, informal processes of language corpus change are immersed in language ideologies and debates whose principal aim is often to constitute changes in political and social relations between different groups of people. Discourse is both the vehicle through which advocacy of such change is made and often the site in which the intended changes are negotiated, devised, and realized. These changes refer to linguistic dimensions of human social identity, and these are discursively realized.

Acquisition planning

Perhaps the most straightforward of the mainstream activities of language policy and planning, acquisition planning (Cooper, 1989) refers to the learning and teaching of additional languages, often within formal systems of education, and is also referred to as language-in-education planning. Acquisition planning might also be applied to the acquisition of literacy and its progressive growth throughout an educational pathway.

The field of language planning appears particularly weak in conceptualizations of language-in-education. This is due to its dependence on theories of language that are structure-centered. A meaning-centered linguistics, such as systemic functional linguistics in the tradition of M.A.K Halliday

(1993), would place acquisition planning (or 'language-in-education planning') very high on its list of priorities, understood principally as the elaboration of the meaning potential of individual learners in the direction of genres of speech and writing that are socially required in different contexts.

Usage planning

Usage planning analyzes fields of activity that extend the domains in which a target language is used. Usually accompanying language revitalization efforts conducted on behalf of dying or marginalized languages, usage planning is both systematic and organizational as well as informal, and it considers pressure, ideology, and social influence. The extension of language planning to the domains of usage of languages engages social planning in direct ways.

Since all language use is intimately connected with social purpose, usage planning inevitably involves social planning as weak languages erode functionally in intimate connections with social purpose and domain, especially when the informal transmission practices of their speakers are disrupted (Fishman, 2001). These practices usually take place in contexts of familial intimacy, and usage planning involves either an artificial substitution for disrupted processes of intergenerational communication or new kinds of extrinsic planning to reconstitute intimacy relations in a targeted language. These all depend on the creation and dispersal of new identity formations, which are discursively realized and enacted.

Esteem planning

Esteem planning is a correlate of usage planning in that it involves action to displace dominant codes from prestigious domains. Prestige planning is often the province of eminent writers. Dante Alighieri is a classic instance (Dante/Botterill, 1996). Dante's code selection of Italian over Latin was a conscious choice to contribute an elevating, standardizing legacy to a vernacular over a more prestigious written variety. Coulmas (1999) attributes a parallel role to William Chaucer in relation to English and Martin Luther in relation to German, among others. A reverse process can also be cited. Post-colonial literature, in which prestige attachments are made to writing in dialectal or varieties of standard colonial languages, establishes literary prestige for national varieties of polycentric languages (Pennycook, 1994). In his 1780 defence of eloquence, the American patriot John Adams urged the first Congress of the new Republic to bolster '... liberty, prosperity, and glory' by devoting '... an early attention to the subject of eloquence and language.' Nine years later, Noah Webster's Declaration of Linguistic Independence called for Americans to 'adorn' English and use it well but also for the separation of 'American' from 'English,' believing this to be both 'necessary and inevitable' (cited in Crawford, 1992: 32–36).

The difference between 'American' and 'English' was a social ideology – namely, its more 'democratical' nature – underscoring ideological language planning for esteem tailored for social relations, not literary culture. H.L Mencken later noted with disdain the 'cultural timorousness' of a class of 'social aspirants' that looked to England for its linguistic esteem (Mencken, 1936), observing the expansion of American English even in his time, which was being carried 'beyond its national borders.' Mencken's hope was not for an Academy, but for a Chaucer or a Dante, who would provide American with 'dignity.' Dignity planning is a kind of prestige attachment, a distinctive form of language planning that poets and writers mostly conduct on behalf of languages struggling against entrenched practices.

Discourse planning

Discourse has already been noted as the means for the negotiation and constitution of the problems, issues, and identities involved in the preceding domains of language planning. However discourse is also planned to constitute new worlds via discursive practice. This kind of language planning is usually called rhetoric, propaganda, PC speech, or political talk, and it is ancient and universal. The language planning of centralized communist states (Calvet, 1998), like its counterpart in Nazi ideologies of language (Hutton, 1999), is concerned with linguistic form only to the extent that it realizes the discursive – and material – project of changing the mental states of citizens. George Orwell's (1974a, 1974b) famous dictum that political language is intended to make lies 'sound truthful and murder respectable' expresses this idea of authoritative control of human mental states, aiming to direct the thinkable by restricting the expressible.

This type of discourse planning – namely, brainwashing – is characterized by little or no concern with linguistic form as an end in itself. Advertising, political language, and indeed all talk and writing with overt persuasive intention is examined within communication studies and more generally as part of attempts to uncover its connections with deception and the subverting of conscious individual action (Carey, 1997). Discourse planning need not be overtly sinister. All institutional talk seeks to give effect to the worldview of the particular institution, involving any kind of ideological field, such that the discourse of membership is taken to be natural.

Language ideology (Schieffelin *et al.*, 1998) is a growing field of scholarship at the intersection of language, society, and cognition, with strong popular and literary antecedents. Heller and Martin-Jones (2001) theorize interaction as a site where contradictions between espoused and often idealistic policies of multilingualism encounter the realities of teaching, classrooms, and relationships, seeking to reconcile the classic sociological conundrum of structure versus agency via the mediation of interaction and talk. It is in this domain that discourse planning is to be located, at the points where the broader social planning of conscious and less conscious types encounters situated realities with local histories and their impact on possibilities and constraints. Discourse planning is rarely conscious, and some will question whether it could therefore be called any kind of planning, a subject for debate and discussion, though discourse is not merely the vehicle for the delivery of pre-determined messages of intention.

Perhaps discourse making cannot easily be conceptualized as 'planning' because the term conjures up images of deliberate, conscious, and overt activity that much discourse, that is, making some discursive regimes prevail over alternatives, does not contain. However, the dialogical, iterative, and deliberative character of what is being proposed as discourse planning is properly a practice of planning to the extent that all planning is an intervention made to help bring about a future desired state.

Making certain discursive understandings prevail over others is an extended and subtle kind of planning; incorporating this as discourse planning within language policy concepts seeks to connect interactional relations with broader social phenomena. A great deal of language policy and planning is conducted not at macro social levels but at micro levels of daily interaction in social contexts. In interactions, beliefs, attitudes, and ideologies of language can constitute a politics of language engaging many layers of society (Schieffelin *et al.*, 1998; Jaffe, 1999; Blommaert, 1999).

A specific instance of the connection between ideology and language is Shannon's (1999) study of bilingual teachers. The absence of overt or deliberate policy or the inability of broad and distant policy to guide local action results in the conversion of ideology as default policy among US bilingual teachers. In this instance, this relates to how the lower public esteem of Spanish in relation to English leads many teachers, even some working in bilingual education, to devalue Spanish speakers' acquisition of English while granting recognition to English speakers' acquisition of Spanish.

In my own work on Australian language policy, this default operation of ideology has often been apparent. During 1986 while preparing the National Policy on Languages report for the Federal Government, I repeatedly encountered the view – often expressed by public officials, government Ministers among them – that language planning is a foreign activity. The underlying idea was that language policies are a kind of national deficiency correction, and therefore something that others do. Three kinds of remarks were made, sometimes as part of a private or personal dialogue, in a process possibly aiming at naming and constituting the activity as appropriate to the jurisdiction or interests of the individual concerned. The first was that language planning was a practice of post-colonial nation making. The second was that language planning is the reaction of older, non-English speaking nations concerned to protect their cherished national language from lexical incursions from English. The third repudiation was that language planning is an activity appropriate to non-English speaking trading nations seeking to advantage their global trading strategies through communication skills in English.

What was decisive in the eventual adoption of the policy and in the subsequent adoption of a series of policies on language education was the elaboration of a national discourse that made the activity itself appropriate to overarching national goals (Lo Bianco, 2004). In Australia's case, these have been Asian integration, indigenous reconciliation, multicultural diversity, and enhanced and more effective English communication (Lo Bianco, 2003). Each of these – and they sometimes contradict each other – reflects the power and ideology configurations of successive administrations, but each has depended on a key component of language planning, namely, discourse planning, and persuasion about the appropriateness of the activity itself. The national policy and language planning commitment has been dramatically changed over the past 15 years, but one of its enduring characteristics has been how each change has been signalled by a discursive construction of realities, especially of which new set of language problems will be given prominence.

Conclusion

Rarely do states or other language planning agencies engage in formal processes of problem definition, position setting, data gathering, formulation of plans, evaluation routines, and refinement of goals. The official English instance in the US tells us about the critical need for agreement about what constitutes the problem that language policy and planning is to address. Also, in the absence of such agreement (which is of course the domain of political struggle), the persistence of this policy problem, without resolution since 1981, points to the lack of a genuinely communicative process where such inter-subjective understanding might be fashioned.

It seems improbable that most actual language policy and planning activity contains more than a small component of professional policy analysis. As Kaplan (1994) pointed out, though language policy and planning is a growing activity, little attention is devoted to it, even in applied linguistics and sociolinguistics programs. Language planning theory ought to explore closer conceptual links with policy analysis scholarship that theorizes power and with the various branches of discourse studies. Potentially productive cross-fertilization addressing the critically important phase of problem definition, both in formal, conscious ways and via what Yeatman (1990) has called 'discursive politics,' might enliven and extend language planning theory further.

Chapter 17
World-Language: Foreign Language Policy in Hungary

PÉTER MEDGYES

Introduction

Until 2002, Hungary did not have a clear and comprehensive foreign language policy or national language program. This is not to say that there had been no attempts at developing such a policy, but earlier strategy documents were haphazard and program implementation never managed to get off the ground.

With the entry of Hungary into the European Union (EU) set to take place in May 2004, it became obvious to the new government taking office in 2002 that the country was lagging behind many member states and candidate countries in terms of its citizens' foreign language competence. Both statistical evidence and everyday experience made it imperative for decision-makers to face this problem and to implement quick measures for improvement. Before taking action, however, they had the foresight to seek expert advice, and even practising teachers, who can seldom make their voices heard beyond the classroom or schools (Kaplan, 1992), were invited to contribute. It is this process of planning the future of foreign language education in Hungary that will be reported in this chapter, in two parts. I first describe the current situation concerning Hungarians' foreign language competence, or rather the lack of it, as well as the place foreign languages occupy in the school curriculum. I then present 'World-Language,' both a strategy document and a set of programs aimed at putting the underlying principles into practice. Throughout the chapter, I emphasize that language planning and language-in-education planning have taken only their first steps in Hungary, and that the challenges must be handled in a never-ending cycle of planning, implementation, and evaluation.

About Hungary

Hungary is a landlocked country, occupying almost the whole of the Carpathian Basin in Central Europe. Its land area is 35,920 square miles

(93,033 square km) and its dwindling population was put at 10.2 million in 2001 compared with 10.7 million 20 years earlier (National Census, 2002). Hungary has always had a turbulent history, and the second half of the 20th century was no exception. Following a Communist takeover in 1949, the Hungarian People's Republic was proclaimed under Stalinist rule. A revolution broke out against this regime in 1956, only to be crushed by the Soviet Union with military force. Between 1956 and 1988, Hungary gradually adopted liberal policies in the economic, educational, and cultural spheres, with the result that it was seen as the most tolerant country behind the 'Iron Curtain.' In 1989, Hungary's communist leaders voluntarily abandoned their monopoly of power, thus facilitating a peaceful shift to a multi-party democracy and free-market economy. Since 1990, four consecutive free elections have been held – an exceptionally long democratic period in the history of the country. In 1994, Hungary applied to be admitted to the European Union (EU), and it became a fully-fledged member in May 2004 along with nine other countries.

It is a truism that every country is multilingual; the concept of monolingual nationhood is a myth. However, it is also true that countries differ in the degree of their multilingualism. Hungary is certainly less multilingual than most of its neighbors: 99.8% of the population speaks Hungarian, and a mere 5.6% identify themselves as non-ethnic Hungarians (National Census, 2002). Even the largest minority group, the Roma population, was found to number only slightly more than 2% in the census, although sociologists put the real figure at 5% or more (Póczik, 1996).

Hungarian is the most unique and isolated language in Central Europe because it belongs to the Finno-Ugric branch of the Uralic family while all the surrounding countries use a language of Indo-European origin as their first language. Thus Hungarians cannot communicate with their neighbors unless they have learned to speak a foreign language. It is little wonder, therefore, that knowledge of foreign languages has always been held in high esteem in Hungary. As a Hungarian proverb puts it, 'You are as many persons as the number of languages you can speak' (Medgyes & Miklósy, 2000).

How many people speak foreign languages in Hungary?

Nevertheless, the foreign language competence of Hungarians leaves a lot to be desired as foreign languages are spoken by only 19.2% of the population (National Census, 2002). Such data, however, should be treated with caution because they draw on self-reports, which reflect stated rather than actual behavior (Marton, 1981). It is assumed that if the claimants were tested for actual proficiency, this figure would be much lower. Moreover, the national census provides no indication of proficiency levels.

The foreign language competence of Hungarians is also unsatisfactory in an international context. The figure of 19.2% in Hungary should be contrasted with 52.7% in the 15 member states before the 2004 enlargement (Europeans and Languages, 2001). But even if compared to the other nine new members, Hungary is far behind as regards knowledge of the five most widely spoken foreign languages in the EU (Eurobarometer, 2002).

This is not to deny that significant progress has been made since the change of regime in 1989. To give just one example, the number of foreign language speakers has more than doubled in 15 years, which is largely to do with increased motivation. In present-day Hungary, stating the vital importance of foreign language proficiency is stating the obvious.

Which languages do Hungarians prefer?

According to the most recent national census, two languages run neck and neck on the popularity scale (Table 17.1): German is spoken by 9.9% of the population and English by 9.8%, and it can be confidently predicted that English will have overtaken German by the time this volume is published. Although the rapid spread of English took place at the expense of German in relative terms, the number of German speakers is also rising. It would be wrong, therefore, to speak of a shift in cultural paradigm between English and German (Sík, 1998). However, the data do show that while German is typically spoken by less educated and older people who live in smaller towns and villages, English is favoured by the better educated and by the young from metropolitan areas (Terestyéni, 1995).

The onslaught of English may also be demonstrated by a survey of 620 top-ranking representatives of Hungarian science (Medgyes & László, 2001), especially if the results are contrasted with those of an identical survey carried out 10 years earlier (Medgyes & Kaplan, 1992). Whereas in 1989, highly proficient English speakers outnumbered highly proficient German speakers by only 1.2%, by 1999 there were nearly four times as many English speakers as German speakers. The relative weight of English was even more pronounced in the area of academic publications. In the 1990s, foreign languages other than English were relegated to a marginal role in academic discourse, a tendency grounded in the view that scientific achievements had a chance of circulation only if they were reported in English. In other words, English has become the unrivalled language of science across the disciplines.

Compared with English and German, all other foreign languages do badly in the ranking (Table 17.1), even though they have all grown in absolute numbers. Interestingly enough, even Russian, considered a pariah after long decades of Soviet dictatorship and mandatory Russian instruction, shows progress, albeit inconsequential, in the number of its speakers. Again, this points to the prominent role that foreign languages play in contemporary Hungary.

Table 17.1 Percentage of Hungarians who speak foreign languages

	1960	1980	1990	2001
English	0.43%	1.07%	2.21%	9.79%
German	4.33%	3.18%	4.01%	9.87%
French	0.45%	na	0.51%	1.14%
Italian	0.11%	na	0.16%	0.60%
Russian	0.67%	1.22%	1.47%	1.91%
Spanish	0.01%	na	0.07%	0.24%

Foreign Languages in the Curriculum

Although the assumption that language-in-education planning is sufficient to promote language learning and language use across a society has been questioned, the importance of school instruction should not be dismissed (Kaplan & Baldauf, 1997).

In the wake of the Communist takeover in 1949, Russian was decreed to be the mandatory 'first' foreign language in all types of schools and, simultaneously, all the other languages were virtually expelled from schools. It was not until the 1960s that 'second' foreign languages began to creep back into the curriculum, though they were overshadowed by Russian until 1989. Typically, even in the last year of communist rule in Hungary, less than 3% of primary and 16.5% of secondary school students had the opportunity to learn English, for example, in spite of the upsurge of interest in the language. Despite a disproportionately huge investment in terms of instructional time and energy, Russian was the worst off: a glance at the figures for 1980 and 1990 (Table 17.1) reveals the extremely low cost-effectiveness of Russian instruction.

Communism imploded in 1989. In the same year, consonant with the historic changes occurring in Hungary and in quick succession over the whole of Central and Eastern Europe, the Russian language was officially stripped of its privileged status. Since then, it has been possible for Hungarian students to learn any foreign language offered by their schools, and thus the distribution of foreign languages at every level of education in Hungary has changed significantly. The magnitude of these changes is illustrated in Figures 17.1, 17.2, and 17.3.

All three figures reveal the growing share of English and German and the negligible proportion that other foreign languages are assigned in the school curriculum. In primary education (grades 1–8) (Figure 17.1), where the study of one foreign language is compulsory from grade 4, English leads with 53.8% and German is the runner-up with 44.0% of the age cohort,

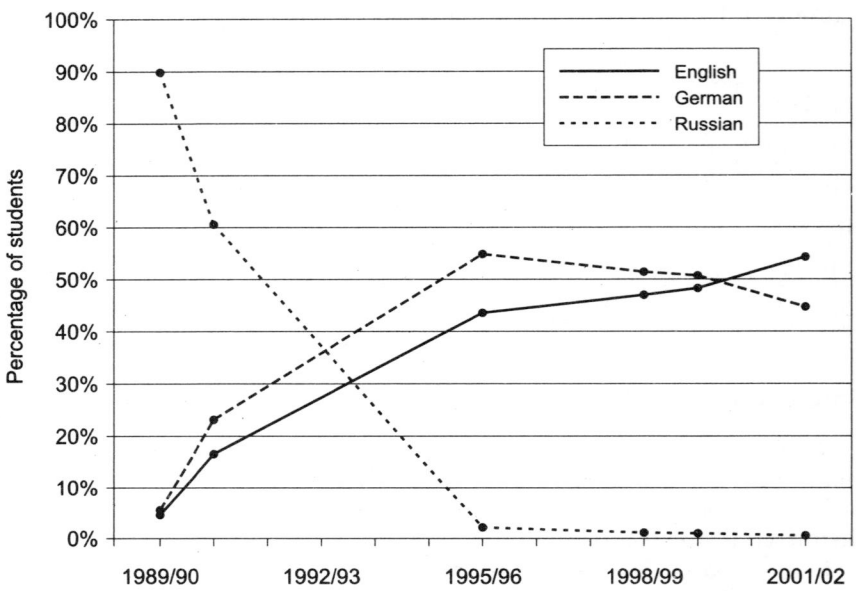

Figure 17.1 Proportion of foreign languages in Hungarian primary schools

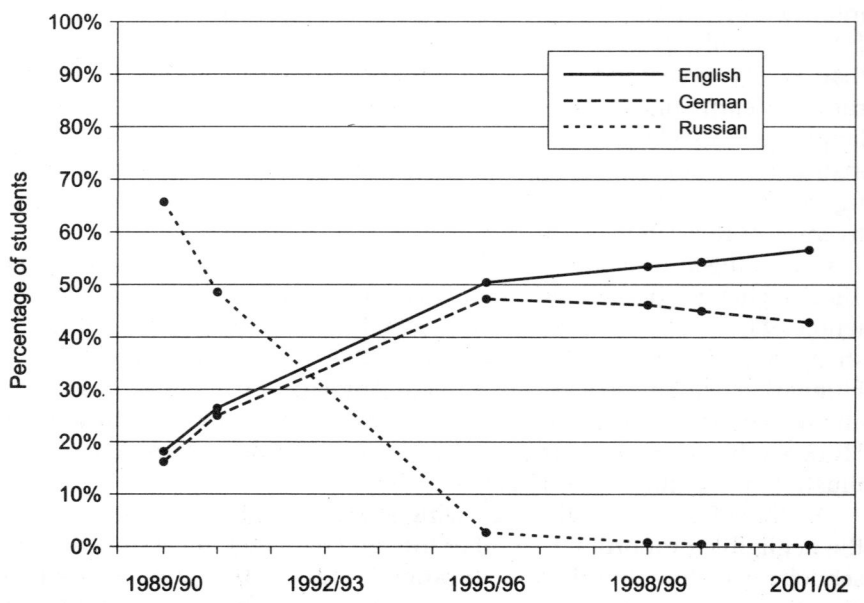

Figure 17.2 Proportion of foreign languages in Hungarian vocational schools

World-Language: Foreign Language Policy in Hungary

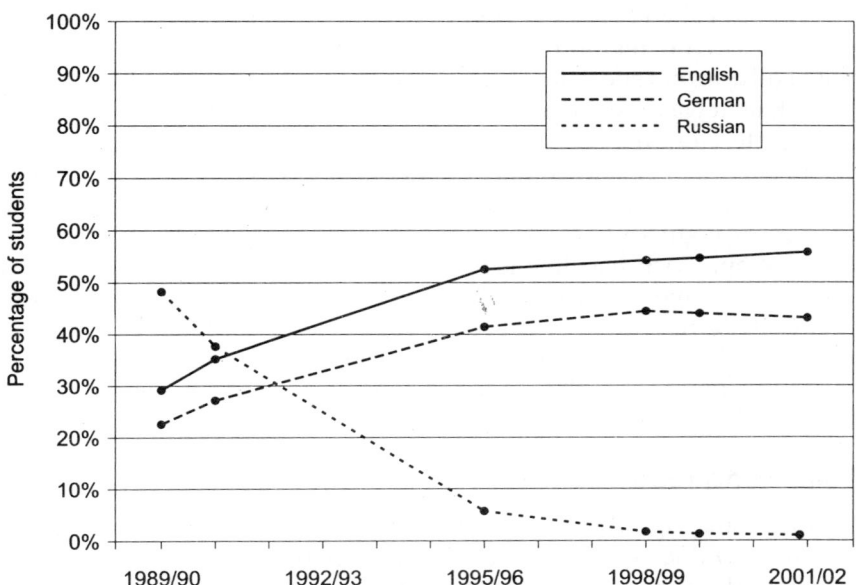

Figure 17.3 Proportion of foreign languages in Hungarian secondary grammar schools

leaving merely 2.2% for the other languages. The situation is only slightly less unbalanced in the three types of secondary education (grades 9–12). Whereas in most trade schools learning a foreign language is not compulsory, in vocational schools, where students are generally required to learn one foreign language, English and German together amount to 94.5% (Figure 17.2). In grammar schools, where the study of two foreign languages is compulsory, the aggregate share of English and German is 82.8% (Figure 17.3). In both vocational and grammar schools, the third place goes to French (2.9% and 6.4%, respectively), followed by Russian (0.5% and 0.8%, respectively).

What Needs to be Done?

As shown above, foreign language needs and hence the provision of foreign languages in Hungary have dramatically changed in the past 15 years. These changes are due to a host of circumstances: while direct political and economic factors have played a decisive role in the spread – or retreat – of foreign languages, individual preferences have also been important. With Hungary's accession to the EU, the process of foreign language study is likely to accelerate. The present state of Hungary bodes well for the teaching and learning of foreign languages.

On the other hand, it has to be admitted that much less has been achieved since the change of regime than had been hoped for: the average Hungarian youth still does not speak foreign languages. Hartinger (1993: 33) is right in saying that 'it was easier to pull down the barbed wire on the border than it has been to cross the [...] language barrier.' A major stumbling block to greater success seems to be the absence of concerted effort in the area of language planning and language-in-education planning. Even though the pressure brought to bear on consecutive governments to take a more proactive approach had intensified, it was not until the socialist-liberal government came to power in 2002 that a breakthrough was made. More specifically, a resolution was passed calling for the design of a foreign language policy and the introduction of a range of concomitant measures to realize this policy. It is this policy document with which the rest of the chapter will be concerned.

World-Language

World-Language (WL) is the campaign logo used by the Hungarian Ministry of Education to publicize its new national strategy for foreign language education. The policy document underlying the campaign is the most complete document of its kind ever produced in Hungary.

At the preliminary stage, a 10-member committee consisting of independent foreign language experts was convened in the summer of 2002, supported by a small team of ministry officials in charge of foreign language education. After a series of meetings, the first draft of the policy document was drawn up. When it had been circulated and reviewed by professional bodies and then revised by the expert committee, the final document was approved by the Minister of Education and subsequently by the Education and Research Committee of the Hungarian Parliament. For the purpose of implementing the program package envisaged in the document, 500 million forints (US$2.5 million) was earmarked for the year 2003.

The policy document itself falls into five major parts. Part 1 briefly describes the general aims and principles, which are as follows:

- Foreign languages should be learned during the most formative years of education, hence the main focus of WL is on primary and secondary education.
- WL also provides opportunities for the adult population, promoting the practice of life-long learning.
- Rather than introducing obligatory measures, WL offers a framework for teachers and learners to freely exploit their creative potential.
- To create equal opportunities, WL supports learners who come from disadvantaged backgrounds and who have learning disabilities.

- While acknowledging the importance of quantitative measures, WL fosters quality education and innovation.
- WL establishes a stimulating environment for language learning not only within the classroom, but also outside the classroom and outside the school.
- WL facilitates the integration of Information and Communication Technology (ICT) into language education, most directly within the framework of the Schoolnet Express program.

Part 2 of the policy document outlines the current situation in Hungary, covering different aspects of language education in schools, pre- and in-service teacher training, the language competence of non-language teachers, specific problems relating to higher education, systems of assessment, and so on.

Part 3 offers a vision of the future, addressing the issues listed above. While stressing the importance of teacher education in general, it urges language provision for non-language teachers so that they become adequately proficient to teach their subject in a foreign language.

Part 4 describes the legislative measures taken to effect radical improvements, and Part 5 elaborates on the 10-item program package designed to achieve the fundamental aims of WL. The next two sections will present in some detail the legislative measures and the program package.

New Elements in Legislation

Intensive language training in secondary schools

A clause in the 2003 Public Education Act concerned foreign language education, and resolved to create an opportunity for a year of intensive language training for 9th graders in every secondary school, both grammar and vocational, with one such class launched in 2004 and one more each year thereafter. This program is optional, but once established, a minimum of 40% of total curriculum time (at least 12 contact hours per week) should be allocated for foreign language study. To follow it up, volunteering schools are obliged to assign a sufficient number of lessons in grades 10–13 for students who participated in the intensive language training program to be able to take the advanced-level school-leaving examination in their first foreign language. These students will leave school after grade 13 – a year later than their peers. Incidentally, the law does not specify whether one or two languages should be taught during the intensive year of study.

Increased contact time in secondary grammar schools

A recommendation was issued by the Ministry of Education with the purpose of improving language instruction in secondary grammar schools, where at present the study of two foreign languages is compulsory, each with three contact hours per week. Most experts agree that the time allotted is not sufficient for attaining a decent level of communicative competence in either language, and the two languages studied simultaneously and unintensively cancel each other out. It is recommended, therefore, that students begin to study only one language for least five lessons a week, and they are advised not to embark on a second language until they have passed the advanced-level school-leaving examination. After this, the second language should also be allocated five lessons per week and post-exam study of the first language should continue in a limited number of lessons according to a special curriculum.

Changes to school-leaving and university entrance examinations

The new Public Education Act, in harmony with the 2003 amended Higher Education Act, abolished entrance examinations, making the school-leaving examination the only eligibility criterion for entry into higher education as from 2005. In all school subjects, the school-leaving examination may be taken at two levels: intermediate and advanced. One of the four compulsory exam subjects should be a foreign language, but school leavers may opt for another foreign language as their fifth subject. Administered to measure communicative proficiency in the four skills and use of language, the language examination consists of an oral and a written component. The expected level of competence corresponds to A2/B1 at intermediate level and to B2 at advanced level as defined in the *Common European Framework of Reference* ... (2001). This new system of school-leaving examination offers an additional possibility. Traditionally, students have been exempt from having to take the school-leaving language exam once they have passed the medium-level state foreign language examination (for which they have to pay). With the new system in place, the reverse now applies: those who have passed the advanced-level school-leaving examination (which is obviously free of charge) are automatically granted the state foreign language examination certificate as well.

Tax incentives

Pursuant to the 2001 Adult Training Act, an amendment to the 2003 Act on Personal Income Tax allows all adult citizens who have participated in an accredited language course to deduct from their personal income tax 30% of the tuition fee up to a limit of 60,000 Hungarian forints (US$300) per year. This scheme acts as a modest incentive to promote the life-long learning of foreign languages.

The Program Package

The package comprises 10 programs and a number of subcomponents, all of which are accessible through an open application system advertised and administered by the Tempus Public Foundation, a support agency of the Ministry of Education. The criteria for bidding are in accordance with the general aims and principles of WL. The catch-phrases used for the application and selection process are self-explanatory: easy access to information, transparency, motivating objectives, innovation, financial reward and professional recognition for participants, measurable achievements, sustainable development, integration with other projects, and so on. Below is a brief summary of the ten programs.

(1) Resource bags

This program supplies schools with authentic foreign language materials for German, English and French, as well as audio and visual equipment to assist self-directed language learning and the establishment of foreign language libraries and resource centers. Applicants from disadvantaged regions and schools are given preference. An in-service training project and the establishment of a network of coordinators are linked to the program.

(2) Content-based teaching

This program encourages schools to introduce modules within the framework, in which certain general or vocational subjects can be taught in a foreign language. It offers: (a) support for infrastructural and technological investments related to the new scheme; (b) the opportunity for non-language teacher trainees to spend 10 months studying in the target language country; (c) in-service training courses for non-language teachers, including a strong element of language improvement; (d) grants to develop content-based syllabuses and teaching materials; and (e) in-service training courses for secondary school teachers to teach European cultural studies.

(3) Help the disadvantaged!

The program is targeted at secondary school students who come from disadvantaged family and/or ethnic backgrounds, or who are dyslexic or dysgraphic, or visually or audially impaired.

(4) The efficient language teacher

Prospective language teachers in pre-service education are supported in three ways: (a) successful candidates may spend a one-semester study period in a target-language country; (b) teacher training institutions may apply for a grant to extend to one semester their period of teaching practice, which is generally not more than 15 contact hours of actual teaching; and (c) mentor training programs exist for practicing teachers to learn how to assist trainee teachers during their teaching practice. A fourth subcomponent is aimed at designing a practice-oriented M.Ed. program for language teachers.

(5) Lesser taught languages

As mentioned above, all foreign languages except English and German fall into the category of 'less widely taught languages' in Hungary. In accordance with the recommendations of the EU and the Council of Europe, which advocate linguistic and cultural diversity and the ideal of the 'trilingual European citizen' (implying the mother tongue plus two foreign languages), this program gives financial aid to schools prepared to launch and/or maintain instruction in any of these languages. The list also includes languages spoken in neighboring countries and those used by ethnic minorities in Hungary.

(6) Test and assess

The chief objective of this program is to develop the expertise of language teachers in assessment, testing, and program evaluation, especially in relation to existing curriculum and ongoing examination reform.

(7) Focus on vocational training

Vocational training in Hungary is provided in trade schools, vocational schools, and post-secondary vocational training centers. The main objective of the program is to raise language and non-language teachers' levels of language proficiency, particularly in the use of specialized language.

(8) Focus on higher education

In this program, institutions of higher education are given financial aid to run in-service training courses for teachers. The main emphasis is on curriculum development for academic and specific purposes.

(9) Life-long learning

This program has been designed to cater for the language needs of the Hungarian adult population employed in different areas of the manufacturing and service sectors. The aim is to improve their job-retaining potential and competitiveness and to enable them to communicate fluently in a culturally and linguistically diverse Europe.

(10) Supplementary programs

Two specific kinds of language program are offered: one supports the hosting of international conferences; the other sponsors the publication of professional journals and books.

The bulk of the first application period was closed in mid-May 2003. Among the applications received, 'Life-long learning,' 'The efficient language teacher,' and 'Resource bags' were the most popular programs, while interest in other programs failed to live up to expectations. The first round of applications also revealed gaps in the program package.

Looking Backward and Forward

Examining the WL program as it was run in 2003, two deficiencies are noticeable. One is the neglect of language teaching at an early age, a concern repeatedly voiced by experts. The need for early learning is most strongly felt by primary school principals, who have to resolve the contradiction between parental pressure for more space in the curriculum to be allocated to foreign language instruction, and a shortage of teachers trained to teach the young. In addition, the integration of ICT and language education was found not to be seamless. While an increasing number of schools are being equipped with adequate computer facilities and free access to the Internet under the auspices of the Schoolnet Program, ICT is still only tangentially applied to language teaching purposes, and few teachers feel at home with its use. To remedy this handicap, many teachers expressed their desire to participate in training programs geared towards ICT in language education.

The main task still facing the program concerns the introduction of the intensive language training program for 9th graders, as stipulated in the new Public Education Act (see above). Although experience from bilingual schools is readily available, intensive work should begin to develop suitable syllabuses and teaching materials as well as to prepare teachers to handle such classes.

To respond to the challenges posed by the pilot year, further developments were planned for 2004, bolstered by the Government's growing interest in boosting foreign language study in Hungary. As signs of this commitment, three initiatives deserve special mention:

- The Ministry of Education hired a professional firm charged with mounting a campaign for foreign language education in Hungary. The primary target group is school-aged youngsters and the slogan is: 'Speaking foreign languages is "cool".'
- The Minister of Education announced that the 2003/04 school year would be dedicated to foreign language study. The official launch took place on September 26, 2003, the European Day of Languages, and was followed by a string of events throughout the year.
- In the spring of 2003, the Hungarian Government submitted to the European Commission its National Development Plan, which included a submeasure aimed at improving the foreign language competence of Hungarian citizens. If the National Development Plan

were to be approved the Commission, considerable EU sources would become available for foreign language teaching and learning to complement the allocation due in the Hungarian national budget for 2004 and beyond.

Issues with the World-Language Program

Although the first year of the World-Language program was met with strong approval by the language teaching profession and beyond, some bones of contention remain. Here are a few examples.

- Many foreign language teachers in Hungary are of the view that the success of the language teaching process is essentially determined by quantitative parameters, such as the number of weekly contact hours and class size. This attitude overlooks the importance of quality assurance, and the need for the continuous assessment of student competences as well as for teacher and program evaluation.
- Advocates of the 'the earlier, the better' concept advocate lowering the compulsory starting age for foreign language teaching and learning from grade 4 to earlier grades. This disregards the fact that an early start can be harmful unless there is a sufficient supply of qualified teachers. Imposing adult methods of education on primary students can only lead to demotivation and frustration.
- The past few decades have witnessed the spread of Communicative Language Teaching (CLT) all over the world. However, some supporters of CLT interpret the concept restrictively, giving equal preference to the spoken over the written mode and to group work and pair work over teacher-fronted work. To others, CLT is an educational philosophy, encompassing far more than methodological concerns. It is this broader concept that was adopted by the decision-makers in charge of devising the policy document.
- Language instructors working in higher education deplore the fact that the program package contains no element aimed at strengthening university language centers. While agreeing that their long-term task should be the development of special-purpose language competence, they argue that since the majority of students arrive with low-level foreign language competence, there is a need for a WL component designed to cater for general language development. In response, policy-makers restated that this would only perpetuate the detrimental practice of providing free basic language training in higher education.
- The conflicting demands of elite and mass education are found in every society. With regard to foreign language education in Hungary, recent data reveal that school children who come from better-off fami-

lies have eight times more opportunity to learn foreign languages in and outside school than do their peers whose circumstances are less auspicious (*Család változóban*, 2002). In an attempt to reduce inequalities, a special program was launched, and in several other programs disadvantaged candidates were granted priority. However, information about the WL program may not always have reached potential candidates while other applicants were rejected because they lacked the skills for writing applications. Oddly enough, some critics have requested that, in later program packages, the elite should be guaranteed 'equal chances'.

- In response to the radical steps taken to promote foreign language education in Hungary, those who worry that foreign languages, especially English, put the mother tongue in jeopardy have become vociferous. They assert that WL is in fact a ruse to marginalize and eventually eliminate the Hungarian language. Incidentally, these are the same nationalists who two years earlier conducted a successful campaign to pass a bill protecting the Hungarian language (Medgyes, 2002). To challenge this view, it is worth remembering the axiom that the knowledge of foreign languages also contributes to a more conscious and sophisticated use of the first language. The trouble is that, since this has always been an emotionally charged and over-politicized issue in Hungary, rational argument tends to fall on deaf ears.

- The most bitter controversies have arisen out of the question of language choice in the curriculum, with ill-feeling emerging in different guises and being expressed with differing degrees of vehemence. After the elimination of Russian as the compulsory foreign language in schools, no other language was declared an official successor, though English gradually became *primus inter pares*. The WL policy is neutral on this issue except for one sentence: 'Since English has become the number one language of international communication, every student must have the opportunity to learn English before leaving school.' This statement has come under attack, spearheaded by diplomats and teachers representing other languages. They cry linguicism (Phillipson, 1992), contending that this is a covert attempt at making English a quasi-mandatory language at the expense of all others. Countering this argument, the Ministry of Education argues that this is merely a strategy paper that carries no legal force and that school principals remain free to choose and prioritize foreign languages.

- A similar wave of discontent has arisen in connection with the distribution of the two languages taught in secondary grammar schools (see above). Opponents claim that WL will reduce the space for foreign languages other than English and runs counter to the notion of the 'trilingual European citizen.' These critics tend to overlook that, contrary to this lofty ideal, English is one of the compulsory foreign languages in schools in 13 of the 30 European countries and in 8 of them is the only one (Key data..., 2002).

Curiously, even the concept of 9th grade intensive language training has been challenged (see above). The criticism has been leveled at a clause in the new Public Education Act that fails to clarify whether this period refers to intensive instruction in only one foreign language or more than one. The answer is that the time frame gives sufficient space for a second language in the 9th grade and possibly even a third in subsequent grades.

Conclusion

This chapter reported on the significant reforms being effected in foreign language education in Hungary. These positive developments are in large measure due to the determination of the government to enhance the knowledge of foreign languages through innovation in its language-in-education policy. Before advancing legislative reforms and program implementation, the Ministry of Education created a conceptual framework in the form of a policy document. In addition to favorable external circumstances, the remarkable success of WL has hinged on establishing adequate internal conditions, such as the proper use of expert advice, critical thinking, and good coordination. Setting the priorities right was another crucial element. Policy-makers managed to avoid the danger of fragmentation, resisting pressure from various professional lobbies to cut the cake into too many pieces. Overall, a sound balance was struck between compromises and firm decisions.

After the tentative steps taken in 2003, WL will continue in a somewhat altered form, in terms both of the policy document and the set of programs envisaged. After all, this is a long-term commitment whose final aim is to catch up with fellow member states in the EU in terms of foreign language competence. It can only be hoped that the language policy presented in this chapter will bridge over consecutive governments on the basis of joint decisions between policy-makers and specialists. Likewise, it is desirable that no innovation should be imposed without the creative participation and consent of teachers and learners (Medgyes & Nikolov, 2002).

Acknowledgement

I would like to thank Eniko Öveges for her dedication and massive support extended in the first year of the World-Language program.

References

Adair-Hauck, B. and Donato, R. (2002) The Pace model: A story-based approach to meaning and form for standards-based language learning. *French Review* 76, 265–276.
Adair-Hauck, B., Donato, R., and Cumo, P. (1994) Using a whole language approach to teach grammar. In K. Shrum and E. Glisan (eds) *Teachers' Handbook: Contextualized Foreign Language Instruction K–12*. Boston: Heinle & Heinle.
Adamson, H.D. (1998) *Academic Competence: Theory and Classroom Practice: Preparing ESL Students for Content Courses*. New York: Longman.
Ager, D. (2005) Prestige and image planning. In E. Hinkel (ed.) *Handbook of Research in Second Language Teaching and Learning*. Mahwah, NJ: Lawrence Erlbaum.
Ainsworth, N. (1981) *Oral Narratives of Bilingual Mexican-American Adults Enrolled in Adult Basic Education*. Washington, DC: National Institute of Education.
Alatorre, A. (1989) *Los 1,001 Años de la Lengua Española [1,001 Years of the Spanish Language]*. México: Tezontle.
Alcalá, M. (1968) Los neologismos y su peligro [Neologisms and their danger]. *Memorias de la Academia Mexicana* 19, 288–289.
Alexander, R. (2000) *Culture and Pedagogy: International Comparisons in Primary Education*. Malden, MA: Blackwell.
Amin, N. (1997) Race and the identity of the nonnative ESL teacher. *TESOL Quarterly* 31, 580–583.
Amin, N. (1999) Minority women teachers of ESL: Negotiating White English. In G. Braine (ed.) *Non-native Educators in English Language Teaching*. Mahwah, NJ: Lawrence Erlbaum.
Amin, N. (2001) Nativism, the native speaker construct, and minority immigrant women teachers of English as a Second Language. *CATESOL Journal* 13, 89–107.
Anderson, F. (1995) Classroom discourse and language socialization in a Japanese elementary-school setting: An ethnographic-linguistics study. Unpublished doctoral dissertation, University of Hawai'i.
Annamalai, E. (1979) Movements for linguistic purism: The case of Tamil. In E. Annamalai (ed.) *Language Movements in India*. Mysore: Central Institute of Indian Languages.
Annamalai, E. (1989) The linguistic and social dimensions of purism. In B.H. Jernudd and M.J. Shapiro (eds) *The Politics of Language Purism*. Berlin: Mouton de Gruyter.
Annamalai, E. and Rubin, J. (1980) Planning for language code and language use: Some considerations in policy formation and implementation. *Language Planning Newsletter* 6, 1–4.
Applebee, A. (1981) *Writing in the Secondary School*. Urbana, IL: National Council of Teachers of English.
Arva, V. and Medgyes, P. (2000) Native and non-native teachers in the classroom. *System* 28, 355–372.
Atkinson, D. (1999) TESOL and culture. *TESOL Quarterly* 33, 625–654.

Atkinson, D. (2001) Reflections and refractions on the *JSLW* special issue on voice. *Journal of Second Language Writing*, 10, 107–124.
Atkinson, D. (2003) Language socialization and dys-socialization in a South Indian college. In R. Bayley and S.R. Schecter (eds) *Language Socialization and Bilingualism*. Clevedon: Multilingual Matters.
Auerbach, E.R. (1993) Re-examining English Only in the ESL classroom. *TESOL Quarterly* 27, 9–32.
Bailey, K. (2002) Declarative knowledge, procedural knowledge, and the varieties of English we speak. *NNEST (Nonnative English Speakers in TESOL Caucus) Newsletter* 4, 3–5.
Baker, C. (2001) *Foundations of Bilingual Education and Bilingualism*. Clevedon: Multilingual Matters.
Baldauf, R.B., Jr (1994) 'Unplanned' language policy and planning. In W. Grabe (ed.) *Annual Review of Applied Linguistics: Language Policy and Planning* 14. New York: Cambridge University Press.
Baldauf, R.B., Jr and Kaplan, R.B. (2003) Who are the actors? The role of (applied) linguists in language policy. In P. Ryan and R. Terborg (eds) *Language: Issues of Inequality*. Mexico City: CELE/Autonomous National University of Mexico.
Baldauf, R.B., Jr. and Kaplan, R.B. (2005) Language-in-education planning. In E. Hinkel (ed.) *Handbook of Research in Second Language Teaching and Learning*. Mahwah, NJ: Lawrence Erlbaum.
Ball, A.F. (1992) Cultural preference and the expository writing of African-American adolescents. *Written Communication* 9, 501–532.
Ball, S.J. (1993) What is policy? Texts, trajectories and toolboxes. *Discourse* 13, 10–17.
Bander, R. (1971) *American English Rhetoric*. New York: Holt, Rinehart, & Winston.
Banks, J. (1995) Multicultural education: Historical development, dimensions, and practice. In J. Banks and C. McGee Banks (eds) *Handbook of Research on Multicultural Education*. New York: Macmillan.
Barbour, S. and Carmichael, C. (eds) (2000) *Language and Nationalism in Europe*. Oxford: Oxford University Press.
Bauer, L. (1983) *English Word-formation*. Cambridge: Cambridge University Press.
Baumgardner, R.J. (1993) *The English Language in Pakistan*. Karachi: Oxford University Press.
Baumgardner, R.J. (1997) English in Mexican Spanish. *English Today* 13, 27–35.
Bawarshi, A. (2003) *Genre and the Invention of the Writer*. Logan, UT: University of Utah Press.
Bean, J. (2001) *Engaging Ideas: The Professor's Guide to Integrating Writing, Critical Thinking, and Active Learning in the Classroom*. San Francisco: Jossey-Bass.
Beason, L. and Lester, M. (2000) *A Commonsense Guide to Grammar and Usage*. Boston: Bedford/St Martin's.
Becka, J.V. (1978) Application of quantitative methods in contrastive stylistics. *Prague Studies in Mathematical Linguistics* 6, 83–92.
Benesch, S. (2001) *Critical English for Academic Purposes: Theory, Politics, and Practice*. Mahwah, NJ: Lawrence Erlbaum.
Bentahila, A. and Davies, E.E. (1993) Language revival: Restoration or transformation. *Journal of Multilingual and Multicultural Development* 14, 355–374.
Bereiter, C. and Scardamalia, M. (1987) *The Psychology of Written Composition*. Hillsdale, NJ: Lawrence Erlbaum.
Berkenkotter, C. and Huckin, T. (1995) *Genre Knowledge in Disciplinary Communities*. Mahwah, NJ: Lawrence Erlbaum.

Berns, M. (2002) Expanding on the expanding circle: Where do WE go from here? Plenary address: 9th International Association of World Englishes (IAWE) Conference, Urbana, IL.
Bernstein, B. (1990) *Class, Codes and Control.* London: Routledge.
Bernstein, D.A., Clarke-Stewart. A., Penner, L.A., Roy, E.J. and Wickens, C.D. (2000) *Psychology.* Boston: Houghton Mifflin.
Bernth, A. and Gdaniec, C. (2001) MTranslatability. *Machine Translation* 16, 175–218.
Bhatia, V. (1993) *Analyzing Genre: Language Use in Professional Settings.* New York: Longman.
Bhatia, V. (2001) Analyzing genre: Some conceptual issues. In M. Hewings (ed.) *Academic Writing in Context: Implications and Applications.* Birmingham: Birmingham University Press.
Bhatt, R.M. (2001) World Englishes. *Annual Review of Anthropology* 30, 527–550.
Bialystok, E. and Sharwood-Smith, M. (1985) Interlanguage is not a state of mind: An evaluation of the construct for second language acquisition. *Applied Linguistics* 6, 101–117.
Biber, D., Conrad, S. and Reppen, R. (1998). *Corpus Linguistics: Investigating Language Structure and Use.* Cambridge: Cambridge University Press.
Biber, D., Conrad, S., Reppen, R., Byrd, P. and Helt, M. (2002) Speaking and writing in the university: A multidimensional comparison. *TESOL Quarterly* 36: 9–48.
Biber, D. and Finegan, E. (1989) Styles of stance in English: Lexical and grammatical marking of evidentiality and affect. *Text* 9, 93–124.
Biber, D., Johansson, S., Leech, G., Conrad, S. and Finegan, E. (1999) *Longman Grammar of Spoken and Written English.* Harlow: Pearson.
Björk, L, Bräuer, G., Reinecker, L. and Jörgenson, P.S. (eds) (2003) *Teaching Academic Writing in European Higher Education.* Dordrecht: Kluwer.
Blachford, D.R. (2000) Language planning and bilingual education for linguistic minorities in China: A case study of the policy formulation and implementation process. *Dissertation Abstracts International* 60: 3242-A.
Blanton, L.L. (1999) Classroom instruction and language minority students: On teaching to 'smarter' readers and writers. In L. Harklau, K.M. Losey and M. Siegal (eds) *Generation 1.5 Meets College Composition: Issues in the Teaching of Writing to US Educated Learners of ESL.* Mahwah, NJ: Lawrence Erlbaum.
Blanton, L.L. (2002) As I was saying to Leonard Bloomfield: A personalized history of ESL/writing. In L.L. Blanton and B. Kroll (eds) *ESL Composition Tales: Reflections on Teaching.* Ann Arbor, MI: University of Michigan Press.
Blommaert, J. (ed.) (1999) *Language Ideological Debates.* Berlin: Mouton de Gruyter.
Blum-Kulka, S., House, J. and Kasper, G. (eds) (1989) *Cross-cultural Pragmatics: Requests and Apologies.* Norwood, NJ: Ablex.
Blythman, M.J., Mullin, J., Milton, J. and Orr, S. (2003) Implementation issues for study support. In L. Björk, G. Bräuer, L. Reinecker and P.S. Jörgenson (eds) *Teaching Academic Writing in European Higher Education.* Dordrecht: Kluwer.
Bodde, D. (1991) *Chinese Thought, Society, and Science.* Honolulu, HI: University of Hawai'i Press.
Bookless, T.C. (1982) Towards a semantic description of English loan-words in Spanish. *Quinquerme* 5, 170–185.
Bookless, T.C. (1984) The semantic development of English loan-words in Spanish. *Quinquerme* 7, 39–53.
Borg, S. (1994) Language awareness as methodology: Implications for teachers and teacher training. *Language Awareness* 3, 61–71.
Borg, S. (1996) Language pedagogy and linguistics. *Language Awareness* 5, 118–124.

Borofsky, R. (1994) *Assessing Cultural Anthropology.* New York: McGraw-Hill.
Bosher, S. and Rowenkamp, J. (1992) Language proficiency and academic success: The refugee/immigrant in higher education. *ERIC Document Service,* ED 353 914.
Bourdieu, P. and Passeron, J.C. (1979) *The Inheritors: French Students and their Relation to Culture.* Chicago: Chicago University Press.
Bowerman, M. and Levinson, S. (eds) (2001) *Language Acquisition and Conceptual Development.* Cambridge: Cambridge University Press.
Boxer, D. (2002) Discourse issues in cross-cultural pragmatics. *Annual Review of Applied Linguistics* 22. New York: Cambridge University Press.
Boxer, D. and Cortes-Conde, F. (2000) Identify and ideology: Culture and pragmatics in content-based ESL. In J.K. Hall and L.S. Verplaetse (eds) *Second and Foreign Language Learning through Classroom Interaction.* Mahwah, NJ: Lawrence Erlbaum.
Boyd, M and Maloof, V.M. (2000) How teachers can build upon student-proposed intertextual links to facilitate student talk in the ESL classroom. In J.K. Hall and L.S. Verplaetse (eds) *Second and Foreign Language Learning through Classroom Interaction.* Mahwah, NJ: Lawrence Erlbaum.
Braddock, R., Lloyd-Jones, R. and Shoer, L. (1963) *Research in Written Composition.* Urbana, IL: National Council of Teachers of English.
Braine, G. (1996) In their own voices: Nonnative speaker professionals in TESOL. Colloquium presented at the annual TESOL meeting: Chicago, IL.
Braine, G. (ed.) (1999a) *Non-native Educators in English Language Teaching.* Mahwah, NJ: Lawrence Erlbaum.
Braine, G. (1999b) From the periphery to the center: One teacher's journey. In G. Braine (ed.) *Non-native Educators in English Language Teaching.* Mahwah, NJ: Lawrence Erlbaum.
Braine, G. (2004) The nonnative English-speaking professionals' movement and its research foundations. In L.D. Kamhi-Stein (ed.) *Learning and Teaching from Experience: Perspectives on Nonnative English-speaking Professionals.* Ann Arbor, MI: University of Michigan Press.
Brecht, R.D., Caemmerer, J. and Walton, A.R. (1995) *Russian in the United States: A Case Study of America's Language Needs and Capacities.* Washington, DC: National Foreign Language Center.
Brecht, R.D. and Ingold, C.W. (1998) *Tapping a National Resource: Heritage Languages in the United States.* Washington, DC: National Foreign Language Center.
Brecht, R.D. and Walton, A.R. (1994) National strategic planning and less commonly taught languages. *Annals of the American Academy of Political and Social Science* 532, 190–212.
Brecht, R.D. and Walton, A.R. (2000) System III: The future of language learning in the United States. In R.D. Lambert and E. Shohamy (eds) *Language Policy and Pedagogy: Essays in Honor of A. Ronald Walton.* Amsterdam: John Benjamins.
Breen, M. (2002) From a language policy to classroom practice: The intervention of identity and relationships. *Language and Education* 16, 260–224.
Brinton, D. (2004) Nonnative English-speaking student teachers: Insights from dialogue journals. In L.D. Kamhi-Stein (ed.) *Learning and Teaching from Experience: Perspectives on Nonnative English-speaking Professionals.* Ann Arbor, MI: University of Michigan Press.
Broukal, M. (1994) *Idioms for Everyday Use.* Lincolnwood, IL: National Textbook Company.
Broukal, M. (1995) *Heinle & Heinle TOEFL Test Assistant.* Boston: Heinle & Heinle.

Brown, H.D. (2000) *Principles of Language Learning and Teaching* (4th edn). Englewood Cliffs, NJ: Prentice-Hall.
Brown, P. and Levinson, S. (1987) *Politeness: Some Universals in Language Use.* Cambridge: Cambridge University Press.
Browning, G., Brinton, D., Ching, R., Dees, R., Dunlap, S., Erickson, M., Garlow, K., Manson, M., Poole, D. and Sasser, L. (1997) *California Pathways: The Second Language Student in Public High Schools, Colleges, and Universities.* Glendale, CA: California Teachers of English to Speakers of Other Languages (CATESOL).
Brye, E. (2003) *A Rapid Appraisal Language Survey of Sharwa, a Language of Cameroon.* Dallas, TX: Summer Institute of Linguistics.
Bygate, M. and Kramsch, C. (2000) Editorial. *Applied Linguistics* 21, 2.
Byrd, P. (2002) Instructed grammar. In Eli Hinkel (ed.) *Second Language Writers' Text: Linguistic and Rhetorical Features.* Mahwah, NJ: Lawrence Erlbaum.
Byrd, P., Reid, J. and Schuemann, C. (eds) (in press) *Houghton-Mifflin English for Academic Success Series.* Boston: Houghton-Mifflin.
Calvet, L.J. (1998) *Language Wars and Linguistic Politics* (M. Petheram, trans.). New York: Oxford University Press.
Canagarajah, S.A. (1999) *Resisting Linguistic Imperialism in English Teaching.* Oxford: Oxford University Press.
Candlin, C.N. and McNamara, T.F. (eds) (1989) *Language Learning and Community, Festschrift in Honour of Terry Quinn.* Sydney: Macquarie University/National Centre for English Language Teaching and Research.
Carey, A. (1997) *Taking the Risk out of Democracy: Corporate Propaganda Versus Freedom and Liberty.* Sydney: University of New South Wales Press.
Carreño, A.M. (1967a) En contra del barbarismo [Against barbarisms]. *Memorias de la Academia Mexicana* 18, 14–16.
Carreño, A.M. (1967b) Anuncios en voces extranjeras [Advertisements in foreign languages]. *Memorias de la Academia Mexicana* 18, 18.
Carver, R. (1994) Percentages of unknown words in text as a function of the relative difficulty of the text: Implications for instruction. *Journal of Reading Behavior* 26, 413–437.
Casanave, C.P. (2002) *Writing Games: Multicultural Case Studies of Academic Literacy Practices in Higher Education.* Mahwah, NJ: Lawrence Erlbaum.
Cazden, C.B. (1988) *Classroom Discourse: The Language of Teaching and Learning.* Portsmouth, NH: Heinemann.
Cecil, N.L and Gipe, J.P. (2003) *Literacy in the Intermediate Grades.* Scottsdale, AZ: Holcomb Hathaway.
Channell, J. (2000) Corpus-based analysis of evaluative lexis. In S. Hunston and G. Thompson (eds) *Evaluation in Text: Authorial Stance and the Construction of Discourse.* Oxford: Oxford University Press.
Chatwin, B. (1987) *The Songlines.* New York: Viking.
Chen, L. (1998) The organization of teacher–student interaction in Chinese EFL classroom lessons. Unpublished masters thesis, San Diego State University.
Chesterman, A. (1998) *Contrastive Functional Analysis.* Amsterdam: John Benjamins.
Cheung, Y.L. (2002) The attitude of university students in Hong Kong towards native and non-native teachers of English. Unpublished masters thesis, Chinese University of Hong Kong.
Chick, J.K. (1988) Contributions of ethnography to applied linguistics and to the in-service education of English language teachers. Paper presented at the annual TESOL meeting: Chicago, IL.

Chick, J.K. (1996a) Safe-talk: Collusion in apartheid education. In H. Coleman (ed.) *Society and the Language Classroom*. New York: Cambridge University Press.
Chick, J.K. (1996b) Intercultural communication. In S.L. McKay and N.H. Hornberger (eds) *Sociolinguistics and Language Teaching*. New York: Cambridge University Press.
Chomsky, N. (1965) *Aspects of the Theory of Syntax*. Cambridge, MA: MIT.
Chomsky, N. (1972) *Language and Mind*. New York: Harcourt Brace.
Christie, F. (1989) Language development in education. In R. Hasan and J.R. Martin (eds) *Language Development: Learning Language, Learning Culture*. Norwood, NJ: Ablex.
Chu, H.C., Swaffer, J., and Charney, D. (2002) Cultural representations of rhetorical conventions: The effects on reading recall. *TESOL Quarterly* 36, 511–541.
Clancy, P. (1986) The acquisition of communicative style in Japanese. In B. Schieffelin and E. Ochs (eds) *Language Socialization across Cultures*. Cambridge: Cambridge University Press.
Clyne, M. (1991) *Community Languages: The Australian Experience*. Cambridge: Cambridge University Press.
Clyne, M. (2002) The use of community resources in immersion. In P. Burmeister, T. Piske and A. Rohde (eds) *An Integrated View of Language Development*. Trier: Wissenschaftlicher Verlag.
Clyne, M. (2003) Towards a more language-centered approach to plurilingualism. In Li Wei, J-M. Dewaele and A. Housen (eds) *Bilingualism: Beyond Principles*. Clevedon: Multilingual Matters.
Clyne, M., Fernandez, S., Chen, I. and Summo-O'Connell, R. (1997) *Background Speakers: Diversity and its Management in LOTE Programs*. Canberra: Language Australia.
Clyne, M., Isaakidis, T., Liem, I. and Rossi Hunt, C. (2004) Developing and sharing community language programs through secondary school programs. *Journal of Bilingual Education and Bilingualism* 7, 255–278.
Cobb, T. (2003) The web vocabulary profiler. On WWW at http://www.eruqam.ca/nobel/r21270/cgi-bin/webfreqs/read_trial.cgi
Common European Framework of Reference for Languages: Learning, Teaching, Assessment (2001) Strasbourg: Council of Europe/Cambridge: Cambridge University Press.
Connelly, M. (2000) *The Sundance Writer*. New York: Harcourt.
Connor, U. (1996) *Contrastive Rhetoric. Cross-cultural Aspects of Second-Language Writing*. Cambridge: Cambridge University Press.
Connor, U. (2000) Variation in rhetorical moves in grant proposals of US humanists and scientists, *Text* 20, 1–28.
Connor, U. (2002) New directions in contrastive rhetoric. *TESOL Quarterly* 36, 493–510.
Connor, U. (2003) Changing currents in contrastive rhetoric: Implications for teaching and research. In B. Kroll (ed.) *Exploring the Dynamics of Second Language Writing*. Cambridge: Cambridge University Press.
Connor, U. and Kaplan, R.B. (eds) (1987) *Writing across Languages: Analysis of L2 Text*. Reading, MA: Addison-Wesley.
Connor, U. and Mauranen, A. (1999) Linguistic analysis of grant proposals: European Union research grants. *English for Specific Purposes* 18, 47–62.
Connors, R.J. and Lundsford, A.A. (1988) Frequency of formal errors in current college writing, or Ma and Pa Kettle do research. *College Composition and Communication* 39, 395–409.

Conrad, S. and Biber, D. (2000) Adverbial marking of stance in speech and writing. In S. Hunston and G. Thompson (eds) *Evaluation in Text: Authorial Stance and the Construction of Discourse.* Oxford: Oxford University Press.

Consolo, D. (2000) Teachers' action and student oral participation in classroom interaction. In J.K. Hall and L.S. Verplaetse (eds) *Second and Foreign Language Learning through Classroom Interaction.* Mahwah, NJ: Lawrence Erlbaum.

Cook, G. (2003) *Applied Linguistics.* Oxford: Oxford University Press.

Cook, H.M. (1999) Language socialization in Japanese elementary schools: Attentive listening and reaction turns. *Journal of Pragmatics* 31, 1443–1465.

Cook, V. (1999) Going beyond the native speaker in language teaching. *TESOL Quarterly* 33, 185–210.

Cooper, R.L. (1989) *Language Planning and Social Change.* Cambridge: Cambridge University Press.

Cope, B. and Kalantzis, M. (2000) Multiliteracies: The beginnings of an idea. In B. Cope and M. Kalantzis (eds) *Multiliteracies: Literacy Learning and the Design of Social Futures.* London: Routledge.

Cornell, C. (1995) Reducing failure of LEP students in the mainstream classroom and why it is important. *Journal of Education Issues of Language Minority Students* 15. On WWW at www.ncela.gwu.edu/miscpubs/jeilms/vol15/reducing.htm.

Corson, D. (1999) *Language Planning in Schools.* Mahwah, NJ: Lawrence Erlbaum.

Corvalán, G. (1998) La educación escolar bilingüe del Paraguay: Avances y desafíos [Bilingual school education in Paraguay. Advances and challenges]. *Revista Paraguaya de Sociología* 35, 101–118.

Costello, R.B. (ed.) (1995) *Random House Webster's College Dictionary.* New York: Random House.

Cotton, E.G. and Sharp, J.M. (1988) *Spanish in the Americas.* Washington, DC: Georgetown University Press.

Coulmas, F. (1999) Language masters: Defying linguistic materialism. *International Journal of the Sociology of Language* 37, 27–38.

Coxhead, A. (2000) A new academic word list. *TESOL Quarterly* 34, 213–238.

Crandall, J. (2000) Language teacher education. *Annual Review of Applied Linguistics* 20. New York: Cambridge University Press.

Crawford, J. (ed.) (1992) *Language Loyalties: A Source Book on the Official English Controversy.* Chicago: University of Chicago Press.

Crowley, S. and Hawhee, D. (1999) *Ancient Rhetorics for Contemporary Students.* Needham Heights, MA: Allyn & Bacon.

Cruse, D.A. (1986) *Lexical Semantics.* Cambridge: Cambridge University Press.

Család változóban (2002) *Család változóban 2001* [*Changing Families 2001*] Budapest: Central Statistical Office.

Cumming, A. (2002) If I had known twelve things. In L.L. Blanton and B. Kroll (eds) *ESL Composition Tales: Reflections on Teaching.* Ann Arbor, MI: University of Michigan Press.

Cummins, J. (1978) Metalinguistic awareness of children in bilingual education programs. In M. Paradis (ed.) *Aspects of Bilingualism.* Columbia, SC: Hornbeam Press.

Cummins, J. (1979) Cognitive/academic language proficiency, linguistic interdependence, the optimum age question and some other matters. *Working Papers on Bilingualism* 19, 121–129.

Cummins, J. (1996) *Negotiating Identities: Education for Empowerment in a Diverse Society.* Los Angeles: California Association for Bilingual Education.

Cummins, J. and Swain, M. (1989) *Bilingualism and Education.* Harlow: Longman.

Dante Alighieri (n.d./1996) *De Vulgari Eloquentia* (S. Botterill, ed. and trans.). Cambridge: Cambridge University Press.
Davies, A. (1991) *The Native Speaker in Applied Linguistics*. Edinburgh: Edinburgh University Press.
Davies, A. (1995) Proficiency and the native speaker: What are we trying to achieve in ELT? In G. Cook and B. Seidlhofer (eds) *Principle & Practice in Applied Linguistics: Studies in Honour of H.G. Widdowson*. Oxford: Oxford University Press.
Davies, A. (1999) Review of Kaplan, R.B. and Baldauf, R.B., Jr, 'Language Planning from Practice to Theory.' *Australian Review of Applied Linguistics* 22, 121–124.
Davies, A. (2002) The native speaker of World Englishes. *Pan-Pacific Association of Applied Linguistics* 6, 43–60.
Davies, A. (2003) *The Native Speaker: Myth and Reality*. Clevedon: Multilingual Matters.
Dawkins, J. (1991) *Australia's Language: The Australian Language and Literacy Policy*. Canberra: Australian Government Publishing Service.
DeLorme, R.S. (1999) Mother tongue, mother's touch: Kazakhstan government and school construction of identity and language planning metaphors. *Dissertation Abstracts International* 60, 984–A.
Delpit, L. (1995) *Other people's children: Cultural conflict in the classroom*. New York: New Press.
Del Valle, S. (2003) *Language Rights and the Law in the United States: Finding our Voices*. Clevedon: Multilingual Matters.
Denzin, N. and Lincoln, Y. (eds) (2002) *The Handbook of Qualitative Research*. Thousand Oaks, CA: Sage.
De Oliveira, C.L. and Richardson, L. (2001) Collaboration between native and nonnative English-speaking educators. *CATESOL Journal* 13, 123–134.
DETYA (2003) Department of Education, Training, and Youth Affairs: Australia. On WWW at http://www.detya.gov.au.
Diller, J., Jordan-Diller, K. and Hamm, C. (2002) *Sentence Repetition Testing (SRT) and Language Shift Survey of the Tuki Language*. Dallas, TX: Summer Institute of Linguistics.
Dillon, S. (2003) On the language of Cervantes: The imprint of the internet. On WWW at http: //www.nytimes.com/library/review/080600spanish-internet-review.html.
Ding, A. (2000) Another multicultural classroom: Non-native teachers of native students. In T. Lavonne Good and L.B. Warshauer (eds) *In Our Voice: Graduate Students Teach Writing*. Boston: Allyn & Bacon.
DiPardo, A. (1990) Narrative knowers, expository knowledge: Discourse as a dialectic. *Written Communication* 34, 59–95.
Domínguez, R. (2002) *Curricular Innovation in Elementary School: A Case for Spanish Language Literacy*. Unpublished doctoral dissertation, Carnegie Mellon University.
Dong, Y.R. (1998) From writing in their native language to writing in English: What ESL students bring to our writing classroom. *College English* 8, 87–105.
Doughty, C.J. and Long, M.H. (eds) (2003) *The Handbook of Second Language Acquisition*. Oxford: Blackwell.
DRAE (1992) *Diccionario de la Lengua Española* [*Dictionary of the Spanish Language*] (21st edn). Real Academia Española. Madrid: Espasa-Calpe.
DRAE (2001) *Diccionario de la Lengua Española* [*Dictionary of the Spanish Language*] (22nd edn). Real Academia Española. Madrid: Espasa-Calpe.

Dua, H.R. (1985) *Language Planning in India*. New Delhi: Harnam.
Dua, H.R. (1986) Language planning and linguistic minorities. In E. Annamalai, B.H. Jernudd and J. Rubin (eds) *Language Planning: Proceedings of an Institute*. Mysore: Central Institute of Indian Languages.
Duff, P.A. (1995) An ethnography of communication in immersion classrooms in Hungary. *TESOL Quarterly* 29, 505–537.
Duff, P.A. (2002) Research approaches in applied linguistics. In R.B. Kaplan (ed.) *The Oxford Handbook of Applied Linguistics*. Oxford: Oxford University Press.
Dumas, B.K. and Short, A.C. (1998) Linguistic ambiguity in non-statutory language. *Forensic Linguistics* 5, 127–140.
Dyson, A.H. (1989) *Multiple Worlds of Child Writers: Friends Learning to Write*. New York: Teachers College Press.
Eckert, P. (1989) *Jocks and Burn-Outs: Social Identity in the High School*. New York: Teachers College Press.
Edelsky, C. (1986) *Writing in a Bilingual Program: Habia Una Vez*. Norwood, NJ: Ablex.
Eggington, W. (2002) Unplanned language planning. In R.B. Kaplan (ed.) *Handbook of Applied Linguistics*. Oxford: Oxford University Press.
Elbow, P. (1991) Reflections on academic discourse. *College English* 53, 135–155.
Elbow, P. (1999) Options for responding to student writing. In R. Straub (ed.) *A Sourcebook for Responding to Student Writing*. Creskill, NJ: Hampton Press.
Elder, C. (2000) Learner performance and its implications for performance of students in LOTEs. *Australian Review of Applied Linguistics* 21, 61–78.
Ellis, R. (1995) *The Study of Second Language Acquisition Theory*. Oxford: Oxford University Press.
Ellis, E. (2002) Teaching from experience: A new perspective on the non-native teacher of adult ESL. *Australian Review of Applied Linguistics* 25, 71–107.
Eurobarometer 2001 (2002) Eurobarometer 2001, Candidate countries. Brussels: European Commission, Directorate-General Press and Communication. On WWW at http://europa.eu.int/comm/public_opinion.
Europeans and languages (2001) Europeans and languages: A Eurobarometer special survey. Brussels: European Commission, Directorate-General for Education and Culture. On WWW at http://europa.eu.int/comm/dgs/education_culture/index_en.htm.
Fahnestock, J. (2003) Visual and verbal parallelism. *Written Communication* 20, 123–152.
Fairclough, N. (1992) *Discourse and Social Change*. Cambridge: Polity Press.
Ferguson, C.A. (1968a) St. Stefan of Perm and applied linguistics. In J.A. Fishman, C.A. Ferguson and J. Das Gupta (eds) *Language Problems of Developing Nations*. New York: Wiley.
Ferguson, C.A. (1968b) Language development. In J.A. Fishman, C.A. Ferguson and J. Das Gupta (eds) *Language Problems of Developing Nations*. New York: Wiley.
Ferguson, C.A. (1982) Religious factors in language spread. In R.L. Cooper (ed.) *Language Spread: Studies in Diffusion and Social Change*. Bloomington, IN: Indiana University Press.
Ferris, D.R. (1991) Syntactic and lexical characteristics of ESL student writing: A multidimensional study. Unpublished doctoral dissertation, University of Southern California.
Ferris, D.R. (1993) The design and implementation of an automatic analysis program for L2 text research: Necessity and feasibility. *Journal of Second Language Writing* 2, 119–129.

Ferris, D.R. (1994a) Lexical and syntactic features of ESL writing by students at different levels of L2 proficiency. *TESOL Quarterly* 28, 414–420.
Ferris, D.R. (1994b) Rhetorical strategies in student persuasive writing: Differences between native and non-native speakers. *Research in the Teaching of English* 28, 45–65.
Ferris, D.R. (1995a) Can advanced ESL students be taught to correct their most serious and frequent errors? *CATESOL Journal* 8, 41–62.
Ferris, D.R. (1995b) Student reactions to teacher response in multiple-draft composition classrooms. *TESOL Quarterly* 29, 33–53.
Ferris, D.R. (1997) The influence of teacher commentary on student revision. *TESOL Quarterly* 31, 315–339.
Ferris, D.R. (1998) Student views of academic oral skills: A comparative needs analysis. *TESOL Quarterly* 32, 289–318.
Ferris, D.R. (2001) Teaching writing for academic purposes. In J. Flowerdew and M. Peacock (eds) *Research perspectives on English for academic purposes*. Cambridge: Cambridge University Press.
Ferris, D.R. (2002) *Treatment of Error in Second Language Writing Classes*. Ann Arbor, MI: University of Michigan Press.
Ferris, D.R. (2003) *Response to Student Writing: Implications for Second Language Students*. Mahwah, NJ: Lawrence Erlbaum.
Ferris, D.R. (2005) Tricks of the trade: The nuts and bolts of L2 writing research. In P.K. Matsuda and T. Silva (eds) *Second Language Writing Research: Perspectives on the Process of Knowledge Construction*. Mahwah, NJ: Lawrence Erlbaum.
Ferris, D. and Hedgcock, J.S. (2005) *Teaching ESL Composition: Purpose, Process, and Practice* (2nd edn). Mahwah, NJ: Lawrence Erlbaum.
Ferris, D.R., Pezone, S., Tade, C.R. and Tinti, S. (1997) Teacher commentary on student writing: Descriptions and implications. *Journal of Second Language Writing* 6, 155–182.
Ferris, D. and Roberts, B. (2001) Error feedback in L2 writing classes: How explicit does it need to be? *Journal of Second Language Writing* 10, 161–184.
Ferris, D. and Tagg, T. (1996a) Academic listening/speaking skills for ESL students: Problems, suggestions, and implications. *TESOL Quarterly* 30, 297–320.
Ferris, D. and Tagg, T. (1996b) Academic oral communication needs of EAP learners: What subject-matter instructors actually require. *TESOL Quarterly* 30, 31–58.
Finocchiaro, M.B. (1983) *The Functional-notional Approach*. London: Oxford University Press.
Firth, J.R. (1952/1968) *Selected Papers of J.R. Firth* (F.R. Palmer, ed.). London: Longman.
Fishman, J.A. (1974) Language planning and language planning research: The state of the art. In J.A. Fishman (ed.) *Advances in Language Planning*. The Hague: Mouton.
Fishman, J.A. (1991) Putting the 'socio' back into the sociolinguistic enterprise. *International Journal of the Sociology of Language* 92, 127–138.
Fishman, J.A. (ed.) (2001) *Can Threatened Languages Be Saved?* Clevedon: Multilingual Matters.
Ford Foundation. (1975) *Language and Development: A Retrospective Survey of Ford Foundation Language Projects, 1952–1974*. New York: Ford Foundation.
Fountas, I. and Hannigan, I. (1989) Making sense of whole language: The pursuit of informed teaching. *Childhood Education* 65, 133–137.
Fox, H. (1994) *Listening to the World: Cultural Issues in Academic Writing*. Urbana, IL: NCTE.

Fox, M.J. (1975) *Language and Development: A Retrospective Survey of Ford Foundation Language Projects 1952–1974*. New York: Ford Foundation.

Frederking, R., Rudnicky, A., Hogan, C. and Lenzo, K. (2000) Interactive speech translation in the Diplomat project. *Machine Translation* 15, 27–42.

Freedman, A. (1987) Development in story writing. *Applied Psycholinguistics* 8, 153–170.

Freeman, D. and Johnson, K.E. (1998) Reconceptualizing the knowledge-base of language teacher education. *TESOL Quarterly* 32, 397–417.

Freeman, Y. and Freeman, D. (2003) Struggling English language learners: Keys for academic success. *TESOL Journal* 12, 5–10.

Frodesen, J. and Starna, N. (1999) Distinguishing incipient and functional bilingual writers: Assessment and instructional insights gained through second-language writing profiles. In L. Harklau, K.M. Losey and M. Siegal (eds) *Generation 1.5 Meets College Composition*. Mahwah, NJ: Lawrence Erlbaum.

Fu, D. (1995) *'My Trouble is my English:' Asian Students and the American Dream*. Portsmouth, NH: Boynton/Cook.

García, E.E. (1995) Educating Mexican-American students: Past treatment and recent developments in theory, research, policy, and practice. In J. Banks and C. McGee Banks (eds) *Handbook of Research on Multicultural Education*. New York: Macmillan.

García, E.E. (2002) Bilingualism and schooling in the United States. *International Journal of the Sociology of Language* 155/156, 1–92.

Gardner, R.C. and Lambert, W.E. (1972) *Attitudes and Motivation in Second Language Learning*. Rowley, MA: Newbury House.

Garvin, P. (1973) Some comments on language planning. In J. Rubin and R. Shuy (eds) *Language Planning: Current Issues and Research*. Washington, DC: Georgetown University Press.

Gass, S.M. and Selinker, L. (2001) *Second Language Acquisition: An Introductory Course*. (2nd edn). Mahwah, NJ: Lawrence Erlbaum.

Gee, J.P. (1996) *Social Linguistics and Literacies: Ideology in Discourses*. London: Routledge/Falmer.

Gifted Development Center (2003) Visual-spatial learner. On WWW at http://www.gifteddevelopment.com/Articles/VSL%20Char%20Comparison.htm.

Gilmore, P. (1986) Sub-rosa literacy: Peers, play, and ownership in literacy acquisition. In B. Schieffelin and P. Gilmore (eds) *The Acquisition of Literacy: Ethnographic Perspectives*. Norwood, NJ: Ablex.

Goldenberg, C. and Patthey-Chavez, G.G. (1995) Discourse processes in instructional conversations: Interactions between teacher and transition readers. *Discourse Processes* 19, 57–73.

Goldman, L. (1981) *Getting Along with Idioms*. New York: Minerva Books.

Gómez de Silva, G. (ed.) (2001) *Diccionario Breve de Mexicanismos [Brief Dictionary of Mexicanisms]*. México: Academia Mexicana and Fondo Cultura Económica.

Goodman, K. (1986) *What's Whole in Whole Language?* Portsmouth, NH: Heinemann Educational.

Grabe, W. (2002) Applied linguistics: An emerging discipline for the twenty-first century. In R.B. Kaplan (ed.) *The Oxford Handbook of Applied Linguistics*. Oxford: Oxford University Press.

Grabe, W. and Kaplan, R.B. (1996) *Theory and Practice of Writing*. New York: Longman.

Grabe, W. and Stoller, F.L. (2002) *Teaching and Researching Reading*. Harlow: Longman/Pearson Education.

Granger, S. (1996) From CA to CIA and back: An integrated approach to computerized bilingual and learner corpora. In K. Aijmer, B. Altenberg and M. Johansson (eds) *Languages in Contrast. Papers from a Symposium on Text-Based Cross-Linguistic Studies: Lund, 2–5 March 1994*. Lund: Lund University Press.

Gregory, G.H. and Chapman, C. (2003) *Differentiated Instruction in Practice*. Thousand Oaks, CA: Corwin Press.

Grenoble, L.A. (2003) *Soviet Language Policy*. Dordrecht: Kluwer.

Griffin, P. and Humphrey, F. (1978) Task and talk. In R. Shuy and P. Griffin (eds) *The Study of Children's Functional Language and Education in the Early Years*. Arlington, VA: Center for Applied Linguistics.

Gringoire, P. (n.d./1979) *Repertorio de Dispartes* [*Repository of Errors*] (1st edn, 1979; 2nd edn, n.d.). México: Costa-Amic Editores.

Gringoire, P. (1982) Defensa de la lengua [In defense of the language]. In *Nuestro Idioma, (Vol. 7). El Español Actual. Contribuciones a su Estudio. Necesidad de una Defensa* [*Our Language (Vol. 7). Modern Spanish. Contributions to its Study. Necessity for a Defense*]. México: CPDIE.

Gudschinsky, S.C. (1976) *Literacy: The Growing Influence of Linguistics*. The Hague: Mouton.

Guitarte, G.L. and Torres Quintero, R. (1968) Linguistic correctness and the role of the Academies. In T.A. Sebeka (ed.) *Current Trends in Linguistics, Vol. IV: Iberia-American and Caribbean Linguistics*. The Hague: Mouton.

Gumperz, J.J. (1983) *Discourse Strategies*. Cambridge: Cambridge University Press.

Gumperz, J.J. and Levinson, S. (eds) (1996) *Rethinking Linguistic Relativity*. Cambridge: Cambridge University Press.

Haarmann, H. (1990) Language planning in the light of a general theory of language: A methodological framework. *International Journal of the Sociology of Language* 95, 109–129.

Hacker, D. (2000) *Rules for Writers*. Boston: Bedford/St Martin's.

Hale, K. (1991) On endangered languages and the safeguarding of diversity. *Language* 68, 1–3.

Hall, D. and Ames, R. (1987) *Thinking through Confucius*. Albany, NY: SUNY Press.

Hall, D. and Ames, R. (1998) *Thinking from the Han: Self, Truth, and Transcendence in Chinese and Western Culture*. Albany, NY: SUNY Press.

Hall, J.K. (1998) Differential teacher attention to student utterances: The construction of different opportunities for learning in the IRF. *Linguistics and Education* 9, 287–311.

Hall, J.K. and Walsh, M. (2002) Teacher–student interaction and language Learning. *Annual Review of Applied Linguistics* 22. New York: Cambridge University Press.

Halliday, M.A.K. (1993) *Language in a Changing World. Occasional Papers 13*. Sydney: Applied Linguistics Association of Australia/University of Sydney.

Halliday, M.A.K. and Hasan, R. (1976) *Cohesion in English*. London: Longman.

Halliday, M.A.K. and Hasan, R. (1989) *Language, Context, and Text: Aspects of Language in a Social-semiotic Perspective*. New York: Oxford University Press.

Hansen, J. (2004) Invisible minorities and the nonnative English-speaking professional. In L.D. Kamhi-Stein (ed.) *Learning and Teaching from Experience: Perspectives on Nonnative English-speaking Professionals*. Ann Arbor, MI: University of Michigan Press.

Harklau, L. (1999) Representing culture in the L2 classroom. In E. Hinkel (ed.) *Culture in Second Language Teaching and Learning*. Cambridge: Cambridge University Press.

Harklau, L. (2000) From the 'good kids' to the 'worst:' Representations of English language learners across educational settings. *TESOL Quarterly* 34, 35–67.
Harklau, L. (2003) L2 writing by 'Generation 1.5 students:' Recent research and pedagogical trends. *Journal of Second Language Writing* 12, 153–156.
Harklau, L., Losey, K.M. and Siegal, M. (eds) (1999) *Generation 1.5 Meets College Composition: Issues in the Teaching of Writing to U.S. Educated Learners of ESL.* Mahwah, NJ: Lawrence Erlbaum.
Hartinger, K. (1993) Why language learning difficulties are not always linguistic. *Perspectives* 1, 33–35.
Hartman, B. and Tarone, E. (1999) Preparation for college writing: Teachers talk about writing instruction for Southeast Asian American students in secondary school. In L. Harklau, K.M. Losey and M. Siegal (eds) *Generation 1.5 Meets College Composition: Issues in the Teaching of Writing to US Educated Learners of ESL.* Mahwah, NJ: Lawrence Erlbaum.
Hartwell, P. (1985) Grammar, grammars, and the teaching of grammar. *College English* 47, 105–127.
Haugen, E. (1983) The implementation of corpus planning: Theory and practice. In J. Cobarrubias and J.A. Fishman (eds) *Progress in Language Planning: International Perspectives.* Berlin: Mouton de Gruyter.
Haugen, E. (1987) *Blessings of Babel: Bilingualism and Language Planning: Problems and Pleasures.* Berlin: Mouton de Gruyter.
Heath, S.B. (1983) *Ways with Words: Language, Life, and Work in Community and Classroom.* Cambridge: Cambridge University Press.
Heath, S.B. (1986) Sociocultural contexts of language development. In Bilingual Educational Office, California State Department of Education (ed.) *Beyond Language.* Los Angeles: Evaluation, Dissemination and Assessment Center, California State University.
Heath, S.B. (1995) Ethnography in communities: Learning the everyday life of America's subordinated youth. In J. Banks and C. McGee Banks (eds) *Handbook of Research on Multicultural Education.* New York: Macmillan.
Heller, M. (1999) *Linguistic Minorities and Modernity: A Sociolinguistic Ethnography.* London: Longman.
Heller, M. and Martin-Jones, M. (2001) *Voices of Authority: Education and Linguistic Difference.* Westport, CT: Ablex.
Hendrickson. J. (1978) The treatment of error in written work. *Modern Language Journal* 64, 216–221.
Heugh, K. (2003) *Language Policy and Democracy in South Africa.* Stockholm: Stockholm University Centre for Research on Bilingualism.
Hicks, D. (1990) Narrative skills and genre knowledge: Ways of telling in the primary school grades. *Applied Psycholinguistics* 11, 83–103.
Hinkel, E. (1999) (ed.) *Culture in Second Language Teaching and Learning.* Cambridge: Cambridge University Press.
Hinkel, E. (2001) Matters of cohesion in L1 and L2 academic texts. *Applied Language Learning* 12, 111–132.
Hinkel, E. (2002) *Second Language Writers' Text: Linguistic and Rhetorical Features.* Mahwah, NJ: Lawrence Erlbaum.
Hinkel, E. (2003a) Adverbial markers and tone in L1 and L2 students' writing. *Journal of Pragmatics* 35, 1049–1068.
Hinkel, E. (2003b) Simplicity without elegance: Features of sentences in L2 and L1 academic texts. *TESOL Quarterly* 37, 275–301.

Hinton, L. and Hale, K. (eds) (2001) *The Green Book of Language Revitalization in Practice.* New York: Academic Press.
Ho, W.K. and Wong, R.Y.L. (2000) *Language Policies and Language Education: The Impact in East Asian Countries in the Next Decade.* Singapore: Times Academic Press.
Holliday, A. (1994) *Appropriate Methodology and Social Context.* New York: Cambridge University Press.
Holten, C. and Marasco, J. (1998) *Looking Ahead: Mastering Academic Writing.* Boston: Heinle & Heinle.
Hornberger, N. (1994) Literacy and language planning. *Language and Education* 8, 75–86.
Hornberger, N. and Skilton-Sylvester, E. (2000) Revisiting the continua of biliteracy: International and critical perspectives. *Language & Education* 14, 96–122.
Hu, H.C.M. and Nation, I.S.P (2000) Unknown vocabulary density and reading comprehension. *Reading in a Foreign Language* 13, 403–430.
Huacuja, D. (1960) En defensa del idioma [In defense of the language]. *Memorias de la Academia Mexicana* 17, 138–149.
Huddlestone, R. and Pullum, G.K. (2002) *The Cambridge Grammar of the English Language.* Cambridge: Cambridge University Press.
Hudelson, S. (1994) Literacy development of second language children. In F. Genesee (ed.) *Educating Second Language Children: The Whole Child, the Whole Curriculum, the Whole Community.* Cambridge: Cambridge University Press.
Hunston, S. (2000) Evaluation and the planes of discourse: Status and value in persuasive texts. In S. Hunston and G. Thompson (eds) *Evaluation in Text: Authorial Stance and the Construction of Discourse.* Oxford: Oxford University Press.
Hunston, S. and Thompson, G. (eds) (2000) *Evaluation in Text: Authorial Stance and the Construction of Discourse.* Oxford: Oxford University Press.
Hutchins, W.J. (2001) Machine translation over fifty years. *Histoire Epistémologie Langage* 23, 7–32.
Hutton, C.M. (1999) *Linguistics of the Third Reich: Mother-tongue Fascism, Race and the Science of Language.* London: Routledge.
Hvitfeld, C. (1992) Oral orientations in ESL academic writing. *College ESL* 2, 29–39.
Hwang, S.J. (1987) *Discourse Features of Korean Narration.* Arlington, TX: Summer Institute of Linguistics and University of Texas.
Hyland, K. (1994) Hedging in academic writing and EAP textbooks. *English for Specific Purposes* 13, 239–256.
Hyland, K. (1998) *Hedging in Scientific Research Articles.* Amsterdam: John Benjamins.
Hyland, K. (2000) *Disciplinary Discourses: Social Interactions in Academic Writing.* Harlow: Pearson Education.
Hyland, K. (2002) Genre-based pedagogies: A social response to process. *Journal of Second Language Writing* 12, 17–29.
Hymes, D. (1974) *Foundations in Sociolinguistics: An Ethnographic Approach.* Philadelphia: University of Pennsylvania Press.
Hymes, D. and Cazden, C. (1980) Narrative thinking and story-telling rights: A folklorist's clue to a critique of education. In D. Hymes (ed.) *Language in Education: Ethnolinguistic Essays.* Washington, DC: Center for Applied Linguistics.
Iedema, R. (2003) Multimodality, resemiotization: Extending the analysis of discourse as a multi-semiotic practice. *Visual Communication* 2, 29–57.

Ikeno, A. (1998) A sociocultural analysis of 'kotae-awase' interaction in Japanese secondary school lessons. Unpublished masters thesis, San Diego State University.
Inbar, O. (2001) Native and non-native English teachers: Investigation of the construct and perceptions. Unpublished doctoral dissertation, Tel Aviv University.
Ivanic, R. and Camps, D. (2001) I am how I sound: Voice as self-representation in L2 writing. *Journal of Second Language Writing* 10, 3–33.
Jacobs, S.E. (1985) The development of children's writing. *Written Communication* 2, 414–433.
Jaffe, A. (1999) *Ideologies in Action: Language Politics on Corsica*. Berlin: Mouton de Gruyter.
James, C. (1980) *Contrastive Analysis*. Harlow: Longman.
James, C. (1990) Learner language. *Language Learning* 18, 89–109.
James, C. (1998) *Errors in Language Learning and Use: Exploring Error Analysis*. London: Longman.
Jensen, V. (1987) Rhetorical emphases of Taoism. *Rhetorica* 5, 219–229.
Johansson, S. (1998) On the role of corpora in cross-linguistic research. In S. Johansson and S. Oksefjell (eds) *Corpora and Cross-linguistic Research: Theory, Method, and Case Studies*. Amsterdam: Rodopi.
Johns, A.M. (1997) *Text, Role, and Context: Developing Academic Literacies*. New York: Cambridge University Press.
Johns, A.M. (1998) The visual and the verbal: A case study in macroeconomics. *English for Specific Purposes Journal* 17, 183–198.
Johns, A.M. (2001) An interdisciplinary, interinstitutional, learning communities program: Student involvement and student success. In I. Leki (ed.) *Academic Writing Programs*. Alexandria, VA: TESOL.
Johns, A.M. (ed.) (2002a) *Genre in the Classroom: Multiple Perspectives*. Mahwah, NJ: Lawrence Erlbaum.
Johns, A.M. (2002b) A story of experimentation and evolving awareness, or why I became an advocate for approaching writing through genre. In L.L. Blanton and B. Kroll (eds) *ESL Composition Tales: Reflections on Teaching*. Ann Arbor, MI: University of Michigan.
Johns, A.M. (forthcoming) *Writing Through Genres*. Boston: Houghton-Mifflin.
Johnson, D. (1985) Error gravity: Communicative effect of language errors in academic writing. *BAAL Newsletter* 24, 46–47.
Johnston, B. and Goettsch, K. (2000) In search of the knowledge base of language teaching: Explanations by experienced teachers. *Canadian Modern Language Review* 56, 438–468.
Jones, M.C. (1996) Language shift in Brittany: The importance of local surveys for the study of linguistic obsolescence. *Journal of Celtic Linguistics* 5, 51–69.
Jones, R. and Spolsky, B. (eds) (1975) *Testing Language Proficiency*. Washington, DC: Center for Applied Linguistics.
Kachru, B.B. (1983) *The Indianization of English: The English Language in India*. New Delhi: Oxford University Press.
Kachru, B.B. (ed.) (1992) *The Other Tongue: English across Cultures*. Chicago: University of Illinois Press.
Kachru, B.B. (1995) World Englishes: Approaches, issues, and resources. In H.D. Brown and S. Gonzo (eds) *Readings on Second Language Acquisition*. Upper Saddle River, NJ: Prentice Hall Regents.

Kachru, B.B. and Nelson, C.L. (1996) World Englishes. In S.L. McKay and N.H. Hornberger (eds) *Sociolinguistics and Language Teaching*. Cambridge: Cambridge University Press.

Kalantzis, M. and B. Cope (2000) The multiliteracies pedagogy: A pedagogical supplement. In B. Cope and M. Kalantzis (eds) *Multiliteracies: Literacy Learning and the Design of Social Futures*. London: Routledge.

Kamberelis, G. (1999) Genre development and learning: Children writing stories, science reports, and poems. *Research in the Teaching of English* 33, 403–460.

Kamhi-Stein, L.D. (1999) Preparing nonnative English-speaking professionals in TESOL: Implications for teacher education programs. In G. Braine (ed.) *Nonnative Educators in English Language Teaching*. Mahwah, NJ: Lawrence Erlbaum.

Kamhi-Stein, L.D., Aagard, A., Ching, A., Paik, A. and Sasser, L. (2001) Teaching in kindergarten through grade 12 programs: Perceptions of native and nonnative English-speaking practitioners. *CATESOL Journal* 13, 69–88.

Kamhi-Stein, L.D., Lee, E. and Lee, C. (1998) Looking at the strengths and needs of nonnative English-speaking teachers-in-preparation. Paper presented at the annual CATESOL meeting: Pasadena, CA.

Kaplan, R.B. (1963) *Reading and Rhetoric*. New York: Odyssey Press.

Kaplan, R.B. (1966) Cultural thought patterns in intercultural education. *Language Learning* 16, 1–20.

Kaplan, R.B. (1971) Composition at the advanced ESL level: A teacher's guide to connected paragraph construction for advanced-level foreign students. *The English Record* 21, 53–64.

Kaplan, R.B. (1972) *The Anatomy of Rhetoric: Prologomena to a Functional Theory of Rhetoric*. Philadelphia: Center for Curriculum Development.

Kaplan, R.B. (ed.) (1980a) *On the Scope of Applied Linguistics*. Rowley, MA: Newbury House.

Kaplan, R.B. (1980b) An instructional technique for advanced ESL writing. *MEXTESOL Journal* 4, 46–65.

Kaplan, R.B. (1980c) *The Language Needs of Migrant Workers*. Wellington: New Zealand Council for Educational Research.

Kaplan, R.B. (1983) Contrastive rhetorics: Some implications for the writing process. In A. Freedman, I. Pringle, and J. Yalden (eds) *Learning to Write: First Language/Second Language*. London: Longman.

Kaplan, R.B. (1987) Cultural thought patterns revisited. In U. Connor and R.B. Kaplan (eds) *Writing across Languages: Analysis of L2 Text*. Reading, MA: Addison-Wesley.

Kaplan, R.B. (1988) Contrastive rhetoric and second language learning: Notes toward a theory of contrastive rhetoric. In A.C. Purves (ed.) *Writing Across Languages and Cultures. Issues in Contrastive Rhetoric*. Newbury Park, CA: Sage.

Kaplan, R.B. (1990) Conference summary. In C. Walton and W. Eggington (eds) *Language: Maintenance, Power and Education in Australian Aboriginal Contexts*. Darwin: NTU Press.

Kaplan, R.B. (1991) Contrastive rhetoric. In W. Bright (ed.) *International Encyclopedia of Linguistics, Vol. 4*. New York: Oxford University Press.

Kaplan, R.B. (1992) Applied linguistics and language policy and planning. In. W. Grabe and R.B. Kaplan (eds) *Introduction to Applied Linguistics*. Reading, MA: Addison-Wesley.

Kaplan, R.B. (1994) Language policy and planning: Fundamental issues. *Annual Review of Applied Linguistics* 14. New York: Cambridge University Press.

Kaplan, R.B. (1997a) Contrastive rhetoric. In T. Miller (ed.) *Functional Approaches to Written Text: Classroom Applications*. Washington, DC: USIA.
Kaplan, R.B. (1997b) An IEP is a many-splendored thing. In M. Christison and F. Stoller (eds) *A Handbook for Language Program Administrators*. Burlingame, CA: Alta Book Center.
Kaplan, R.B. (1999) The ELT: Ho(NEST) or not Ho(NEST)? *NNEST (Nonnative English Speakers in TESOL Caucus) Newsletter* 1, 5–6.
Kaplan, R.B. (2000) Contrastive rhetoric and discourse analysis: Who writes what to whom? When? In what circumstances? In S. Sarangi and M. Coulthard (eds) *Discourse and Social Life*. Harlow: Longman.
Kaplan, R.B. (2001) Foreword: What in the world is contrastive rhetoric? In C. Panetta (ed.) *Contrastive Rhetoric Revisited and Redefined*. Mahwah, NJ: Lawrence Erlbaum.
Kaplan, R.B. (ed.) (2002) *The Oxford Handbook of Applied Linguistics*. New York: Oxford University Press.
Kaplan, R.B. (2005) What is contrastive rhetoric? In E. Hinkel (ed.) *Handbook of Research on Second Language Teaching and Learning*. Mahwah, NJ: Lawrence Erlbaum.
Kaplan, R.B. and Baldauf, R.B., Jr (1997) *Language Planning from Practice to Theory*. Clevedon: Multilingual Matters.
Kaplan, R.B. and Baldauf, R.B., Jr (eds) (1999) *Language Planning in Malawi, Mozambique, and the Philippines*. Clevedon: Multilingual Matters.
Kaplan, R.B. and Baldauf, R.B., Jr (eds) (2000) *Language Planning, in Nepal, Taiwan and Sweden*. Clevedon: Multilingual Matters.
Kaplan, R.B. and Baldauf, R.B., Jr (2003) *Language and Language-in-Education Planning in the Pacific Basin*. Dordrecht: Kluwer.
Kaplan, R.B., Touchstone, E.E. and Hagstrom, C.L. (1995) Image and reality: Banking in Los Angeles. *Text* 15, 427–456.
Kasper, G. and Blum-Kulka, S. (eds) (1993) *Interlanguage Pragmatics*. New York: Oxford University Press.
Kasper, G. and Schmidt, R. (1996) Developmental issues in interlanguage pragmatics. *Studies in Second Language Acquisition* 18, 149–169.
Keefer, L.E. (1988) *Scholars in Foxholes: The Story of the Army Specialized Training Program in World War II.* Jefferson, NC: McFarland.
Kelch, K. and Santana-Williamson, E. (2002) ESL students' attitudes toward native- and nonnative-speaking instructors' accents. *CATESOL Journal* 14, 57–72.
Kemmis, S. and McTaggart, R. (2000) Participatory action research. In N.K. Denzin and Y.S. Lincoln (eds) *Handbook of Qualitative Research*. Thousand Oaks, CA: Sage.
Kerpan, N. (1991) Temps forts ou temps faibles pour la terminologie en entreprise? [Strong times or weak times for industrial terminology?]. *Meta* 36, 234–239.
Key Data on Education in Europe 2002 (2002) Brussels/Luxembourg: European Commission.
Kim, H. (2000) Teacher–student interaction in Korean classrooms. Unpublished masters thesis, San Diego State University.
Kiniry, M. and Rose, M. (1993) *Critical Strategies for Academic Thinking and Writing*. Boston: Bedford/St. Martin's.
Kirkpatrick, A. (1997) Traditional Chinese text structures and their influence on the writing in Chinese and English of contemporary mainland Chinese students. *Journal of Second Language Writing* 6, 223–244.
Kloss, H. (1969) *Research Possibilities on Group Bilingualism: A Report*. Quebec: International Center for Research on Bilingualism.

Knoblauch, C.H. and Brannon, L. (1981) Teacher commentary on student writing: The state of the art. *Freshman English News* 10, 1–4.

Kochman, T. (1981) *Black and White Styles in Conflict*. Chicago, IL: University of Chicago Press.

Koda, K. (2002) Learning to read and writing systems in a second language. In W. Li, J. Gaffney, and J. Packard (eds) *Chinese Children's Writing Acquisition*. Dordrecht: Kluwer.

Koshik, I. (2002) Designedly incomplete utterances: A pedagogical practice for eliciting knowledge displays in error correction sequences. *Research on Language and Social Interaction* 35, 277–309.

Kramsch, C. (1998a) *Language and Culture*. Oxford: Oxford University Press.

Kramsch, C. (1998b) The privilege of the intercultural speaker. In M. Byram and M. Fleming (eds) *Language Learning in Intercultural Perspective: Approaches Through Drama and Ethnography*. Cambridge: Cambridge University Press.

Krashen, S.D. (1981) *Second Language Acquisition and Second Language Learning*. Oxford: Pergamon.

Krashen, S.D. (1984) *Writing: Research, Theory, and Application*. Oxford: Pergamon Press.

Krauss, M. (1991) The world's languages in crisis. *Language* 68, 4–10.

Krauss, M. (1998) The condition of Native North American languages: The need for realistic assessment and action. *International Journal of the Sociology of Language* 132, 9–21.

Kress, G.R. and van Leeuwen, T. (1996) *Reading Images: The Grammar of Visual Design*. London: Routledge.

Kroll, J.F. and Dijkstra, T. (2002) The bilingual lexicon. In R.B. Kaplan (ed.) *The Oxford Handbook of Applied Linguistics*. New York: Oxford University Press.

Krzeszowski, T.P. (1981) Tertium comparationis. In J. Fisiak (ed.) *Contrastive Linguistics: Prospects and Problems*. Berlin: Mouton de Gruyter.

Krzeszowski, T.P. (1990) *Contrasting Languages: The Scope of Contrastive Linguistics*. Berlin: Mouton de Gruyter.

Kuhn, T. (1962) *The Structure of Scientific Revolutions*. Chicago: University of Chicago Press.

Kuo, E.C.Y. and Jernudd, B.H. (1993) Balancing macro- and micro-sociolinguistic perspectives in language management: The case of Singapore. *Language Problems & Language Planning* 17, 1–21.

Labov, W. (1972a) *Sociolinguistic Patterns*. Philadelphia: University of Pennsylvania Press.

Labov, W. (1972b) *Language in the Inner City: Studies in the Black English Vernacular*. Philadelphia: University of Pennsylvania Press.

Labov, W. (1988) The judicial testing of a linguistic theory. In D. Tannen (ed.) *Linguistics in Context: Connecting Observation and Understanding*. Norwood, NJ: Ablex.

Labov, W. and Walezky, S. (1967) Narrative analysis. In J. Helm (ed.) *Essays on the Verbal and Visual Arts*. Seattle, WA: University of Washington Press.

Lalande, J.F. (1982) Reducing composition errors: An experiment. *Modern Language Journal* 66, 140–149.

Lara, L.F. (ed.) (1982) *Diccionario Fundamental del Español de México* [Fundamental Dictionary of Mexican Spanish]. México: El Colegio de México and Fondo de Cultura Económica.

Lara, L.F. (1993) Crónica de una política del lenguaje abortada: la Comisión para la Defensa del Idioma Español [Chronicle of an aborted language policy: The Commission for the Defense of the Spanish Language]. *Iztapalapa* 29, 147–176.
Lara, L.F. (ed.) (1996) *Diccionario del Español Usual en México* [Dictionary of Everyday Mexican Spanish]. México: El Colegio de México.
Lara, L.F. (1997) Mexican Spanish. In M.S. Werner (ed.) *Encyclopedia of Mexico: History, Society and Culture.* Chicago: Fitzroy Dearborn.
Lasagabaster, D. and Sierra, J. M. (2002) University students' perceptions of native and non-native speaker teachers of English. *Language Awareness* 11, 132–142.
Laufer, B. (1990) Why are some words more difficult than others? Some intralexical factors that affect the learning of words. *International Review of Applied Linguistics* 28, 293–307.
Learner – learning styles – the auditory learner (2003) On WWW at http://www.sasked.gov.sk.ca/curr_content/adapthandbooklearner/auditory.html.
Leki, I. (1990) Coaching from the margins: Issues in written response. In B. Kroll (ed.) *Second Language Writing: Research Insights for the Classroom.* Cambridge: Cambridge University Press.
Leki, I. (1999a) *Academic Writing: Techniques and Tasks.* New York: Cambridge University Press.
Leki, I. (1999b) Pretty much I screwed up: Ill-served needs of a permanent resident. In L. Harklau, K.M. Losey and M. Siegal (eds.) *Generation 1.5 Meets College Composition: Issues in the Teaching of Writing to US Educated Learners of ESL.* Mahwah, NJ: Lawrence Erlbaum.
Leki, I. (2003) A challenge to second language writing professionals: Is writing overrated? In B. Kroll (ed.) *Exploring the Dynamics of Second Language Writing.* Cambridge: Cambridge University Press.
Leki, I. and Carson, J. (1997) 'Completely different worlds:' EAP and the writing experiences of ESL students in university courses. *TESOL Quarterly* 31, 39–69.
Lemke, J.L. (1990) *Talking Science: Language, Learning, and Values.* Norwood, NJ: Ablex.
Lensmire, T. (1994) *When Children Write: Critical Re-visions of the Writing Workshop.* New York: Teachers College Press.
Lewis, G. (1999) *The Turkish Language Reform: A Catastrophic Success.* Oxford: Oxford University Press.
Liang, K.Y. (2002) English as a Second Language (ESL) students' attitudes towards non-native English-speaking teachers' accentedness. Unpublished masters thesis, California State University, Los Angeles.
Liddicoat, A.J. (2005) Corpus planning. In E. Hinkel (ed.) *Handbook of Research in Second Language Teaching and Learning.* Mahwah, NJ: Lawrence Erlbaum.
Linfante, F.A. (2002) Students' success in college-level English composition after completing developmental English in an urban community college. *Dissertation Abstracts International* 63: 70A.
Liu, J. (1999) Nonnative-English-speaking-educators. *TESOL Quarterly* 33, 85–102.
Liu, J. (2001) Confessions of a nonnative English-speaking professional. *CATESOL Journal* 13, 53–67.
Lo Bianco, J. (1987) *National Languages Policy.* Canberra: Australian Government Publishing Service.
Lo Bianco, J. (2001) From policy to anti-policy: How fear of language rights took policy-making out of community hands. In J. Lo Bianco and R. Wickert (eds) *Australian Policy Activism in Language and Literacy.* Melbourne: Language Australia.

Lo Bianco (2002) Real world language politics and policy. In S.J. Baker (ed.) *Language Policy: Lessons from Global Models*. Monterey, CA: Monterey Institute of International Studies.

Lo Bianco, J. (2003) Language education in Australia: Italian and Japanese as symbols of cultural policy. In J. Bourne and E. Reid (eds) *Language Education: World Yearbook of Education 2003*. London: Kogan Page.

Lo Bianco, J. (2004) *A Site for Debate, Negotiation, and Contest of National Identity: Language Policy in Australia. Guide for the Development of Language Education Policies in Europe: From Linguistic Diversity to Plurilingual Education*. Strasbourg: Council of Europe.

Long, M.H. (1991) Focus on form: A design feature in language teaching methodology. In K. de Bot, D. Coste, R. Ginsberg and C. Kramsch (eds) *Foreign Language Research in Cross-Cultural Perspective*. Amsterdam: John Benjamins.

Long, M.H. (2000) Focus on form in task-based language teaching. In R.D. Lambert and E. Shohamy (eds) *Language Policy and Pedagogy*. Amsterdam: John Benjamins.

Longman Advanced American Dictionary (2000) Harlow: Pearson Education.

Lunsford, A. (2001) *The Everyday Writer*. New York: St Martin's Press.

Lunsford, A and Connors, R. (1997) *The Everyday Writer: A Brief Reference*. New York: St Martins.

Mac Giolla Chriost, D. (2002) Language planning in Northern Ireland. *Current Issues in Language Planning* 3, 425–476.

Mahboob, A. (2004) Native or nonnative: What do students enrolled in an intensive English program think? In L.D. Kamhi-Stein (ed.) *Learning and Teaching from Experience: Perspectives on Nonnative English-speaking Professionals*. Ann Arbor, MI: University of Michigan Press.

Mahboob, A., Uhrig, K., Newman, K. and Hartford, B. (2004) Children of a lesser English: Status of nonnative English speakers as college-level ESL teachers in the United States. In L.D. Kamhi-Stein (ed.) *Learning and Teaching from Experience: Perspectives on Nonnative English-speaking Professionals*. Ann Arbor, MI: University of Michigan Press.

Maier, P. (1992) Politeness strategies in business letters by native and non-native speakers of English. *English for Specific Purposes* 11, 189–205.

Majone, G. (1989) *Evidence, Argument and Persuasion in the Policy Process*. New Haven, CT: Yale University Press.

Markee, N. (1997) *Managing Curricular Innovation*. New York: Cambridge University Press.

Martin, J.R. (1985) *Factual Writing: Exploring and Challenging Social Reality*. Oxford: Oxford University Press.

Martin, J.R. (1993) *Genre and Literacy: Modelling Context in Educational Linguistics*. Sydney: University of Sydney.

Marton, F. (1981) Phenomenography: Describing conceptions of the world around us. *Instructional Science* 10, 177–200.

Matsuda, P.K. (2001) Voice in Japanese written discourse: Implications for second language writing. *Journal of Second Language Writing* 10, 35–54.

Maum, R. (2003) A comparison of native and nonnative English-speaking teachers' beliefs about English as a second language to adult English language learners. Unpublished doctoral dissertation, University of Louisville.

Maurais, J. and Morris, M.A. (eds) (2003) *Languages in a Globalising World*. Cambridge: Cambridge University Press.

Mauranen, A. (1993a) Contrastive ESP rhetoric: Metatext in Finnish-English economics texts. *English for Specific Purposes* 12, 3–22.
Mauranen, A. (1993b) *Cultural Differences in Academic Rhetoric*. Frankfurt-am-Main: Peter Lang.
May, S. (2001) *Language and Minority Rights: Ethnicity, Nationalism and the Politics of Language*. New York: Longman.
May, S. (2003) Rearticulating the case for minority language rights. *Current Issues in Language Planning* 4, 95–125.
May, S. (2005) Linguistic human rights. In E. Hinkel (ed.) *Handbook of Research in Second Language Teaching and Learning*. Mahwah, NJ: Lawrence Erlbaum.
Maynard, S. (1997) *Japanese Communication: Language and Thought in Context*. Honolulu, HI: University of Hawai'i Press.
Maynard, S. (1998) *Principles of Japanese Discourse*. Cambridge: Cambridge University Press.
McCabe, A. and Peterson, C. (1990) What makes a narrative memorable? *Applied Psycholinguistics* 11, 73–82.
McCarthy, M. (1990) *Vocabulary*. Oxford: Oxford University Press.
McCollum, P. (1989) Turn-allocation in lessons with North American and Puerto Rican students: A comparative study. *Anthropology & Education Quarterly* 20, 133–158.
McConnell, G.D. (1977a) Language treatment and language planning in Canada. *Language Planning Newsletter* 3, 3–6.
McConnell, G.D. (1977b) Language treatment and language planning in Canada: Part 2: The Provinces. *Language Planning Newsletter* 3, 1–6.
McCutchen, D. and Perfetti, C. (1982) Coherence and connectedness in the development of discourse production. *Text* 2, 113–139.
Meara, P. (1997) Towards a new approach to modeling vocabulary acquisition. In N. Schmitt and M. McCarthy (eds) *Vocabulary: Description, Acquisition and Pedagogy*. Cambridge: Cambridge University Press.
Medgyes, P. (1983) The schizophrenic teachers. *ELT Journal* 37, 2–6.
Medgyes, P. (1986) Queries from a communicative teacher. *ELT Journal* 40, 107–112.
Medgyes, P. (1992) Native or nonnative: Who's worth more? *ELT Journal* 46, 340–349.
Medgyes, P. (1994) *The Non-native Teacher*. London: Macmillan.
Medgyes, P. (2001) When the teacher is a non-native speaker. In M. Celce-Murcia (ed.) *Teaching English as a Second or Foreign Language*. Boston: Heinle & Heinle.
Medgyes, P. (2002) 'Very English, very good!' – Gondolatok az angol nyelv magyarországi térhódításáról ['Very English, very good!' – On the spread of English in Hungary]. In J.M. Kovács (ed.) *A zárva várt Nyugat: Kulturális globalizáció Magyarországon* [*The West Closed Shut: Cultural Globalisation in Hungary*]. Budapest: 2000/Sík Kiadó.
Medgyes, P. and Kaplan, R.B. (1992) Discourse in a foreign language: An empirical survey of the foreign language competence of leading Hungarian scholars. *International Journal of the Sociology of Language* 98, 67–100.
Medgyes, P. and László, M. (2001) The foreign language competence of Hungarian scholars: Ten years later. In U. Ammon (ed.) *The Dominance of English as a Language of Science*. Berlin: Mouton de Gruyter.
Medgyes, P. and Miklósy, K. (2000) The language situation in Hungary. *Current Issues in Language Planning* 1, 148–242.

Medgyes, P. and Nikolov, M. (2002) Curriculum development in foreign language education: The interface between political and professional decisions. In R.B. Kaplan (ed.) *The Oxford Handbook of Applied Linguistics*. New York: Oxford University Press.

Mehan, H. (1979) *Learning Lessons*. Cambridge, MA: Harvard University Press.

Mencken, H.L. (1936) *The American Language*. New York: Alfred Knopf.

Merton, T. (1965) *The Way of Chuang Tzu*. New York: New Direction.

Meyer, M.C., Sherman, W.L. and Deeds, S.M. (2003) *The Course of Mexican History*. New York: Oxford University Press.

Michaels, S. (1981) 'Sharing time:' Children's narrative styles and differential access to literacy. *Language in Society* 10, 423–442.

Miller, C. (1984) Genre as social action. *Quarterly Review of Speech* 70, 151–167.

Montaño-Harmon, M. (1988) Discourse features in the compositions of Mexican, English-as-a-second-language, Mexican-American/Chicano, and Anglo high school students: Considerations for the formulation of educational policies. Unpublished doctoral dissertation, University of Southern California.

Moreno, A.I. (1996) *Estudio Contrastivo Inglés–Español de la Expresión de las Relaciones de Coherencia Causal Interoracional: El Artículo Académico sobre Economía y Empresa*. [*English–Spanish contrastive study of the expression of causal intersentential coherence relations: The academic article in business and economics*]. Published doctoral dissertation, University of León, Spain.

Moreno, A.I. (1997) Genre constraints across languages: Causal metatext in Spanish and English. *English for Specific Purposes* 16, 161–179.

Moreno, A.I. (1998) The explicit signalling of premise-conclusion sequences in research articles: A contrastive framework. *Text* 18, 545–585.

Moreno de Alba, J.G. (1996) Seudoanglicismos [Pseudoanglicisms]. In J.G. Moreno de Alba (ed.) *Nuevas Minucias del Lenguaje* [*New Minutiae of Language*]. México: Fondo de Cultura Económica.

Motta-Roth, D. (1998) Discourse analysis and academic book reviews: A study of text and disciplinary cultures. In S. Fortanet, S. Posteguillo, J.C. Palmer and J. F. Coll (eds) *Genre Studies in English for Academic Purposes*. Castelló, Spain: Universitat Jaume I.

Moussu, L. (2002) English as a second language students' reactions to nonnative English speaking teachers. Unpublished masters thesis, Brigham Young University.

Muchisky, D. and Tangren (1999) Immigrant student performance in a academic intensive English program. In L. Harklau, K.M. Losey, and M. Siegal (eds) *Generation 1.5 Meets College Composition: Issues in the Teaching of Writing to US Educated Learners of ESL*. Mahwah, NJ: Lawrence Erlbaum.

Mühlhäusler, P. (2000) Language planning and language ecology. *Current Issues in Language Planning* 1, 306–367.

Murie, R. and Thomson, R. (2001) When ESL is developmental: A model program for the freshman year. In J. Higbee (ed.) *2001: A Developmental Odyssey*. Warrensburg, MO: NADE Monograph Series.

Nagy, W. (1997) On the role of context in first- and second-language vocabulary learning. In N. Schmitt and M. McCarthy (eds) *Vocabulary: Description, Acquisition, and Pedagogy*. Cambridge: Cambridge University Press.

Nahir, M. (1984) Language planning goals: A classification. *Language Problems & Language Planning* 8, 294–327.

Nahir, M. (1998) Micro language planning and the revival of Hebrew: A schematic framework. *Language in Society* 27, 335–357.

References

Nassaji, H. and Wells, G. (2000) What's the use of 'triadic dialogue'? An investigation of teacher–student interaction. *Applied Linguistics* 21, 376–406.
Nation, I.S.P. (1990) *Teaching and Learning Vocabulary.* New York: Newbury House.
Nation, I.S.P. (2001) *Learning Vocabulary in Another Language.* Cambridge: Cambridge University Press.
Nation, I.S.P. and Wang, K. (1999) Graded readers and vocabulary. *Reading in a Foreign Language* 12, 355–380.
National Census (2002) *National Census 2001, Summary Data* (Vol. 1). Budapest: Central Statistical Office.
Nattinger, J.R. and DeCarrico, J.S. (1992) *Lexical Phrases and Language Teaching.* Oxford: Oxford University Press.
Nayar, P.B. (1994) Whose English is it? *TESL-EJ* 1. On WWW at http://www-writing.berkeley.edu/TESL-EJ/ej01/f.1.html.
Neustupný, J.V. (1974) Basic types of treatment of language problems. In J.A. Fishman (ed.) *Advances in Language Planning.* The Hague: Mouton.
Neustupný, J.V. (1989) Language purism as a type of language correction. In B.H. Jernudd and M.J. Shapiro (eds) *The Politics of Language Purism.* Berlin: Mouton de Gruyter.
Neustupný, J.V. and Nekvapil, J. (2003) Language management in the Czech Republic. *Current Issues in Language Planning* 5, 181–366.
Nettle, D. and Romaine, S. (2000) *Vanishing Voices.* Oxford: Oxford University Press.
Niedzielski, N. and Preston, D. (2003) *Folk Linguistics.* Berlin: Mouton de Gruyter.
Ochs, E. (1986) Introduction. In B.B. Schieffelin and E. Ochs (eds) *Language Socialization Across Cultures.* New York: Cambridge University Press.
Ochs, E. (1988) *Culture and Language Development: Language Acquisition and Language Socialization in a Samoan Village.* Cambridge: Cambridge University Press.
Oliver, R. (1972) *Communication and Culture in Ancient India and China.* Syracuse, NY: Syracuse University Press.
Olsen, L. and Jaramillo, A. (1999) *Turning the Tides of Exclusion: A Guide for Educators and Advocates for Immigrant Students.* Oakland CA: California Tomorrow.
Orellana, M. F. (1995) Literacy as a gendered social practice: Tasks, texts, talk, and take-up. *Reading Research Quarterly* 30, 674–708.
Orwell, G. (1974a) The principles of Newspeak. In J.F. Somer and J. Hoy (eds) *The Language Experience.* New York: Dell.
Orwell, G. (1974b) Politics and the English language. In J.F. Somer and J. Hoy (eds) *The Language Experience.* New York: Dell.
Oxford Advanced Learner's Dictionary (1995) Oxford: Oxford University Press.
Padrón, Y.N., Waxman, H., Brown, A.P. and Powers, R.A. (2000) Improving classroom instruction and student learning for resilient and non-resilient English language learners. Research Brief #7: Center for Research on Education, Diversity and Excellence (CREDE). Washington, DC: Center for Applied Linguistics.
Paikeday, T.M. (1985) *The Native Speaker is Dead!* Toronto: Paikeday.
Palmberg, R. (1987) Patterns of vocabulary development in foreign-language learners. *Studies in Second Language Acquisition* 9, 201–220.
Paltridge, B. (2001) *Genre in the Language Learning Classroom.* Ann Arbor, MI: University of Michigan Press.
Panetta, C.G. (2001) *Contrastive Rhetoric Revisited and Redefined.* Mahwah, NJ: Lawrence Erlbaum.

Pasternak, M. and Bailey, K.M. (2004) Preparing nonnative and native English-speaking teachers: Issues of professionalism and proficiency. In L.D. Kamhi-Stein (ed.) *Learning and Teaching from Experience: Perspectives on Nonnative English-speaking Professionals*. Ann Arbor, MI: University of Michigan Press.

Patterson, W. and Urrutibéheity, H. (1975) *The Lexical Structure of Spanish*. The Hague: Mouton.

Patthey-Chavez, G.G. (1993) High school as an arena for cultural conflict and acculturation for Latino Angelinos. *Anthropology & Education Quarterly* 24, 33–60.

Patthey-Chavez, G.G. and Clare, L. (1996) Task, talk, and text: The influence of instructional conversation on transitional bilingual writers. *Written Communication* 13, 515–563.

Paulston, C.B. (ed.) (1988) *International Handbook of Bilingualism and Bilingual Education*. New York: Greenwood Press.

Paulston, C.B. and Peckham, D. (eds) (1998) *Linguistic Minorities in Central and East Europe*. Clevedon: Multilingual Matters.

Paulston, C.B. and Tucker, G.R. (eds) (1997) *The Early Days of Sociolinguistics: Memories and Reflections*. Dallas, TX: Summer Institute of Linguistics.

Pawley, A. and Syder, F.H. (1983) Two puzzles for linguistic theory: Native-like selection and native-like fluency. In J. Richards and R. Schmidt (eds) *Language and Communication*. London: Longman.

Penny, R. (1991) *A History of the Spanish Language*. Cambridge: Cambridge University Press.

Pennycook, A. (1994) *The Cultural Politics of English as an International Language*. New York: Longman.

Pennycook, A. (1998) *English and the Discourses of Colonialism*. London: Routledge.

Pennycook, A. (2001) *Critical Applied Linguistics: A Critical Introduction*. Mahwah, NJ: Lawrence Erlbaum.

Peterson, C. and McCabe, A. (1983) *Developmental Psycholinguistics*. New York: Plenum Press.

Phillipson, R. (1992) *Linguistic Imperialism*. Oxford: Oxford University Press.

Pinker, S. (1994) *The Language Instinct: How the Mind Creates Language*. New York: William Morrow.

Pinzur, M.I. (2003) Even after English lessons, foreign kids lag on tests. *The Miami Herald*, January 31.

Póczik, S. (1996) Rendszerváltás és kriminalitás: külföldiek és cigányok a bunpiacon [Change of regime and criminality: Foreigners and Gypsies on the crime market]. *Valóság* 39, 73–102.

Polio, C. (2003) Research on second language writing: An overview of what we investigate and how. In B. Kroll (ed.) *Exploring the Dynamics of Second Language Writing*. Cambridge: Cambridge University Press.

Pomerantz, A. (2002) Language ideologies and the production of identities: Spanish as a resource for participation in a multilingual workplace. *Multilingua* 21, 275–302.

Poole, D. (1990) Contextualizing IRE in an eighth-grade quiz review. *Linguistics and Education* 2, 85–211.

Poole, D. (1992) Classroom turn-allocation strategies: Motivations and consequences for learning. Paper presented at the Annual Meeting of the American Association for Applied Linguistics: Seattle, WA.

Prague School (1973) General principles for the cultivation of good language (P.L. Garvin, trans.) In J. Rubin and R. Shuy (eds) *Language Planning: Current Issues and Research*. Washington, DC: Georgetown University Press.

Pratt, M.L. (1977) *Toward a Speech Act Theory of Literary Discourse.* Bloomington, IN: Indiana University Press.
Precht, K. (2003). 'Great vs. lovely:' Stance differences in American and British English. In P. Leistyna and C.F. Meyer (eds) *Corpus Analysis: Language Structure and Language Use.* Amsterdam: Rodopi.
Prior, P. (1998) *Writing/Disciplinarity: A Sociohistoric Account of Literate Activity in the Academy.* Mahwah, NJ: Lawrence Erlbaum.
¿Qué es la Comisión para La Defensa del Idioma Español? *[What is the Commission for the Defense of the Spanish Language?]* (1982). México: Secretaria de la Educación Pública.
Raimes, A. (1999) *Keys for Writers: A Brief Handbook.* Boston: Houghton Mifflin.
Ramanathan, V. (2002) *The Politics of TESOL Education: Writing, Knowledge, Critical Pedagogy.* New York: RoutledgeFalmer.
Ramanathan, V., Davies, C.E. and Schleppegrell, M.J. (2001) A naturalistic inquiry into the cultures of two divergent MA-TESOL programs: Implications for TESOL. *TESOL Quarterly* 35, 279–305.
Ramanathan, V. and Kaplan, R.B. (1996a) Audience and voice in current L1 composition texts: Some implications for ESL student writers. *Journal of Second Language Writing* 5, 21–34.
Ramanathan, V. and Kaplan, R.B. (1996b) Some problematic 'channels' in the teaching of critical thinking: Implications for L2 student-writers. *Issues in Applied Linguistics* 7, 225–249.
Ramanathan, V. and Kaplan, R.B. (2000) Genres, authors, discourse communities: Theory and practice for (L1 and) L2 writing instructors. *Journal of Second Language Writing* 9, 171–191.
Rampton, B. (1990) Displacing the 'native speaker:' Expertise, affiliation, and inheritance. *ELT Journal* 44, 97–101.
Rampton, B. (1995) *Crossing: Language and Ethnicity among Adolescents.* London: Longman.
Rampton, B. (1997) Retuning in applied linguistics. *International Journal of Applied Linguistics* 7, 3–25.
Reese, L. (2002) Parental strategies in contrasting cultural settings: Families in Mexico and 'El Norte.' *Anthropology & Education Quarterly* 33, 30–59.
Reeves, G. (1975) *Idioms in Action.* Cambridge, MA: Newbury House.
Reid, J. (1988) Quantitative differences in English prose written by Arabic, Chinese, Spanish, and English students. Unpublished doctoral dissertation, Colorado State University.
Reid, J. (1995) (ed.) *Learning Styles in the ESL/EFL Classroom.* Boston: Heinle & Heinle.
Reid, J. (1998a) 'Eye' learners and 'ear' learners: Identifying the needs of international students and US resident writers. In J. Reid and P. Byrd (eds) *Grammar in the Composition Classroom: Essays on Teaching ESL for College-Bound Students.* Boston: Heinle & Heinle.
Reid, J. (1998b) *Understanding Learning Styles in the Second Language Classroom.* Upper Saddle River, NJ: Prentice Hall Regents.
Reid, J. (2000) *The Process of Composition.* New York: Longman.
Reid, J. (2005) *Essentials of College Writing.* Boston: Houghton-Mifflin.
Reves, T. and Medgyes, P. (1994) The non-native English speaking ESL/EFL teacher's self-image: An international survey. *System* 22, 353–367.

Rhodes, N. and Branaman, L. (1999) *Foreign Language Instruction in the United States: A National Survey of Elementary and Secondary Schools*. Washington, DC/ McHenry, IL: Center for Applied Linguistics/Delta Systems.

Ricento, T. (2000a) Historical and theoretical perspectives in language policy and planning. In T. Ricento (ed.) *Ideology, Politics and Language Policies: Focus on English*. Amsterdam: John Benjamins.

Ricento, T. (2000b) (ed.) *Ideology, Politics and Language Policies: Focus on English*. Amsterdam: John Benjamins.

Richards, J.C. and Lockhart, C. (1994) *Reflective Teaching in Second Language Classrooms*. Cambridge: Cambridge University Press.

Richek, M. (2000) *The World of Words*. Boston: Houghton Mifflin.

Robbins, F.E. (1992) Standardization of unwritten vernaculars. In S.J.J. Hwang and W.R. Merrifield (eds) *Language in Context: Essays for Robert E. Longacre*. Dallas, TX: Summer Institute of Linguistics/ University of Texas at Arlington.

Roberge, M.M. (2002a) California's Generation 1.5 immigrants: What experiences, characteristics, and needs do they bring to our English classes? *CATESOL Journal* 14, 107–130.

Roberge, M.M. (2002b) Institutional responses to immigrant college students: An ethnographic case study of a college composition, basic writing, and English as a second language program. *Dissertation Abstracts International* 63: 584A.

Rodríguez González, F. and Lillo Baudes, A. (eds) (1997) *Nuevo Diccionario de Anglicismos [New Dictionary of Anglicisms]*. Madrid: Gredos.

Rubin, J. and Jernudd, B.H. (eds) (1971) *Can Language Be Planned?* Honolulu, HI: University of Hawai'i Press.

Rubin, J., Jernudd, B.H., Das Gupta, J., Fishman, J.A. and Ferguson, C.A. (1977) *Language Planning Processes*. The Hague: Mouton.

Rudd, K. (1994) *Asian Languages and Australia's Economic Future*. Canberra: Australian Government Publishing Service.

Ruiz-de-Velasco, J., Fix, M. and Clewel, B.C. (2001) *Overlooked and Underserved: Immigrant Students in US Secondary Schools*. Washington, DC: The Urban Institute.

Rumbaut, R.G. and Ima, K. (1988) The adaptation of Southeast Asian refugee youth: A comparative study. Final report to the Office of Resettlement. San Diego, CA: San Diego State University.

Rusikoff, K. (1994) Hidden expectations: Faculty perceptions of SLA and ESL writing competence. *ERIC Document Service*, ED 370 376.

Sacks, H., Schegloff, E. and Jefferson, G. (1974) A simplest systematics for the organization of turn-taking in conversation. *Language* 50, 696–735.

Samimy, K.K. and Brutt-Griffler, J. (1999) To be a native or non-native speaker: Perceptions of 'non-native' students in a graduate TESOL program. In G. Braine (ed.) *Non-native Educators in English Language Teaching*. Mahwah, NJ: Lawrence Erlbaum.

Samraj, B. (2002) Texts and contextual layers: Academic writing in content courses. In A.M. Johns (ed.) *Genre in the Classroom: Multiple Perspectives*. Mahwah, NJ: Lawrence Erlbaum.

Santamaría, F.J. (1974) *Diccionario de Mejicanismos [Dictionary of Mexicanisms]*. México: Porrua.

Santos, T. (1988) Professors' reactions to the academic writing of non-native speaking students. *TESOL Quarterly* 18, 671–688.

Santos, T., Atkinson, D., Erickson, M., Matsuda, P.K. and Silva, T. (2000) On the future of second language writing: A colloquium. *Journal of Second Language Writing* 9, 1–20.
Schieffelin, B.B. and Ochs, E. (1986) Language socialization. *Annual Review of Anthropology* 15, 163–191.
Schieffelin, B.B., Woolard, K.A. and Kroskrity, P.V. (1998) *Language Ideologies: Practice and Theory*. Oxford: Oxford University Press.
Schiffman, H.E. (1996) *Linguistic Culture and Language Policy*. London: Routledge.
Schmitt, N. (2000) *Vocabulary in Language Teaching*. Cambridge: Cambridge University Press.
Schmitt, N. and Zimmerman, C.B. (2002) Derivative words forms: What do learners know? *TESOL Quarterly* 36, 145–171.
Scollon, R. (1997) Contrastive rhetoric, contrastive poetics, or perhaps something else? *TESOL Quarterly* 31, 352–358.
Scollon, R. and Scollon, S.B.K. (1981) *Narrative, Literacy, and Face in Interethnic Communication*. Norwood, NJ: Ablex.
Seal, B. (1991) Vocabulary learning and teaching. In M. Celce-Murcia (ed.) *Teaching English as a Second or Foreign Language*. Boston: Heinle & Heinle.
Seidlhofer, B. (1999) Double standards: Teacher education in the expanding circle. *World Englishes* 18, 233–245.
Seidlhofer, B. (ed.) (2003) *Controversies in Applied Linguistics*. Oxford: Oxford University Press.
Selinker, L. (1972) Interlanguage. *International Review of Applied Linguistics* 20, 201–231.
Selinker, L. (1995) *Rediscovering Interlanguage*. Boston: Addison-Wesley.
Semke, H.D. (1984) The effects of the red pen. *Foreign Language Annals* 17, 195–202.
Senate (1984) *A National Language Policy. Report of the Senate Standing Committee on Education and the Arts*. Canberra: Australian Government Publishing Service.
Sengupta, S. (1999) Rhetorical consciousness raising in the L2 reading classroom. *Journal of Second Language Writing* 8, 291–319.
Shannon, S.M. (1999) The debate on bilingual education in the US: Language ideology as reflected in the practices of bilingual teachers. In J. Blommaert (ed.) *Language Ideological Debates*. Berlin: Mouton de Gruyter.
Shaughnessy, M.P. (1977) *Errors and Expectations: A Guide for the Teacher of Basic Writing*. New York: Oxford University Press.
Shim, R.J. (2002) Changing attitudes toward TEWOL in Korea. *Journal of Asian Pacific Communication* 12, 143–158.
Shulman, L.S. (1986) Those who understand: Knowledge growth in teaching. *Educational Researcher* 15, 4–14.
Shulman, L.S. (1987) Knowledge and teaching: Foundations of the new reform. *Harvard Educational Review* 57, 1–22.
Sík, E. (1998) Minden ötödik magyar beszél idegen nyelvet [Every fifth Hungarian speaks a foreign language]. *Magyar Hírlap*: 28 December.
Silva, T. (2005) On the philosophical bases of inquiry in second language writing. In P.K. Matsuda and T. Silva (eds) *Second Language Writing Research: Perspectives on the Process of Knowledge Construction*. Mahwah, NJ: Lawrence Erlbaum.
Simpson, J.A. and Weiner, E.S.C. (eds) (1989) *The Oxford English Dictionary*. Oxford: Clarendon Press.
Sinclair, J.M. (1985) Selected issues. In R. Quirk and H.G. Widdowson (eds) *English in the World*. Cambridge: Cambridge University Press.

Sinclair, J.M. (1991) *Corpus, Concordance, Collocation*. Oxford: Oxford University Press.
Sinclair, J.M. (1997) Corpus evidence in language description. In A. Wichmann, S. Fligelstone, T. McEnery and G. Knowles (eds) *Teaching and Language Corpora*. London: Longman.
Sinclair, J.M. and Coulthard, R.M. (1975) *Toward an Analysis of Discourse: The English Used by Teachers and Pupils*. New York: Oxford University Press.
Singleton, D. (2000) *Language and the Lexicon: An Introduction*. London: Edward Arnold.
Skilton, E.E. (1992) Acquisition policy planning and litigation: Language planning in the context of Y.S. v. School District of Philadelphia. *Working Papers in Educational Linguistics* 8, 55–87.
Skilton-Sylvester, P. (1998) Putting school/work back together?: A comparison of organizational change in an inner city school and a Fortune 500 company. Unpublished doctoral dissertation, University of Pennsylvania.
Skutnabb-Kangas, T. (2000) *Linguistic Genocide in Education, or Worldwide Diversity and Human Rights?* Mahwah, NJ: Lawrence Erlbaum.
Skutnabb-Kangas, T. and Cummins, J. (eds) (1988) *Minority Education: From Shame to Struggle*. Clevedon: Multilingual Matters.
Skutnabb-Kangas, T. and Phillipson, R. (1995) Linguistic human rights, past and present. In T. Skutnabb-Kangas, R. Phillipson and M. Rannut (eds) *Linguistic Human Rights: Overcoming Linguistic Discrimination*. Berlin: Mouton de Gruyter.
Smalley, R., Ruetten, M. and Kozyrev, J. (2000) *Refining Composition Skills*. Boston: Heinle & Heinle.
Smead, R.N. and Clegg, J.H. (1996) English calques in Chicano Spanish. In A. Roca and J.B. Jensen (eds) *Spanish in Contact: Issues in Bilingualism*. Somerville, MA: Cascadilla Press.
Smitherman, G. (1977) *Talkin and Testifyin*. Boston: Houghton Mifflin.
Smoke, T. (1999) *A Writer's Workbook*. New York: Cambridge University Press.
Spolsky, B. (1968) Language testing: The problem of validation. *TESOL Quarterly* 2, 88–94.
Spolsky, B. (1970) Linguistics and language pedagogy: Applications or implications? In J.E. Alatis (ed.) *Twentieth Annual Round Table on Languages and Linguistics*. Washington, DC: Georgetown University Press.
Spolsky, B. (1971) Reduced redundancy as a language testing tool. In G.E. Perren and J.L.M. Trim (eds) *Applications of Linguistics: Selected Papers of the Second International Congress of Applied Linguistics, Cambridge, September 1969*. Cambridge: Cambridge University Press.
Spolsky, B. (1973) Linguistics and language pedagogy: Applications or implications? In M. Lester (ed.) *Readings in Applied Transformational Grammar*. New York: Holt, Rinehart, & Winston.
Spolsky, B. (1974) The Navajo Reading Study: An illustration of the scope and nature of educational linguistics. In J. Quistgaard, H. Schwarz and H. Spong-Hanssen (eds) *Applied Linguistics: Problems and Solutions: Proceedings of the Third Congress on Applied Linguistics, Copenhagen, 1972, Vol. 3*. Heidelberg: Julius Gros Verlag.
Spolsky, B. (1978) *Educational Linguistics: An Introduction*. Rowley, MA: Newbury House.
Spolsky, B. (1980) The scope of educational linguistics. In R.B. Kaplan (ed.) *On the Scope of Applied Linguistics*. Rowley, MA: Newbury House.
Spolsky, B. (1990) Educational linguistics: Definitions, progress, problems. *Journal of Applied Linguistics* 6, 75–85.

Spolsky, B. (1995) The impact of the Army Specialized Training Program: A reconsideration. In G. Cook and B. Seidlhofer (eds) *Principle & Practice in Applied Linguistics: Studies in Honour of H.G. Widdowson*. Oxford: Oxford University Press.

Spolsky, B. (1998) *Sociolinguistics*. Oxford: Oxford University Press.

Spolsky, B. (2003) Educational linguistics. In W.J. Frawley (ed.) *International Encyclopedia of Linguistics*. New York: Oxford University Press.

Spolsky, B. (2004) *Language Policy*. Cambridge: Cambridge University Press.

Spolsky, B. and Kaplan, R.B. (1976) Warning: CAL may be hazardous to the profession. *TESOL Newsletter* 10, 2.

Sternglass, M.S. (1997) *Time to Know Them: A Longitudinal Study of Writing and Learning at the College Level*. Mahwah NJ: Lawrence Erlbaum.

Strauss, V. (2003) English-language learners called at risk. *The Washington Post*, February 17. On WWW at washingtonpost.com/wp-dyn/articles/A22994-2003Feb17.html.

Stubbs, M. (1980) *Language and Literacy*. London: Routledge & Kegan Paul.

Stubbs, M. (1983) *Discourse Analysis*. Oxford: Blackwell.

Sullivan, P. (2000) Spoken artistry: Performance in a foreign language classroom. In J.K. Hall and L.S. Verplaetse (eds) *Second and Foreign Language Learning through Classroom Interaction*. Mahwah, NJ: Lawrence Erlbaum.

Sulzby, E. and Teale, W. (1991) Emergent literacy. In R. Barr, M.L. Kamil, P. Mosenthal, and P.D. Pearson (eds) *Handbook of Reading Research* (Vol. 2). New York: Longman.

Swain, M. (1998) Focus on form through conscious reflection. In C. Doughty and J. Williams (eds) *Focus on Form in Classroom Second Language Acquisition*. Cambridge: Cambridge University Press.

Swain, M. (2000) French immersion research in Canada: Recent contributions to SLA and applied linguistics. *Annual Review of Applied Linguistics* 20. New York: Cambridge University Press.

Swales, J.M. (1990) *Genre Analysis: English in Academic and Research Settings*. Cambridge: Cambridge University Press.

Swales, J.M. and Feak, C.B. (1994) *Academic Writing for Graduate Students: Essential Tasks and Skills*. Ann Arbor, MI: University of Michigan Press.

Swerdlow, J.L. (2001) Changing America. *National Geographic*, September: 42–61.

Tandefelt, M. (1992) Some linguistic consequences of the shift from Swedish to Finnish in Finland. In W. Fase, K. Jaspaert, and S. Kroon (eds) *Maintenance and Loss of Minority Languages*. Amsterdam: John Benjamins.

Tannen, D. (1982) Oral and literate strategies in spoken and written narratives. *Language* 58, 1–21.

Taylor, I. (1995) *Writing and Literacy in Chinese, Korean, and Japanese*. Amsterdam: John Benjamins.

Terestyéni, T. (1995) Helyzetkép az idegennyelv-tudásról [State of the art in foreign language knowledge]. *Jel-kép* 1, 47–60.

TESOL (1991) A TESOL Statement on Nonnative Speakers of English and Hiring Practices. On WWW at http://nnest.moussu.net/articles/hiring.pdf.

Tharp, R.G. and Gallimore, R. (1988) *Rousing Minds to Life: Teaching, Learning, and Schooling in Social Context*. New York: Cambridge University Press.

Thomas, J. (1999) Voices from the periphery: Non-native teachers and issues of credibility. In G. Braine (ed.) *Non-native Educators in English Language Teaching*. Mahwah, NJ: Lawrence Erlbaum.

Thompson, G. and Hunston, S. (2000) Evaluation: An introduction. In S. Hunston and G. Thompson (eds) *Evaluation in Text: Authorial Stance and the Construction of Discourse*. Oxford: Oxford University Press.
Tobin, Y. (1993) Showing native speakers what and why they say what they do say: Awareness raising from a semiotic point of view. *Language Awareness* 2, 143–158.
Tollefson, J.W. (1981a) Centralized and decentralized language planning. *Language Problems & Language Planning* 5, 175–188.
Tollefson, J.W. (1981b) The role of language planning in second language acquisition. *Language Learning* 31, 337–348.
Touchstone, E.E., Kaplan, R.B. and Hagstrom, C.L. (1996) 'Home, sweet casa:' Access to home loans in Los Angeles. A critique of English and Spanish home loan brochures. *Multilingua* 15, 329–349.
Trudgill, P. (2002) *Sociolinguistic Variation and Change*. Edinburgh: Edinburgh University Press.
Tucker, G.R., Donato, R. and Murday, K. (2001) The genesis of a district-wide Spanish FLES program. In R.L. Cooper, E.S. Shohamy, and J. Walters (eds) *New Perspectives and Issues in Educational Language Policy. In Honour of Bernard Dov Spolsky*. Amsterdam: John Benjamins.
Ulijn, J.M. and Strother, J.B. (1995) *Communicating in Business and Technology: From Psycholinguistic Theory to International Practice*. Frankfurt: Peter Lang.
Valdes, G. (1992) Bilingual minorities and language issues in writing. *Written Communication* 9: 85–136.
van Dijk, T. and Kintsch, W. (1983) *Strategies of Discourse Comprehension*. New York: Academic Press.
van Els, T. (2005) Status planning. In E. Hinkel (ed.) *Handbook of Research in Second Language Teaching and Learning*. Mahwah, NJ: Lawrence Erlbaum
Vann, R., Lorenz, F., and Meyer, D. (1991) Error gravity: Faculty response to errors in written discourse of nonnative speakers of English. In L. Hamp-Lyons (ed.) *Assessing Second Language Writing in Academic Contexts*. Norwood, NJ: Ablex.
Vann, R., Meyer, D.E. and Lorenz, F.D. (1984) Error gravity: A study of faculty opinion of ESL errors. *TESOL Quarterly* 18, 427–440.
Vasquez, O., Pease-Alvarez, L. and Shannon, S. (1994) *Pushing Boundaries: Language and Culture in a Mexicano Community*. New York: Cambridge.
Velasco-Martin, C. (2004) The nonnative English-speaking teacher as an intercultural speaker. In L.D. Kamhi-Stein (ed.) *Learning and Teaching from Experience: Perspectives on Nonnative English-speaking Professionals*. Ann Arbor, MI: University of Michigan Press.
Victoria (2002) *Languages for Victoria's Future: An Analysis of Languages in Government Schools*. Melbourne: Victorian Department of Education and Training.
Voegelin, C.F. (n.d.) On the probability of autonomous linguistics converging with hyphenated linguistics. Unpublished manuscript, Philadelphia, PA.
Werlich, E. (1976) *A Text Grammar of English*. Heidelberg: Quelle & Meyer.
Whorf, B.L. (1956) *Language, Thought, and Reality: Selected Writings of Benjamin Lee Whorf* (J.B. Caroll, ed.). Cambridge, MA: MIT Press.
Widdowson, H.G. (1979) *Explorations in Applied Linguistics*. Oxford: Oxford University Press.
Widdowson, H.G. (1998) The theory and practice of critical discourse analysis. *Applied Linguistics* 19, 136–151.
Widdowson, H.G. (2000a) On the limitations of linguistics applied. *Applied Linguistics* 21, 3–25.

Widdowson, H.G. (2000b) Object language and the language subject: On the mediating role of applied linguistics. *Annual Review of Applied Linguistics* 20. New York: Cambridge University Press.

Widdowson, H.G. (2003) *Defining Issues in English Language Teaching*. Oxford: Oxford University Press.

Widdowson, H.G. (2004) *Text, Context, Pretext: Issues in Discourse Analysis*. Oxford: Blackwell.

Wilkins, D.A. (1976) *Notional Syllabuses: A Taxonomy and its Relevance to Foreign Language Curriculum Development*. Oxford: Oxford University Press.

Wolfram, W. and Schilling-Estes, N. (1998) *American English: Dialects and Variation*. Malden, MA: Blackwell.

Wollman-Bonilla, J.E. (2000) Teaching science writing to first graders: Genre learning and recontextualization. *Research in the Teaching of English* 35, 35–65.

Yamashita, T. (1993) The organization of teacher–student interaction in Japanese classroom lessons. Unpublished masters thesis, San Diego State University.

Yeatman, A. (1990) *Bureaucrats, Technocrats, Femocrats: Essays on the Contemporary Australian State*. Sydney: Allen & Unwin.

Yoshimitsu, K. (2000) Japanese school children in Melbourne and their language maintenance efforts. *Journal of Asian Pacific Communication* 10, 255–278.

Zamel, V. (1982) Writing: The process of discovering meaning. *TESOL Quarterly* 16, 195–209.

Zamel, V. (1983) The composing processes of advanced ESL students: Six case studies. *TESOL Quarterly* 17, 165–187.

Zamel, V. (1985) Responding to student writing. *TESOL Quarterly* 19, 79–102.

Zimmerman, C.B. (1997) Do reading and interactive vocabulary instruction make a difference? An empirical study. *TESOL Quarterly* 31, 121–140.

Robert Kaplan: Biography and Publications

Biography

Robert B. Kaplan PhD is Professor Emeritus of Applied Linguistics and past Director of the American Language Institute at the University of Southern California, where he was a faculty member from September 1960 to January 1995. He currently resides in Port Angeles, Washington. In 1998–99, he served as Professor of Applied Linguistics in the Graduate School of Applied Language Study, Meikai University, Japan. Kaplan is a past Editor-in-Chief of the *Annual Review of Applied Linguistics*, which he founded in 1980, and from 1980 to 2000 was a member of its Editorial Board. He is Editor-in-Chief *of Current Issues in Language Planning*, which he co-founded with Richard B. Baldauf Jr in 2000. Kaplan is also Editor-in-Chief of the *Oxford Handbook of Applied Linguistics*, is a member of the Editorial Board of the Oxford University Press *International Encyclopedia of Linguistics* (1st and 2nd editions), and serves on the editorial boards of several scholarly journals.

Robert Kaplan has authored or edited more than 40 books, more than 160 articles in scholarly journals and as chapters in books, and more than 90 book reviews and other ephemeral pieces in various newsletters, as well as nine special reports to government in the US and elsewhere.

Over a long career, Kaplan has presented more than 200 talks, papers, and invited plenary addresses at national and international conferences. He has specialized in written discourse analysis, and his name has been widely linked with the notion of 'contrastive rhetoric.' He has performed language planning research in some dozen countries in Australasia, East Asia, and the Middle East, and he has lectured at universities in some 35 countries around the world. He has held three separate Senior Fulbright Fellowship Awards (Australia, 1978; Hong Kong, 1986; New Zealand, 1992), two Vice-Chancellors' Awards (Britain, 1977; New Zealand, 1978), and a special research award from the New Zealand Council for Educational Research (1979). Kaplan received a Distinguished Alumni Citation Award from Willamette University (2002), the American Association for Applied Linguistics Award for Distinguished Scholarship and Service (1998), the first Distinguished Faculty Service Award from the Academic Senate, University of Southern California (1995), and the first Distinguished Service Award from the Black Administrators' Alliance, County of Los Angeles (1989). He has previously served as President of the following:

- the American Association for Applied Linguistics (AAAL) [founding member; life member 1998];
- the Association of Teachers of English as a Second Language (ATESL);
- the California Association of Teachers of English to Speakers of Other Languages (CATESOL) [founding member];
- the National Association for Foreign Student Affairs (NAFSA) [life member 1995];
- the international organization Teachers of English to Speakers of Other Languages (TESOL) [founding member; life member 1994];
- the University of Southern California Faculty Senate.

Publications

Books

1963 *Reading and Rhetoric: A Reader in English as a Second Language.* New York: Odyssey Press.
1965 *The Catcher in the Rye Notes: A Critical Study of J.D. Salinger.* Lincoln, NE: Cliff's Notes.
T.S. Eliot: A Critical Study of the Major Poems. Lincoln, NE: Cliff's Notes.
1966 *Bibliography of Materials for Teachers of English as a Second Language* (ed.). Los Angeles: Field Service Program of the National Association for Foreign Student Affairs.
Selected Conference Papers of the Association of Teachers of English as a Second Language (ed.). Los Angeles.
1967 *Bibliography of Materials for Teachers of English as a Second Language* (ed.). Los Angeles: Field Service Program of the National Association for Foreign Student Affairs.
1968 *Transformational Grammar: A Guide for Teachers* (with J. Aurback, P. Cook and V. Tufte). Washington, DC: English Language Services. [Introduction reprinted in J.S. DeStefano and S.E. Fox (eds) *Language and the Language Arts.* Boston: Little Brown.]
1969 *Learning English Through Typewriting* (with C.W. Gay and R.D. Schoesler). Washington, DC: English Language Services. [Reprinted as *English at Your Fingertips.* Culver City, CA: English Languages Services.]
1971 *Guidelines: English Language Proficiency.* Washington, DC: National Association for Foreign Student Affairs.
The Anatomy of Rhetoric: Prolegomena to a Functional Theory of Rhetoric. Philadelphia: Center for Curriculum Development. [Subsequently distributed by Heinle & Heinle.]
1979 *The Language Needs of Migrant Workers.* Wellington: New Zealand Council for Educational Research.
1980 *On the Scope of Applied Linguistics* (ed.). Rowley, MA: Newbury House. [Translated into Japanese by T. Shimaoka and T. Haga. Tokyo: Kenkusha, 1986.]

1981	*Annual Review of Applied Linguistics 1* (ed.). Rowley, MA: Newbury House.
1982	*Annual Review of Applied Linguistics 2* (ed.). Rowley, MA: Newbury House.
1983	*Annual Review of Applied Linguistics 3* (ed.). Rowley, MA: Newbury House.
1984	*Annual Review of Applied Linguistics 4* (ed.). Rowley, MA: Newbury House. *Exploring Academic Discourse: A Textbook for Advanced-level ESL Reading and Writing* (with P. Shaw). Rowley, MA: Newbury House.
1985	*Annual Review of Applied Linguistics 5* (ed.). New York: Cambridge University Press.
1986	*Annual Review of Applied Linguistics 6* (ed.). New York: Cambridge University Press. *Writing Across Languages: Analysis of L2 Text* (with U. Connor, eds). Reading, MA: Addison Wesley.
1987	*Annual Review of Applied Linguistics 7* (ed.). New York: Cambridge University Press.
1988	*Annual Review of Applied Linguistics 8* (ed.). New York: Cambridge University Press.
1989	*Annual Review of Applied Linguistics 9* (ed.). New York: Cambridge University Press.
1990	*Annual Review of Applied Linguistics 10* (ed.). New York: Cambridge University Press.
1991	*Introduction to Applied Linguistics* (with W. Grabe, eds). Reading, MA: Addison Wesley.
1996	*Theory and Practice of Writing: An Applied Linguistic Perspective* (with W. Grabe). London: Longman.
1997	*Language Planning From Practice to Theory* (with R.B. Baldauf Jr). Clevedon: Multilingual Matters.
1999	*Language Planning in Malawi, Mozambique, and The Philippines* (with R.B. Baldauf Jr, eds). Clevedon: Multilingual Matters. [Also in *Journal of Multilingual and Multicultural Development* 19, 5–6.]
2000	*Language Planning in Nepal, Sweden, and Taiwan* (with R.B. Baldauf Jr, eds). Clevedon: Multilingual Matters. [Also in *Journal of Multilingual and Multicultural Development* 20, 5–6.] *Current Issues in Language Planning* 1 (1): *Language Planning in Côte d'Ivoire and Vanuatu* (with R.B. Baldauf Jr). Clevedon: Multilingual Matters.
2001	*Current Issues in Language Planning* 1 (2): *Language Planning in Botswana and Hungary* (with R.B. Baldauf Jr). Clevedon: Multilingual Matters. *Current Issues in Language Planning* 2 (1): *Language Planning in Tunisia and Paraguay* (with R.B. Baldauf Jr). Clevedon: Multilingual Matters. *Current Issues in Language Planning* 2 (4): *Language Planning in the European Union and South Africa* (with R.B. Baldauf Jr). Clevedon: Multilingual Matters.
2002	*Oxford Handbook of Applied Linguistics*. New York: Oxford University Press.
2003	*Language and Language-in-Education Planning in the Pacific Basin* (with R.B. Baldauf Jr). Dordrecht: Kluwer. *Africa* (Vol. 1): *Botswana, Malawi, Mozambique, and South Africa* (with R.B. Baldauf Jr). Clevedon: Multilingual Matters.

Articles

1958	Cyclops at the lectern. *Today's Speech*.
1960	Eliot's 'Journey of the Magi' (with R.J. Wall). *Explicator* 19 (8).
1961	Eliot's 'Gerontion' (with R.J. Wall). *Explicator* 19 (36).

1964 The predictive validity of a modified battery of tests in language skills for foreign students at an American university (with R.A. Jones and W.B. Michaels). *Educational and Psychological Measurements* 24 (4).
1965 Evaluation of relative foreign student success (with R.A. Jones). *Language Learning* 14: 3–4.
1966 Cultural thought patterns in intercultural education. *Language Learning* 16: 1–20. [Reprinted in R.G. Bander. *American English Rhetoric.* New York: Holt, Rinehart, & Winston, 1971; H.B. Allen and R.N. Campbell (eds) *Teaching English as a Second Language.* New York: McGraw-Hill, 1972; K. Croft (ed.) *Readings on English as a Second Language for Teachers and Teacher-trainees.* Cambridge, MA: Winthrop, 1972, 1979; J.S. Wurzel (ed.) *Toward Multiculturalism.* Yarmouth, ME: Intercultural Press, 1988; D.S. Lottgen (ed.) *Cultural Studies in the Second Language Classroom: Needs, Problems and Solutions.* Murcia, Spain: University of Murcia Press, 1997; etc.]
   Teaching language rhythm: Unstressed function words (with J. Aurbach). *Speech Teacher* 15 (1), 78-81.
   A contrastive rhetoric approach to reading and writing. In R.B. Kaplan (ed.) *Selected Conference Papers of the Association of Teachers of English as a Second Language.* Los Angeles: NAFSA.
1967 Seeing the world through language-colored glasses. *TESOL Journal* 1 (4), 10–16.
   Teaching English as a second language. *California English Journal* 3 (3), 11–18.
1968 Teaching English and international exchange. *Exchange* (Winter), 43–47. [Reprinted in *Pacific Bridge* 12 (12), 4–8.]
   Contrastive rhetoric: Teaching composition to the Chinese student. *Journal of English as a Second Language* 3 (1) 1–13.
1969 On a note of protest (in a minor key): Bidialectism vs. bidialectalism. *College English* 30 (5), 386–389. [Reprinted in A.C. Aarons (ed.) *Linguistic-cultural Differences and American Education* 8 (1), 86, 165; R.E. Porter and L.A. Samovar (eds) *Intercultural Communication: A Reader.* New York: Wadsworth.]
   The criterion-related validity of English language screening instruments for foreign students entering the University of Southern California (with J.D. Burke, W.B. Michaels and R.A. Jones). *Educational and Psychological Measurement* 29: 503–506.
   491391625162541253661 [sic]. *Journal of English as a Second Language* 4 (4), 7–18.
1970 On language learning and language teaching. *English Quarterly* 3 (1), 21–28.
   NAFSA in the mod mod world (or the moon and I). *Exchange* 6 (2), 68–75.
   Notes toward an applied rhetoric. In R.C. Lugton (ed.) *Preparing the EFL Teacher: A Projection for the 70s.* Philadelphia: Center for Curriculum Development.
   On the conditions of bilingualism. In R.P. Fox (ed.) *Essays on Teaching English as a Second Language and as a Second Dialect.* Urbana, IL: National Council of Teachers of English.
   On the present failure to educate the American Indian. In W.W. Brickman and S. Lehrer (eds) *Education and the Many Faces of the Disadvantaged: Cultural and Historical Perspectives.* New York: Wiley.
   English language testing for university entrance. In *English Language Testing.* Singapore: RELC.
1971 What do you say? *The Asian Student Orientation Handbook.* San Francisco: The Asia Foundation. [Reprinted annually until 1978.]
   Composition at the advanced ESL level: A teacher's guide to connected

paragraph construction for advanced-level foreign students. *English Record* 21 (4), 53–64.

Towards a theory of applied linguistics. In E.C. Polome, W. Winter and M.A. Jazayery (eds) *Linguistics and Literary Studies in Honor of Professor Archibald A. Hill*. Berlin: Mouton.

1972 On language learning and language teaching: Phase II. *The English Quarterly* 5 (1–2), 73–82.

On linguistics and applied linguistics. *ELEC Bulletin* 39: 28–34.

The teacher education program (TEP) in retrospect and prospect. *Report of the Regional Seminar on Instructional Materials for English Language Teaching*. Singapore: RELC.

1976 An experiment in industrial–academic cooperation in second-language teaching. In G. Nickle (ed.) *Proceedings of the 4th World Congress of the International Association for Applied Linguistics*. Stuttgart.

A theoretical base for applied linguistics. In G. Nickle (ed.) *Proceedings of the 4th World Congress of the International Association for Applied Linguistics*. Stuttgart.

A further note on contrastive rhetoric. *Communication Quarterly* 24 (2), 12–19.

1977 Contrastive rhetoric: Some hypotheses. *ITL* (39–40), 61–72.

1978 On the scope of linguistics, applied and non-. In R.B. Kaplan (ed.) *On the Scope of Applied Linguistics*. Rowley, MA: Newbury House. [Translated into Japanese by T. Shimaoka and T. Haga. Tokyo: Kenkusha, 1986.]

On the notion of topic in written discourse. *Australian Review of Applied Linguistics* 2: 1–10.

Language and learning. *Babel* 14: 4–9.

Defining terms in bilingual education. *Polycom* 20: 4–9. [Reprinted in *Kaleidoscope: Readings in Migrant Education*. Brisbane: Queensland Department of Education.]

Bilingualism in the United States. *Forum of Education* 1, 19–25.

...To do what, and with what, and to whom. *Ethnic Studies* (March), 1–12.

On the notion of contrastive rhetoric. *Creativity: New Ideas in Language Teaching* 24, 1–2.

1979 Forging cultural links. *Modern Language Teachers Association of Queensland Journal* 5, 7–19.

Contrastive rhetorics: Some implications for the writing process. In A. Freeman, I. Pringle and J. Yalden (eds) *Learning to Write: First Language/ Second Language*. London: Longman.

The language situation in Australia. *The Linguistic Reporter* 22 (5), 2–3.

1980 An instructional technique for advanced ESL writing. *MEXTESOL Journal* 4 (2), 46–65.

1981 A language-planning rationale for English for special purposes. In J. Povey (ed.) *Language Policy and Language Teaching: Essays in Honor of Clifford H. Prator*. Culver City, CA: English Language Services.

Error in advanced-level discourse. *TECFORS* 4 (3), 2–3.

The language situation in New Zealand. *The Linguistic Reporter* 23 (9), 1–3.

1982 The language situation in the Philippines. *The Linguistic Reporter* 24 (5), 1–4.

Contrastive rhetoric: Some implications for the writing process. *English Teaching and Learning* 6 (3), 24–38; 6 (4), 16–28.

The language situation in Taiwan. *The Linguistic Reporter* 25 (2), 1–5.

Lectures in applied linguistics. *Proceedings of the 2nd International Conference on the Teaching of English*. Seoul: College English Teachers Association of Korea.

The Taiwan English language survey revisited (with J.K.P. Tse). *English Around the World* 27, 6–8.

US education: An invisible export. In H.M. Jenkins (ed.) *Educating Students from Other Nations*. San Francisco: Jossey Bass.

1983   An introduction to the study of written text: The 'discourse compact.' In R.B. Kaplan et al. (eds) *Annual Review of Applied Linguistics*. Rowley, MA: Newbury House.

Electronic media, instructional technology, and language instruction in planning the use of English as a language of wider communication in non-English speaking countries. In K. Ando et al. (eds) *FLEAT Special Lectures*. Tokyo: Otsuma Women's College Press/Language Laboratory Association of Japan.

Reading and writing, technology, and planning: To do what and with what and to whom? In J.E. Alatis, H.H. Stern and P. Strevens (eds) *Applied Linguistics and the Preparation of Second Language Teachers: Toward a Rationale*. Washington, DC: Georgetown University Press.

Language and science policies in new nations (guest editorial). *Science* 221, 4614.

1984   Reading and writing: Assumptions and presuppositions. *American Language Journal* 2 (2), 39–48.

Immigrant Polynesians in New Zealand. In W. Enninger and L.M. Haynes (eds) *Studies in Language Ecology*. Wiesbaden: Franz Steiner.

Bilingual/bicultural students and competency testing. *SLATE*. Urbana, IL: National Council of Teachers of English.

Applied linguistics, the state of the art: Is there one? *AAALetter* 6 (3), 10–12. [Reprinted in *English Teaching Forum:* ERIC.]

English as a second language: An overview of the literature. In E.G. Barber, P.G. Altman and R.G. Myers (eds) *Bridges to Knowledge: Foreign Students in Comparative Perspective*. Chicago: University of Chicago Press.

1985   Science, technology, language, and information: Implications for language and language-in-education planning (with W. Grabe). *International Journal of the Sociology of Language* 59, 47–71. [Reprinted in *Social science Information Studies* 5 (3), 99–120.]

On writing, reading and rhetorics. *New Settlers and Multicultural Issues* 2 (1), 68–74.

1986   On the structure of text and its pedagogical implications. *Lenguas Modernas* 13, 67–78.

Cultural thought patterns revisited. In U. Connor and R.B. Kaplan (eds) *Writing Across Languages: Analysis of L2 Text*. Reading, MA: Addison-Wesley.

Culture and the written language. In J.M. Valdes (ed.) *Culture-bound: Bridging the Culture Gap in Language Teaching*. New York: Cambridge University Press.

1987   Foreign students: Developing institutional policy. *College Board Review* 43, 7–9, 28–30.

Language and science (with M. Van Naerssen). In R.B. Kaplan et al. (eds) *Annual Review of Applied Linguistics*. New York: Cambridge University Press.

Current trends in second/foreign language teaching. *Language Laboratory* 24, 3–24.

English in the language policy of the Pacific rim. *World Englishes* 2 (6), 137–148.

1988 Contrastive rhetoric and second language learning: Notes toward a theory of contrastive rhetoric. In A.C. Purves (ed.) *Writing Across Languages and Cultures: Issues in Contrastive Rhetoric*. Beverly Hills, CA: Sage.

Process vs. product: Problem or strawman? *Lenguas Modernas* 15, 35–44.

1989 Writing in a second language: Contrastive rhetoric (with W. Grabe). In D.M. Johnson and D.H. Roen (eds) *Richness in Writing*. London: Longman.

The life and times of ITA programs. *English for Specific Purposes* 8 (2). 109–124.

Applied linguistics. *Academic American Encyclopedia* (pp. 90–91). Danbury, CT: Grolier.

Language planning vs. planning language. In C.N. Candlin and T.F. McNamara (eds) *Language Learning and Community: Festschrift for Terry Quinn*. Sydney: National Centre for English Language Teaching and Research, Macquarie University.

1990 Introduction: Language planning in theory and practice. In R.B. Baldauf Jr and A. Luke (eds) *Language Planning and Education in Australasia and the South Pacific*. Clevedon: Multilingual Matters.

A Magyar Kutatók Idegennyelv-Tudása [The foreign language competence of Hungarian scholars (in the Hungarian Academy of Sciences)] (with P. Medgyes). *Magyar tudomány* [*Hungarian Science*] 90 (10), 1219–1232.

Writing in a multilingual/multicultural context: What's contrastive about contrastive rhetoric. *The Writing Instructor* 10 (1), 7–18.

Literacy and language planning. *Lenguas Modernas* 17, 81–91.

Conference summary. In C. Walton and W. Eggington (eds) *Language: Maintenance, Power and Education in Australian Aboriginal Contexts*. Darwin: Northern Territory University Press.

1991 On applied linguistics and discourse analysis. In W. Grabe *et al.* (eds) *Annual Review of Applied Linguistics* 11. New York: Cambridge University Press.

Language-related problems of advanced non-native English speakers during an extended stay in the United States (with P. Medgyes). *Journal of Intensive English Studies* 4, 21–45.

Applied linguistics and language policy and planning. In W. Grabe and R.B. Kaplan (eds) *Introduction to Applied Linguistics*. Reading, MA: Addison-Wesley. [Reprinted in D. Oaks (ed.) *Linguistics at Work*. New York: Harcourt Brace, 1997.]

Literacy and applied linguistics (with J.D. Palmer). In W. Grabe and R.B. Kaplan (eds) *Introduction to Applied Linguistics*. Reading, MA: Addison-Wesley.

Becoming an applied linguist (with W. Grabe). In W. Grabe and R.B. Kaplan (eds) *Introduction to Applied Linguistics*. Reading, MA: Addison-Wesley.

The fiction in science writing (with W. Grabe). In H. Schröder (ed.) *Subject-oriented Text: Languages for Special Purposes and Text Theory*. Berlin: Walter de Gruyter.

Literacy, language planning, and pedagogy. In M. Travis (ed.) *Equity: Report of the 17th Annual Bilingual Multicultural Education Equity Conference*. Fairbanks, AS: Alaska State Department of Education.

Applied linguistics: An overview (with H.G. Widdowson). In W. Bright *et al.* (eds) *International Encyclopedia of Linguistics*. New York: Oxford University Press.

Contrastive rhetoric. In W. Bright et al. (eds) *International Encyclopedia of Linguistics*. New York: Oxford University Press.

1992 Summary comments. In W. Grabe et al. (eds) *Annual Review of Applied Linguistics* 12. New York: Cambridge University Press.

The hegemony of English in science and technology. In G. Jones and A.C.K. Ozug (eds) *Papers Presented at the Conference on Bilingualism and National Development*. Bandar Seri Begawan: Universiti Brunei Darussalam.

Discourse in a foreign language: The example of Hungarian scholars (with P. Medgyes). *International Journal of the Sociology of Language* 98, 67–100.

What is really involved in reading and writing. *Lenguas Modernas* 19, 77–87.

1993 The hegemony of English in science and technology. *Journal of multilingual and multicultural development* 14, 1–2.

New Zealand National Languages Policy. *Working Papers in Language Education* 1. Hamilton: The University of Waikato Language Institute.

Conquest of paradise: Language planning in New Zealand. In M. Hoey and G. Fox (eds) *Data, Description, Discourse: Papers on the English Language in Honour of John McH. Sinclair on his 60th Birthday*. London: Harper-Collins.

TESOL and applied linguistics in North America. In S. Silberstein (ed.) *State of the Art TESOL Essays*. Alexandria, VA: TESOL.

The role of the English language in our developing world. *International Educator* 3 (2), 16–18.

1994 Language policy and planning: Fundamental issues. In W. Grabe et al. (eds) *Annual Review of Applied Linguistics* 14. New York: Cambridge University Press.

Language policy and planning in New Zealand. In W. Grabe et al. (eds) *Annual Review of Applied Linguistics* 14. New York: Cambridge University Press.

On abstract writing (with S. Cantor, C.L. Hagstrom, L. Kamhi-Stein, Y. Shiotani and C. Zimmerman). *Text* 14 (3), 401–426.

Translated! A new breed of bilingual dictionaries (with M. Baker). *Babel* 40 (1), 1–11.

Language-in-education policy: Relevance for developing nations. *Lenguas Modernas* 21, 39–58. [Reprinted in E. Miliani de Ferrero et al. (eds) *Proceedings of the XIth Venezuelan TESOL (VENTESOL) Conference*. Valencia: University of Carabobo.]

1995 Foreword. In R.B. Kaplan (ed.) *The Teaching of Writing in the Pacific Basin*. Special issue of *Journal of Asian Pacific Communication* 6 (1–2), 1–3.

The teaching of writing around the Pacific Basin. *Journal of Asian Pacific Communication* 6 (1–2), 5–12.

Contrastive rhetoric. In T. Miller (ed.) *Functional Approaches to Written Text: Classroom Applications*. Paris: TESOL France/USIS France.

Image and reality: Banking in Los Angeles (with E.E. Touchstone and C.L. Hagstrom). *Text* 15 (4), 427–456.

1996 Audience and voice in current L1 composition texts: Some implications for ESL student-writers (with V. Ramanathan). *Journal of Second Language Writing* 5 (1), 21–34.

'Home sweet casa:' Access to home loans in Los Angeles: A critique of English and Spanish home loan brochures (with E.E. Touchstone and C.L. Hagstrom). *Multilingua* 15 (3), 329–349.

Language teaching: Causes of failure, causes of success. In J. Sarkissian (ed.)

Perspectives in Foreign Language Teaching (Vol. IX). Youngstown, OH: Youngstown State University Press.

Some problematic channels in the teaching of critical thinking in current L1 composition textbooks: Implications for L2 student-writers (with V. Ramanathan). *Issues in Applied Linguistics* 7 (2), 225–249.

1997 The writing course (with W. Grabe). In K. Bardovi-Harlig and B.S. Hartford (eds) *Beyond Methods: Components of Second Language Teacher Education.* New York: McGraw Hill.

Palmam qui meruit ferat. In W. Eggington and H. Wren (eds) *Language Policy: Dominant English, Pluralist Challenges.* Amsterdam: John Benjamins/Canberra: Language Australia.

Contrastive rhetoric. In T. Miller (ed.) *Functional Approaches to Written Text: Classroom Applications.* Washington, DC: United States Information Agency.

An IEP is a many-splendored thing. In M.A. Christison and F.L. Stoller (eds.) *A Handbook for Language Program Administrators.* San Francisco: Alta Book Center.

On the writing of science and the science of writing: Hedging in science text and elsewhere (with W. Grabe). In R. Markkanen and H. Schröder (eds) *Hedging and Discourse: Approaches to the Analysis of a Pragmatic Phenomenon in Academic Texts.* Berlin: Walter de Gruyter.

Hedging in science text and elsewhere (with W. Grabe). In R. Markkanen and H. Schröder (eds) *Hedging and Discourse: Approaches to the Analysis of a Pragmatic Phenomenon in Academic Texts.* Berlin: Walter de Gruyter.

Is there a problem in writing and reading texts across languages? In M. Pütz (ed.) *The Cultural Context in Foreign Language Teaching.* Frankfurt: Peter Lang.

1998 The language planning situation in... (with R.B. Baldauf Jr). *Journal of Multilingual and Multicultural Development* 19 (1), 1–11.

The language planning situation in... (with R.B. Baldauf Jr, eds). *Language Planning in Malawi, Mozambique and the Philippines.* Clevedon: Multilingual Matters.

Language education policy in the Pacific region. In B. Spolsky (ed.) *Concise Encyclopedia of Educational Linguistics.* Amsterdam: Elsevier Science.

Who cares about language policy? *Meikai Roundtable in Applied Languages Studies* 1, 23–37.

Introduction (with R.B. Baldauf Jr, eds) to *Language Planning in Nepal, Taiwan, and Sweden.* Clevedon: Multilingual Matters.

1999 Applied linguistics and the *Annual Review of Applied Linguistics* (with W. Grabe). In W. Grabe et al. (eds) *Annual Review of Applied Linguistics* 20. New York: Cambridge University Press.

Introduction. In J.K. Hall and W.G. Eggington (eds) *The Sociopolitics of English Language Teaching.* Clevedon: Multilingual Matters.

2000 Language planning in Japan. *Conference Papers of the 6th International Conference on World Englishes.* Tsukuba, Japan (July 1999).

Genres, authors, discourse communities: Theory and application for (L1 and) L2 writing instructors (with V. Ramanathan). *Journal of Second Language Writing* 9 (2), 171–191.

Why is English a global language? Problems and perplexities. In W.H. Ho and C. Ward (eds) *Language in the Global Context: Implications for the Language Classroom.* Singapore: RELC.

Introduction (with R.B. Baldauf Jr) to *Current Issues in Language Planning* 1 (1), 1–10.

Language Planning in Japan. In L.S. Bautista, T.A. Llamzon and B. Sibayan (eds) *Parangalcang Brother Andrew: Festschrift for Andrew Gonzales on his Sixtieth Birthday*. Manila: Linguistic Society of the Philippines.

Applied linguistics: (Yesterday) today and tomorrow. In AILA '99 Tokyo Organizing Committee (eds) *Selected Papers from AILA '99 Tokyo*. Tokyo: Waseda University Press.

Contrastive rhetoric and discourse analysis: Who writes what to whom? When? In what circumstances? In S. Sarangi and M. Coulthard (eds) *Discourse and Social Life*. London: Pearson Education.

2001 Foreword: What in the world is contrastive rhetoric? In C.G. Panetta (ed.) *Contrastive Rhetoric Revisited and Redefined*. Mahwah, NJ: Lawrence Erlbaum.

Not only English: 'English only' and the world (with R.B. Baldauf Jr). In R.D. Gonzalez and I. Melis (eds) *Language Ideologies: Critical Perspectives on the Official English Movement* (Vol. 2), *History, Theory and Politics*. Urbana, IL: National Council of Teachers of English.

English: The accidental language of science? In U. Ammon (ed.) *The Dominance of English as a Language of Science: Effects on Other Language Communities*. Berlin: Mouton de Gruyter.

Language teaching and language policy. *Applied Language Learning* 12 (1), 81–86.

2002 Foreword to The wall: Teaching heuristics of English writing among language learners. In E. Hinkel (ed.) *Second Language Writers' Text: Linguistic and Rhetorical Features*. Mahwah, NJ: Lawrence Erlbaum.

A modern history of discourse analysis (with W. Grabe). *Journal of Second Language Writing* 11 (3), 191–223.

2003 Language policy decisions and power: Who are the actors? (with R.B. Baldauf Jr). In P.M. Ryan and R. Terborg (eds) *Language: Issues of Inequality*. Mexico City: Universidad National Autónoma de México.

Applied linguistics (Concerns and related disciplines) (with H.G. Widdowson). In W. Frawley (ed.) *Oxford International Encyclopedia of Linguistics* (2nd edn) New York: Oxford University Press.

Text (Applied aspects: Contrastive rhetoric). In W. Frawley (ed.) *Oxford International Encyclopedia of Linguistics* (2nd edn). New York: Oxford University Press.

CATESOL Yesterday and Today. *CATESOL Journal* 15 (1), 7–18.

In press

Language-in-education policy and planning (with R.B. Baldauf Jr). In E. Hinkel (ed.) *Handbook of Research in Second Language Teaching and Learning*. Mahwah, NJ: Lawrence Erlbaum.

In preparation

Contrastive rhetoric. In E. Hinkel (ed.) *Handbook of Research in Second Language Teaching and Learning*. Mahwah, NJ: Lawrence Erlbaum.

Is language-in-education policy possible? In D. Cunningham (ed.) *Festschrift in Honor of David E. Ingram*.

Applied linguistics in North America (with W. Grabe). In *Encyclopedia of Language and Linguistics* (2nd edn). Amsterdam: Elsevier Science.

Foreword: Literacy in the educational race after cultural integrity. In X. Li and C.P. Casanave (eds) *Multiple perspectives on L1 and L2 academic literacy* in Asia Pacific and diaspora contexts. (Special issue of Journal of Asian Pacific Communication).

Editing contributed scholarly articles from a language management perspective (with R.B. Baldauf Jr). *Submitted to Journal of Second Language Writing.*

Reviews

1967 Test of English as a second language (ETS). In D.C. Wigglesworth (ed.) *Selected Conference Papers of the Association of Teachers of English as a Second Language.* Los Altos, CA: Language Research Associates.

1976 J. Ney, *Linguistics, Composition and the Grades. Modern Language Journal* 60 (5–6), 296–299.

L. Trimble, M. T. Trimble and K. Drobnic, *English for Special Purposes: Science and Technology. TESOL Quarterly* 13 (4), 583–596.

1980 P. Strevens, *New Orientations in the Teaching of English. Applied Linguistics* 1 (2), 177–178.

1982 A. Gonzalez, *Language Planning in the Philippines. Philippine Studies Review* 30, 120–124.

H. Giles and R. St Clair (eds) *Language and Social Psychology. Language Problems and Language Planning* 6 (2), 185–188.

1983 G.N. Robinson, *Issues in Second Language and Cross-cultural Education. Applied Linguistics* 4 (1), 77–79.

R. Rodriguez, *Hunger of Memory. Language Learning* 33 (1), 123–126.

M.G. Clyne, *Multilingual Australia: Resources, Needs, Policies. Ethnic Studies* 5 (1), 27–29.

1988 L.E. Smith, *Discourse Across Cultures. World Englishes* 7 (3), 317–323.

1993 R. Tinio, *A Matter of Language: Where English Fails. Journal of Language and Social Psychology* 12 (4), 369–372.

1996 M.G. Clyne, *Intercultural Communication at Work: Cultural Values in Discourse. Language in Society* 25 (3), 452–456.

M. Herriman and B. Burnaby (eds) *Language Policies in English-dominant Countries: Six Case Studies. TESOL Quarterly* 30 (3), 626–630.

D.L. Rubin (ed.) *Composing Social Identity in Written Language. Language in Society* 25 (4), 623–626.

1997 B. Kenny and W. Savage (eds) *Language and Development: Teachers in a Changing World. Asian Journal of English Language Teaching* 7, 121–126.

T.G. Wiley, *Literacy and Language Diversity. Journal of Multilingual and Multicultural Development* 18 (5), 430–432.

1998 T. Crooks and G. Crewes (eds) *Language and Development. ESP Journal* 17 (3), 317–320.

M. Pennington (ed.) *Language in Hong Kong at Century's End. Journal of Asian Pacific Communication* 8 (1), 81–85.

2001 K. Johnson and H. Johnson, *Encyclopedic Dictionary of Applied Linguistics. Journal of Multilingual and Multicultural Development* 22 (4), 358–360.

2002 A. Duranti (ed.) *Key Terms in Language and Culture. Journal of Multilingual and Multicultural Development* 22 (6), 540–543. [See erratum in *Journal of Multilingual and Multicultural Development* 23 (1–2), 155–157.]

U. Clark, *War Words: Language, History, and the Disciplining of English. Current Issues in Language Planning* 2 (2–3), 305–309.

J.E. Alatis and A. H. Tan (eds) *Language in our Time: Bilingual Education and Official English, Ebonics and Standard English, Immigration and the Unz Initiative. Journal of Multilingual and Multicultural Development* 23 (5), 446–448.

Short reports, columns, letters, responses, interviews and book notes

1968 On part-time English teachers. *NAFSA Newsletter* 19 (5), 10–11
ATESL and the regions. *NAFSA Newsletter* 19 (6), 8–9.
English proficiency-criterion for admission. *NAFSA Newsletter* 20 (2), 4–5.
1969 Report of the 1968 summer ESOL institute at USC. *TESOL Newsletter* (February).
It was a good year. *NAFSA Newsletter* 20 (8), 4.
TOEFL in 1969: A reappraisal. *NAFSA Newsletter* 21 (1), 7–8, 10.
Fifth Inter-American Conference on Language and Linguistics. *NAFSA Newsletter* 21 (3), 4.
1970 TOEFL in 1970: A second look. *NAFSA Newsletter* 21 (9), 6–7.
The President's column. *CATESOL Newsletter* 2 (1), 1–3
The President's column. *CATESOL Newsletter* 2 (2), 1–2.
The SEAMEO/RELC testing conference and English teaching in Southeast Asia. *NAFSA Newsletter* 22 (1), 6, 12.
Recommendations from the publications task force. *NAFSA Newsletter* 23 (3), 1–2.
1971 The President's column. *CATESOL Newsletter* 2 (3), 1–3.
The President's column. *CATESOL Newsletter* 2 (4), 1–2.
1975 Some problems concerning language learning. *ELEC Newsletter* 20.
1976 Book note. *Language* 53 (3), 728–730.
1978 Book note. *Language* 54 (3), 773–774.
Book note. *Language* 54 (4), 1009–1010.
Book note. *Language* 56 (3), 688–690.
The future of NAFSA. *NAFSA Newsletter* 35 (4), 86.
1985 Book note. *Language* 61 (3), 727.
1988 Hong Kong: Fragrant harbour. *Standpoints* 1 (3), 13–17.
Book note. *Language* 64 (4), 822–823.
Book note. *Language* 64 (4), 830–831.
1989 English as language of science. *Vox* 2, 49–53.
Contrastive thought patterns – yet again. *Idiom* 19 (1), 1, 3.
The evidence speaks for itself. *Standpoints* 2 (4), 22–26.
President's page, *USC Faculty Newsletter* 25 (1), 1–2, 3, 4–5; 25 (2), 3; 25 (3), 3.
Book note. *Language* 65 (1), 194–195.
1990 President's page, *USC Faculty Newsletter* 25 (4), 3; 25 (5), 3; 25 (6), 3; 25 (7), 3, 8; 25 (8), 3.
Organizational stability and change. *TESOL Newsletter* 22 (6), 1, 14, 16.
Fiscal problems? Comments made before the Faculty senate. *USC Faculty Newsletter* 26 (2), 1, 4.
1991 President's message. *TESOL Matters* 1 (1), 3.
April 1991 IATEFL Conference. *TESOL Matters* 1 (3), 23.
Debate on English Plus and English Only at NAFSA Conference. *TESOL Matters* 1 (4), 5.
TESOL summer institute a great success. *TESOL Matters* 1 (5), 1.
Just the facts, Ma'am (response to a letter to the editor by Ann Raimes, at the editor's request). *TESOL Matters* 1 (5), 6.
ALAA meets in the deep north of Australia. *TESOL Matters* 1 (6), 23.
1992 Annual meeting update. *AAALetter* 14 (3), 1–2.
Writing or grammar? *Practical English Teaching* 13 (2), 11–12.

1993 Conference update. *AAALetter* 15 (1), 1–2.
 From the President... *AAALetter* 15 (2), 1–3, 6.
 Internationalizing USC's Curriculum. *Academic Senate Forum* (September/October), 7–9.
 From the President... *AAALetter* 15 (3), 1–2, 11.
1994 From the Past President.... *AAALetter* 16 (1), 2–3.
 Book note. *Language* 70 (4), 856–857.
1995 The US certification maze (special guest). *EFL Gazette* 128.
 Iceberg tips and first steps: A call to action (guest editorial). *TESOL Matters* 5 (2), 16.
 Response to letters to the editor. *TESOL Matters* 5 (4), 23.
 Applied linguistics, AAAL, and the political scene. *AAALetter* 17 (2), 2–3.
 Response to letters to the editor *TESOL Matters* 5 (5), 23.
1996 Letter to the editor: Privatizing ESL instruction. *TESOL Matters* 6 (5), 6.
 Rhetorical questions and contrastive answers: An interview with Dr Robert Kaplan. E. Meija (ed.) *WAESOL Newsletter* 22 (2), 1, 6–7.
1997 Where to now? *BBC English (BBC World Service Magazine for Learning English* 16 (121), Insert 2.
 Response to Raimes and Zamel (with V. Ramanathan). *Journal of Second Language Writing* 6 (1), 83–87.
 Letter to the editor. *International Educator* 6 (2), 2.
 Language-in-education planning: Questions to guide program development (with R.B. Baldauf Jr). *Australian Language Matters* 5 (3), 9–10.
 Introducing contrastive rhetoric: What is it? What is it for? How can it be used? (with W. Grabe). *SPELT Newsletter* 12 (1), 2–28.
1998 Putting out fires; lighting fires. *International Educator* 7 (2–3), 80–81.
 On TESOL and research. *TESOL Matters* 8 (3), 16.
 Death by mindlessness: Thoughts on faculty governance. *USC Academic Senate Newsletter*.
1999 Culture speaks through language. *International Educator* 8 (1). 46–47.
 The ELT: Ho(NEST) or not HO(NEST)? *NNEST Newsletter* 1 (1), 1, 5–6.
 An endless study. *Asahi Evening News* (Tokyo). July 31, 11.
2000 Foreign language issue demands national policy. *Asahi Evening News* (Tokyo). July 3, 7.
 Response to 'On the future of second language writing,' T. Santos (ed.) *Journal of Second Language Writing* 9 (3), 311–314.
2001 The language of policy and the policy of language. *FORUM: Official Newsletter of the TESOL Applied Linguistics Interest Section* 21 (1), 1, 9–10.
 Kaplan Interview. In A. Teemany and S. Pinnegar (eds) Understanding language acquisition video segments (videotape recordings). Provo, UT: Brigham Young University/Public School Partnership.
 Kaplan Interview. In A. Teemany and S. Pinnegar (eds) The second language acquisition case: A video ethnography of second language learners: Parts I, II, III (CD-ROM). Provo, UT: Harris Video Cases.
2002 Editorial (with R.B. Baldauf Jr). *Current Issues in Language Planning* 2 (2–3), 135–136.
2003 Language requirements: Problem or opportunity? *International Educator* 12 (2), 12–19.

Government and organization reports

1970 Feasibility study: Regional centers. Conducted for the Field Service Program of the National Association for Foreign Student Affairs. Under a grant from the Bureau of Educational and Cultural Affairs, US Department of State.
1971 A follow-up evaluation and a model for utilization of the ELS teacher-education program. Under a grant from the US Agency for International Development.
1976 An experiment in industry–university cooperation in the teaching of English to Asian engineers. RELC, Singapore, in cooperation with the Northrop Corporation.
1980 Report to the Select Commission on Immigration and Refugee Policy: Non-resident aliens, specifically foreign students.
1983 Report on a visit to the Kingdom of Saudi Arabia, May 1–20, 1983: Institutional linkages: The great chain of mind. Under a grant from The United States Information Agency and the Saudi Arabian-US Joint Economic Advisory Commission.
1986 The foreign student in tertiary and post-tertiary chemical education in the US: Report on a symposium. Jointly sponsored by the American Chemical Society and the National Association for Foreign Student Affairs.
1992 Evaluation report on UCIEP–Eastern-European Project. Grant agreement between the Government of the United States of America and Ohio University on behalf of UCIEP: Consortium of University and College Intensive English Programs.
  New Zealand national languages policy: Making the patient more comfortable. Report to the Policy Division, New Zealand Ministry of Education.
1998 English as a world language and the US national interest. Commissioned paper for the English Language Programs Division: United States Information Agency.

Index

academic discourse 7, 87, 150, 158-159, 161-162, 187, 190-191, 196, 211, 266
academic literacy 59-60, 63, 67, 88-89, 101-102, 104-105, 107-108, 110, 116, 119, 121-122, 165, 167-168
academic writing 3, 5-8, 89, 94, 96, 100-101, 104, 106-107, 109-112, 114-115, 117, 120-125, 127-129, 131, 134, 151, 153-154, 158, 186-199
accentedness 79, 82, 118
acquisition planning 27, 30, 225, 229-230, 258-260, 262
African-American students 8, 126, 151, 165, 167-171, 173, 175-176, 178-185
alphabetization 35, 257
Anglicisms 241-242, 244, 246-248, 253
Anglo-American culture 5, 7, 115, 161, 168, 186-187, 199-200, 203, 205-206, 210, 253
argumentative writing 102, 107, 186, 189, 191, 195, 199
Aristotelian rhetoric 186
audience 6, 103-105, 107, 109-110, 112-113, 153, 162, 166, 168-169, 173, 179

Basic Interpersonal Communication Skills (BICS) 119
bilingual education 43-44, 49-50, 232, 234, 262, 275
bilingualism 32, 39-40, 42-44, 49, 52, 54, 75, 103, 111, 130, 209, 234, 237, 252
biliteracy 51

Chinese rhetoric 151, 186-188, 197, 199-200
classroom discourse 8, 14, 91, 99, 104, 121, 151-152, 165-166, 169, 201-219, 261
Cognitive Academic Language Proficiency (CALP) 119
cohesion 154-155, 157, 160-163, 167-169, 172, 175, 178-179, 183
college writing 6, 88, 101-102, 104, 117, 119, 122, 124, 129, 153, 191-192, 199

collocation 7, 132, 134-135, 137, 139-142, 145
communicative language teaching 61, 208, 276
community languages 5, 40, 42-52, 54, 121, 233-234, 237
connotation 132, 134-135, 139-145
constituent analysis 17
content-based instruction 6, 58-59, 61, 68, 101-102, 111, 113-114, 273
context 61, 94, 104-105, 107-110, 112, 116, 122, 127, 137, 154-155, 157, 160-161, 168, 183, 186-187, 191
contrastive rhetoric 3-4, 7-8, 10, 26, 88-89, 102, 115, 149-165, 167-168, 201-219, 257
corpus linguistics 14, 16-17, 20, 28, 36, 94-95, 105, 107, 150-151, 154-164, 190
corpus planning 30, 33, 223-225, 229-230, 247, 258-259, 291
critical framing 110
critical linguistics 22, 91, 98, 106, 110, 184, 229, 232, 257
crosscultural communication 3, 8-9, 51, 77, 87, 149-151, 154, 156-157, 162-163, 165, 186-187, 199, 201-219
curricular innovation 5, 40, 56, 61-62, 65-67, 112, 267, 274-275

dignity planning 261
discourse 10-11, 61, 104-107, 111, 113, 130, 153, 186-187, 189-191, 199, 225, 228, 256-259, 262-263
discourse analysis 4, 7, 9, 11, 91, 93, 116, 150, 171, 184, 257-258
discourse communities 94, 105, 109, 166-167, 169, 184, 187, 199
discourse planning 255-258, 261-263
discourse structures 7-8, 87, 102, 104, 107, 112, 116, 135, 154, 158, 163

ear learners 6-7, 117-126, 128, 130
educational linguistics 4, 26, 29, 133, 149

Index

English as a foreign language 5, 26, 28, 44, 74-75, 77, 80-83, 119, 125, 153, 201, 206-207, 214-215, 217-218, 229, 237
English as a second language 5, 7, 39, 43-44, 48, 73, 75, 77-83, 98, 102-106, 111, 116-122, 124, 130, 132, 136, 138, 142-145, 149-150, 153, 155, 187, 191-192, 201, 217-218, 237
English for academic purposes 4, 6-7, 87, 91, 94, 101, 131, 134, 192, 274
English for special purposes 87
Englishization 9, 225, 240, 249
error gravity 125, 127-129
esteem planning 225, 246, 258, 260-262
ethnographic research 24, 94, 100, 107, 154, 168-169, 178, 185, 232
ethnography of speaking 30
exemplification 8, 87, 102, 186-191, 193-194, 196-199
expository writing 87, 105, 166, 168, 172, 189
expressivism 101, 103-105
eye learners 6, 118-121, 123, 126

first language education 7-8, 35, 48, 57, 78, 96, 120, 136, 234
first language learners 48, 73-75, 77, 115, 118, 120, 124-128, 191, 193, 201, 204, 265, 277
first language transfer 125, 153, 156, 187, 199
first language writing 149-151, 154-156, 163, 186-187, 191, 200
folk linguistics 15-17, 19-25
foreign language education 5, 8, 10, 30, 35-36, 40, 43-44, 56-58, 60-64, 66-68, 104, 225-226, 230, 264-278
formal grammar 3, 7, 17, 27, 36
formal language 123, 159, 186-187, 189, 191, 197, 199-200
formal linguistics 132
functional meaning 7, 173, 175, 260

Gallicisms 246, 253
general education 101-102, 133
Generation 1.5 89, 98, 130
genre 6, 104-105, 107, 110-116, 150-151, 153-154, 157-159, 162-164, 166-167, 169, 182, 184, 187, 190, 199, 260
grammar errors 7, 96-98, 102, 117-118, 120, 122-129
grammatical description 16, 136, 249

grammatical knowledge 27, 61, 63, 73, 80, 89, 102-103, 123-124, 128

heritage languages 42, 210

idioms 121, 125, 128, 135, 138, 140, 142, 144-145
indigenous languages 34-35, 42, 45, 246, 263
informal language 89, 115, 122-123, 128, 145
information technology 15, 50, 67, 109, 224, 237, 239, 245, 247, 271, 275
intensive English programs 79, 81, 149, 192, 271, 275, 278
interdisciplinarity 3-4, 6, 8, 12-20, 22-25, 256
interlanguage 125-126, 155
interlanguage pragmatics 204-205
international students 89, 117-119, 121-123, 125-126, 129, 149

Japanese rhetoric 151, 186-189, 199-200, 210, 214

Korean rhetoric 151, 186-187, 189, 199-200, 209

language and power 5, 10, 43, 49, 74, 110, 117, 128, 184-185, 225, 256, 258, 263
language cultivation 29, 31-33, 229
language deficit 43, 49, 76, 125
language diversity 12-13, 16-17, 34, 44-45, 51, 120, 152, 187, 254, 263, 274
language ecology 229, 300
language education 4, 39
language ideology 21-22, 30, 103, 105, 111, 224, 255-257, 259-263
language-in-education policy 5, 27, 30, 42-43, 46, 53, 226, 229-230, 236, 247, 259-260, 264, 267, 270, 278
language maintenance 35, 229-230, 234
language management 29-30, 33-35, 229, 231
language norms 29, 31-32, 153, 259
language pedagogy 3, 6-7, 14, 20, 26-27, 74-75, 78-80, 82, 88, 91, 94-95, 98-104, 110-112, 128, 133, 204, 208, 229
language policy and planning 3-5, 9-11, 26-27, 29-31, 33-36, 40, 43-47, 53-54, 57-58, 67, 88, 223-229, 231, 233, 236-238, 255-264, 270, 276-278, 292

language politics 18, 29, 36, 40, 103, 115, 186, 208, 225, 228, 232-233, 244-245, 255-259, 261-263
language problems 9, 12-15, 20-25, 28-29, 33, 36, 39, 88-89, 98-100, 117-120, 122, 125, 130, 132, 188, 256-257, 259, 261, 263-264, 271
language proficiency 5, 27, 30, 50-51, 72, 74-78, 82, 94, 96, 98, 118-119, 122, 191, 199, 208, 265-266, 271-272, 274
language purism 31-32, 246-247, 254
language reform 31, 41, 230, 257, 278
language rights 34, 229
language socialization 149, 152, 168, 204-205, 210, 214
language standards 16, 19, 31-32, 49, 52, 73, 111, 129-131, 159, 171, 245, 253
language testing 26, 36, 44-45, 47-49, 99, 107, 113, 121, 166, 191, 265, 271-272, 274
languages of wider communication 224
languages other than English 39-40, 42-44, 46, 48-49, 52-53, 55, 72, 117, 229, 266, 277
learner-centered instruction 103, 217
learning styles 120, 130
lexical acquisition 7, 90, 131-132
lexical errors 7, 90, 125, 131-132, 134-143, 145
lexical knowledge 73, 118, 122-123, 130-132, 134-135, 138, 253
lexical phrases 134, 141-142, 145, 156, 172, 177-178, 181, 190
limited English proficiency 119, 130
literacy 3, 45-46, 52-53, 75, 88, 103, 109, 111-112, 114, 120, 126, 168, 184, 234, 259
literacy instruction 29, 35, 40, 53, 56-57, 60-64, 66-67, 81, 88, 103-104, 108-109, 112, 116, 168, 185

macro language policy 9-10, 223, 227-228, 231-236, 238, 262
metacognitive development 103, 115
Mexican Academy of Language 225, 246-247, 254
Mexican-American students 8, 88, 151, 165, 167-171, 173, 175-176, 178-181, 183-185
Mexican Spanish 9, 225, 240-244, 247-253
Mexicanisms 243, 253
micro language policy 3, 9-10, 223-224, 227, 231, 233, 235-236, 238-239, 262

missionary linguistics 35
modernization 31, 230
monolingualism 31, 43-44, 49, 53-54, 60, 73, 104, 265
morphology 246
moves analysis 104-105, 107, 112, 163
multilingualism 5, 40-41, 44-45, 50-52, 54, 74, 226, 234, 237, 261, 263, 265
multiliteracies 89, 104, 108-112, 115-116

narrative writing 8, 81, 151, 165-173, 175-176, 178-186, 189, 194-200
native speakers 5, 8, 14, 17, 32, 34, 40, 50, 72-83, 115, 117, 119, 121-123, 125, 127-129, 131-132, 135, 155-156, 186, 189, 191-199, 217, 246, 248, 251
nativization 249
nonlinear text 108-109
non-native speakers 5, 32, 40, 72-83, 89, 115, 119, 126, 186-187, 189, 191-200

oracy 234
oral language 60, 65, 68, 81, 89, 100, 118-119, 121, 126-127, 132, 153
orthography 29, 243, 252

performative language 169, 225, 256-258
phonetic spelling 122, 128
phonetics 29, 243, 252
phonology 3, 29, 156
postsecondary education 90, 101, 111, 119, 127, 274
pragmatics 3, 17, 102, 105, 156, 160, 163
prestige planning 229-230, 238, 260-261
primary education 40, 44, 47, 49-50, 53-54, 58, 117, 169, 178, 185, 208, 226, 231, 238, 267-268, 270, 275-276
process writing 101, 103-104, 109-110, 112-113
professional discourse 10, 25, 102, 109, 159, 256-257
pseudoanglicisms 240-241, 243

qualitative research 62, 91, 94-95, 97-100, 160-164, 172-173, 176
quantitative research 94-95, 97, 99-100, 154-155, 157, 161-164, 173, 214, 271, 276

Royal Spanish Academy 225, 245-246

scientific discourse 15, 21, 88, 122, 150, 158-159, 229-230

Index

second language acquisition 3, 7, 20-21, 29, 36, 45, 48, 50, 61, 94, 98, 118-120, 125-126, 129, 131-137, 144, 201, 230, 267
second language education 76-77
second language learners 48-49, 52, 54, 74-76, 96, 119-120, 125-127, 129-130, 134, 151-152, 201, 204-205, 208, 216-218
second language research 7, 92-93, 98-99, 201, 204, 235
second language writing 7-8, 91, 93-94, 96, 98-99, 117, 120, 124, 126-130, 143, 149-151, 153, 156, 186, 190-191, 195, 197, 199-200
secondary education 47-51, 53-54, 56, 58, 101, 111, 120, 151, 169, 185, 267, 269-271, 273, 277
semantic shift 240-242, 249-250
semantics 3, 7, 30, 90, 131-132, 135-136, 156, 160, 242
social construction 6, 89, 101, 104-106, 109-111, 115-116
social psychology 30
socialization 168, 175, 178, 180, 184
sociocultural factors 11, 21, 39-40, 67, 97-98, 204, 216, 218, 244, 253
sociolinguistics 3-4, 9-10, 13-14, 16-18, 29-30, 33, 35-36, 67, 98, 184, 204, 224, 227, 255, 257, 263
stance 104-108, 110, 115, 173, 176-177, 179-181, 183
standardization 29, 35, 230, 237, 245, 259-260
status planning 30, 32-33, 35, 52, 223-225, 229-230, 258-259, 267

structuralism 16, 28, 101, 103-104, 112
stylistic features 102, 104, 158, 160, 172-173, 179-181, 183-185, 190, 230
stylistics 105, 175, 183
syntax 3, 122-123, 126, 131-132, 136-137, 142, 151, 156, 190, 246
systemic-functional linguistics 105, 259

target language 48, 51, 74, 77, 87, 89, 102, 126, 155, 201, 204, 260, 273
teacher education 7, 78, 82, 96, 99, 133, 232, 235, 238, 271, 273-276
TESOL 26, 81-82, 89, 103, 116
text analysis 6-7, 22, 53, 91-92, 94-100, 105, 116, 150-164, 166, 171, 186, 189-190, 193, 195-197, 199, 218, 256
text processing 103, 115, 187
third language learners 51-52, 54, 269, 278
TOEFL 191
translation 7, 28, 30, 35, 45-46, 136, 155-156, 164, 227, 233-237, 243
trilingualism 274, 278
turn allocation 8
turn taking 121, 151-152, 201-219

US-resident learners 6, 117-130, 209-210
usage 131, 138-139, 145
usage planning 33, 225, 235, 246, 248, 254, 258, 260

voice 104-107, 110, 115

Whorfian hypothesis 150